Waste Works

Waste Works

Vital Politics in Urban Ghana

Brenda Chalfin

DUKE UNIVERSITY PRESS
Durham and London
2023

© 2023 DUKE UNIVERSITY PRESS
All rights reserved
Printed in the United States of America on acid-free paper ∞
Project editor: Liz Smith
Cover designed by Courtney Leigh Richardson
Text designed by A. Mattson Gallagher
Typeset in Adobe Text Pro and Helvetica Neue LT Std
by BW&A Books, Inc.

Library of Congress Cataloging-in-Publication Data
Names: Chalfin, Brenda, author.
Title: Waste works : vital politics in urban Ghana /
Brenda Chalfin.
Description: Durham : Duke University Press, 2023.
| Includes bibliographical references and index.
Identifiers: LCCN 2022040820 (print)
LCCN 2022040821 (ebook)
ISBN 9781478019589 (paperback)
ISBN 9781478016946 (hardcover)
ISBN 9781478024217 (ebook)
Subjects: LCSH: Sociology, Urban—Ghana—Tema.
| Public toilets—Ghana—Tema. | Sanitation—Political
aspects—Ghana—Tema. | City planning—Political aspects—
Ghana—Tema. | Infrastructure (Economics)—Political
aspects—Ghana—Tema. | BISAC: SOCIAL SCIENCE /
Sociology / Urban | SOCIAL SCIENCE / Anthropology /
Cultural & Social
Classification: LCC HT148.G4 C43 2023 (print) | LCC HT148.G4
(ebook) | DDC 307.7609667—dc23/eng/20221208
LC record available at https://lccn.loc.gov/2022040820
LC ebook record available at https://lccn.loc.gov/2022040821

Cover art: Sakumono Beach, Tema, Ghana. Staged photo-
graph, 2022. © Henry Obimpeh.

Contents

List of Illustrations vii

Preface xi

Acknowledgments xix

Introduction. Infrastructural Intimacies 1
The Vital Politics of Waste in Urban Ghana

1. Assembling the New City 45
From Infrastructure to Vital Politics

2. Tema Proper 96
Infrastructures and Intimacies of Disrepair

3. The Right(s) to Remains 133
Excremental Infrastructure and Exception in Tema Manhean

4. Ziginshore 181
Infrastructure and the Commonwealth of Waste

5. Dwelling on Toilets 212
Tema's Breakaway Republic of Ashaiman

Conclusion. From Vital Politics to Deep Domesticity 268
Infrastructure as Political Experiment

Notes 295

References 315

Index 339

Illustrations

Figures

I.1 Tema Development Corporation promotional materials, 2009 3

I.2 "The Big Squat," 2013 7

I.3 Tema's high modernity: high-rise built ca. 1967 (© Constantinos and Emma Doxiadis Foundation) 10

I.4 Tema high-rise, ca. 2011 10

I.5 Clerk, Alcock, and Robinson 1955 master plan for Tema 15

I.6 Tema tabula rasa, 1965 (© Constantinos and Emma Doxiadis Foundation) 16

I.7 Sewage system sea outfall, 1959 (Ghana Information Services Division) 16

I.8 Large-scale biodigester under construction, 2011 20

1.1 President Kwame Nkrumah commissioning Tema Harbor, 1962 (Tema Development Corporation Archives) 47

1.2 President Kwame Nkrumah and Constantinos Doxiadis in Ghana, 1960 (© Constantinos and Emma Doxiadis Foundation) 50

1.3 Fully serviced residential units, built ca. 1965 (© Constantinos and Emma Doxiadis Foundation) 52

1.4 Fully serviced residential units, built ca. 1965 (© Constantinos and Emma Doxiadis Foundation) 52

1.5 Tema final master plan with distribution of incomes, designed by Doxiadis Associates, 1962 (Tema Development Corporation Archives) 56

1.6 President Kwame Nkrumah visiting Tema exhibition with Queen Elizabeth and Mr. A. Otoo, chief development officer, Tema Development Organization, 1961 (© Constantinos and Emma Doxiadis Foundation) 62

1.7 Tema master plan house layouts across income levels indicating bathrooms (Kairon Aiken / Tema Development Corporation Archives) 71

1.8 Circumscribed centers and minipublics, 1962 (Tema Development Corporation Archives) 76

1.9 Sanitary baseline: Tema sewage system, 1967 (Tema Development Corporation Archives) 81

1.10 Trunk sewer lines cutting across Tema's Chemu Lagoon, 1965 (© Constantinos and Emma Doxiadis Foundation) 87

2.1 Construction of Community 5, 1967 (© Constantinos and Emma Doxiadis Foundation) 97

2.2 TMA waste management yard, 2014 (Eliot Chalfin-Smith) 99

2.3 TMA sewage pumping station, 2014 102

2.4 Pumping station wet well, 2014 (Eva Egensteiner) 105

2.5 Original map of sewage manholes (Tema Waste Management Office) 116

2.6 Booking complaints, 2013 118

2.7 Final layout for Tema, Community 5, 1961 (Tema Development Corporation Archives) 122

2.8 Broken pipes and flooded manhole, 2014 125

3.1 Canoe harbor, Port of Tema, 2014 (Eliot Chalfin-Smith) 134

3.2 Awudung streetscape, 2013 (Marina Ofei-Nkansah) 135

3.3 Manhean public toilet interior corridor, 2013 (Marina Ofei-Nkansah) 137

3.4 Manhean public toilet stalls, 2013 (Marina Ofei-Nkansah) 137

3.5 Removal from Old Tema and resettlement in Tema Manhean, 1959 (Ghana Information Services Division) 140

3.6 *Wulomo* and Tema Traditional Council members at Durbar, ca. 1962 (Tema Development Corporation Archives) 142

3.7 Final Drew and Fry plan for Tema Manhean with residential compounds and public toilets, ca. 1956 (Kairon Aiken) 146

3.8 Compound design from *Village Housing in the Tropics* 149

3.9 Tema Manhean public toilet layout, ca. 2012 (Kairon Aiken) 152

3.10 Conversing with toilet managers in Tema Manhean, 2011 158

3.11 Public toilet plastered with political posters, 2010 (Marina Ofei-Nkansah) 164

3.12 Public toilet courtyard as worksite and living space, 2010 (Marina Ofei-Nkansah) 170

4.1 Chemu Lagoon management plan, ca. 1965 (Tema Development Corporation Archives) 183

4.2 Chemu Lagoon, 2014 (Eliot Chalfin-Smith) 183

4.3 Floshin Taifi interior: toilets, 2014 (Eva Egensteiner) 184

4.4 Floshin Taifi interior: showers, 2014 (Eva Egensteiner) 184

4.5 Floshin Taifi standpipe and entryway, 2014 (Eva Egensteiner) 187

4.6 Floshin Taifi veranda, 2014 (Eva Egensteiner) 187

4.7 Diagram of Ziginshore's Floshin Taifi and surrounding infrastructure complex (Kairon Aiken) 190

4.8 Uncle Director's proposal for self-contained waste and water infrastructure, 2014 194

4.9 Hostel interior, 2012 198

4.10 Makeshift shelter established from excess construction materials on the roof of the Floshin Taifi hostel, 2014 (Eliot Chalfin-Smith) 201

4.11 Children and infrastructure, 2014 (Eva Egensteiner) 203

4.12 Building large-scale DIY excremental infrastructure: biogas, 2011 206

4.13 Building large-scale DIY excremental infrastructure: septic system, 2013 (Marina Ofei-Nkansah) 206

4.14 Biogas kitchen, outdoor, 2011 207

5.1 Ashaiman's private commercial toilets tax rates, 2011 215

5.2 "An immigrant removed from Tema Zongo outside of his house in Ashaimang," ca. 1959 220

5.3 Government toilet exterior, 2013 (Mustapha Mohamed) 222

5.4 Government toilet interior, 2014 (Eva Egensteiner) 222

5.5 Stomach toilet layout (Xhulio Binjaku) 228

5.6 Stomach: making wealth conspicuous, 2014 (Eva Egensteiner) 231

5.7 Orders of Gentility, 2014 (Eva Egensteiner) 233

5.8 Toilet stall augmented with rebar, 2013 234

5.9 Adepa Modern layout (Xhulio Binjaku) 240

5.10 "I care for you," 2013 242

5.11 Adepa Modern entrance, 2013 245

5.12 Infrastructural adjustments, 2013 253

5.13 Conspicuous labor, 2014 (Eva Egensteiner) 257

5.14 Toilet stall with graffiti, 2014 (Eva Egensteiner) 257

Maps

I.1 Map of Ghana and Tema (Kairon Aiken) 2

I.2 Map of Tema Acquisition Area and four research areas: Tema Central, Tema Manhean, Ziginshore, and Ashaiman (Kairon Aiken) 34

5.1 Map of Ashaiman within Tema Acquisition Area (Kairon Aiken) 213

Tables

I.1 Survey of urban sanitation in Tema 19

I.2 Excremental infrastructure and private/public nexus in Tema 37

I.3 Excremental infrastructure in relation to the state in Tema 37

1.1 House types, income distribution, and floor area, 1961 70

5.1 Ashaiman's domestic public toilet typology 225

Plates

1   Tema Development Corporation, 2011

2   Trunk sewer lines across Chemu Lagoon from defunct sewage pumping station, 2014 (Eva Egensteiner)

3   Discarded Nkrumah-era maps and models on the premises of the TDC, 2010

4   Tema Central original house plans and modifications, 2011

5   Tema Central original house plans and modifications, 2011

6   Tema Central original house plans and modifications, 2011

7   Pumping station engineers, 2014 (Eva Egensteiner)

8   TMA engineer assessing pipe replacement and repair, 2013

9   Rodding team prepares for work, 2014 (Eva Egensteiner)

10 Objects of contention: Their mains and our extensions, 2014

11 Neighborhood and neighborly repairs, 2014

12 Fish processing in Tema Manhean, 2010

13 Awudung streetscape, 2010 (Marina Ofei-Nkansah)

14 Manhean public toilet exterior, 2014 (Eva Egensteiner)

15 Manhean public toilet and shower house, 2010 (Marina Ofei-Nkansah)

16 Manhean's multifunctional gathering space, 2010 (Marina Ofei-Nkansah)

17 Ziginshore panorama, 2014 (Eliot Chalfin-Smith)

18 Preparing fish for market, 2014 (Eva Egensteiner)

19 Floshin Taifi veranda, 2014 (Eva Egensteiner)

20 Emissah mopping entry, 2014

21 Floshin Taifi toilets: sitting style, 2014 (Eva Egensteiner)

22 Floshin Taifi toilets: squat style, 2014 (Eva Egensteiner)

23 Hostel exterior, 2014 (Eliot Chalfin-Smith)

24 Women create personal space in unfinished hostel, 2014 (Eva Egensteiner)

25 Building large-scale DIY excremental infrastructure: hand-dug wells, 2011

26 Biogas kitchen, indoor, 2014 (Eva Egensteiner)

27 Ashaiman street scene, 2014 (Eva Egensteiner)

28 Stomach Has No Holiday signboard, 2013

29 Stomach: male toilet entrance, 2014 (Eva Egensteiner)

30 Mr. and Mrs. Stomach, 2014 (Eva Egensteiner)

31 Adepa Modern Toilet signage, 2013

32 Adepa Modern's founder, Madame Halima, 2013

33 Adepa toilet stall, 2013

34 Adepa sanitary lane, 2013

35 Lady Di entrance and shower area, 2014 (Eva Egensteiner)

36 Kitchen turned filter room, 2014 (Eva Egensteiner)

37 Daughters turn waste into gold at Lady Di, 2014

Preface

I did not initially intend to write a book about urban sanitation and the politics of human waste. I came to Ghana's city of Tema interested in infrastructure and the interplay of urban planning and governance in the lives of urban dwellers. As I investigated infrastructural form and functioning in this West African city famous for its planned communities, modernist architecture, parks, greenways, and expansive container port, waste emerged as a recurring theme. Debates about norms, responsibilities, and the very nature of human excreta as burden or asset rose to the fore. I realized Tema's wide-ranging sanitary infrastructures offered novel solutions to citywide dilemmas even as they sparked contestation. Indeed, rather than singularly reflecting the heavy hand of centralized planning for which the city was known, the arrangements I encountered are largely shaped by urban residents from across class strata.

From a study of infrastructure as a means of governance, my research shifted to waste and infrastructure as vibrant sites of political negotiation. The more I paid attention to the composition, operation, and design of sanitary infrastructure, the more I noticed that complicated the well-worn script of high modernity. The popularly devised excremental infrastructures I came upon in Tema offered grounds for collective and individual empowerment and recognition despite the convoluted inheritance of midcentury sanitary design. Though built on the body's most base condition, they enhanced human dignity and public good in the face of waning state capacity and inadequate international fixes.

Ghanaian society prides itself on tact and propriety, and conventionally shrouds intimate bodily functions. Bringing these issues to the fore is thus a delicate matter, exposing class, cultural, and generational divisions. I offer my account with utmost respect for those who opened their infrastructural and experiential worlds to me. I hope these stories of urban problem solving do not provoke rancor or embarrassment. In sharing the details of urban practice, I stand in solidarity with urban residents who push the boundaries of urban planning and reveal the blind spots of received norms in order to serve pressing urban needs on their own terms.

I take inspiration from the growing ranks of Ghanaian artists, activists, and members of the urban underclass who speak directly to taboo topics in order to enable more effective and inclusive problem solving and social policy. In a cultural setting premised on hierarchy and deference, they expose entrenched norms and enforced silences on the subject of human excrement. These sentiments are evident, for instance, in David Comrade Sedi Agbeko's conceptual art, Henry Obimpeh's installations (pictured on the cover), and Wanlov Kubalor's popular music, and in community-led sanitation campaigns such as "Let's Talk Shit." This book contributes to these wider social and political projects through its frank discussion of human waste and waste politics across Ghana's city of Tema.

My goal is not to discredit Tema's standing as a model city typically celebrated for its efficient urban design, social mobility, and cosmopolitan outlooks. Rather, I draw attention to the hidden underpinnings of Tema's apparent elegance and efficiency. Forged largely by working-class residents as well as more prosperous citizenry, these interventions actively challenge the limits of inherited urban infrastructures and ideals. I argue that they are a formative arena of urban political imagination and mobilization. Resisting claims of success or failure based on abstract norms, the book examines the functional and expressive potential of these arrangements in situ.

I began research for this book in 2009 and continued through 2016, spending several weeks to several months a year in Ghana. After conducting several years of research in northern Ghana in the 1990s (see Chalfin 2004), I first visited Tema in 2000 in the course of a new project on sovereignty and border controls at the city's container port (see Chalfin 2010). When I passed through the city center on my way to the shipping harbor, the city struck me as quiet and contained in comparison with the dynamism of Ghana's capital, Accra, and the working-class Ga suburbs of Teshi and Nungua occupying the coastline between them. Once I turned my back on the port and took a hard look at the city in its own terms, Tema reemerged as a place of fascinating complexity with depth and creativity of its own despite the heavy hand of the city's planning authority.

I am indebted to Marina Ofei-Nkansah for enabling me to see Tema anew. A longtime resident, youth advocate, and former nurse in one of Tema's main clinics, and my primary research assistant, Ofei-Nkansah showed me the many sides of Tema well before the full contours of the project were clear. We walked through neighborhoods to survey midcentury architectural gems and capture the rhythms and layouts of Tema's carefully orchestrated urban scheme. Through Ofei-Nkansah, I learned about the city's double history as a place of middle-class upward mobility and as a site of displacement built on indigenous lands and the labors of an urban underclass.

Ofei-Nkansah brought me to Tema Manhean, where Tema's original residents were forcibly resettled to make way for the new city in the early years of Ghanaian independence. As we scoped out Manhean's subdivisions, rows of public shower houses marked by high walls and raised clusters of PVC pipe and spigots caught my eye. I soon learned that many contained public toilets. Unlike Tema's core communities, where the neatly built concrete-block flats and semidetached homes were equipped with piped water, electricity, and individual household toilets and bathrooms, only a tiny percentage of Manhean residents had toilets, baths, or working taps in their homes. Instead, public toilets remained from Tema's mid-twentieth-century founding, spaced at regular intervals across Manhean's streetscape. Through the counsel of Manhean toilet manager and community activist Solomon Tetteh, I became aware of the long-standing politics of public toilet operation and upkeep. Attracting the claims of political party activists and traditional and municipal authorities, and the counterclaims of residents, in these public spaces the violations of resettlement were subtly replayed.

Tetteh also shared news of a public toilet that was being resurrected decades after being abandoned by city authorities. Faint outlines of buried pipes and fixtures were visible beneath the dirt and rubble. This was the work of a fellow waste-entrepreneur and activist, Kwame Enyimayew. The worldly Enyimayew was one of the first children born in the new city, where he grew up before departing for university and the United Kingdom. Along with his abundant technical expertise, he voiced endless ideas of what the public toilets could be, from community centers to learning spaces and polling places. He also revealed his knowledge of the full gamut of waste infrastructure in and around Tema, including sewage treatment ponds under construction and the city's original sewage outfall at Paradise Beach. I realized this was the tip of a much larger, multilayered system, part functioning, part frozen in time. I began to see the logic of deciphering the city—its aspirations, inequities, and alternatives—through its sanitary underground. Crystalizing this sentiment, I visited Ziginshore, an informal settlement built upon the accumulated waste of Tema's industrial zone at the edge of Chemu Lagoon. Here, Enyimayew had constructed a massive public toilet complex for the transient populace who worked at the port and fishing harbor. He was building an adjoining hostel and had plans for a waste-fueled biodigester to provide power for the complex.

Attuned to the heavy hand of Ghanaian bureaucracy from my earlier research on Tema's seaport, alongside my introduction to the city through its infrastructural subterrain I sought to understand the official conventions and intentions of urban governance and public provisioning. I approached Tema's joint planning and governing body, the Tema Development Corporation (TDC). After approving of my credentials, the longtime public relations officer shared a pile of old photographs he had hastily gathered when the TDC's original office blocks were demolished. Attesting to the importance of Tema to Ghanaian nation-building, they included numerous images of Ghana's independence leader and first president, Dr. Kwame Nkrumah. A sign of Tema's international standing, there were images of African heads of state and a picture of Queen Elizabeth inspecting models of the city.

The following year I sorted through maps, blueprints, and drawings guided by the TDC's chief archivist. These were not PR images but the nuts and bolts of the city-building created by a new generation of technocrats— planners, draftsmen, architects, surveyors, typists, and health officers—in the early years of Ghana's independence. Most prominent was the imprint of Greek urban planning firm Doxiadis Associates displayed on report covers, serials, and rolls of crisp vellum. Although Tema was built by and for Ghanaians for the purpose of national development, design and construction specs were largely outsourced to Doxiadis's planning team, in residence at the TDC for much of the 1960s and 1970s.

The site maps and building plans in the TDC's collection, though in poor condition, provided an institutional bedrock across which I could trace links and layers. Sanitation was a persistent subtext connecting the different sections of the city and the past to processes still in train. I came upon contour maps of water courses and drawings intended to guide installation of drainage pipes. There were plumbing catalogs and studies to determine the ideal size and configuration of bathing areas and water closets. Visible as soon as one started to look for it, here was a point of entry that could be read across Tema's varied urban plans and scales. It was also unfolding around me as

I relocated from Accra to lodge in Tema's core. While I admired Tema's well-preserved midcentury architecture, it was not unusual to see sewage trucks siphoning spills from burst pipes or puddles left from overflowing manholes. Alleys surrounding Tema's main market were often blocked to permit replacement of spoiled underground pipes. Local blogs and news reports shared residents' complaints, spanning the gamut from open defecation to inoperable donor-built sewage treatment plants. Clearly, sanitation was a matter of concern to current residents, much as it had preoccupied planners and politicians in the wake of new nation-building.

I learned from residents the confusing terms of accountability and jurisdiction surrounding urban sanitation between the TDC and the city's administrative body, Tema Metropolitan Assembly (TMA). The director of waste management confirmed this point. On a tour of internationally funded sewage treatment ponds, he explained their demise and shared his own progressive vision of sanitation for the city, which posed waste less as scourge than as opportunity. Technicians invited me to join them on site visits and inspections. I shadowed engineers at Tema's main sewage pumping station. As they explained the system's operation, they articulated a sensorial sympathy with the materials under their control. Common among waste workers elsewhere in the world and indicative of the interplay of human and nonhuman agency in waste work, it spurred me to think about what I eventually came to call "infrastructural intimacy." This dynamic was also evident as I followed the trail of sewage complaints and tracked interactions among neighbors, repair crews, and local political representatives. Bringing to the fore the status of waste as an agent and object of political negotiation, even in the city's middle-class neighborhoods it became apparent that Tema's infrastructural underground was not an invisible media of interconnection but actively debated and recomposed by residents. Waste, in short, was a political object in its own right.

My research concerns shifted from waste management as means of political suppression to waste and waste infrastructure as sources of self-determination and collective claims making. It was apparent that sanitary infrastructures were not simply the ambit of technical experts. Large-scale solutions were being formulated from within Tema's urban communities, at once correcting, supplementing, and subverting received sanitary technologies and associated models of urban order. Alongside the tensions and overlaps of urban planning schemes and do-it-yourself urban survival strategies, metalevel questions about the place of private bodily processes in the organization of public and collective life rose the fore. Evident in the unsettled terms of urban sanitation stemming from systems externally imposed without the full means to sustain them, the allocation of responsibility for bodily processes and outputs was perennially unresolved in the city.

While these ideas percolated, I had yet to come upon my final case study: Tema's satellite settlement of Ashaiman. I visited Ashaiman in the 1990s to see relatives of my host family in northern Ghana and was unaware it was founded in the 1950s as a labor reserve for the new city of Tema. Ashaiman gained standing as an autonomous municipality in 2008. Sanitation was a centerpiece of urban reform in Ashaiman, denied the infrastructural inputs of its sister city. With few government-provided facilities or a centralized sewage system, residents relied on hundreds of privately built public toilets located in or attached to residential space. Serving urban needs when the municipality could not, Ashaiman's case affirmed my hunch that waste and sanitation were leading vectors of urban political activism across Tema. A further indication of a new political and cultural economy of waste afoot, private commercial toilets in Ashaiman were associated with status attainment for customers and proprietors alike.

As I parsed the theoretical resonances of my findings in Tema, prevailing frameworks addressing the capacity of the modern liberal state to simultaneously harness and restrict the body as a political object offered important starting points. Yet they ultimately proved inadequate. The hard-won realities of Tema's citizen-driven infrastructural exceptions pointed to fissures in these much-replicated orders. Taken together, Hannah Arendt's discussions of bodily labor, Georges Bataille's ideas about power's heterogeneity, and Bruno Latour's conception of actor networks and nonhuman agency offered theoretical traction. Informing what I eventually came to term the "vital politics of infrastructure," the case of Tema revealed the never fully containable force of vital materials—human bodies and bodily excreta included—and associated infrastructures. Full of life and essential to it, they are doubly vital. Despite city founders' intention to use large-scale urban infrastructure to imprint individuals and constrain collectivity, the dynamic mix of human necessity and organic and inorganic forces renders these systems unstable. In turn, I realized, they are critical to crafting alternative infrastructural arrangements and enabling unscripted political outcomes.

My juxtaposition of social theory and the lived realities of urban sanitation in West Africa is both deliberate and jarring. I take inspiration from feminist and antiracist scholars such as Carol Pateman and Charles Mills, who return to classic theoretical precepts in order to correct and confound their normative assumptions and deficits. An ethnographic account of the afterlives of postwar high-modernist infrastructure offers a window on the cracks, gaps, and lapses in the theoretical armature of modernity and an opening to see how people formulate infrastructure—and lives—within, around, and against its strictures and possibilities. Following Bruno Latour's methodological impulse to locate the political empirically, I argue that putting the base facts of life in the global South in conversation—not just contention—with social theory is an important step in advancing "theory from the South." Such a move avoids confusing "theory *from* the South" with assertions of "theory *for* the South" and the risk of theoretical-territorial essentialism tying theory—and people—to fixed locations. Challenging narrow understandings of theory's emplacement is part and parcel of recognizing Africans as actors in, not passive recipients of, modernity's inheritance, whether seamless citywide sewage systems or grand theories of human progress.

Alongside the social scientific claim that historical experience can be theorized is the companion point that theory has a history. That is, theoretical precepts emerge out of distinct historical junctures that transcend singular locales. The theorists I draw on in my analysis of late modern infrastructural exigencies in Ghana are part of the same world-historical shift of postwar modernization that resulted in rendering the city of Tema a paragon of African progress. Case in point, Arendt and Tema's founding figures Kwame Nkrumah and Greek urbanist Constantinos Doxiadis were all students of classical philosophy and deeply invested in rebuilding and making sense of the post–World War II world. Indeed, Tema residents, like Arendt, are heirs to postwar internationalism's paired projects of modern state-building and city-building. Other theoretical propositions I bring into the discussion of Ghana's postcolonial infrastructural experiments, namely those of Walter Benjamin and Georges Bataille, are likewise born from the same forces of radical displacement—from the disruptions of the Holocaust to the eruptions of the atomic bomb—that produced the city of Tema. Seventeenth-century Thomas Hobbes, whose *Leviathan* also provides a theoretical fulcrum for the text, is certainly a historical outlier in this regard. However, recognizing the diverse logics of nature encapsulated within the state form, Hobbes speaks to foundational modernist precepts—and tensions—long suppressed, which claim a durable presence in the course of urban restructuring in Tema.

Finally, historicizing theory requires situating my own perspectives and preoccupations. I completed this book amid the uncertainty and enforced stasis of the 2020–21 coronavirus pandemic. During that time a final conceptual frame emerged. What I gloss as "deep domesticity," it addresses the expansion and intensification of domestic functions when state and international institutions fail to provide or protect. In Tema, the process is evident in privately built public toilets that double as working-class community hubs, middle-class households' collective efforts to rebuild and safeguard shared sewage lines, and city engineers' self-conceptions as caretakers of public infrastructure. Enlarging the scope and reach of the privatized domestic realm and encompassing practices otherwise deemed government responsibility, I remain struck by their resonance with the recalibrations of daily life induced by COVID in the United States. Street-corner fridges and food banks, the personal sacrifices of essential workers to ensure the survival of others, and the overlay of work, school, and leisure in domestic space—all publicly exposed by private media infrastructure—these shifts gather people and basic life practices together in unexpected ways, not entirely different from arrangements evident in Tema.

These cases remind us that geographically distant corners of the world can be linked by shared structural conditions. They indicate, moreover, the ways cities in the global South map out historical trajectories overlooked in theories of urban life derived from the global North yet surprisingly relevant to them both. As long as humanity is on this planet, waste—including bodily waste—is not going away, regardless of one's geographic or class location. As recent works such as Chelsea Wald's *Pipe Dreams: The Urgent Global Quest to Transform the Toilet* (2021) and Catherine Coleman Flowers's *Waste: One Woman's Fight against America's Dirty Secret* (2020) likewise attest, if excrement is part of our shared human condition, inadequate and inefficient waste infrastructures are a global problem. It is thus critical to pay attention to the individuals and communities who forge workable alternatives to the received script of late modernity and the political as well as practical implications of their infrastructural solutions.

Excremental arrangements in Tema demonstrate that the orchestration of human waste in the city by the public and for the public offers an alternative to the social power of the state. Serving as an enduring basis of association and collective action by means of infrastructure, bodily waste's inevitable excesses and instabilities, both cultural and organic, are political resources in their own right and continuously harnessed to new ends.

Acknowledgments

This book is a product of the generosity of countless friends, colleagues, and acquaintances in Ghana across a decade of visits and returns. Most of all, I am indebted to residents of the city of Tema who generously shared their homes, workplaces, stories, and daily routines with me. I am grateful for the honesty, dignity, and conviction with which they made me aware of the challenges of urban sanitation and the hard-won solutions they devised in turn.

Although I was no stranger to Ghana, my presence as a white American female academic interested in the intimate details of household sanitation demanded explanation and the establishment of trust and personal credibility on my part. To understand these matters and to facilitate, Marina Ofei-Nkansah provided research assistance, friendship, and wise counsel drawing on her academic training, deep ties to Tema, and knack for connecting with people. A skilled fieldworker with a masters of philosophy from University of Ghana's Institute of African Studies, she carried out research with me and on her own in Tema Manhean, Ziginshore, and Tema's core, where she also aided with archival work at TDC. Mohammed Mustapha contributed substantial research assistance in Ashaiman and aided research in Ziginshore. Alhassan Bilal Yunis helped with research in Ashaiman.

At Tema Development Corporation, managing director Joe Abbey graciously approved my affiliation and provided permission for institutional research, as did architect and board member E. O. Adjetey. I was welcomed by TDC staff and provided with workspace thanks to communications director Dorothy Asare-Kumah. In return for access to the TDC Archives I assisted TDC archivist Cosmos Anane with cataloging and digitizing materials. Public relations assistant David Donya was ever ready to participate in document searches, digitization, and site visits across the city. Samuel Yeboah in the TDC Drawing Room was also a source of expertise and insight on the city's architectural history and design.

In Tema Manhean, Tema *mantse* Nii Adjei Kraku II enabled my request to conduct research in the community on public space and public goods, as did *wulomo* Nuumo Ashiboye Kofi II and chief fisherman *woleiatse* Nii Odametey II. The owners and operators of public toilets, water taps, and bathhouses in Manhean patiently cooperated with interviews and observational and participatory research. Local residents and political representatives also made themselves available for discussion. Following these preliminary walkabouts, in 2009 I met two individuals who would become guides, friends, and key informants in their own right: one, Solomon Tetteh, a toilet manager and community activist; the other, Kwame Enyimayew, a sanitation entrepreneur. Tetteh graciously introduced me to his extended family, putting me at ease in the courtyard of his family home and offering a convenient perch during my many visits to the public toilet he managed. Though the names of Manhean's public toilets and toilet franchise groups and leaders have been changed to preserve confidentiality, all were generous with time, access, and information.

In Ziginshore, Enyimayew taught me more than I ever imagined was possible about the uses and abuses of public sanitation and urban waste. His investment in the infrastructural and social transformation of Ziginshore's wastelands piqued my curiosity early on and continued to fascinate me during the prolonged process of constructing an off-grid toilet, bath, and waste recycling complex in this marginalized settlement. I appreciate the openness of staff members and residents to my presence and that of the larger research team. I acknowledge in particular cleaners, technicians, and attendants Mr. Montey, Nana Sam, Emissah, Steven, Enoch, Matthew, Augustine, Grace, Vida, Efua, and Kekey. Office managers Jennifer and Joshua were also of help. I am especially grateful to the residents of Ziginshore's adjoining hostel who took time to share their lives and experiences with us despite the demands of work, childcare, and precarity of livelihood and living conditions.

In pursuit of further information on Tema's development I visited London's Architectural Association School (AA), where Tema's early designers, Jane Drew and Maxwell Fry, founded the Department of Tropical Studies. Archivist Edward Bottoms connected me to Patrick Wakely at University College of London's Development Planning Unit. Wakely had worked in Ghana in the 1960s and more recently served as a development consultant in

Tema's satellite city of Ashaiman. Wakely told me about Ashaiman's unique sanitation solutions and its drive to become an autonomous municipality challenging the oversight of TDC. Wakely introduced me to his project partners in Ashaiman: Ibrahim Baidoo, Ashaiman assemblyman, activist, and eventual mayor, and urban planner and community organizer Erika Mamley Kisseih. Upon my return to Ghana, I sought their counsel. Both offered and have continued to provide in-depth understanding of Ashaiman's unique history, demographics, and politics, along with ongoing feedback on my research findings. Kisseih was among the first to read and comment on the manuscript in full.

My debts to those in Ashaiman span from city government to managers, attendants, and customers of the city's vast array of privately owned dwelling-based public toilets. Ashaiman's environmental sanitation officer, Eric Kartey, was a patient guide to the city and shared the details of national policy and waste management challenges and solutions in Ashaiman. With the help of Innocent Adamadu, in 2013 I conducted initial surveys of Ashaiman's sanitary landscape. The work was completed with the assistance of Mohammed Mustapha, then a masters of philosophy candidate in Archaeology and Heritage Studies at the University of Ghana, and later a doctoral student at the University of Florida. Mustapha's UG classmate and longtime Ashaiman resident Alhassan Bilal Yunis soon joined the Ashaiman research team. Bilal's home and his family, Fati Adam and Amina Alhassan, became my base in Ashaiman, offering a space of rest, refreshment, conversation, and support. Their own efforts to install private water closets and a small-scale sewage system in their house provided additional insight on the price and politics of sanitary upgrading in the city.

The owners and operators of Ashaiman's many dozens of private commercial toilets patiently responded to research questions and participated in site surveys as we sketched, measured, and mapped each installation. I thank Pius Opuku, Ali Imran, and Agnes Agirron and their families, staff, and customers, who contributed to the case studies featured in this book. Their kindness allowed me and my research team to feel at ease as we learned about the inner workings and social worlds of their facilities over numerous visits and conversations. I also thank customers, staff, and proprietors of the following commercial toilets in Ashaiman: Wisdom, Otumfo, Base 10, God's Way, Fine, Donkor, Taifa, 2010, and Shower House, among many others.

Personnel of Tema Metropolitan Assembly were instrumental to my research on urban sanitation in Tema's core neighborhoods of Communities

1 through 12. At TMA headquarters, I benefited from conversations with Emmanuel Avenogbor, Sevlo Adjei, and assemblyman Sumailah Issah. Officials and employees of Tema's Waste Management Department played an especially critical role in the research process. Waste management director Edward Mbah was exceptionally helpful as he mapped out the multiple models of waste management operating in the city. His successor, Jonas Dunnebon, was also a source of guidance. So too was James Lamina, another "brother" from northern Ghana and longtime leader of TMA's sewage repair squad. TMA engineers Adu Gyamfi, George McCarthy, and Emmanuel Mensah shared their expertise with the work of maintenance and repair. Manager Lucy Tetteh shared her expertise on liquid waste. George Ferguson, Henaku Joseph, and other administrative staff shared their extensive knowledge of the wider scope of system breakdown and rebuilding. In Tema's core middle-class communities, Community 1, Community 4, Community 5, and Community 7, I am grateful to the families and households who so frankly and graciously shared their experiences. I do not name them or TMA workers and use pseudonyms for the sake of confidentiality. Rev. E. A. Armah and Joseph Yedu Bannerman imparted extensive knowledge of the first decades of the new city's management and settlement.

Research outside of Ghana offered additional insight on Tema's infrastructural and political underpinnings. At Belgium's Catholic University of Leuven, I met urban studies scholar Viviana D'Auria, who conducted her PhD research on Ghana's Volta River Project and continues to research and publish on Tema along with a talented group of MA students. Attuned to Tema's program of incremental modification of dwelling units, D'Auria put Tema residents' do-it-yourself approach to large-scale infrastructure in new perspective, offering especially important insight into Tema Manhean. Travel to Greece brought me to the Constaninos A. Doxiadis Archives at the Benaki Museum in Athens, masterfully managed by Giota Pavlidou. Here I found personal correspondence between Nkrumah and Doxiadis attesting to shared ideas about the course of national development. I also came upon original photographs of the city under construction, including massive sewage mains that remain in use today.

A summer visit to Ghana in 2014 afforded the opportunity for follow-up. With support from the University of Florida, photographer/videographer Eva Egensteiner accompanied me to visually document the four communities that form the heart of this book. Building upon relationships forged by Ofei-Nkansah and ties to Enyimayew, staff, and hostel residents, Tetteh and Mustapha joined the research team in Ziginshore, as did my son, Eliot Chalfin-Smith. We collected workers' and residents' occupational and geographic profiles and watched the waste complex expand before our eyes, with hand-dug wells, a biogas-powered café, and a homemade waste treatment plant. Besides tracing the site's overall infrastructural development, we paid close attention to the relationship between bodies and infrastructure, taking a phenomenological approach to the lifeworlds incited by waste.

Along with that of Tema residents and officials, the support of scholars and educational institutions in Ghana remains invaluable to my research endeavors. The Institute of African Studies at University of Ghana–Legon was my academic home away from home and offered research affiliation through the many phases of the project. The directors of IAS, initially Takyiwaah Manuh, and then Akosua Adamako Ampofo, warmly welcomed me. I benefited from the intellectual support of IAS faculty Richard Asante, Debrah Atobrah, and Albert Awedoba. My ties to Legon extend to Department of Archeology and Heritage Studies faculty Wazi Apoh and Kwadzo Gavuah. This is in addition to ongoing exchange with Akosuah Darkwah in Legon's Department of Sociology, who with Debrah Atobrah provided critical feedback on the manuscript.

At Commonwealth Hall, where my family and I resided in 2011 while on a Fulbright-Hays fellowship, we were aided by hall bursar, porters, and staff. Hall librarian Francis Atsu and family were also a source of advice and support, as were Legon Hospital transportation chief Sammy Dansoh and family. Fellow Fulbrighters Theresa Morrow and Bill Ristow shared their love of campus and spirit of adventure. The US Embassy Cultural Affairs unit also facilitated visas and other documents necessary for research and residence. Special thanks to Cultural Affairs officer Sarpei Nunoo.

Emily Asiedu and the Asiedu Institute provided a second home for me in Ghana, for visits long or short, alone or accompanied by friends and family members. The warmth and unfailing welcome of Auntie Asiedu and her extended family, Dinah Dentaa, Ebenezer Afful, Solomon Ofosu Appea, and Daniel Ohene Appea; UK-based family Comfort, Mary, and Steven; and Evelyn Asiedu in the United States, are beyond compare. I thank Nana Kwame Fosu for Twi lessons, may he rest in peace. A vast network of Ghana scholars provided intellectual and moral support during shared time in Kokomlemle. They include Jennifer Hasty, Lauren Adrover, Chris Richards, Cati Coe, Jen Boylan, Michael Stasik, Jean Allman, John Parker, Stephan Miescher, Lane Clark, and many others. I recall the many conversations with Stephan Miescher driving to and from Tema in 2010, as we compared notes on his project on Ghana's Volta River Dam and the early stages of my research on Tema.

A host of other Ghana scholars in one way or another contributed to this work, including Jeff Paller, Waseem Bin-Kasin, Ann Cassiman, Nana Osei-Opare, Abena Dove Osseo-Asare, D. K. Asare, Elisabeth Sutherland, Nate Plageman, Rod Alence, Paul Nugent, R. B. Bening, Jeff Ahlman, and Benjamin Talton. Nate Plagemen was particularly generous in providing feedback on the manuscript as a whole. The long-standing friendships and intellectual network of the Accra-based Center for Democracy and Development also helped to ground my research inquiries. I am grateful to E. Gymah-Boadi, Franklin Oduro, Kojo Asante, and Baffour Agyeman-Duah, who is now with the Kufuor Foundation.

The influence of a broad-ranging group of infrastructure-focused anthropologists and urbanists informs my approach to waste politics in Tema. I benefited from conversations, conference panels, and sharing ideas and works in progress with Brian Larkin, Antina von Schnitzler, Mike Degani, Danny Hoffman, Antonio Tomas, Omulade Adunbi, Hannah Appel, Akhil Anand, Kris Peterson, Filip De boeck, Dominic Boyer, Laura Bear, Charles Piot, Daniel Mains, Greg Feldman, Kristin Phillips, Rosalind Fredericks, Sophia Stamatopoulou-Robbins, Kareem Buyana, Peter Redfield, and Steven Robins. I sincerely appreciate Robins's and Feldman's willingness to read and comment on the draft manuscript.

At the University of Florida, I benefited from the support of colleagues in the Center for African Studies and Department of Anthropology. Donna Cohen in UF's School of Architecture has been a source of great wisdom and insight, helping me to place Tema within the wider context of tropical modernism and to recognize the boundary between architectural history and anthropological approach to architecture. This book would not have been possible without her ongoing support and enthusiasm and blunt admonition to stay grounded in my home discipline. Our cotaught course and 2015 conference "Design and Development in Africa" was especially valuable for gaining perspective on these matters. Students Ben Burgen and Xhulio Binjaku brought important insights of their own into the conversation. Binjaku prepared initial sketches from my research findings. Binjaku and I later worked together to design architectural models displayed at a Mellon Foundation–funded conference in Durban in 2016 and published in *Limn* in 2017. Binjaku's drawings are included in chapter 5. Kairon Aiken, another graduate of UF's architecture program, did the final maps and drawings that appear throughout the book, demonstrating creativity, efficiency, and skill.

Colleagues in UF's Department of Anthropology inspired me to keep the conversation going despite the distractions and demands of teaching, advising, and administration. I am most of all indebted to Susan Gillespie, Ken Sassaman, Mike Heckenberger, Richard Kernaghan, John Krigbaum, Augusto Oyuela-Caycedo, and Marit Ostebo for their encouragement and feedback as well as the model they each provide of original, theoretically informed scholarship challenging disciplinary strictures. Department chairs Susan DeFrance and Pete Collings likewise accommodated requests for research leave and fellowship support making this project possible. I also thank Anthropology's indefatigable administrative corps, Karen Jones, Patricia King, Pam Freeman, and Juanita Bagnall for their aid throughout.

Center for African Studies colleagues offered invaluable friendship and intellectual input and a model for academic research grounded in real-world challenges and accomplishments on the African continent. During my appointment as director of the Center for African Studies, College of Liberal Arts and Sciences dean David Richardson and associate dean Mary Watt encouraged research and scholarship as an integral element of program-building. The committed scholarship of CAS faculty Renata Serra, Luise White, Terje Ostebo, Abdoulaye Kane, Ben Soares, Alioune Sow, Agnes Ngoma Leslie, Joan Frosch, Todd Leedy, Akintunde Akinyemi, James Essegbey, Leo Villalon, and Fiona McLaughlin informed and inspired me. Exposure to Africa-based scholars and experts through the center's many programs helped to keep African agency at the fore of my discussion. This was especially so in the case of African architecture and design. Visiting scholars and practicing architects Joe Osae-Addo and James Inedu George shared my interest in living architecture in West Africa.

In addition to faculty, a dynamic group of Africa-focused UF graduate students contributed to the conversation about infrastructure, built environment, and the politics of everyday life: Cady Gonzalez, Megan Cogburn, Felicien Maisha, Jamie Fuller, Shambhavi Bhusan, Jenny Boylan, Chris Richards, and Netty Carey. Carey, in addition, provided assistance with archival materials and book references. Lia Merivaki provided translations of Doxiadis Greek-language documents pertaining to Ghana. Tracy Yoder assisted with organizing and cataloging archival material at TDC. Felicity Tackey-Otoo helped analyze and organize Doxiadis Associates reports on Tema commissioned by Ghana's Ministry of Housing. Mohammed Mustapha, initially in the capacity of fieldwork assistant, and later, UF graduate student, was readily available to offer feedback and bring his combined archaeological and ethnographic sensibility to bear.

A residential fellowship from Harvard University's Radcliffe Institute for Advanced Study in 2015–16 enabled me to focus exclusively on research and writing among a diverse group of scholars and artists in an atmosphere of openness and exchange cultivated by associate dean Judtih Visniak and dean Liz Cohen. In 2015–16 I took a first stab at pulling a book manuscript together thanks to a residential fellowship at Harvard University's Radcliffe Institute for Advanced Study. I profited from fruitful interaction with fellows Daniel Ziblatt, Bill Hurst, Mary Lewis, Lesley Sharpe, and Kris Manjarapa. I was fortunate to have access to the immense resources of Harvard University Libraries and the outstanding collection of the Graduate School of Design. Weekly workshops moderated by Jean and John Comaroff offered an engaged and well-informed Africanist community, including Emmanuel Acheampong, Lucie White, George Mieu, Suzanne Blier, and Delia Wendel. Added to this were the social and intellectual sustenance of Tarik Dahou, Helene Sow, Sue Cook, and Oteng Acheampong. Time at Cambridge was further sustained by the unfailing warmth and generosity of my sister, Sonia Chalfin, and brother-in-law, John Wakeley, and the willingness of my daughter, Safi Chalfin-Smith, to explore new urban horizons.

Opportunities to share and receive feedback on earlier versions of book chapters helped me to hone my argument and clarify core themes. Portions of this work were presented at the University of Washington (2019), the University of Oslo (2019), the European Conference on African Studies (2018), the Africa Center for Cities at University of Capetown (2018), Stellenbosch University (2017), the Graduate Center of City University of New York (2016), the University of Michigan/University of Witwatersrand Mellon Seminar in Durban (2016), the Radcliffe Institute for Advanced Study (2016), American Anthropological Association Annual Meetings (2014), African Studies Association Annual Meetings (2014, 2013), the University of Chicago African Studies Program (2014), Northwestern University (2012), the Catholic University Leuven (2012), and the Cambridge University Center for Research in the Arts, Social Sciences and Humanities (2012).

Research and write-up were made possible by the following grants and fellowships: Fulbright-Hays Faculty Research Abroad, US Department of Education, "Socializing the City: Middle-Class Lives and High-Modernist Urban Planning in Ghana's Port City of Tema," 2010–11 Award PO19A

100035; Harvard University Radcliffe Institute for Advanced Study 2015–16 Faculty Fellowship; University of Florida 2014 Humanities Enhancement Award; University of Florida 2012 Faculty Enhancement Opportunity Award; and UF Center for Humanities and the Public Sphere 2010 Library Enhancement Award. In addition to research clearance from the Institute of African Studies at the University of Ghana, research was conducted according to the ethical guidelines of the American Anthropological Association and in accord with University of Florida Institutional Review Board UFIRB#2009-U-543, UFIRB#2010-U-1036, UFIRB#2014-U-544.

Material from chapter 3 appeared in "Public Things, Excremental Politics, and the Infrastructure of Bare Life in Ghana's City of Tema," *American Ethnologist* 41, no. 1 (February 2014): 92–109. An earlier version of chapter 4 was published as "'Wastelandia': Infrastructure and the Commonwealth of Waste in Urban Ghana," *Ethnos: Journal of Anthropology* 82, no. 4 (January 2016): 648–71. Portions of chapter 5 can be found in "Excrementa III: The Leader in Upscale Sanitary Solutions?," *Limn*, no. 9, "Humanitarian Goods," October 2017. Archival photographs are courtesy of Constantinos A. Doxiadis Archives, Ghana Information Service, Ghana Universities Press. In addition to my own, field photographs are the work of Eva Egensteiner, Marina Ofei-Nkansah, and Eliot Chalfin-Smith. Eva Egensteiner also provided photo editing for the book.

A writing retreat at University of California Irvine Anza-Borrego Desert Research Center (DOI:10.21973/N3Q9F) in January 2020 organized by Kris Peterson and Elizabeth Chin pushed me to renew my focus on manuscript completion. Soon thereafter, when the rest of our work lives were thrown into disarray by the fears and uncertainties of COVID, participation in UF's Center for Humanities and Public Sphere Summer 2020 writing collective offering comradery and shared purpose. Denise Trunk Krigbaum assisted with copyediting. Check-ins with writing partner Leah Rosenberg along with the tool kit offered by the National Council for Faculty Diversity and Development were instrumental to completion of this work. Since our initial conversations in 2019, Elizabeth Ault, acquisitions editor at Duke University Press, has been a great source of encouragement and insight in shaping the manuscript for a broad audience.

My family has stuck with me throughout the long decade it has taken to research and write this book. My son, Eliot, and daughter, Safi, adjusted early to parental absence, family trips to Ghana, and school abroad. Navigating cultural differences from a young age, they have honed their own ethnographic sensibilities and ease in diverse settings. For three decades now my husband, Daniel A. Smith, has cultivated his own ties to Ghana and gained a shrewd awareness of the vagaries of anthropological research and publication. He has learned great patience in the process, evident in his support across the weeks of pandemic confinement that I devoted to writing, editing, and revision in 2020–21. This work is devoted to them. All errors are my own.

Introduction. Infrastructural Intimacies
The Vital Politics of Waste in Urban Ghana

Sɛbi taflatse (Ga, "I beg your pardon").

With all due respect to those in Ghana whose lives and experiences I touch on, this book probes the politics of human waste, *taifi* in Ga and Akan (Twi) languages.[1]

The stories I share are conveyed with utmost respect for the dignity and problem-solving capacities of urban residents and city officials navigating infrastructural decline in a city long considered a paragon of technical progress and socioeconomic attainment. The city is Tema, built under the aegis of Ghana's first president, Kwame Nkrumah.

After several months of extended visits to Tema's working-class neighborhoods, it was a change of pace to find myself in a cement-lined courtyard behind a three-bedroom home in Tema's well-laid-out residential core. I was following up with a retired accountant for one of the city's factories who had lodged a complaint at the municipal waste management authority about a burst sewage pipe flooding his home. He shared:

> The old pipes are broken and collect mud and sand and soil for that matter. It chokes the entrance of where it enters the main. When that happens, the toilet rises. You see it rising. The manhole, you can see the manhole increasing. The water level comes up from the sewage in the shower area. It comes up. Because the sewer is choked it comes up. The water comes up in the bathroom and you are standing in the water. It happens in these four [neighboring] houses: There was one day it came from the street. My whole yard was flooded with sewage with the *poos* in it. It was like that for three or four days. It affected the whole street. It was very disgusting.

Map I.1. Map of Ghana and Tema (Created by Kairon Aiken)

Figure I.1. Tema Development Corporation promotional materials, 2009

The response took me by surprise. Besides the frank description, I was caught unaware by the pervasive problems of breakdown and disrepair in the well-planned, well-kept, if sometimes timeworn middle-class neighborhoods that marked residence in Tema as a path to upward mobility. While infrastructural failure and inadequacy were clearly evident in the underserved working-class neighborhoods that sustained Tema, waste management issues were kept under wraps in more prosperous parts of the city. The more I paid attention, the more I noticed that breakdown of sanitary infrastructure was a common occurrence despite the neat homes, spacious apartments, and parks and greenways of the planned city. I soon realized that across Tema's varied communities, populations, and locations, residents—as well as waste workers and officials—were involved in complex problem solving and workarounds to ensure access to basic urban infrastructure. It also became clear that much more than waste was at stake. Most of all, the infrastructural solutions pursued by urban residents address broader issues of power and powerlessness in the city. By redistributing control over urban bodies and bodily outputs by means of urban infrastructure, they alter the terms of public and private life and counter inherited norms and associated claims of state ascendance.

Reversing expectations regarding access to the means of waste management and self-care, the greatest range of successful infrastructural innovation
comes not from Tema's more prosperous core but from less resourced settlements in and around the city. Descendants of the city's original inhabitants,
for instance, turn public toilets into vehicles of protest, self-determination,
and revenue generation. Along the way, they challenge negative connotations of bodily waste that are the norm in Ghanaian society. Elsewhere in
the city, on an unofficially claimed tract of urban wetland, a Tema native son
back from abroad runs a massive public toilet–cum–residential complex for
a transient urban underclass. Populist in spirit, though far from egalitarian,
the apparatus functions as a means to both satisfy and influence customers'
daily needs, aspirations, and loyalties. In turn, they garner a modicum of
municipal recognition.

Back in the city's core, sanitary engineers inured to the harms of fecal
materials and worn technologies invested themselves in system repair. Attributing system breakdown to the domestic ills of middle-class residents
and mismanaged international fixes, they position themselves as protectors
of national heritage. In a peri-urban working-class settlement at the city's
edge, better-off households convert domestic space into public toilet facilities to fill the void of municipal incapacity and state exclusion. Turning excrement from a source of shame to gateway to influence and material gain,
waste infrastructures reorganize status hierarchies and recode sources of
social power. Democratizing urban infrastructure and broadening access to
basic urban services, taken together these interventions rob the state of its
professed control over the terms of public and private responsibility in this
showcase West African city. Reworking inherited systems to novel ends,
some intended, some unexpected, they seed an ongoing cycle of negotiation and recalibration.

On Excrement, Infrastructure, and Urban Politics

Succinctly put, in Tema, excrement and associated infrastructures are political matters bringing to the fore what in high-modernist cities is largely
shrouded or suppressed. There is no shortage of literature on fecal matter
from the perspective of medicine, public and environmental health, and
psychology. The account shared here takes an entirely different tack and
reveals the centrality of human waste and waste infrastructures to urban
politics and public life. A close reading of the lifeworlds built around and

through waste and waste infrastructure offers a means to understand the fraught boundary between private interest and public good in the making of urban political order. Foremost, ethnographic investigations of the range of actually existing excremental solutions in Tema upend presumptions about human excreta as a singularly private concern and reveal the political significance of infrastructures that transform bodily waste from individual output to collective responsibility. While highlighting the experience of a single West African location, the argument is relevant to other spaces where state responsibility for essential public services is being rejected, withdrawn, or both, and alternative solutions to basic urban needs devised by urban residents rise to the fore.

A profound "politics from below," Tema's diverse waste management systems, and the social and material struggles they organize and express, push us to look beyond conventional arenas of political participation—parliaments, protests, voting booths, legal battles—to account for the quotidian spaces and processes through which the contemporary polis is forged. As noted by Bruno Latour (2005a, 4), "The time seems right to shift our attention to other ways of considering public matters." Bodily waste is an insistent locus for the negotiation of urban political order, whether state power is ascendant, as argued in Dominique Laporte's provocative *History of Shit* (2002), or on the wane, as described here.

Just as excreta is a source of emotional ambivalence per psychoanalytic theory (Freud [1905] 1947), and a site of semantic excess per cultural studies (Mbembe 2001; Stallybrass and White 1986), bodily waste is an enduring source of political contention. It is, in the political and material sense, "undecidable," at once irreducible, unresolvable, and impossible to escape, fully capture, or repress.[2] To paraphrase Sophia Stamatopoulou-Robbins on waste more generally (2019, 23), "Shit never truly disappears, it merely changes place and form." In any city for that matter, excrement is an enduring undercurrent of social and political life, sometimes erupting, sometimes hovering below the surface, yet ever present. As the proprietor of a public toilet complex in Tema's edge-city of Ashaiman puts it, "Stomach has no holiday."

Excrement's undecidability is a perennial problem not only for urban residents but also for the state authorities that seek to govern the city. Tapping into the defining dilemmas of urban existence—how do we, as embodied beings, live together—bodily waste and its manifold infrastructures are ever ready to surface in the tug-of-war between and among the agents and subjects of urban governance. Scholarly, technoscientific, and political interventions regarding the proper management of human excreta abound. These conventions reinforce a decisively modernist script with excreta's management the arbiter of civility and incivility, the social and the primal, progress and stagnation. According to this widely accepted frame, the natural disorder of human waste is expected to give way to political administration and the sequestering of fecal matter as base substance and private act (Elias 1994; Laporte 2002; Morgan 2002). In a powerful sleight of hand interlinking the discipline of individual bodies and populations (Foucault 1979), such renderings naturalize the paired emergence of self-regulating private citizens and the overarching apparatus of the modern state (Laporte 2002). In turn, they underwrite what is taken to be the "modern infrastructural ideal" (Graham and Marvin 2001): centralized administration of urban infrastructural systems.

Despite its problematic assumptions about bodily discipline and responsibility, this model of human scatological organization, embodying what Bhaskar Mukhopadhyay (2006, 226) calls "the municipal-civic master discourse," remains an enduring preoccupation of urban planning, international development, and public health (Barton and Tsourou 2000; Melosi 2008; Osinde 2008; Rosen 1993; van der Geest and Obirih-Opareh 2008). When orchestrated by the state or its proxies, all pose the interiorization of sanitation and bodily waste as fundamental to individual well-being and a broader project of societal improvement (Anderson 2006; Corburn 2009; McFarlane 2008a, 2008b).[3] The World Bank's (2011) "No Open Defecation" scheme promoting private, in-home toilets across Africa and South Asia demonstrates the enduring hold of this widely accepted scatalogic. The United Nations Millennium Development Goals (2015) likewise promote private toilets for every household, branding public facilities as inadequate and undesirable. Evident in UNICEF's "Water, Sanitation and Hygiene" campaign for Ghana (UNICEF 2018; Baddoo 2019), the more recent UN global Sustainable Development agenda (UNDP 2019b) endorses the same position.

The story told here offers an alternative to this dominant sanitary thesis by putting infrastructure, theories of material agency, and, most of all, actually existing sanitary solutions devised by city residents at the fore. Evidence drawn from urban lives and localities demonstrates that it is misleading to look at sanitation in the global South through an overarching optic of inadequacy, whether lack of facilities, privacy, hygiene, or infrastructural capacity. This assumption not only denies the long historical legacy of sanitary provisioning within cities across the world (Appadurai 2002; Bouju 2008;

Figure I.2. "The Big Squat," 2013 (Photo by Brenda Chalfin)

Joshi et al. 2011; Molotch 2010; Mukhopadhyay 2006).⁴ It equally obscures the vital engagement of social actors with waste and hygiene in organizing urban politics and public life in other than high-modernist terms, including in contexts of entrenched exclusion.

Notably, this book, rather than reproduce modernist suppositions by calling attention to their absence in spaces where they never materialized, probes the presumptions and contradictions of the modernist script by looking closely at the alternatives that emerge in its wake. Known as "defamiliarization," this is a classic strategy of anthropological critique (Marcus and Fischer 1986), putting what is presumed common, best, or inevitable in new light. It is also posed as a mode of political engagement in its own right. As Mukhopadhyay (2006, 226) notes, and I concur: "Putting shit and filth up for reconsideration does not mean a passive withdrawal from activism. On the contrary, it means engaging with popular or subaltern practices as ethico-political responses and reflecting on their sources of authority rather than simply denigrating them from the vantage point of some absolute wisdom."

Although Tema's excremental experiments are certainly replicable, the goal is not to pose them as ideal types but to historicize them as emanations of distinct political conjunctures. By fusing political analysis and excremental evidence from urban Ghana, the work resists the claim that political practice in Africa demands a special lens attuned to what Jean-François Bayart (1993) calls "belly-politics" or Achille Mbembe (2003) "necro-politics." Rather, consideration of urban politics through the lens of excrement, and excrement through the lens of urban politics, joins other challenges to the tunnel vision of political analysis around the institutional canon of elections, legislative bodies, law, and executive authority (see also Paller 2019). Left out is the broad spectrum of public life formative of urban political experience, what Asef Bayat (2013) calls "life as politics." A focus on formal institutional processes furthermore denies power's fundamental, indeed elemental, "heterogeneity," as Georges Bataille (1985) puts it. Made vivid in the account of excremental infrastructure, the substantive approach to urban politics proposed here is of broad relevance.[5] Certainly, shit is not going away. Indeed, at a planetary moment when the possibilities and limiting conditions of the material world are undeniable (Jobson 2020; Haraway 2016; Latour 2018; Moore 2015), the commingling of human and other-than-human agents, including bodily waste, in the orchestration of urban plurality is all the more consequential.

In sum, a series of core propositions drive this text. First, excrement is an essential element of urban politics and public life—that is, a political matter—due to its perennial presence, elemental vitality, and "undecidable" character as public or private, resource or risk, human or other than human.[6] Second, the political potentials and struggles surrounding bodily waste in urban settings are powerfully evident in the infrastructures used, designed, or avoided by urban residents to manage individual and collective excremental outputs. Third, these realities confound the received sanitary script of high modernity. They not only reveal viable solutions to urban sanitation otherwise ignored. Joining other recent interrogations of the politics of urban waste (Fredericks 2018; Millar 2018; Stamatopoulou-Robbins 2019), they bring to the fore a broad arena of urban collective action considered insignificant or deemed inscrutable.

Looking beyond examples of self-conscious urban protest around sanitation and the lack thereof, evidence from Ghana turns away from excremental activism per se (cf. Appadurai 2002; Jackson and Robins 2018; Robins 2014; Robins and Redfield 2016; von Schnitzler 2016). The work instead trains its lens on infrastructural arrangements designed and modified by urban residents and treats them as a form of political action in their own right. In contrast to episodic expressions or reactions against received forms, the character of waste-based infrastructures affects urban routines, relationships, and the built and natural environment in enduring ways. While infrastructural interventions in Tema may provoke the attention of urban authorities, they are devised first and foremost for use, not demonstration effect (cf. Appadurai 2002). A "politics of the ordinary," to borrow from Steven Robins (2008), this is what I term deep urbanism at work. Indeed, because excremental infrastructures serve as a node of individual and collective well-being in the city, the effects of their revival and restructuring are multiplied across urban lives and the wider urban landscape.

The approach developed in this work differs from studies of infrastructure through the predominant lens of techno-politics and genealogy of Michel Foucault (cf. Anand 2017; Carse 2014; Chalfin 2010; Mains 2019; Mitchell 2002; von Schnitzler 2016). Notably, the book puts the vitality of things at the fore, specifically, the vitality of human waste and its associated infrastructures. Underwriting what I call the "vital politics of infrastructure," this vitality complicates and confounds the workings of techno-politics.[7] While the scatalogics of the postcolony have provoked substantial discussion attuned to "the aesthetics of vulgarity" (Esty 1999; Mbembe 2001), the discursive bias of these approaches sidesteps the vital materialities of human ordure and the natural and infrastructural systems sustaining them. These are matters Brian Larkin (2008) and Kerry Chance (2018) start to unpack elsewhere in Africa.[8] Larkin, focused on urban Nigeria, addresses the interplay of infrastructural functioning and breakdown. Chance, training her lens on urban South Africa, investigates how essential elements of urban survival, including their unpredictability, are repurposed for political ends.[9] Contributing to the dual focus pursued here, together they draw attention to the elemental vitality of bodily matters and the vitality of infrastructural things.

A point of crucial importance to my argument, sanitary infrastructures should not and cannot be understood solely through a biopolitical lens privileging discipline and domination (cf. Anderson 2006; Foucault 1979), even if they are a predominant legacy of colonial and national state-building. Driven by the vitality of things themselves—bodily cycles, bodily wastes, and the remains of earlier infrastructural orders—excremental arrangements can be the basis of solidarity, self-determination, and counterpolitics of all sorts (Aretxaga 1995; A. Feldman 1991).[10] Open to restructuring and reinvention,

Figure I.3. Tema's high modernity: high-rise built ca. 1967 (© Constantinos and Emma Doxiadis Foundation)

Figure I.4. Tema high-rise, ca. 2011 (Photo by Brenda Chalfin)

excremental infrastructures provide a formative arena for forging alternative political possibilities. Again, "undecidable," at once human and nonhuman, individual and collective, spent and ever active, intimate and foreign, these matters are impossible to fully suppress and ever ready to be politicized.

Ghana and the Sanitary-Political Paradox

Pushing us to think both politics and human waste anew, Ghana presents a profound sanitary-political paradox. The first African nation to achieve independence, in 1957, Ghana has long been considered a beacon of progress and prosperity on the African continent. It is touted for its political stability, history of democratic rule, and rising incomes and living standards (Adams and Asante 2020; Agyeman-Duah 2005; Gyimah-Boadi 2007; Nathan 2019; Paller 2019). Yet here, more than in any other country in the world, the urban populace relies on public toilet facilities outside of their homes for bodily relief (Appiah-Effah et al. 2019, 400; Ayee and Crook 2003; Crook and Ayee 2006; Oteng-Ababio 2011; Peprah et al. 2015; Thrift 2007; van der Geest and Obirih-Opareh 2008). Less than one-quarter of Ghana's populace has access to private toilets dedicated to the exclusive use of household residents. In terms of what the World Health Organization defines as "improved sanitation" based on private household facilities utilizing waterborne sewerage, the figure is cut in half again (Appiah-Effah et al. 2019, 399, 402). Instead, a preponderance of urban dwellers rely on shared toilets.[11] In-home toilets are lacking for middle-class and upwardly mobile urban residents as much as for their working-class neighbors. This remains the case in Ghana despite the country's standing as a rising middle-income nation meeting global development targets for clean water, basic education, and women's rights, with a more than twenty-year span of competitive elections and an upward trajectory of economic growth (UNDP 2019a). Is this an anomaly, a holdover of underdevelopment that detracts from Ghana's progress, or could it be part and parcel of Ghana's democratic, participatory dispensation? Both? Or something other?

Shedding light on this sanitary-political paradox, the city of Tema serves as the book's analytic focus. A space of vast infrastructural diversity, Tema has a rare citywide sewage system that was considered one of a kind in West Africa when this planned city was constructed circa 1960 as a model of industry-based high modernity for independent Africa. Despite Tema's continued standing as a bastion of upward mobility and middle-class attainment marked by attractive flats and private homes, it is the very site where the sanitary alternatives described above have come to thrive. Here, the political undecidability of waste and waste infrastructures are on full display. Danny Hoffman (2017, 17) remarks, "Nowhere, perhaps, are the contradictory and confusing legacies of modern built forms more evident than in contemporary African cities," which he calls "laboratories of modernism's and modernity's successes and failures." This is fully evident in Tema, where the writing and rewriting of the high-modernist script and the transformative force of ordinary lives pursued among modernism's promises and remains can be read in the city's excremental infrastructural order.

Excremental Colonialism

Ghana has an early and uneven legacy of excremental intervention. In the annals of colonial hygiene, Ghana, like elsewhere in West Africa's tropics, did not fare well. Beginning in 1844, colonial occupation brought increased commerce and the concentration of subject populations (Parker 2000). Amid the salt ponds and lagoons of the West Atlantic littoral, Gold Coast settlements and growing urban zones lacked drains, septic systems, or easy access to fresh water for Europeans and Africans alike. Yet there was minimal investment in sanitation by the fledging colonial administration for the urban populace (Patterson 1979). Though sanitary reform swept the nineteenth-century British metropole (Melosi 2008; Wright 1980), sanitary infrastructural investment in West Africa remained out of the picture (Gale 1995, 187). The relocation of the colony's administrative capital to Accra in 1877 brought little change (Parker 2000). Urban planning revolved around a built environment in the service of rule: office blocks, housing, and leisure spaces for European administrative personnel, with limited regard for the living conditions of African urban dwellers (Freund 2007). Proponents of colonial hygiene in the Gold Coast were instead geared toward the protection of Europeans from tropical disease (Curtin 1985; Bashford 2004; Worboys 2000).

All of this was a prelude to an extended era of sanitary "indirect rule" not entirely different from broader administrative tactics imposed across the region in which residents were essentially commanded to "police" themselves (Killingray 1986; Mamdani 1996). Demonstrating the colonial regime's preoccupation with sanitation and hygiene as a prime logic of urban governance, what Warwick Anderson (1995) calls "excremental colonialism," there was no lack of rhetoric or policy on the matter (Bin-Kasim 2019). Once opened, the gap between sanitary discourse, the actualities of rule, and the realities of excremental practice in the Gold Coast's urban centers continued to grow.[12] Sanitary servicing was made the founding responsibility of town councils (Gale 1995, 194). Commuting political inclusion into responsibility for one's own waste, early municipal ordinances demanded tax revenue from African residents to pay for sanitary schemes (Hess 2000, 39). Resistance to "taxation—and sanitary responsibilization—without representation" sparked protests across the colonial capital Accra (Gale 1995, 196; Patterson 1979, 252). Merchants and mining companies were left to fill the gap.[13] An early example of the privatization of waste management, commercial interests took charge, building sanitary facilities for their workers, and monitoring use and maintenance (Dumett 1968, 168; 1993, 217).[14]

The colonial government finally installed pan latrines in Accra at the turn of the century.[15] However, they refused to be held accountable for urban sanitary conditions, blaming "the lack of reliable water supplies" and "the filthy and lazy habits of the large majority of the native population" (Patterson 1979, 252). The lack of anything but the most rudimentary of infrastructural investments on the part of colonial authorities was no hindrance to the rise of waste- and infrastructure-centered institutions. Employing infrastructure as a means of social and spatial division, "slum clearance" involving demolition of urban African settlements and dwellings was at the heart of a growing Public Works Department mission carried out with the input of medical authorities (Dumett 1968, 196; Gale 1995; Simpson 1909). Bodily waste remained a "niche" matter. Scant effort was made to accommodate the waste flows of the expanding urban populace (Bin-Kasim 2019). Water-based toilets and sewage systems were deemed too expensive for urban Africans (Bohman 2010, 82; Patterson 1979, 254). In Accra, pan latrines persisted as the primary urban sanitary infrastructure well into the 1930s, while the number of structures and the nature of the facilities remained wholly inadequate to urban needs (Appiah-Effah et al. 2019, 403).[16]

In the process, pushing and pulling at the boundaries of the properly political through the play of regulatory intervention and infrastructural neglect, waste and sanitation had become a vibrant terrain of urban public life. Accra's latrines were deemed physically as well as spiritually unclean by residents. Administrative records indicate "[excremental] concealment matters not at all. . . . A walk around Accra in the evening will prove . . . that many prefer not to use a latrine" (Patterson 1979, 254). "Just as plans for collection of water rates aroused popular resentment, the lack of enough clean latrines was a continuing public grievance" (255). All the while, the town council adamantly rejected pleas for intervention. Herein lies the festering root of Ghana's sanitary-political paradox: having become a source of governmental scrutiny and sanction, sanitation was deemed a public good yet was made a private responsibility heaped on urban residents by city authorities.

The Rise of Tema

The sanitary-infrastructural fabric of imperial rule would soon be disrupted by the sanitary designs of decolonization, complicating the sanitary-political paradox anew. These rearrangements found their most vivid expression not in the capital Accra, nor in any existing city, but in the newly imagined and yet-to-be-built city of Tema.[17] In 1949, the colonial government, on the heels of its departure, proposed constructing a massive hydroelectric dam on the Volta River to jump-start industry and maintain a hold on the economy (D'Auria 2014, 339; D. Hart 1980; Miescher 2012, 2014; Moxon 1969).[18] A new seaport to export the anticipated output was added to the plan (R. B. Davidson 1954; Hilling 1966, 113).[19] The elements of what was known as the Volta River Scheme formed West Africa's most ambitious industrial-infrastructural project to date (D'Auria 2010). A proposal for an industrial hub and residential zone adjacent to the port followed. The city of Tema was born, as was the nation-state of Ghana.

In 1951, the very year of Tema's founding, a new constitution stipulating the appointment of the African prime minister, African cabinet, and African legislative assembly was ratified by the Gold Coast legislature (Apter 1963; B. Davidson 1989). *Osagyefo* Dr. Kwame Nkrumah, a Pan-African statesman and visionary, was designated prime minister. With Tema and the Volta River Scheme at the fore, Ghana launched its first national development plan. Through government decree, a sixty-four-square-mile tract of land twenty miles east of Accra was acquired from customary authorities to site the port and city (Hilling 1966, 115). Considered an engine of Ghanaian and indeed African progress signaling Ghana's equivalence with other modern nation-states, the new city was to contain all the infrastructures of modern living. Described by Ghana's newly established Ministry of Information as "enjoying all the advantages of modern civilization" (Jopp 1961, 6), Tema was to be serviced with the full complement of infrastructural modernity, from power stations, phone lines, and an electrical grid to street drains, culverts and waterworks, and a hierarchy of roads, streets, and bridges designed exclusively for vehicular traffic.

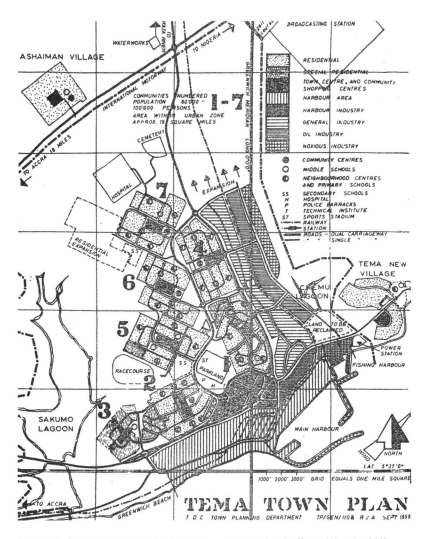

Figure I.5. Clerk, Alcock, and Robinson 1955 master plan for Tema (Alcock 1963)

Most important for the story told here, among Tema's many infrastructural firsts was an expansive, gravity-driven, subterranean sewerage system. It remains today the largest and most ambitious sanitary infrastructure in the subregion, linking individual homes and industrial installations to local trunk lines and sewage mains, and sewage mains to a series of citywide sewage pumping stations. Waste would be channeled to offshore outflows

Figure I.6. Tema tabula rasa, 1965 (© Constantinos and Emma Doxiadis Foundation)

Figure I.7. Sewage system sea outfall, 1959 (Ghana Information Services Division)

extending miles into the Atlantic. Thus, to the lore of Ghana's midcentury political and economic exceptionalism can be added the high-modernist city of Tema and the innovations of its waste management system.[20] Reports convey the alignment of Ghanaian progress with the new city, its sewage system included: "Tema is the first city in West Africa to be built with a waterborne sewerage and mains-water system serving each individual house irrespective of income group. Elimination of septic tanks and open-sewage ditches has removed the smell and risk of disease, and as the sewerage system is automatic, recurring costs are low. All grades of housing have flushing toilet, shower and kitchen-sink with mains water supply" (Alcock 1963, 3).

For architectural historians, Tema is regarded as an artifact of modernist internationalism virtually frozen in time (Jackson and Holland 2014). Read through the lens of its vital infrastructure however, Tema is a more lively form: dynamic, unsettled, and functionally de- and recomposed behind the façade of its master plan and cement-block buildings. Undermining the grand claims and infrastructural aspirations of new nation-building, a half century later, Tema's once idealized sewage system is in massive disrepair. Belying the neat appearance of Tema's homes and the calm ambiance of its residential streets and public thoroughfares compared to the hustle and bustle of nearby Accra, a different reality lies underground and inside the walled-off installations of the city's Waste Management Authority.[21] Across this diverse urban zone, the remains of the new city's original sanitary arrangements are supplemented and sustained by a wide range of excremental infrastructural alternatives forged by the residents themselves. Here again, we see the heavy hand—and contradictions—of state impositions regarding the disposition of urban waste. Despite the substantial investment in waste infrastructure in the name of national progress and public good, bodily waste turns into a realm of private responsibility, this time amid an already established expansive public system.

Evidence from locations across Tema reveals sanitation and sewerage to be substantially orchestrated by urban dwellers grappling with the remnants of the citywide system (see table I.1). Tema's infrastructural innovators include residents still dependent on household facilities left over from the city's founding, who actively monitor and modify the remains of the midcentury order to keep it operable. For the more than half of city residents currently untethered to the sewage system, public toilets are a predominant popular solution. Of households surveyed across the city, barely half still have access to a household-based water closet. Nearly one-third of residents utilize public toilet facilities (Rohilla et al. 2018, 4). While some residents use government-built toilets reminiscent of the barely maintained installations of colonial-era Accra, these installations are overshadowed in number and popularity by public facilities largely devised, maintained, and managed by private persons, families, households, and community collectives. Flush, pit, septic tank, sit, and squat, found on street corners, in back alleys, on remote lots, and inside residential dwellings, toilet access is open to stranger, kin, resident, and transient alike for a nominal fee. All offer alternatives to open defecation and the deposition of fecal matter in plastic baggies before tossing them to the wind (Appiah-Effah et al. 2019, 406)—a practice referred to as "flying toilets"—scorned by public health experts and urban dwellers alike (*New Humanitarian* 2012). Rather than a source of shame or excremental last resort, a substantial proportion of Tema's public facilities are a source of comfort, dignity, and, for some, profit.

In this mix, Ghana's sanitary-political paradox takes a new turn. Bodily waste comes to the fore as an essential element of urban public life, again politically undecidable. What was decreed a private matter to be guaranteed by state authorities is turned back into a public issue to be managed by private persons. In these breakdowns and adjustments, the received script of sanitary and political modernity articulated by urban and political theorists alike is upended (pace Arendt 1958; Elias 1994; Mumford 1938). Excrement and its infrastructures, as Laporte (2002) reminds us, have a history. But rather than the straight line of excremental progress by way of suppression in the private realm and exclusion from the public, in Tema's diverse neighborhoods shit has resurfaced as a private responsibility and a public one in lieu of the state. In turn, individual bodily needs and outputs push into public space, and public needs and concerns push into the ostensibly private domain of the household. Not only do these sanitary solutions supplant the state's claim to primacy over the terms of urban waste management; in the process, they rework the expected relation between bodily waste, public life (the res publica), the locus of collective decision making (the polis), and the domus, taken to be the space of domicile and primary affiliation (Swanson 2018).[22]

This book unpacks the unexpected political possibilities, some emancipating and enabling, others creating new forms of dependence and inequality, born from the reinvention of excremental infrastructure in the city. The point is not to argue that anywhere there is centralized urban sanitation

Table I.1. Survey of urban sanitation in Tema

Types of sanitation facilities	Households	Percentage of total households
No facility—bush, beach, field	6,701	9.5
Water closet	37,626	53.1
Pit latrine	1,465	2.1
Ventilated latrine	2,498	3.5
Bucket/pan	115	0.2
Public toilet	21,775	30.8
Other	617	0.9
Total	70,797	

Source: Rohilla et al. 2018, 3.

the same vital politics found in Tema will be in play. To the contrary, building on the insights of a long line of social theorists (Elias 1994; Foucault 1979; Harvey 2005; Laporte 2002; Mumford 1939), the case of Tema is both norm and exception. State-based, mandated, or delegated waste management, paired with the privatization of waste production outside the public sphere, is more often largely expected and little objectified in urban political life. Only rarely or sporadically does this metastructure of urban order come to the fore, typically in the case of breakdown, massive inequality, or gross mismanagement.[23] In some cities, water and water infrastructure spur activism and contestation (Anand 2017). In others, it is electricity (Degani 2018; von Schnitzler 2016). In others still, such as Tema, it is human waste (Appadurai 2002; Robbins 2016).

Tema represents a special case, illustrating and complicating norms in several ways. First, Tema's sanitation system, rather than an after-the-fact organic feature of the city's urban built environment, was on the leading edge of urban design, planning, and settlement. In place before many of the residential zones were complete, the system was self-consciously promoted by city founders in terms of the work it could do—at once technical, political, and ideological—as a sign of industrial modernity and a means to orient citizens inward. Second, not only do the breakdown and inadequacy of the system betray its dashed promises and unrealizable intentions, but the real-

Figure I.8. Large-scale biodigester under construction, 2011 (Photo by Brenda Chalfin)

ities of excremental order in Tema foreground an array of alternative pathways to large-scale urban waste management that carry their own political implications and presumptions. In short, the sanitary alternatives evident in Tema do not just bring the norm to attention but call it into question by laying out other viable solutions to urban bodily and infrastructural needs. Circling back to the very constitution and character of urban polities, actually existing sanitary arrangements at work in the city each configure the relationship between public, private, and the state in distinct ways. In turn, they offer urban planners and analysts as well as city residents a means to actualize alternative visions of urban living and propose new paths to urban futures. As the massive infrastructural outlays of the heyday of industrial modernity fall into disrepair (Fortun 2014), much like Tema, such reconfigurations are likely to become all the more prevalent. Coming full circle, Tema's extant exceptions may well map new norms.

In making the case for close examination of Tema's infrastructural alternatives, it is crucial to recognize that the novel excremental arrangements found in the city are not isolated attempts at infrastructural self-provisioning.

They are fine-tuned modalities of claims making and political imagining vital to urban functioning. Sometimes cooperative, sometimes competitive, these excremental interventions give order to the wider urban milieu as state bodies and initiatives struggle for reach and relevance. Born of necessity and biopolitical proscription yet moving in directions all their own, Tema's novel excremental solutions expose a largely overlooked realm of urban public life expressive of urban dwellers' "right to the city" (Lefebvre 1996) that is relevant beyond the case at hand. Phrased in terms of Raymond Williams's (1977) classic analytic triad "dominant, emergent, residual," built on and around "residual" forms, in Tema we find a set of "emergent" urban orders taking shape in response to the rollback of state services and capacities alongside unprecedented urban growth that marks a "dominant" trend across the global South and global North.

If there is one thing that brings urban dwellers together across the social and spatial distinctions of the city, it is the need for bodily relief. An enduring urban motif, the predicament of bodily waste is the prevailing metaphor of Ghanaian Ayi Kwei Armah's *The Beautyful Ones Are Not Yet Born* (1969). In this novel, written during the very era of Tema's founding, a humble bureaucrat and corrupt politician both seek escape through the glory hole of a common bucket latrine. What Joshua D. Esty (1999) describes from a literary stance as "excremental post-colonialism" surfaces anew decades later from an infrastructural stance via the collective reshaping of Tema's built environment. Less about the heavy hand and laden ideals of Ghana's immediate postcolonial state, Tema's excremental realities reflect much more the light touch of the twenty-first-century neoliberal state (Chalfin 2010) amid the ruins of high modernity.

Vital Politics of Infrastructure: Central Arguments

Tema's excremental infrastructures, while shaped by limited state capacity and faulty international fixes, and sometimes less than ideal from a public health standpoint, are meaningful social and political formations not to be overlooked when assessing the lived terms of urban democracy and development, whether in Ghana or elsewhere. Sophia Stamatopoulou-Robbins (2019, 4), regarding Palestine's waste infrastructure, states, "The ways in which and the extent to which a population is exposed to waste can thus be diagnostic of the nature of governance." The study of Ghana's city of Tema indicates that what happens in response are diagnostic of "vital politics"—a term I use to capture the interplay of that which is full of life—human and nonhuman—along with essential human needs and struggles for dignity and bodily well-being.

From the vantage point of "vital politics," anchored in living bodies and vital needs and substances, the sanitary solutions created and transformed by Tema residents are political on multiple fronts. They are prime domains of urban contention where urban residents confront and challenge the limits of centralized political authority. Moreover, serving as small p "parliaments of things" (Latour 1993, 142; 2005a, 24), Tema residents' novel infrastructural outlays extend the limit of what is possible and permissible in both the public and private realms for a large swath of urban dwellers. Despite their ostensibly private ends and location in privately owned and managed spaces, they are formative arenas of public claims making where residents push back on state promises and inherited technologies and reengineer the urban social contract in concrete terms. At once harnessing and stabilizing excrement's elemental volatility and social undecidability, Tema's infrastructural experiments are furthermore political in their capacity to organize, reproduce, and legitimize the lived conditions of urban "plurality," a relation that simultaneously encompasses human "equality and distinction" (Arendt 1958, 175). In toto, these conditions attest to a vital politics by means of infrastructure at work.

In Tema, I argue, three features of infrastructure's vital politics prevail. The first, substantive, I call "vital remains." The second, relational, I term "infrastructural intimacy" (Chalfin 2015).[24] The third, institutional, I label "deep domesticity." Each one shapes the other in turn. Doubly constituting "vital remains," both infrastructure and bodily excreta are never inert. This perspective aligns frameworks of new materialism (Bennet 2010) and anthropologies of waste (Fredericks 2018; Millar 2018; Reno 2015). Along with the bodies and bodily cycles of Tema residents, the liveliness of the materials that make up and move through the city's infrastructural outlays are central to their political possibilities. These materials undergo decay and recomposition just as the bodies of city residents follow their own cycles of consumption and expulsion, production, and evacuation. Like them, the infrastructures in which they are entangled may break down but never completely go away. A point Brian Larkin (2008) makes clear in his discussion of media infrastructure in Nigeria, old systems evince unexpected elements in the course of decline, available to be harnessed anew. As Steven Jackson (2014, 221, 227) asserts, "When we take erosion, breakdown and decay ... as starting points," the interdependence of innovation and repair becomes self-evident. That's because breakdown seeds innovation, both human and nonhuman. Likewise complicating received understandings of infrastructural decline, infrastructural decay can also be read as "signs of life" (Hetherington 2019, 9), keeping in mind the disruptions and disadvantages as well as potential opportunities that ensue.

When it comes to the vitality and unpredictability of spent things, feces, sewage, and associated infrastructures are bioactive forms with their own agency and energetics divorced from human intention despite their intimate association with human bodies. As Georges Bataille's (1985) application of the logics of thermodynamics to political life asserts, the excesses of human existence, whether bodily waste or otherwise, can never be completely captured. Given the "ongoingness" of life and the "ongoingness" of things (Haraway 2016), excremental infrastructures thus bring an elemental force to urban politics and serve as a threshold of political possibility. Although they are often suppressed by the heavy hand of the state, they are susceptible to eruption, from the unexpected flooding of markets, homes, and streets in Tema due to broken sewage mains, or more gradual, quotidian transformations of pipes, pumps, water closets, and septic pits.

Vital remains constitute the substrate of infrastructure's vital politics. Surpluses never fully contained, they enliven connections and tensions among urban residents and between urban residents and municipal bodies. Bound up with the relational aspects of infrastructure's vital politics, the play of vital remains in Tema inspires attachments between people and infrastructure and among people through infrastructure that I term "infrastructural intimacy"—the second critical term in the triad.[25] Enabled by bodily processes and outputs in which they are entangled, infrastructural intimacies exceed relations of bodily copresence and play out through an array of affective, sensory, and operational correspondences and interdependencies across persons and infrastructural things. Infused by the force and possibility of vital remains, the sociotechnical remix of infrastructural intimacy offers a formative means through which new political orders and accountabilities materialize in the stead of the city's official infrastructural fabric, moving beyond restoration to sustain innovation (cf. Jackson 2014, 222). They set the stage for new configurations of public order and accountability as well as new social and technical arrangements in the private sphere of household and community.[26]

A kind of relational glue, infrastructural intimacy transforms emergent orders into enduring formations by tapping into, channeling, and containing the vitality of material remains. In the face of the base substances and practices of human excretion, infrastructural intimacies mobilize emotional attachments and identifications to routinize new infrastructural arrangements. Differing from discussions of infrastructure's capacity to shape intimate forms of sociality (Appel, Anand, and Gupta 2018, 22), I use the term "infrastructural intimacy" to address intimate sociality's capacity to instantiate, stabilize, and harness infrastructure. Such inversions of infrastructural figure and ground, prevalent across Tema's infrastructural outlays, underwrite what I call the "infrastructural inchoate." Through the lens of infrastructural intimacy, attention to the inchoate allows a finer-grained understanding of situations otherwise glossed as "breakdown" (pace Star 1999). The inchoate signals the possibility of transformation as infrastructural context and content intertwine, provider and user switch places, material flows prevail over fixed forms, and popular needs unseat state ideals.

Similarly integral to the vital politics of infrastructure in Tema, excremental solutions formulated by city residents are rooted in and transformative of domestic spaces and practices. Notably, domestic arenas demonstrate a capacity to concentrate vital remains, and seed and sustain infrastructural intimacies. The results are institutional formations marked by what I call "deep domesticity," which provide the work's third conceptual anchor. Undergirding Tema's excremental innovations, deep domesticity involves the expansion and extension of domestic functions, membership, and spatial and operational reach. Drawing persons and things into domestic spaces and networks, deep domesticity provides a foundation for wider infrastructural and political realignments. The "depth" of deep domesticity" lies in multilayered linkages and entailments at once state-facing, public-facing, and internally focused. Like Clifford Geertz's (1972) "deep play," deep domesticity is multivalent. Articulating claims to resources, rights, and recognition and sustaining residents' coordinated response to state exclusions and intrusions, deep domesticity turns inside out Tema's founding plan of excremental infrastructural internalization and centralized control. Rather than infrastructural elaboration and tight enclosure of the domestic sphere walled off from the polis per the conventional modernist sanitary script, by means of infrastructure's vital politics the domus encroaches on the polis and res publica to claim earlier suppressed possibilities. Whether these popular modalities of urban infrastructural provisioning should be replicated or championed is a matter for health experts to determine. For those concerned with the realities of urban politics and public life in African cities, they offer important grounds for political critique and theorization.

Theoretical Anchors: From Actor Network Theory to Vita Activa

Making Latourian Associations

I draw inspiration from what on the surface may appear to be two rather different camps of political theory to understand the nature of Tema's excremental infrastructures as engines and outcomes of urban political praxis. Bruno Latour's (1990, 1993, 1996, 2005a, 2005b) rendering of Actor Network Theory (ANT) is essential to the discussion. So too is Hannah Arendt's multifaceted conception of political life articulated in *The Human Condition* (1958). Though infrequently conjoined (Chalfin 2014, 2015, 2017; Honig 2017),[27] they share roots in Martin Heidegger's (1971, 2008) phenomenological approach to lifeworlds. Relevant to and revealed by infrastructure's vital politics, the juxtaposition of Arendt and Latour offers generative tensions and unexpected intersections both theoretical and methodological. Drawing on Heidegger's theorization of "gatherings," Latour (1993, 2005a, 2005b) focuses on never entirely predictable processes and outcomes of "associations." Arendt's *The Human Condition*, by contrast, seeks to capture historical trends and transhistorical continuities, fostering comparison and *longue dureé* perspectives. Despite the originality of its historical sweep and conceptual frames, hers is a more conventional approach to politics focused on institutions and individual and collective rights and recognition.

Through the combined optics of Arendt and Latour, it is possible to unpack the multifaceted origins of the excremental infrastructural solutions devised and utilized by Tema residents and their sociopolitical and institutional impacts given infrastructural arrangements' capacity to shape and remake the functionally entangled realms of domus, polis, and res publica. By reflecting on Tema via the conceptual and methodological lens of Arendt and Latour, and Arendt and Latour through the lens of Tema, the ability of excremental infrastructures to express and orient urban political experience and expressions of plurality in enduring, even if contested, ways comes to the fore. *Demos*—including participatory forms of public goods provisioning such as waste management that are the lived terrain of urban coexistence and self-governance—is built not on rote consensus but on constant negotiation across difference, as Latour's (2005a, 14) discussion of the varied and dynamic character of political assembly reminds us.

Eschewing ideal types, Latour's Actor Network Theory is attuned to actually existing entanglements of human and nonhuman and the unscripted possibilities that emerge in the immediate flow of social life. Drawing on Gilles Deleuze's notion of "assemblage," ANT builds on the premise that human and nonhuman agency coconstitute social and technical worlds (Latour 1993). By enabling and reproducing "associations," practices of human and nonhuman assembly establish the material contours of public life and give them durable form (Latour 2005a, 1990). The value of ANT to anthropological investigations of infrastructure is well established (Barry 2006, 2013; Jensen and Morita 2017; Von Schnitzler 2016). With regard to political processes, ANT offers an important alternative to Michel Foucault's (1979) and Giorgio Agamben's (1998) much stricter disciplinary optics. In contrast to these theorists, ANT is attuned to the interacting agencies of humans and nonhuman things, and makes visible infrastructure's multiplex, often unstable technopolitics and its unscripted political outcomes.[28]

The political entailments of public life engendered via gatherings of people and things are core concerns for Latour (2005a). Centered on the concept of "dingpolitics" ("thing-politics"), from the archaic definition of "ding" as a mix of "meeting and matter," Latour (2005a, 5, 12) asserts, "The body politik is not only made of people. They are thick with things" (6). He founds this contention on the premise that "objects—taken as so many issues—bind all of us in ways that map out a public space profoundly different from what is usually recognized under the label of 'the political'" (5). Rooted in the sustained admixture of people and things by means of infrastructure, these configurations enable and orchestrate human plurality amid the vagaries of public life. For Latour (24), as for those who reside in urban Ghana, such assemblies are the "real" parliaments of public life distinct from formal institutions of representation and deliberation. In a similar vein, Bonnie Honig (2017, 90), drawing on Latour and Arendt, asserts, "Public things are one of democracy's necessary conditions"; if we neglect them, "we end up theorizing the demos . . . without the things that give them purpose."

Actor Network Theory speaks to infrastructure's political potentials in another critical way as it moves beyond the dichotomy between human and nonhuman matters. Urging recognition of the intractable presence and agential potential of bioactive materials, the murky middle grounds of the more-than and not-quite human come into the analytic ambit (Murdoch

1997; Haraway 2004, 2016; Kirksey and Helmreich 2010).[29] Excreta prime among them, these are substances of both life and decay. Of the body but not fully human, they are a by-product of human life yet have a life of their own and can threaten or bolster human vitality.[30] Alert to the varied half-lives of human bodily waste, this strand of ANT, falling under the rubric of "vital materialism" (Bennett 2010), lends to the study of infrastructure an appreciation of material arrangements essential to human life and material forms full of life. Not recognized in Arendt's rendering of politics or plurality despite her attunement to human vitality (1958, 47), attention to the dynamics of the "other than human" offers a fuller picture of infrastructure's vital politics appropriate to the case of Tema's excremental experiments.[31]

Arendt on Bodies, Infrastructure, and Urban Publics

Driven by the conditions at work in Tema, I pair ANT's consideration of the Gordian knot of material agency en masse with investigation of the specific ways human interests and intentions are actively materialized to represent and enforce political claims. A conceptual couplet, this approach encodes a double question of how materiality becomes agential and human agency is materialized. Though related and intersecting, the agency of material forms cannot be assumed to be identical to the material dimensions of human agency. In this regard, Arendt's *The Human Condition* offers crucial insight on matters overlooked or conflated by Latour. For Arendt, "the human condition is an active condition": what she calls the *vita activa*. Human existence depends on the engagement of the human body as both agent and object of activity. Such activity takes multiple forms. Arendt divides them in three—labor, work, and action. She poses each as a sequential move in the full realization of human political potential (Arendt 1958, 7):

> Labor is the activity that corresponds to the biological processes of the human body . . . life itself.

> Work provides an artificial world of things distinctly different from natural surrounds.

> Action, the only activity that goes on directly between men [*sic*] without the intermediary of things or matter, corresponds to the human condition of plurality, to the fact that men, not Man, live on the earth and inhabit the world. While all aspects of the human condition are somehow related to politics, this plurality is specifically the condition . . . of all political life.

Together, the conditions of human experience compose the *vita activa* (Arendt 1958, 17), a form of dually collective and individual existence. Also referred to as the "unquiet," it exceeds the life of contemplation by being in the world with others and with things. Though posed in terms at times contradictory, Arendt's triad of labor, work, and action complicates the prevailing political dichotomization of public and private by speaking to their various overlaps and middle grounds (Honig 1995, 4). In the case of Tema, where public needs enter into private domains and private needs spill over to the public realm, this analytic alternative offers critical conceptual traction. In this work, I make the bold move to attend to action as conceived by Arendt not by privileging speech but instead by treating actions' material manifestations as forms of individual and collective practice.

Appeal to Arendt is not without consequence. Like the work of her teacher-mentor Heidegger, Arendt's political philosophy is marred by presumptions of inherent human hierarchies and exclusions.[32] Where Heidegger is taken to task for his anti-Semitism, Arendt is guilty of a deep misunderstanding of race and racial politics in Africa as well as in the United States (Allen 2004; Bernasconi 1996; Gines 2014; King and Stone 2007; Norton 1995). Attuned to these limitations, my engagement with Arendt partakes of a larger intellectual effort to "think with Arendt against Arendt," as feminist political theorist Seyla Benhabib (2000, 198) puts it. To make Arendt relevant to the present, Benhabib (198) asserts, scholars need to "leave behind the pieties of textual analysis and ask Arendtian questions and be ready to provide non-Arendtian answers." In this vein, my examination of political life in Ghana builds on the growing reappraisal of Arendt among scholars of the global South. Alongside those in allied fields of history (Lee 2008) and political science (Bernstein 2018; Samnotra 2016), anthropologists and their ethnographic interlocutors have a growing stake and voice in this project (Bear 2015; de Genova 2010; G. Feldman 2013, 2015).[33]

Arendt's core ideas—about the body, public life, politics, plurality, and the human-made world—are marked by towering intellectual insights as well as impasses. In these gaps, Latour and Arendt illuminate one another and are illuminated by the case at hand. Of fundamental relevance to the investigation of infrastructure's vital politics in the city of Tema, Arendt, unlike most political theorists of her day—not to mention Latour—deigns to address bodily processes. The body is integral to her distinctive conception of labor, defined as "practices necessary for the maintenance of life itself" (Arendt 1958, 7) and encompassing the biological processes and metabolic needs of the human body. Arendt, again unusual for theorists of her day, dares to speak directly to the presence and significance of the body in the political realm. However, representing a telling fissure in her conceptual apparatus, she shuts down this conceptual opening. After discussing the details of bodily sustenance and reproduction, Arendt asserts that bodily needs as a realm of bare necessity reflect humans' animal nature. Thus, she deems them prepolitical, preconditional to political life. Provoking scholars to accuse Arendt of both condemning and silencing the political body—especially a body gendered female (Zerilli 1995, 167)—Arendt blatantly rejects any polity in which intimate concerns are publicized and dismisses the body as an inappropriate subject or object of political action. She grounds these claims in her much-idealized polis of Ancient Greece, where "the citizens' freedom derived from their capacity to disregard the fact that they too were ... as beholden to bodily needs as anyone else" (Tsao 2002, 106).

Taken at face value, Arendt's diatribe against the public body, treating it as not only out of place but also antithetical to the polis and political action, is unable to comprehend the political possibilities of Tema's excremental orders. Yet amid these "pieties," Arendt expresses flashes of insight regarding the place of the body in the public realm. Apposite to the case of Tema, she remarks, "Whether an activity is performed in private or in public is by no means a matter of indifference. The character of the public realm must change in accordance with the activities admitted to it. To a large extent the activity changes its own nature too" (1958, 46). To draw on terms introduced earlier, the "vital remains" of the body are likewise the "vital remains" of Arendt's theorization of labor. Indeed, offering unexpected resonance with Tema's excremental infrastructural innovations, despite Arendt's ardent effort to treat bodily necessity as prepolitical, bodily processes and substances creep into her formulations, suggesting that the body too is politically undecidable.[34] Resonating with the collective management of bodily waste in Tema, Arendt (1958, 100) mentions the "natural metabolism of the living body," and "processes of growth and decay through which nature forever invades the human artifice." From this perspective, the vitalities of things—both human and nonhuman—are recognized to inform political process.

Rather than conforming to Arendt's explicit contention that activities of *animal laborans* corrupt the political realm, Tema's excremental solutions raise the question of how "practices necessary for the maintenance of life itself" (Arendt 1958, 7) shape the character of urban plurality, pushing us to "think with Arendt against Arendt" (Benhabib 2000, 198). Arendt's subtended intuitions regarding the bodily processes and the polis may well serve to strengthen Latourian assemblage theory, which is widely accused of "ontological flattening" in its tendency to equate human and nonhuman agency (Harman 2014). Such recognition of the forms, forces, and consequences of bodily presence in the modern public sphere, even if couched in dismissal per Arendt (1958), puts the multiplex presences, concerns, and capacities of the body into ANT's political ontology, offering a vantage point in line with infrastructure's vital politics in Tema.

Bringing Latour and Arendt to bear on each other as well as the case at hand, Tema's excremental arrangements likewise pry open Arendt's rendering of what she calls "the social." A core—and much debated (Honig 1995)—contention of *The Human Condition*, Arendt furiously maligns what she identifies as the rise of the "social" in modern public life. Coming to the fore with industrial modernity, the social, as she sees it, undermines the capacity for open-ended in-depth exchange and debate that marks the properly political (Arendt 1958, 45). Characterized by Arendt as an explanation for modernity's downfall, "the social" in her rendering is an expansive if unruly concept collapsing multiple claims. Three stand out. Most pronounced is the surfacing of bodily labors in public. Also wrapped into the social is the force of social conformism in modern consumer society, inhibiting autonomy and expression of difference (Arendt 1958, 46; Pitkin 1995, 59; Tsao 2002, 106). The third is the tendency toward self-interest, summed up by Hanna Pitkin (1995, 54) as the scourge of "housekeeping," whether pushing the preoccupations of the household in the political realm or turning away from public life and collective well-being toward superficial self-interest rather than political things (Arendt 1958, 52). Arendt's disdain for "the social" is evident in her much-remembered discussion of modern enchantment with "small things" in the private space of the household, such that the collective potentials of the public realm are supplanted by a penchant for comfort and "charm" (52). Ultimately undermining what she considers to be the all-important workings of plurality in the public realm, Arendt argues that the social detracts from the pursuit of collective interests and breeds passivity rather than collective negotiation of difference (Canovan 1992; Norris 2002; Pitkin 1995).[35]

Taken at face value, Arendt's concept of the social wholly disqualifies Tema's excremental infrastructures as properly political spaces of plurality. Of the body, the household, and entering into public life in the name of self-care, social inclusion, and status advancement, on the surface at least,

Tema's excremental experiments represent all the ills of Arendt's grand category. Again, looking beyond Arendt's "textual pieties" (per Benhabib 2000, 198) with the aid of Latourian method and the reference point of Tema's lived reality, a closer examination of Arendt's claims offers an analytic opening in its own right. Countering a narrow model of political possibility, a much less restrictive understanding of political community and associated forms of mutual recognition and self-determination rise to the top. Relevant to, and visible in Tema, namely, the demise of the public realm Arendt sketches in her rendering of "the social" opens the door for the politization of the private. In addition, what is initially posed as an impediment to meaningful public life becomes a means to return to and revitalize public space and interaction.

Arendt herself provides the tool kit for this reversal. *The Human Condition* is at root a materialist meditation on human experience. It starts with things, or more precisely, a broad category of things that Arendt labels "work." Work, the middle term in her triad, stands between and also connects and bleeds into labor and action. Work also transcends the categories of public and private. Arendt's is not a Marxian materialism built around relations of production but one rooted in an expansive understanding of work. Work, for Arendt, revolves around fabrication: those who fabricate (whom she labels "*homo faber*," human who fabricates), machines, as well as tools, and the things that result, from objects to the built environment of the city.[36] Indeed, for Arendt, things and their makers are the bedrock of plurality and *vita activa*. Paraphrasing Arendt (1958, 182), Linda Zerilli (1995, 183) states: "Action, which creates the 'web of human relationships,' the intangible 'in-between which consists of deeds and words,' must be supported by 'a physical worldly in-between,' by objective worldly interests that constitute something which inter-est, which lies between people and therefore can relate and bind them."

Aided by the insights of Latour and the lived truths of Tema, all of which address hybrids rather than absolutes, gatherings rather than containment, and how things are constituted rather than instituted, Arendt's stipulations can be turned toward a more inductive approach to urban political space and practice. Eschewing the strict divide of public and private, it becomes possible to notice rather than assume the material forms—burst pipes, wastes, wetlands, alleyways, boreholes, and pour-flush toilets—that provide the context for and object of coparticipation and collectivity. Attuned to "association" in the vein of Latour, Arendt's conceptualization of labor, work, and action as separate spheres rather than interlinked dimensions of human experience proves inadequate to social reality (see also Markell 2011). Turning from Arendtian orthodoxy to the possibility of a more heterodox perspective recognizing intersection and overlap, the essence of what I call "infrastructural intimacy" comes into view. In this analytic, bodies, waste, infrastructural things, and articulations of human interest commingle and coimbricate, creating complex attachments.[37]

With this in mind, building on Arendt's reluctant admission that the modern *oikos* allows the "outside" in, the household can be understood as a space of plurality in its own right. Whether material things, persons, values, or social accountabilities, it is actively shaped by and reflects back on externalities, not a static closed space as purported by Arendt's strict classicism. Likewise, Arendt's baseline description of the properly public realm as restricted to appearances, utterances, and abstract issues appears surprisingly shallow compared to the taint of living bodies, fabricated and decaying things, and self-interest that invade the public sphere alongside "the social." Laying the ground for bodily and waste-based associations—what I gloss as "intimacies," infrastructural and otherwise—public places and public things (including public toilets) offer a space of fulsome possibility that grapple with and organize the complexities of human and nonhuman plurality in the city. Made evident in Tema's excremental infrastructures, at these junctures, conventions of deep or expansive domesticity coalesce. Usurping the ambit and promise of governmental provisioning, they either draw inward into the space of household or extend outward claiming public space and resources for collective, albeit private, use.

While the alignment of Latourian empiricism and the realpolitik of Tema's excremental outlays unsettle Arendt's sanitized representations of public life, we cannot dispense with the important insights of her work. These include attention to institutional forces and impasses that structure political possibility across different epochs and in the present. In this regard, Arendt's claims regarding the broad contours of the *longue dureé* and multilayered historical realities call for continued consideration. Kim Fortun (2014, 315, 318) sharpens this critique, pointing to the failure of Latour-inspired ANT to adequately address cross-scale interactions and externalities, privileging the emergent over the weight of history and the "soiled grounds" left in its wake (see also Bessire and Bond 2014; Gordillo 2014).[38] In this light, to give analytic pride of place to Tema's excremental experiments is not to treat them as deus ex machina. Rather, refracted through the combined lens of Actor Network Theory and Arendtian political analysis, Tema's waste management solutions stand as a material index and anchor of shifting strategies of urban collective life across political epochs. Forged in the face of neoliberal developmentalism and the long, drawn-out, multilayered process of industrial modernity's decomposition in a location once considered its leading edge on the African continent, they build on the persistent, transhistorical rhythms of the human body. At once accommodating governmental failures and reproducing urban inequalities as they enable new interdependencies and solidarities, in Tema these interventions remake the urban landscape and alter routines, accountabilities, and expectations by harnessing intimate bodily processes through novel means of essential infrastructural provisioning.

Manufacturing Infrastructural Exception in Tema

Attuned to disparities and interdependencies across Tema's urban expanse, the book's chapters investigate the vital politics of urban waste through in-depth portraits of excremental infrastructures in four parts of the city (see map I.2). Each chapter is situated in a different urban locale to reveal a distinctive nexus of infrastructure, bodily processes, and urban public life expressing and delimiting the possibilities of the polis via the res. Across these locations and examples, Tema's excremental arrangements simultaneously connect and separate the city's inhabitants and serve as a focal point for negotiating the terms of urban plurality above, below, beyond, and alongside governing authorities.

It is important to recognize that Tema, despite being designed and conceived as a whole, was and remains a divided city with sharply demarcated sections and zones. Not only is Tema's infrastructure-laden built environment divided into distinct functional areas dedicated to port, industry, residence, and commerce, but from the start, Tema's urban landscape was also marked by implicit codes of social differentiation. Similar to other large-scale modernist experiments in the tropics from the same era, such as Brasília, designed by Oscar Niemeyer in 1956 (Holston 1989), and Chandigarh in India's Punjab, designed by modernist master Le Corbusier in 1952 (Fynn 2017; Shaw 2009), Tema's actualization was predicated on strict rules of form and spaces of exception. These are the social, geographic, and infrastructural outliers and exclusions on which urban functioning has come to depend.

The deliberate management of difference was part of the city's design early on. Gold Coast town planning advisor A. E. S. Alcock sketched the

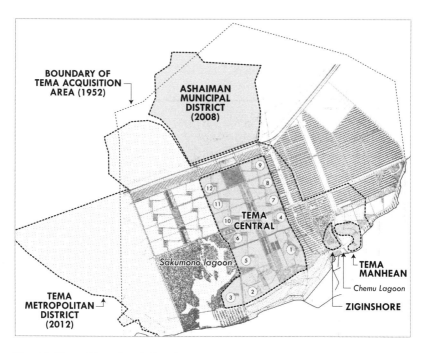

BOUNDARY OF
TEMA ACQUISITION
AREA (1952)

ASHAIMAN
MUNICIPAL
DISTRICT
(2008)

9

8

12

11

7

TEMA
CENTRAL

10

4

6

Sakumono lagoon

5

1

TEMA
MANHEAN

TEMA
METROPOLITAN
DISTRICT
(2012)

3

2

Chemu Lagoon

ZIGINSHORE

Map I.2. Map of Tema Acquisition Area and four research areas: Tema Central, Tema
Manhean, Ziginshore, and Ashaiman (Created by Kairon Aiken)

first comprehensive scheme for Tema in 1951. The initial plan centered on
small residential neighborhoods, described as "village-size units" (Alcock
1955, 52), designed to reproduce what he called the "feeling of belonging"
characteristic of African village life and "avoid the estrangements common
to urban living." Organic in shape and tightly clustered, by independence in
1957 only a small fraction of new residential, industrial, or commercial areas
were completed. In 1961, after sidelining the inputs of Soviet bloc planners
(Stanek 2015),[39] the master plan for the city was finalized with the input of
the Athens-based engineering and architecture firm Doxiadis Associates.
Eschewing the more naturalistic approach of Alcock, the plan included
twelve distinct communities of nearly equal size organized around a central spine at the city's core. Persons deemed not fit for residence in the new
city's center were relocated to outlying zones.

Despite the promise of upward mobility for all, the realization of Tema's master plan depended on a series of carefully orchestrated displacements. The first was claiming land to build the city (Gold Coast Ordinance
1952). Designated the Tema Acquisition Area, the land was carved from the

customary property of Ga-Adangbe fishing and farming communities and long-inhabited villages of Tema and Sakumono.[40] Replete with shrines, burial grounds, lagoons, and fishing beaches, under the Public Lands Ordinance, the entire parcel was fully vested in the government, "with the native chieftaincies retaining only residual custodial rights" (Kirchherr 1968, 210).[41] Officials in the Ministry of Housing swiftly recommended the removal and resettlement of persons of Ga-Adangbe heritage, whom they considered indigenous to Tema (D'Auria 2014, 339, 340). Buffered from the rest of the city's residential areas by the port and industrial zone, there was to be a new village with a plan all its own. It was designated "Tema New Village" and designed to offer transitional living arrangements reminiscent of traditional forms. Popularly called Tema New Town, it was also known as Tema Manhean, meaning "new town in Ga" (Amarteifio 1966).

The strict injunctions of planning led to further separation of urban spaces, functions, and populations. Confounding the professed commitment to nation-building and the cultivation of national belonging over and above "tribalism," native Ga were not the only ones removed from the area designated to become the city's core. A settlement of over two hundred multi-roomed homes and many more associated households (Field 1940), also residing in Old Tema and adjoining areas, were persons vaguely identified as "Northerners" and "Nigerians" (Amarteifio 1966). Despite having recognized leaders, family homes, and histories in place, they were considered by urban authorities illegitimate occupants of the city yet to come. Members of this diverse demographic were relocated in 1959 to the far reaches of the new township. The area eventually became "point zero" of Tema's working-class community of Ashaiman. Functionally linked to Tema, it was largely exempt from the tight logics of urban governance and municipal provisioning found in of the rest of the city despite the labor residents provided to sustain Tema's seaport, industrial zone, and service economies.

Beneath the promise of political and infrastructural entitlements of the model city, these initial fissures in Tema's urban fabric continue to infiltrate urban life and reflect the type of "splintering urbanism" described by Stephen Graham and Simon Marvin (2001) when high-modernist ideals of urban infrastructural integration give way to differentiation and decentralization. While Graham and Marvin address the rise of urban inequalities in the face of uneven external ties and investments, Tema's infrastructural underground highlights internal and organic processes of disintegration. Reproducing and deepening inequalities, these processes also seed unscripted outcomes. Revealing the complex political entailments of infrastructural reordering for both public and private life, a view of Tema through these emergent and embedded formations puts Arendt's *vita activa* and Latour's dingpolitics in a new light. In the face of seemingly quotidian technical rearrangements mixing human and nonhuman, living and inert, spent and new, the material and experiential contours of political inclusion and exclusion in the city rise to prominence as sites of transformation even if they do not take the familiar form of polis.

Chapter Overviews

The book begins with a discussion of the founding figures and forces driving Tema's midcentury master plan, highlighting the central role of sanitary infrastructure in entraining urban political possibility. A backdrop to the dilemmas faced by Tema residents and city authorities a half century later, chapter 1 provides a historical touchstone for the rest of the book. Subsequent chapters offer in-depth profiles of four sections of the city. Chapter 2 addresses the core of the planned residential zone, what I call Tema proper. Chapter 3 focuses on the resettlement village of Tema Manhean. An informal settlement built on the polluted wetlands of Tema's industrial area known as Ziginshore is the subject of chapter 4. And the working-class township of Ashaiman is featured in chapter 5. With distinct histories, demographics, and built environments, each section reveals different arrangements of excremental infrastructure composed in response to the gaps, lacks, failures, and possibilities of the received order. Each arrangement carries its own political implications, where excremental infrastructural improvisation turns into political experiment. Through the play of vital remains and the work of infrastructural intimacy, these sections evince and embody different configurations of public and private life. Each ultimately deepens the political reach of the domestic domain to alter the terms of urban coexistence and distinction.

The solutions forged in the different areas of the city represent contrasting patterns of excremental provisioning. Tema's core, built according to a postwar "new town" template, exemplifies the public provisioning of private sanitation. Tema Manhean contains public sanitation facilities provided by public sources, both municipal and community-based. The informal settlement of Ziginshore is the site of an expanse of public facilities built and serviced by a private waste entrepreneur. Ashaiman offers sanitary solutions

Table I.2. Comparison of excremental infrastructure and private/public nexus in Tema

Section of city	Provided by	Provided for
Tema Central	Public authorities	Private use
Tema Manhean	Public authorities	Public use
Ziginshore	Private sources	Public use
Ashaiman	Private sources	Private use

Table I.3. Excremental infrastructure in relation to the state in four sections of Tema

Section of city	Relationship to state
Tema Central	Negotiation of boundary between private property and public responsibility serves to "instate" the state
Tema Manhean	Communal toilets challenge transcendent claims of state and traditional authority and reject the state
Ziginshore	Waste infrastructure forms the foundation of proxy sovereignty both alternative to and simulating state practices
Ashaiman	Enlargement of private excremental provisioning fuses the domestic and public to supplant the state

located in private households for public use and sponsored by private individuals (see table I.2).

In each locale, vital bodily processes and infrastructural breakdown inspire diverse forms of political assembly and serve as the basis of urban collectivity and claims making. Whether with, against, or outside of state authority, they enable new hierarchies and fealties alongside opportunities for security, self-care, and self-determination (see table I.3). In Tema proper, infrastructural breakdown provides grounds for renegotiation of the urban social contract regarding the boundaries between private property and public responsibility. In Manhean, residents utilize public toilets status as a community inheritance to challenge the transcendent claims of state and traditional authorities and while catering to individual and collective needs. In the case of Ziginshore, waste infrastructure forms the foundation of a proxy sovereignty alternative to the state, with excreta an irrepressible force impossible to fully harness or tame. In Tema's sprawling satellite settlement of Ashaiman, a city in its own right, private provisioning of hundreds of public toilets, most within the confines of domestic space, prevails. Insisting on acceptance by the municipal government by default, these facilities rewrite the terms of urban public life to enable new conventions of urban status and civility.

Chapter 1, "Assembling the New City: From Infrastructure to Vital Politics," delineates the infrastructural and ideological underpinnings of Tema's founding and the consequences for urban politics and public life. Tema melds the infrastructure-heavy vision of nation-building of Ghana's first president, Kwame Nkrumah (1958), with the designs of Greek engineer turned planner Constantinos Doxiadis (1968). Like their contemporary, Arendt, both Nkrumah and Doxiadis were invested in the restoration of the rightful order of humanity in the aftermath of the violence of colonization, occupation, and world war. Whereas Arendt privileged participation and self-determination, Nkrumah and Doxiadis saw the built environment and technological advancement as a primary means to achieve societal progress. All three, however, treated the satisfaction of bodily needs as prior to full-fledged processes of political inclusion. In contrast to colonial-era denials of basic services and supports, the approach of Nkrumah and Doxiadis to the new city depended on deliberate strategies of urban provisioning and turned household and neighborhood infrastructure into the prime loci of urban control under the aegis of the Tema Development Corporation. Serving basic needs, these efforts sidestepped the more difficult issue of political mobilization among the city's new working class.

Driven by the 1960s master plan, the disposition of bodily waste became a marker of urban order and parity across Tema's neighborhoods and income categories. Each residence was equipped with private household toilets linked to the municipal sewerage system. By substituting planning for participation, the city's infrastructure-heavy design was intended to serve the liberal project of "self-rule." Alongside the new nation's embrace of self-government, these arrangements encompassed an atomized governance of the self, anchored in the domestic realm. As the urban population and associated waste flows grew, the limits of Tema's sewage system and planning authority became apparent, instigating sanitary alternatives built from the vital remains of the old order, still visible today.

Chapter 2, "Tema Proper: Infrastructures and Intimacies of Disrepair," sticks close to the residential neighborhoods in the planned city's core. A half century after Tema's founding, the sewage system is in the throes of collapse. With Walter Benjamin's idea of "ruination" as the chapter's theoretical fulcrum, drawing on Ann Laura Stoler (2013, 13), it asks, "How do lives accumulate around ruins and ruins around lives?" Told from the perspective of the engineers who operate Tema's sole functioning sewage pumping station, the chapter recounts the centrality of bodily knowledge and corporal risk in sustaining urban public services. Here, the res publica is supplanted by "the labor of life itself" (Arendt 1958, 7) lodged in the discrete bodies of infrastructure's caretakers. Such infrastructural intimacies, merging human and nonhuman, private and public, bioactive and machinic, prove integral to upholding the façade of municipal capacity.

Tema residents experience infrastructural intimacies of their own. Revealed in the sewage diary of a cluster of middle-class homes, residents confront overflowing manholes and the backed-up excrement of neighbors, tenants, and family members flooding streets, bathrooms, and courtyards. As an example of vital bodily materials spurring political assembly (Latour 2005b), errant excreta enliven the "connective tissue" (Stoler 2013) of community as neighbors pool resources to clear pipes and clean spills. Facing overstretched municipal repair teams, residents prevail on local representatives—aptly designated "assemblymen"—to bring complaints to city authorities. In doing so they invite intrusion into domestic space and inadvertently incite allegations of abuse of public infrastructure as the sewage system's cycle of breakdown and repair reveals a looming gulf between public and private responsibility. While Tema's middle-class urban dwellers continue to look to city authorities for input and oversight, at this political cum technical juncture, it is residents' stopgap measures that ensure the functioning of a fragile system.

Chapter 3, "The Right(s) to Remains: Excremental Infrastructure and Exception in Tema Manhean," employs Henri Lefebvre's (1996) notion of the "right to the city," to examine the rise, fall, and restoration of fee-based public toilet facilities by residents of Tema's resettlement area established in the 1950s to house those removed from their lands and homes to make way for the new city. Manhean's compact neighborhoods retain public toilet and bath complexes from its founding, initially linked to the city's centralized sewage system and for decades bereft of adequate municipal input. In the earliest plans for the urban core, sanitation was largely out of sight. However, in Manhean, standalone public structures with shared toilets and baths, designed by British architects Jane Drew and Maxwell Fry, were located between clusters of residential dwellings to enable public access and monitoring by urban authorities.

Over time, Manhean residents mobilized the self-proclaimed "right(s) to shit" to make public toilet facilities their own. Treating them as vital remains rather than ruins despite their substantial disrepair, residents effectively rendered them community property. In the process, they undermined the claims of Tema's municipal government, political party hacks, and traditional leaders who deem themselves rightful owners of independence-era infrastructure. With septic pits and sewer lines at the fore, a political dynamic around the stuff of bare life is at play. Demonstrating Arendt's (1958, 46) insight that the "public realm must change in accordance with the activities admitted into it, [and] the activity itself changes its nature too," these spaces and contestations fuel a profound reworking of the urban political topos. Namely, driven by vital needs, Manhean's public toilets pull a range of reproductive activities—sleeping, cooking, childcare, petty trade, prayer, medicinal aid, and other forms of self-care—into the public sphere for the urban poor. A graphic example of deep domesticity at work, these spaces enable a public staging of intimate forms of self-determination.

Chapter 4, "Ziginshore: Infrastructure and the Commonwealth of Waste," focuses on a settlement in the wetlands between Tema's port and industrial zone. Turned dumping ground and shantytown, it is built on the sedimentation and recycling of human, environmental, and industrial waste. Akin to a Hobbesian ([1651] 1994) social contract, in this unstable locale—a political and material inchoate—a putative "state of nature" is transformed into waste-based commonwealth by means of infrastructure. The marginality of the landscape is matched by the marginality of Ziginshore's inhabitants: a highly transient array of men, women, and children who lack permanent housing, reliable jobs, or the basic guarantees of social and bodily reproduction. They use this spit of reclaimed land for respite between stints of work at Tema's harbor and movement to and from hometowns elsewhere. Lacking any "privately owned place," these urban dwellers live in a public realm where even the most intimate functions can be "seen and heard by everyone" (Arendt 1958, 50, 52).

While Ziginshore's fluid ecology, human and otherwise, places it beneath the radar of official state recognition or oversight, a more opportunistic sovereign fills the void. At the heart of the settlement is a native son home from abroad who has turned infrastructure into political experiment. A massive public toilet and bath complex and adjoining excrement-based biogas plant is the font of public life and of his own empowerment. Spawning subsidiary functions and structures: schoolroom, hostel, meeting place, communal kitchen, and more, these infrastructural experiments, built on vital needs and vital essences, make public Arendtian (1958) "labors of living." Entraining bodies and inculcating compliance through a broad range of infrastructural intimacies, they doubly instantiate and suppress the body politic in this corner of the city. Public but by no means polis, Ziginshore's homespun biogas plant and associated waste-based infrastructures rule over sovereign and subjects alike. Here, the ever-productive forces of vital human and nonhuman natures contained by Ziginshore's infrastructure power a crude Leviathan.

Chapter 5, "Dwelling on Toilets: Tema's Breakaway Republic of Ashaiman," focuses on Tema's sister settlement of Ashaiman. Ashaiman is Tema's inverse: an unplanned, periurban catchment area on whose labor, goods, and services the functioning of the planned city depends. If Manhean can be understood as a zone of abandonment marked by the evacuation and eventual rejection of formal government, and Ziginshore as an underground polity, Ashaiman stands as a breakaway republic. For fifty years a part of the Tema metropolitan area, Ashaiman fought for and won municipal autonomy in 2008 and now holds legal authority but lacks the means to actualize its goals. Ashaiman's development depends on the full-blown privatization of public works, toilets included. With more than two hundred privately owned and managed public toilet facilities covering the whole of the community, these arrangements are remarkable for their scope, scale, and class character. A compelling testimony to the force of deep domesticity, most are associated with domestic space, attached or adjacent to dwellings, and offer different degrees of service, comfort, and cleanliness.

Resembling displays of "conspicuous waste" (Veblen [1899] 1994), Ashaiman's dwelling-based public toilets offer upward economic mobility for owners and users alike. The chapter highlights three toilet complexes: one geared to working-class livelihoods, another built on merchant capital, and a third promoting middle-class assimilation. Using what the state refuses to acknowledge, these complexes expose what Bataille (1985) describes as the "heterogeneous nature of power" built on unclaimed excess. With toilets serving as the basis of influence and recognition in a public sphere largely abdicated by city authorities, evidence from Ashaiman affirms Arendt's (1958, 160) reluctant admission that "*homo faber* is fully capable of having a public realm ... even though it may not be a political realm, properly speaking." The polis here is alive and well but privatized in content and control despite its public locus.

The conclusion, "From Vital Politics to Deep Domesticity: Infrastructure as Political Experiment," uses the case of Tema to offer an alternative means to comprehend urban political currents via human bodily waste. Beyond the "splintered urbanism" (Graham and Marvin 2001) of the underclass, brought to light are the broader repressions, work-arounds, and leakages on which urban functioning, whether for rich or poor, depends. Here, waste matter and its infrastructures provide a source of what Benjamin (1968) calls "profane illumination." Building on the potentials of vital remains, Tema's excremental infrastructural experiments are the lived terrain of the polity and engender and sustain new configurations of urban plurality beyond state sanctions.

Notably, evidence from Tema shows that excremental infrastructures can be a means and ends of political engagement and recognition despite the exclusions and inequalities that fuel them. The city's excremental experiments thus offer a theory of urban political life that recognizes the disordered yet vital remains of and around bodily waste to be a central player rather than suppressed agency in the organization of urban political experience. Taking what Arendt relegates to the apolitical realm of labor and turning it into an active arena of work and fabrication, and ultimately action, the infrastructural adjustments and innovations forged by Tema's residents demonstrate how built forms and sedimented routines alter the fundamental conditions of urban coexistence contra state expectations and interventions.

A vital politics from below, Tema's excremental experiments bring to bear widely shared urban realities. Whether in the global North or global South, cities worldwide are unified by the overwhelming excess of human waste matter, organic and inorganic, and the limits to the Leviathan as the will and capacity of the modern state to manage them wanes. In its face, wastes—both bodily outputs and the remains of defunct infrastructures—spur human and other-than-human agency and aggregation sustained by a range of infrastructural intimacies. A growing locus of urban political activity in cities such as Tema, where residents as well as public officials cope with the breakdown of high modernity's infrastructural inheritance, these arrangements simultaneously alter the character of public life along with domestic spaces, practices, and sodalities. They restructure access to and organization of basic urban services and pull the locus of urban politics and service provision inward. Intensifying and expanding on processes already in place, these routines deepen domestic capacities and responsibilities. Public-facing infrastructure surfaces in domestic space; all the while, domestic practices, accountabilities, and infrastructural installations move into public domains. Different from the shrouded intentions and "quiet encroachments" of the urban underclass described by Bayat (2013), Tema's excremental infrastructural installations and adjustments directly alter the domestic realm by harnessing the staying power and unpredictability of vital remains, at once letting the state off the hook and calling it to attention.

1. Assembling the New City
From Infrastructure to Vital Politics

Ten years ago I wandered about here alone with my driver. There were no roads and I had to do a considerable amount of walking to be where I wanted to be. But so real was the harbor I built around myself that evening that I imagined I could already hear the scream of winches, sirens of ships and clamor and chatter of men at work.
—Kwame Nkrumah, speech opening Tema Harbor, February 10, 1962

Before men began to act, a definite space had to be secured and structure built where all subsequent actions could take place.
—Hannah Arendt, *The Human Condition* (1958)

We must clarify that we always speak of Anthropos (Man) with a capital "A" and therefore use the case of an average person in the broadest sense of the word, because only by defining him in such a way can we conceive the city, where people live together with their common desires and characteristics. But, at the same time, we must recognize that people, as individuals, tend to be different and ensure that this will be the city of free human beings and not bees or ants. Since I am speaking of common desires and characteristics, we must recall the established and unchanging constants several of which are now overlooked. This can be proved by the fact that we forget completely what the human scale is, a scale defined by Anthropos (Man) as an organism, his body, his senses, his mind and probably his soul: this composite, total Anthropos (Man) has not changed at all for at least ten thousand years.
—Constantinos Doxiadis, *Anthropopolis: City for Human Development* (1974)

Imagining the African City Anew

It is not difficult to locate the inspiration for Tema's design and realization in the postwar New Towns of the United Kingdom (Alexander 2009; Provoost 2006). In this regard, it is important to recognize that the planned city of

Tema emerged in parallel with, not as a "secondhand," latecomer copy of, the metropolitan model with which it is chronologically coincident. Built to contain the panoply of infrastructures that signaled the fusion of industrial modernity and national self-sufficiency, Tema demonstrates the early alignment of strategies of postwar reconstruction in the global North and new-nation-making in the global South. From the start, Tema was designed to do the work of national transformation, from the productivity of its port and factories to the new lifestyles it made possible. Such "designs for living" were written into Tema's overarching urban form and high-modern industrial installations (cf. Scott 1998) as well as its residents' day-to-day routines.

Evident in the master plans for the new settlement, provisioning for bodily needs via well-developed sanitation systems served as the basis of membership in the polity. These infrastructures were and remain a formative arena for negotiation between city residents and planning authorities, as well as expression of deeper ideals about the proper composition of public and private life. In Arendtian (1958) terms, infrastructure—situated under her broad mantel of "work"—reaches "backward" to organize the "labors of living," and "forward" to organize the terms of urban collectivity. For a new nation in the process of becoming, here was a formula for liberal self-making that could be achieved without the fully formed polis urgently sought by President Kwame Nkrumah and the wider Ghanaian populace.

Formative of the city of Tema, decolonization and post–World War II reconstruction would leave an indelible mark on Ghana's urban landscape.[1] Driven by a machinic logic of nation-building, the result was an urban scheme encompassing housing, industry, and infrastructure, all linked to the world beyond by an expansive shipping harbor. From drawing board to full-fledged built environment, Tema's founding designs hinged on three linked principles: first, the use of planning as a proxy for governance; second, a highly orchestrated private sphere and a truncated public realm; and third, the assertion of a firm divide between indigenous, ideal, and undesirable residents.

Motivating this technology-centered urban platform were the political ideologies and aspirations of its founding figures: notably, Ghana's nationalist hero and first president, Dr. Kwame Nkrumah, and a Greek engineer, Constantinos Doxiadis, whose firm was responsible for the city's master plan. Devoted to promoting social solidarity and individual well-being while avoiding the risks of social upheaval, these two postwar visionaries expressed a common concern with political community and nation-building

Figure 1.1. President Kwame Nkrumah commissioning Tema Harbor, 1962 (Tema Development Corporation Archives)

in the aftermath of world-historical destruction. A telling convergence of postwar political thought, this too was a prime preoccupation of leading political theorist and public intellectual of the day Hannah Arendt. Nkrumah's and Doxiadis's contemporary, Arendt, though seemingly far apart in vocation and reputation, shared with them the status of globalist intellectual and émigré. In different ways and for different reasons, each of these figures contemplated—and in some cases, advocated—distinctive modalities of self-governance sidestepping the risks, struggles, and potentials of designated realms of participatory rule.

In Tema, the manifestation of this shared midcentury urban vision substituted individual material security for the uncertain spoils of collective mobilization, deliberately containing rather than cultivating public life. The intent was a fundamentally materialist (de)orchestration of political community, privileging work, shelter, and the satisfaction of basic human needs over participation, deliberation, and collective self-determination, all in the name of national progress and public good. Indeed, in terms of the system's techno-political logic, what Hannah Appel, Nikhil Anand, and Akhil Gupta (2018) call "the promise of infrastructure" was at the fore.

A close reading of Tema's early planning documents, settlement layouts, infrastructures, and built environment through the lens of Nkrumah, Doxiadis, and Arendt reveals the inner workings and impasses of a dually humanist and technology-centered urban template. Evident across the city, this double agenda was strikingly manifest in the city's expansive infrastructural installations, sanitation prime among them. As subsequent chapters detail, ultimately unsettled or "undecidable," these interventions would soon put in motion the very sort of political engagements they were meant to contain.

A complete story in its own right, this chapter describes the intertwined philosophical and infrastructural foundations of political processes still at work in Tema more than a half century later. These lessons undergird a broader argument regarding the political contentions of urban infrastructure relevant in other locales. Namely, the intended "ante" or "prepolitical" character of vital infrastructure does not exclude the unscripted possibilities of plurality. This insight pertains even in cases such as Tema, where public life was deliberately circumscribed by city planners in favor of the cultivation and satisfaction of basic human needs in the private sphere—excretion included—under the control of centralized authorities. Instead, Tema's vital sanitary infrastructures operate as an armature of both political suppression and popular mobilization, emerging as a primary site of urban state and subject formation. This is because Tema's toilets, sewage mains, pumping stations, settling tanks and outflows, and the human waste they channel and contain directly embody the impossible division of private and public matters they were intended to enforce. Entangled with bodily processes and outputs as well as state authorities, the design, disposition, breakdown, and reassembly of these shared forms make tangible the ongoing negotiation of ways of living together and apart in the city.

New Plans, New Principles, New Partnerships

Over the course of World War II, town planning gained a prime position within the colonial tool kit (Jackson and Holland 2014, 159). Agencies crossing colony and metropole were established to provide resources, personnel, and policy frameworks for the management of urban locations and populations at home and abroad (Harris and Parnell 2012, 140). Demonstrating what Viviana D'Auria and Victor Sanwu (2010, 2) describe as the "proximity between disciplinary shifts and the changing culture of imperialism," in the Gold Coast the looming reality of decolonization enhanced the already rising sway of expat architects and planners.[2] With the push for political independence all but assured at the war's end (Apter 1963; B. Davidson 1989), the agents and agencies of empire pursued a last-gasp effort. Architecture, infrastructure, and urban design—forms durable, transposable, and readily assimilated into the landscape of daily life—offered the promise of lasting impact (Hargreaves 2014, 118).

A medium of transition, these same material forms served the mission of independent nation-state making. Despite contending political platforms, for those whose power was on the wane and those for whom it was on the rise, architecture and planning provided a common idiom of public legitimation marking the investment of governing authorities in collective futures and shared betterment. Over and above the sheer spectacle of political authority, for regimes on their way out and those on their way in, architectural and infrastructural "fabrication," to borrow from Arendt's (1958, 139) distinct vocabulary, had become essential to crafting collective futures, political and otherwise.

When Ghana achieved national independence in 1957, only a small portion of the new city of Tema, Community 1 and Community 2 and some temporary residential blocks, were close to completion.[3] It was not until 1959, two full years after independence, that Tema's master plan was fast-tracked.[4] Rather than turning inward in pursuit of expertise necessary to realize the new city, the Nkrumah government adopted a brand of urban internationalization different from the conventional hierarchical coupling of colony and metropole of earlier proposals penned by colonial planners. Nkrumah forged ties with up-and-coming Greek urbanist Constantinos Doxiadis and his Athens-based firm, Doxiadis Associates International Consultants on Development and Ekistics. Widely known as Doxiadis Associates, or DA, the firm was founded in 1951. Constantinos or "Dinos" Doxiadis, DA's principal, was a civil engineer turned World War II army captain, and resistance member turned international technocrat (Doxiadis 1968, 1; Menoret 2014, 68, 69; Theocharopoulou 2009).[5] After leading Greece's Ministry of Housing and Reconstruction, he earned an international reputation in charge of Marshall Plan reconstruction in Greece and Southern Europe (Bromley 2003).

In the brief span of a decade between 1950 and 1960, Doxiadis established himself as leading figure in the building, design, and execution of new urban agglomerations the world over (Bromley 2003, 317). Urban plans for recently evacuated outposts of British imperial occupation were high on his project list. According to heirs of postwar internationalism like Doxiadis,

Figure 1.2. President Kwame Nkrumah and Constantinos Doxiadis in Ghana, 1960
(© Constantinos and Emma Doxiadis Foundation)

these locations were in urgent need of large-scale infrastructure to deal with the responsibilities of self-administration and the challenges of urban agglomeration expected to follow. Tema was one of numerous overseas projects executed by DA. By time the firm began its work in Ghana, Doxiadis had already initiated major projects in Islamabad in 1959 (Hull 2012), Baghdad in 1955 (Pieri 2008), and Dhaka in 1957 (Karim 2016). Plans were also underway for the new city of Aspra Spitia in Doxiadis's homeland, Greece (Pyla 2008). A master plan for Riyadh would come a few years later (Meneret 2014).[6] Like Tema, they too were conceived as "Cities of the Future" built in the present to stave off the more uncertain, unsavory outcomes of mass urbanization in empire's wake.

More than a planning template, Tema anchored a shared personal and political project allying Nkrumah and Doxiadis. Pursuing the possibilities of postwar parity from different corners of the global South, these two midcentury visionaries sought to escape the assumptions and impositions of colonization and occupation (D'Auria 2010, 42). For newly elected President Nkrumah, driven by the ends of nation- and state-building, Doxiadis's ready-made approach to urban organization had obvious appeal. One cannot overlook the hard facts of Nkrumah's political inheritance. Along with inheriting the administrative apparatus of the outgoing colonial government, he faced intense party and elite competition and the high expectations of a newly nationalized citizenry (Apter 1963). Doxiadis's tool kit offered concrete solutions for Nkrumah as he faced the challenge of both building and containing the polity.

Besides the proximate end of fulfilling the basic urban requirements of work and shelter, Doxiadis's tight-knit city plan made real the possibility of urban order without the tricky processes of popular deliberation. Promising the large-scale satisfaction of urban needs in the service of both national development and individual well-being, the messy give-and-take of public debate could be avoided all the while promoting material entitlement. Managing the "political consequences of urban growth," under Doxiadis's mantle "urban planning would prevent urban unrest by raising standards of living, creating conditions for prosperity and fostering the development of consumption-based economies," as Pascal Menoret (2014, 70) explains of the Doxiadis-planned Saudi capital Riyadh. Aligning their aims, Nkrumah already shared Doxiadis's focus on shelter, and placed housing at the core of his populist socialist platform (Nkrumah 1958, 51). For Nkrumah's newly established government, housing was part of a deliberate strategy to "prevent public discontent ... perceived [as an] essential requirement for political longevity" at the same time as it worked to "enhance social development" (Arku 2006, 342). In an early speech in Tema, Nkrumah (1997a, 176) touted the efforts of his Convention People's Party regarding housing (October 16, 1963): "In the Party 'Programme for Work and Happiness' we have recognized the fundamental right of everyone living in Ghana to adequate housing for himself and his family. Our aim, therefore[,] is to see that everyone[,] whether he is a civil servant, a teacher, a farmer, a carpenter, a clerk, a market woman or an ordinary worker, can—if he so wishes—acquire a decent house or flat to live in at a reasonable rate and without too much difficulty or red tape."

Doxiadis, with the assistance of the Athens-based training institute he founded, translated a focus on housing and common human needs into a highly portable urban plan that could be easily replicated and adjusted to fit the circumstances at hand. Bridging the roles of bureaucrat, technical expert, and philosopher-scientist, he developed a distinctive theory of urbanization he branded "ekistics," defined as the "science of human settlements"

Figure 1.3. Fully
serviced residential
units, built ca. 1965
(© Constantinos
and Emma Dox-
iadis Foundation)

Figure 1.4. Fully
serviced residential
units, built ca. 1965
(© Constantinos
and Emma Dox-
iadis Foundation)

(Doxiadis 1968). Taking shelter to be fundamental to all human relationships, Doxiadis applied the principles of ekistics to the smallest social unit of mother/child dyads, to cities, and to uncontained urban sprawl. A comprehensive theory combining psychology, anthropology, philosophy, cell biology, and systems engineering, ekistics was founded on ideas of shared human nature and common human needs rather than social hierarchies or immutable distinctions. Consisting of five essential elements—nature, people, society, shell, networks—the logic of human shelter and settlement was treated as scientific truth. Attuned to what humanity already held in common, including a common historical present, Doxiadis saw his thesis as universally applicable.

Similarly committed to building a new world order in the aftermath of World War II and the simmering collapse of colonial rule, Nkrumah, like Doxiadis, was driven by political pragmatics and philosophical ideals. Before the war both traveled abroad for higher education. In 1935, Nkrumah left Ghana for the United Kingdom and the United States, where he pursued his PhD in philosophy and developed his platform of Pan-African solidarity (Nkrumah 1957; B. Davidson 1989). Doxiadis left Greece a few years earlier to study in Berlin. His 1936 PhD thesis on architectural space in Ancient Greece was grounded in classical political thought (Daechsel 2015, 210; Theocharopoulou 2009; Zarmakoupi 2015, 3). Informed by these concerns, Doxiadis took the polis as starting and end point of his work as a planner: "The 'polis' of antiquity was a daily life system of equal people, and the human settlements of the future are going to tend in the same direction. Only in scale and structure will they be different. The new 'City' of Anthropos will follow the laws of the past" (Doxiadis and Papaioannou 1974, 318).

Amid these conceptual and experiential crossroads, a complex common ground linking the lives and ideas of Doxiadis, Nkrumah, and political theorist Arendt comes into view. A master of classical and modern philosophy, Arendt was steeped in the values of classical Greece (Tsao 2002). Though not focused on the developing world, as were her contemporaries Doxiadis and Nkrumah, her driving intellectual concern was postwar political reconstruction (Krimstein 2018).[7] Arendt's *The Human Condition* (1958) is ultimately a meditation on the origins, character, and corruption of the polis and the possibility of its restoration at a historical moment marked by the tyranny of world war on the one hand and the tyranny of self-interest and conformism of mass society on the other. For all three figures this was deeply felt. The lives of each had been transformed by the destructions and displacements of World War II and by ethnic and racially driven violence and domination. All shared the status at one time or another of expat and émigré, at once outsider and member of elite circles of knowledge, influence, and activism. All turned to philosophy to inform wider projects of political repair.

Despite their shared ends and common grounding in classical humanist thought, their means of repair were fundamentally different. For Arendt, it involved the search for a renewed—if ever imperfect—moral foundation for humanity's future. According to her, this possibility could be found only in the expressive domain of the public realm, via "sharing words and deeds" and "acting and speaking together" (1958, 198). Idealizing political participation among equals, Arendt writes (26), "To live in the polis meant that everything was decided through words and persuasion and not through force and violence." For Doxiadis, engineer, planner, and "ekistician," the means of human renewal was shelter—whether scaled down to the protective cocoon of the mother/child dyad, the roof and walls of a human abode, or scaled up to settlement, town, city, conurbation, and beyond. Nkrumah, committed to modern nation-building on the basis of global parity and domestic accord, hitched his hopes for Tema to this materially grounded model of modern city and citizen-making.

Notwithstanding their evident differences, these political platforms contained significant overlaps. An analytic conundrum at the crux of this book, each gave extensive consideration to the proper place of the body in modern political life. Albeit in distinct ways for each, bodies and bodily processes were substantively present in their formulations of political order. Allying these three figures' political ideas, though not their political ends, the body held a prepolitical (or counterpolitical) status related, yet prior to bona fide political endeavor. A perspective encapsulated in Arendt's notion of *animal laborans*, bodily needs are properly outside of the realm of politics. For Arendt, "public life was possible only after the much more urgent needs of life itself had been taken care of" (Arendt 1958, 65). Not only should the satisfaction of these needs precede participation in political activity, they should also not mix with it. Precipitating what Arendt considers the scourge of "the social" in the modern world, the privilege accorded to base private interests corrupts the express public purpose of the polis (45–46).

A proposition at once surprising similar and markedly different from Arendt's perspective, as Doxiadis saw it, the management of bodily needs was a cornerstone of political society. Bodily labors constituted a basic yet hidden foundation, prior yet contiguous to political society. Again, closely aligned but not identical to Doxiadis, from Nkrumah's perspective, government satisfaction of the populace's basic bodily needs was a way to sidestep the formulation of a full-blown political sphere yet still preserve the premises of participation and give concrete purpose to a centralized state. Complicating these claims, as subsequent chapters reveal, in Tema human bodily waste and its affiliated infrastructures became a subject of individual and collective contention and claims making—that is, politics—in the very contexts where they were to be sequestered and "invisibly" managed, whether from on high by the state (per Nkrumah), from within by the responsible citizen (per Arendt), or below through the built environment (per Doxiadis). Instead of the private taking over the public, as in Arendt's (1958, 44) assessment of the intrusions of the social in modern industrial societies, when it came to sanitation in Tema and its environs, the polity in the name of public good would conscript and circumscribe the private while protecting and legitimizing the expanded reach of the state.

Assembling the New City

Although readily endorsed by the Nkrumah government, the philosophical and political implications of Doxiadis's designs for Tema were not initially clear. Doxiadis Associates' involvement in the new city was at first a small piece of the 1959 National Development Plan tied to the completion of the Volta River Scheme.[8] The Ministry of Works and Housing had engaged DA as a consultant (TDC Archives, MR-GHA 1, 1960, 3). With the firm's input eagerly embraced, Doxiadis took it upon himself to propose an integrated urban plan coordinating the development of Ghana's already established capital city of Accra and the new city of Tema. A testament to the effort's timeliness, the plan was accepted in January 1960, barely a month after submission.[9] Based in Athens and Accra, DA project teams were immediately assembled.

By August DA submitted a regional plan to Ghana's Ministry of Works and Housing, encompassing not just Accra and Tema but also a new urban scheme for Akosombo, located next to the new Volta Dam. Soon thereafter, in November 1960, the firm delved into detailed discussion of the Tema Township Project, conceived as the linchpin. Less than a year later, in 1961 DA was officially "entrusted with full responsibility for future development and planning of the town" and given the mandate to get the new city up and running "without further delay" (Doxiadis 1971). The firm's plan for the city

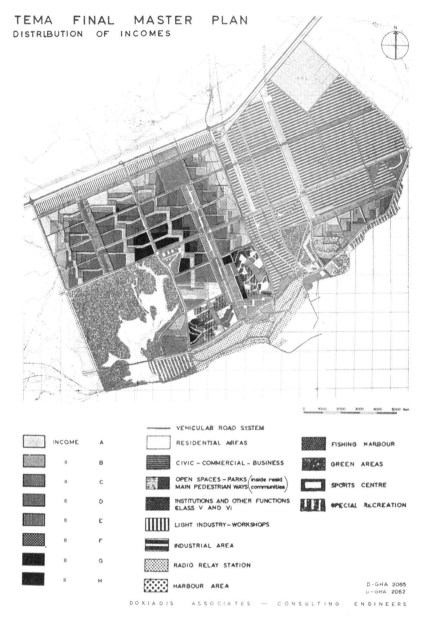

TEMA FINAL MASTER PLAN
DISTRIBUTION OF INCOMES

INCOME	A
	II B
	II C
	II D
	II E
	II F
	II G
	II H

VEHICULAR ROAD SYSTEM
RESIDENTIAL AREAS
CIVIC – COMMERCIAL – BUSINESS
OPEN SPACES – PARKS (inside resid. communities)
MAIN PEDESTRIAN WAYS
INSTITUTIONS AND OTHER FUNCTIONS CLASS V AND VI
LIGHT INDUSTRY – WORKSHOPS
INDUSTRIAL AREA
RADIO RELAY STATION
HARBOUR AREA

FISHING HARBOUR
GREEN AREAS
SPORTS CENTRE
SPECIAL RECREATION

D-GHA 2065
D-GHA 2062

DOXIADIS   ASSOCIATES — CONSULTING   ENGINEERS

Figure 1.5. Tema final master plan with distribution of incomes, designed by Doxiadis Associates, 1962 (Tema Development Corporation Archives)

included twelve residential communities neatly organized on two sides of a central spine. The industrial area filled out a parallel corridor abutting the new harbor and dividing the new city from the resettlement area of Tema Manhean, with plans for a cement factory, oil refinery, textile factory, and fish cannery.

Propelling these developments, Doxiadis and Nkrumah forged ties of their own built out of letters, telegrams, and diplomatic mementos. Alongside the numerous reports they circulated blueprints and plans that guided and authorized the new city's construction. Seen through the lens of Latourian (2005a) readings of political ordering, this was an "epistolary assembly" of a sort. Situating cities, civilizations, and political projects on the same plane, this assembly was not just about gathering together but also about spreading out, forging lateral connections and networks of parity. In addition, in these circulations of text, objects, and image, the placemaking sought by Doxiadis and discursive exchange sought by Arendt occupied a common ground. Indeed, in the case of Tema, this was the stuff of "city-building" (Arendt 1958, 195). As Arendt (194) reinforces, according to the Ancient Greeks, "Before men began to act, a definite space had to be secured and structure built where all subsequent actions could take place." This was an ideal well familiar to Doxiadis, as his PhD thesis on Ancient Greek city planning attests (Zarmakoupi 2015).

Doxiadis was most certainly a man of letters, as was his planning outfit, Doxiadis Associates. The firm was steeped in the compilation and publication of reports, serials, white papers, maps, projections, graphs, charts, and a scholarly journal devoted to ekistics.[10] As Matthew Hull's (2012) study of Tema's sister city of Islamabad, also designed and managed by DA, demonstrates, this documentary corpus was formative to urban political order. Far from epiphenomenal, linking DA's many projects, it was an operative modality of urban political assembly within DA-designed cities as well as across them. Evident in the trashed archive of Tema's development office, where plans for Dhaka and Islamabad mingled with those of Tema, records and reports circulated among DA international offices and urban outposts, as did a highly international corps of roving professionals.[11] Fast-tracking urban mass production, DA's paper trail was a material means through which order within individual cities and structural sympathies across them were forged and legitimized.

The decisive role played by DA in the realization of the city of Tema hinged on these exchanges, not least of which was the correspondence—epistolary, intellectual, and philosophical—between its principal, Dinos Doxiadis, and Ghana's President Nkrumah. When Ghana was officially deemed a republic on July 1, 1960, Doxiadis personally cabled the new president: "Congratulations for new task of historic importance and best wishes for success" (Doxiadis Archives, C-GHA 68, 1-7-60). The two met on several occasions, for discussions, commissionings, and celebratory photo shoots. One of the firm's early reports notes, "Dr. CA Doxiadis, President of Doxiadis Associates, visited Ghana in March. HE the President of Ghana, Dr. Kwame Nkrumah, received Dr. Doxiadis on the 21st March and discussed with him major aspects of the overall programme under study or implementation by DA" (TDC Archives, MR-GHA 43, 1962, 1).

Though Nkrumah and Doxiadis came from different corners of the world, both worked from the margins to influence global configurations of power. They were likewise committed to the interlinked midcentury projects of modernization and nation-building. It is important to recall that Doxiadis's native Greece, like Ghana, was also in the throes of postwar transformation. Still colored by its agrarian roots, Greece was grappling with the aftermath of wartime destabilization. For both Nkrumah and Doxiadis, investment in large-scale re/construction offered the promise of internationalist parity (Kelly and Kaplan 2001). This shared vision and the relationship on which it depended were assiduously cultivated by Doxiadis and his team.

As much as Ghana's new leadership was in search of a plan to correct the colonial tinge of earlier urban designs, DA too was working to establish itself internationally. A large-scale commission in Ghana, the first African state to achieve independence, would do much to gain influence in and access to Africa after building a reputation in South Asia and the Middle East. In correspondence with Ghanaian colleagues, Dinos Doxiadis readily asserted, "My Associates and myself are very proud to be working for such a big program and plan, in such an important moment in the development of the major urban area of Ghana, and I am confident that this can become a leading example in proper urban planning of major urban areas of Africa" (Doxiadis Archives, C-GHA 131, 10-9-60).

On receiving his first contract with the Ministry of Works and Housing and meeting with Nkrumah in April 1960, Doxiadis wrote at length to the president in a bid to establish common ground and secure the new nation's business. Doxiadis's correspondence with Nkrumah encodes recognition of both cultural difference and common needs across nation-states: "Our professional organization is Doxiadis Associates, Consulting Engineers, which provides services on development, especially in ekistics, which range from the conception of national housing programs to regional plans, highway programs, master programs and plans for cities, community facilities, water supply, sewage, etc, housing schemes, public buildings which we try to study from the economic, social, technical, cultural points of view" (Doxiadis Archives, C-GHA 41, 26-4-60, 3).

Beyond the technicalities of selling his firm's services to the president, Doxiadis emphasized the two men's shared intellectualism, from their intellectual parity to their shared appreciation of intellectual pursuits. On the one hand asserting the gap between more and less industrialized societies, on the other Doxiadis spoke to cultural achievements that transcended time and place, conveying a classic humanist perspective. Allying a builder's view of the world with the values of Ancient Greece, Doxiadis expressed this in decisively materialist terms. In an early note to Nkrumah he compared the Attic Greek vase he gave to him with the fine carvings he purchased from Ghanaian craftsman: "I was so enthusiastic that I took them in the plane with me straight to Athens and have them in my home. The first is an armchair, carved in wood. Anyone understanding how furniture is made, will recognize that the man who has cut this chair is a real artist. You can sit more comfortably than in many European-made chairs of timber; it is a well-balanced construction, very safe to sit on, and artistically very complete" (Doxiadis Archives, C-GHA 41, 26-4-60).

A statement of common human values afforded by technical and aesthetic acuity, Doxiadis's pitch was all about expertise. This expertise, however, was never about ideas alone. It was embodied and expressed via material means. Doxiadis touted the precepts of his combined consultancy and educational organization, the Athens Institute for Ekistics, "combining theoretical training with practical, on-the-job training" (Athens Technological Institute 1963). These ideals fit well with Nkrumah's pride in and promotion of Ghanaian industry and industriousness. Central to Nkrumah's Second Five-Year Plan for National Development , Ghana's industrial promise was touted in speeches and public relations materials that were a core part of the newly minted national imaginary, such as the glossy brochures promoting the city of Tema.

For Doxiadis, Ghanaian expertise was to be preserved. In the same letter Doxiadis goes on state, "Allow me to say, Sir, that the people who have carved these two pieces are people who require special care by your government. There is a real danger that these people, if asked to pass through the stages of evolution as the Western artists did, may lose the skill that they have; be-cause they will then have to jump over to a new era, and they themselves, or their children, will not be able to recapture the skill and tradition they have inherited" (Doxiadis Archives, C-GHA 41, 26-4-60). Wary of down-grading expertise to mere labor via the exertions of an unskilled working class, Doxiadis sought knowledge transfer through training in architecture and engineering. He offered opportunities at his Athens-based institute for Ghanaian students "to become experts in the development of human set-tlements . . . the beginning of a broader training program which will allow, some day, experts from Ghana to replace our own experts in the field of ek-istics" (Doxiadis Archives, C-GHA 41, 26-4-60). Eventually a branch was opened in Ghana, just as Doxiadis had done for architecture and engineer-ing students from Pakistan when the firm received its commission for Islam-abad. By means of exposure and education, expertise, including the elitism it harbored, was ecumenical. In Nkrumah and Doxiadis's eyes, it was there for the taking for a new generation of Ghanaian city and nation builders.

Embedded in Doxiadis's approach were strains of Nkrumah's own am-bivalence about the potentials of Ghana's working class in spite of the new government's declared socialist platform. Though a prime vector of national transformation and Nkrumah's and his party's ascendance, Ghana's work-ing class also harbored the seeds of the newly independent government's demise. Nkrumah and the Convention People's Party's staying power there-fore required a delicate dance with a growing urban workforce. From an initial stance of accommodation and participation at independence, ten-sions between workers and Ghana's designated Trade Union Congress grew in scope (Ahlman 2017). By 1958, the union was made an arm of the ruling party. "Chip[ing] away at worker autonomy and self-expression in favor of productivity and socialist collectivity" (19), facing persistent threats of strikes, the government asserted that workers were expected to contrib-ute to nation-building, not alter existing social and economic hierarchies (Fitch and Oppenheimer 1966).[12] In short, for Nkrumah, working-class self-determination, while noble in the abstract, was in practice secondary to the alignment of party, union, and presidency. Driven by political expedience, this perspective reflected a like-mindedness with internationalist intellec-tuals such as Doxiadis, whose elite achievements and exposures, and inter-est in order and containment, Nkrumah shared.

From Expertise to Oversight

For Doxiadis and Nkrumah alike, shared ideas about education and expertise over and above undisciplined labor served to link humanist precepts to statist practice. A harsh reality underlying President Nkrumah's professed socialist proclivities was that the new nation's working classes were to be carefully managed (Biney 2011). In correspondence with Nkrumah, Doxiadis made a strong argument for a top-down approach to urban development. Doxiadis asserted early on, "Both profit and oversight of property development should be in the hands of the state, not private interests.... Should at very least be executed and overseen by state at outset and can later share or devolve responsibility to private interests ... ensures a proper plan will be put into place" (TDC Archives, DOX-GHA 3, 1960, 62). With this charge, the DA team took the reins of Tema's design and building, an assignment that lasted through the early 1970s, long after Nkrumah was toppled in a 1966 coup. In Tema, in a path nearly identical to what Pascal Menoret (2014, 94) describes for DA's operations in Riyadh, "the Greek experts' mission had dramatically evolved. From mere consultants they had become actual urban planners, who were opening new roads, widening existing avenues and participating in day-to-day planning operations."

In Tema, it wasn't only DA's planning authority that rose to the fore. Posed as a model polity within a larger model nation-state, the city of Tema was overseen by a singular administrative body. Via special legislation, authority over the city was made the purview of the state-owned and -commissioned Tema Development Corporation (TDC). The operations of TDC exploited the ambiguity between planning and governing, with planning largely serving as a proxy for municipal government. Doxiadis Associates' Tema offices were located on TDC premises. With DA on-site, both up-front and behind the scenes, TDC readily emerged as the prime overseer of the new city responsible for the building and development as well as the management. The TDC was the city's "go-to" authority, in charge of everything from rent collection and housing repair to the drawing of maps; allocation of homes, plots, and contracts; and issuing of permissions for any and all land use in the Tema Acquisition Area outside of the port. Even when local administration was established for more general law enforcement in Tema, TDC remained at the fore as the first line of inquiry and the last word on how things were to be done in the city.[13] With the capacity to collect revenue as well as demolish structures and requisition resources, TDC was and remains the de facto

Figure 1.6. President Kwame Nkrumah visiting Tema exhibition with Queen Elizabeth and Mr. A. Otoo, chief development officer, Tema Development Organization, 1961 (© Constantinos and Emma Doxiadis Foundation)

seat of power in the city, making the most of its unique mandate coincident with the founding of the Republic of Ghana (see plate 1).

Tema Development Corporation was founded in 1952 and in operation by 1953, and its charter endowed it with exclusive local control and full vesting of land rights in the state—"free from all adverse or competing rights, title, interests, trusts, claims and demands whatsoever" (Kirchherr 1968, 210). Its mandate was to oversee the creation, implementation, and enforcement of the master plan for the new city: from building design and construction to the allocation and maintenance of services and properties, and the destruction of nonconforming sites and structures (Kirchherr 1968). Planning—and the infrastructures imagined and instituted via those plans—became the prime modality of urban social ordering and control. In the handover from colonial rule to national government, TDC's first charge was to "secure the layout and development of the new town and port of Tema" (TDC Archives, DOX-GHA 64, 1962, 2–3) (Kirchherr 1968). As harbor construction moved forward and city plans stalled, TDC's ambit soon moved to the town alone.[14]

Incorporated into the same administrative rubric and shared workspace, DA's Tema office and Tema-based officers worked hand in hand with TDC personnel, providing substantial direction and expertise alongside their Ghanaian counterparts. With the input of the highly mobile Doxiadis and an expanding cast of associates,[15] they marshaled the technical know-how of a wide-ranging team of Ghanaian and expatriate planners, architects, engineers, and draftsmen.[16] Most important was TDC's chief architect, the Ghana-born Scotland-trained T. S. Clerk.[17] Eventually serving as TDC's first chief executive officer, starting in 1963 until his untimely death two years later, he played a major role in planning for Tema's first three communities, overseeing a team of expatriate planners and architects, including Alcock and Denis Curtis Robinson. Geared to accommodating the city's initial cadre of factory and dockworkers, this was a project started but still unfinished by the time Doxiadis's contract was finalized (Provoost 2020).

Besides TDC chief architect T. S. Clerk, DA's team worked alongside an extensive, newly professionalized national administrative corps eager to build their own futures in the new city. Adapting the firm's template to the demographic and topographic features of the new city, they wielded a decisive influence over urban living standards and the city's built environment. In the few short years following the launch of the 1961 master plan, the collective ambit of the DA and TDC team encompassed housing and neighborhood layouts, community spaces and services, and the overarching and underlying infrastructural conditions of the new city.

A firm example of Bruno Latour's (2005a) claim that "infrastructure gathers people together," by the beginning of 1961, these partnerships were in full swing. One of a long series of monthly reports published by DA notes, "Our Tema office during the month of January occupied 21 expatriate and 104 Ghanaian personnel directly employed by Doxiadis Associates or seconded by the Tema Development Organisation, making a total of 125, out of which 37 were directly employed by Doxiadis Associates and 38 were seconded to Doxiadis Associates by Tema Development Organization" (TDC Archives, MR-GHA 37, 1962, 71).

The Organic Turns Technical

With TDC up and running and Doxiadis on board, by 1962 investments in the grand schemes of port and dam for the new city were matched by concerted investment in the distributed systems of day-to-day living and urban functioning, including the details of sanitary arrangements. Propelled by the Nkrumah government's financial support and ideological buy-in, DA's vision of urban order in Ghana was turned into a material reality. Rooted in the coupled humanism and scientism of ekistics theory, the resulting urban scheme was strongly machinic in both means and ends, applying the materials and mechanical logics of modernist mass production to the details of daily life, justified by the wider ends of new nation-building.

These interventions were composed and imposed on a pretense of an urban tabula rasa authorized by the newly independent government. Also notable was their comprehensive rollout in an effort to override prior histories of habitation and political organization. In this regard Tema finds a parallel in the better-known tropical modernist cities Brasília and Chandigarh over and above the many New Town developments of the metropole. Certainly, countless cities—Paris, London, New York—have been subject to infrastructural "makeovers" in the name of public health and improvement (Halliday 1999; Laporte 2002; Melosi 2002). In those settings a substantial urban population and established polity was already in place. Infrastructure was used as a means to tighten the net of urban order and accountability. In Tema, however, once the original populace had been (forcibly) dispersed and replaced by newcomers with few ties to place or to one another, sanitary infrastructure was not a secondary affectation of established urban arrangements and affinities but a first-order political instrument intended to both draw people in and to keep them apart.

The coupled humanist and machinic roots of the new city and their inherent limits and contradictions would inform the infrastructural impasses and inventions in play decades later. Namely, in the breach between the technical and the human-centered, an overlooked past and a desired future, the Nkrumah/Doxiadis plan suppressed the formation of a full-blown public sphere. As subsequent chapters make clear, the inadequacies of these investments offered an inadvertent platform for the expression of urban plurality. Though far from the classic polis described by Arendt, what emerged was an arena of collective possibility. Spawning new ways of being and living together and making durable claims on the urban order, here we see an unsettled assemblage seeding active *agencement*: an "event of becoming" anew beyond disparate parts and points of origin (J. Phillips 2006, 108–9), in the vein of Gilles Deleuze and Félix Guattari's (1987) original conception of the term.

The remainder of this chapter discloses Doxiadis's plan for the city and the distinct registers and rationales driving the details of household, neighborhood, and city design. Conveyed in Doxiadis's first letters to Nkrumah praising what "humanity held in common," the resulting installations were devised around shared human needs and standards. Representing the unique orientation of DA and its founder, they were pegged to the scale and functions of the human body. According to this conceptual scheme, the body is the starting point and enduring condition of human—including urban—existence. A contention in line with Arendt's (1958) recognition of bodily labors as the baseline of political membership, what for Arendt was precondition was for Doxiadis and Nkrumah in Tema sufficient end point.

In Arendt's words (1958, 30–31), the plight of *animal laborans*, "mastering the necessities of life ... a condition for freedom in the polis ... is primarily a prepolitical phenomenon." However, for Doxiadis, when it came to design, the human body was not solely a first-order problem: it was the ultimate one. Offered as corrective to the missteps of modern urbanism, ekistics theory hinged on "preserving the human scale" (Doxiadis 1968). The human-centered unit was held to be both foundational and generative, spurring growth as well as stability. In a cellular conception of urbanization, Doxiadis explained (431), "the smaller the parts, the more stable it should be.... On the macro-scale the ecumenopolis will be dynamic while on the micro-scale it should remain stable and static."

Human-centered, the notion of human sameness was translated by DA into a common set of urban solutions.[18] Generative of a distinct set of urban designs and associated sociopolitical orders, ekistics was a framework that privileged the body as well as the *oikos*. From this vantage point, the city of Tema was not solely conceived as urban machine for the production of national futures, it was also *oikos*: that is, built of and around households. Of prime importance to the plan's execution and fallout, it was also managed as one, whether via the heavy hand of the Nkrumah government or the managerial claims of Doxiadis Associates in partnership with TDC. Indeed, when Doxiadis (1958, cited in Zarmakoupi 2015) first coined the term "ekistics," he pointed to its etymological roots: "from feminine of *oikistikos* of settlement, from Greek, from *oikizein* to settle, colonize, from *oikos* house."[19]

As opposed to a Marxian outlook that places the making of modern man in the factory, or an Arendtian one that locates it in the polis, from the perspective of Tema's urban plan, modern humanity could be made in the most basic of social units: the household.[20] Orienting bodies and domestic space and, through them, the city writ large, sanitary installations were put toward this end, marking their centrality to Tema's overall design. For Doxiadis and colleagues, when it came to the mass production of urban modernity in the tropics, sanitation was an essential matter, not an afterthought to be put in place once the integuments of urban rule were set. Explaining the firm's grand plan for Tema, an early DA report on the city states, "The basic requirement of designing a house, regardless of income group, is that it should be complete in all essential components. This means that the unit should include all the spaces needed to serve the basic family functions: food preparation and eating, cleanliness, sleeping, recreation. These four basic functions are carried out by the whole range of incomes. The design of the housing unit is based on the above-mentioned functions" (TDC Archives, DOX-GHA 27, 1961, 22–23).

Sanitation was encompassed within the category of "cleanliness," rather than excised via categorical exclusion, as in earlier town plans. Translating organic bodily processes onto built forms, the DA report continues, "The function of cleanliness involves the following[:] a. water closet b. shower, laundry c. clothes hanging space d. clothes storage space. The Function of sleeping involves the following. . . . The Function of recreation involves the following. . . . These functions embrace the life of the whole family. They occupy the three basic spaces of the house: outdoor, sheltered and indoor spaces" (TDC Archives, DOX-GHA 27, 1961, 22–23).

Emphasizing the parity of human needs and the associated equivalence of persons based on these needs—again, a parity materially based and expressed—DA's sanitary arrangements for Tema share a common set of infrastructural and architectural features. Given and giving structure by means of aggregation of basic body-centered units, these details range from the location and layout of toilets and bathing facilities to types of fixtures, pipe depths, and wind and outflow directions. Exemplifying the firm's scientific approach to human settlements, DA's planning for Tema began with the square footage of human survival. Considered a universal measure, the bare minimum was calculated at ninety-eight square feet for a bed, a closet, and a space to stand (TDC Archives, DOX-GHA 52, 1962, 20). Found in the lowest grade of housing designed for single male laborers, the calculation of basic needs was progressively scaled up for larger units and higher income levels. Across diverse income groups and house designs, however, sanitary functions, fixtures, and features were largely constant. The ultimate arbiter of urban and, indeed, human equivalence, they adhered to the same configurations, fittings, and technical specifications.

As an exercise in urban mass production, identical inputs were assembled across the different sections of the city. Doxiadis Associates' records inventory the full range of sanitary procurements: "¾" and ½" copper and galvanized steel pipes. Brass bib taps, fireclay sink, fireclay lavatory basin, chrome plated shower rose, 2½ imperial gallon capacity cast iron flushing cistern at high level. 4" dia pitch fibre and 2½" dia gray syntex heavy duty pipes. Manholes according to design. White glazed fireclay pedestal type WC pan" (TDC Archives, DOX-GHA A 94, 1964, 40).

An early report on imported building materials lists the purchase of twenty-five thousand sanitary fixtures ordered from UK suppliers for £281,400 (TDC Archives, DOX-GHA A 96, 1965, 9, table 3, "Imports of Building Materials"). Among the detritus of DA's dismantled Tema Development Corporation library could be found dusty catalogs of plumbing hardware. Once enabling the production of sanitary uniformity across the city, they sat beside a 1950 handbook for *British Standard Water Fittings* and the 1960 Overseas Architects Standards Catalog with several pages devoted to purveyors of bathroom wall and floor tiles. Part of a wider project of urban mass production across the former outposts of empire, these materials likewise facilitated Doxiadis's replication of a common template among far-flung locales. From Islamabad to Aspra Spitia and beyond, Doxiadis worked from a single template amenable to replication and modification.

Not only were sanitary installations identical throughout the new city, but they were nearly exclusively private in character. Asserting its cultural relevance, the DA team defended this stipulation: "It is also known that Ghanaian people like to have privacy in their houses. A fundamental requirement, therefore, is that, irrespective of income group, each house should be complete and independent" (TDC Archives, DOX-GHA 27, 1961, 18). Translating this human scale into specified technical-cum-infrastructural correlates, toilet facilities were dedicated to the exclusive use of household residents, a privacy both social and spatial. Toilets and baths were tucked away in the interior spaces of each dwelling and deliberately situated downwind to avoid the accumulation of "offensive odors."[21] These conditions prevailed across the residential units planned for the new settlement, barring just a few exceptions left over from the first phases of the city's development before Doxiadis and company arrived on the scene.[22] Attuned to privacy and parity, this was considerably different from the mores of colonial hygiene, which hinged on supervision rather than self-sufficiency, and developmental differences instead of equivalence.

Domesticating Class Difference

Despite different ideas about the place of the body in the polity, Nkrumah and Doxiadis, like Arendt, favored self-determination over ascription as the basis of modern political membership. Devoted to the linked goals of modernization and nation-building, planner and president similarly dismissed cultural difference as an appropriate basis of urban order in the new city. Nkrumah spoke and wrote vehemently against the scourge of tribalism (Nkrumah 1958, 1962a). Doxiadis's techno-humanism focused on the fundamental equality of humanity despite varied outward expression. Giving tangible form to these sociopolitical proscriptions yet tiptoeing around the fraught concept of class, the housing stock proposed for Tema was organized on the basis of earnings rather than race, tribe, or ethnicity.[23] An early report on the city preceding Doxiadis's involvement makes clear:

> As urbanization takes effect in Ghana, tribal ties and disciplines must be superseded by other loyalties if a coordinated law-abiding society is to emerge. It is therefore important to give urban Ghanaians a sense of community membership. The policy in Tema has been to discourage racial, tribal, religious or class segregation, in the hope that citizens' loyalty will be to neighborhood, community and town. This policy requires nontraditional types of housing accommodation. The tribal compound has no place in Tema and is replaced by the private family dwelling. Differentiation of dwelling standards is purely by income, and all income-groups are represented in each community. (Robinson and Anderson 1961, 5)

Demonstrating his distinctive state and household-centric socialist proclivities, President Nkrumah, likewise sidestepping the subject of class, placed "work" at the core of national belonging. In a dramatic speech commissioning Tema's industrial zone, he proclaimed on August 24, 1963: "The ability of the Ghanaian must reveal itself in work. Love and respect for work and concern for State and cooperative property must be the cornerstone and backbone of our Ghanaian society. To the Ghanaian, work must not only be an obligation, it must also be a civic duty. By the sweat of thy brow thou shalt eat bread" (Nkrumah 1997c, 79–80). Commuting production to reproduction and class to earnings, income was made the measure of urban man in the DA-designed city. The architecture firm divided Tema's population into four tiers: lower, lower-middle, middle, and high income. Reflecting the scientific pretensions of DA's model and the wider technocratic tenor of postwar national planning, income measures were derived from successive surveys of wage rates along with estimates of the projected labor needs of Tema's industries.

With income level considered a common denominator of urban membership, housing costs and styles in Tema were calculated according to the pragmatics of affordability along with the basic functionalities of urban shelter—eating, hygiene, sleep, and recreation—earlier identified. Housing stock was skewed toward the provision of low-cost dwellings to attract and keep low-paid industrial, harbor, and construction workers in the new city (TDC Archives, DOX-GHA 31, 1962). This was so even if it meant TDC would need to subsidize the rents of those on the bottom rungs of the income ladder (TDC Archives, DOX-GHA 31, 1962, 3). Reiterating the critical importance of housing as the foundation of urban order, as DA saw it, "Workers who own their own homes are usually an important factor in promoting social order, political equilibrium and economic progress" (TDC Archives, DOX-GHA 27, 1961, 7). Though much in order with Arendt's tripartite schema shielding bodily reproduction from public life, the circumscription of difference within the private household in Tema could also be construed as a means to mitigate politicized self-expression in the public sphere, a move that undermined the plurality of public life prized by Arendt as the core of political existence.

In addition, at once recognizing and holding at bay President Nkrumah's commitment to socialism, by making the private life of the household the crux of urban order and emphasizing equivalence across income groups, the Doxiadis plan essentially domesticated class difference. Not only could a focus on domestic needs mitigate the potential for workplace mobilization and urban proletarianization despite Tema's industrial base; DA's plan also worked against the formation of class-based affiliations in any given residential zone. In an avowed effort of social engineering (D'Auria 2010, 47), each community was to contain a mix of income levels, promoting aspirations of class mobility over and above intraclass solidarities.[24]

In keeping with this logic, Tema's housing scheme was organized according to eight income tiers, classified low to high (see table 1.1). These tiers were distributed across a progression of housing types, styles, and sizes: houses, hostels, and flats; attached and detached; storied and single-level; and more (D'Auria 2010, 45). Types A, B, and C, spanning around four hundred, five hundred, and six hundred square feet per unit, respectively, were reserved for the lowest-income tiers. At around seven hundred and nine hundred square feet, types D and E were for Tema's middle-income residents. The

Table 1.1. House types, income distribution, and floor area according to 1961 master plan for Tema

House type	Income level	Floor area	Percentage of structures
A	Low	400 sq. ft.	15
B	Low	540 sq. ft.	35
C	Low, middle	630 sq. ft.	25
D	Middle	740 sq. ft.	10
E	Upper middle	900 sq. ft.	7
F	Upper	1,100 sq. ft.	4
G	Upper	1,270 sq. ft.	2
H	Upper	1,610 sq. ft.	2

Source: DOX-GHA 20, 44.

homes of types F, G, and H, for the highest-income group, were measured at 1,000, 1,300, and 1,600 square feet, not counting the garage or boy's quarters (TDC Archives, DOX-GHA 20, 1961, 44). Further differentiated by layout and slight variations in size, there were fourteen styles of low-income housing alone (TDC Archives, DOX-GHA 31, 1962, 36).

Sanitary arrangements, however, were a constant across the wide array of housing types and income levels. Though city plans were numerically dominated by the very lowest income tiers and house types, and residential styles further differentiated for higher-income groups, the same sanitary forms prevailed across the spectrum of high-, middle-, and low-income housing. In each, the doubly private condition of interior location and exclusive residential access to toilets and bathrooms obtained. From the lowest rung of worker hostel to lower-middle-income row house, middle-income multistory flat and high-income detached home, each was appointed with a self-contained water closet and adjoining hand sink, and a shower/bath, all accessed from the interior of the dwelling (TDC Archives, DOX-GHA 40, 1962). Despite the considerable variation and clear intentionality devoted to the details of residential design, this was a telling indication of city planners' commitment to sanitary parity (see figure 1.7).

BATH   HOUSE TYPE

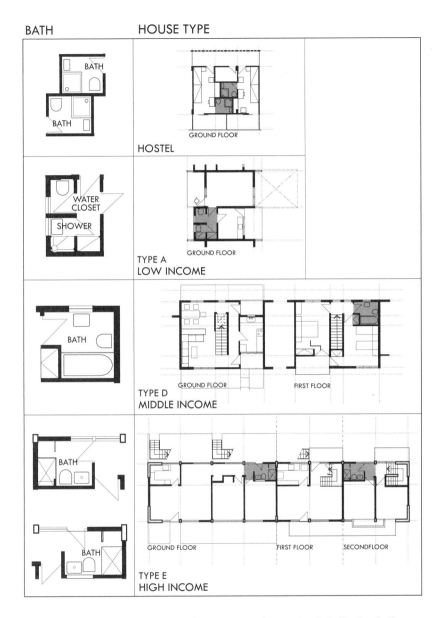

Figure 1.7. Tema master plan house layouts across income levels indicating bathrooms (Kairon Aiken, adapted from Doxiadis Associates Reports for Government of Ghana, DOX-GHA 83, DOX-GHA A91, MR-GHA 65, Tema Development Corporation Archives)

The multistory three-bedroom apartments designed for Tema's upper-middle-class residents, called "maisonettes" by DA, contained a single bathroom with toilet, sink, and shower stall identical to those of working-class homes (TDC Archives, MR-GHA 65, 17). Across the many styles of low-income dwelling, regardless of building contractor or corporate client, the same conditions were maintained. These two- and three-room dwellings were all equipped with enclosed water closet and adjoining sink and shower stalls (TDC Archives, DOX-GHA A 94, 1964, 14). While the smaller dwellings of four to five hundred feet might have only a partial wall separating the toilet from the bath, all were fully contained within domestic space. Planners were attentive to consistency in layout and placement. One of DA's many planning reports made clear the intentionality of these design decisions: "The WC and shower are located toward the entrance as the prevailing wind is northerly and would cause nuisance to the inhabitants if these spaces were placed toward the courtyard" (TDC Archives, DOX-GHA 20, 1961, 16).

Even as other domestic functions in these compact dwelling spaces were allocated to the semi-enclosed space of porch and veranda, the bathroom and toilet remained at the core of the dwelling, occupying square footage nearly equal to that designated to kitchen and food preparation (TDC Archives, DOX-GHA A 94, 1964, 14). At the higher end of the spectrum of low-income dwellings containing three to four rooms with a veranda and front and back entry, water closet and bath were accessible from all corners. Middle-income homes with multiple bedrooms as well as a large living room had the very same bathrooms, save the addition of a tub in place of the shower stall (TDC Archives, DOX-GHA A 91, 1964, 45, 51).

Urban theorist Lewis Mumford (1938, 419) comments on the logics of such arrangements of mid-twentieth-century infrastructural equity:

> We do not have one type of electric light for the rich and another for the poor. All these instruments have an objective standard of performance, determinable by experiment: they are products of a collective economy and are meant to fit into a collective whole. One's economic position may entitle one to a greater or smaller quantity, but the quality is fixed. . . . In order to make collective production and distribution possible on a scale that will embrace a whole society, economy must be a regulating principle in all design: for it is only by saving on the means and instrumentalities of life that a community can command the necessary abundance at

the higher levels of art, science, education and expression. Holding on to this principle means having enough to go around.

Depluralization and Urban Body Politics

The political implications of Tema's domestic arrangements are manifold. To begin with, bodily needs—both individual and collective—are explicitly addressed rather than deemed insignificant to public life. In addition, with sanitary infrastructure serving as an "equalizer" cutting across income categories, class appears a transient category perched on a common embodied personhood. In contrast to Arendt's (1958) understanding of bodily labors as entirely private, this sanitary rubric simultaneously individuates and equalizes private persons as a co-condition of membership in the urban public sphere via interference in the domestic realm. Such an approach to biopolitics upheld the purportedly apolitical foundations of Tema, where the city's planning authority, Tema Development Corporation, and its primary agent and partner, Doxiadis Associates, were essentially equated with government. Implied in this model and serving the nascent national government and city planners alike, as bodily functions and household infrastructure and organization enabled urban membership, there was little need or opportunity to cultivate other avenues of political participation and belonging for Tema residents.

Mixing tenets of socialism and consumerism, Tema's urban plan cultivated the body in lieu of the body politic. In Tema's mixed-class communities, bodily and infrastructural parity were envisioned as an ideal foundation for the kind of interclass mobility sought by Nkrumah for Ghana's citizenry, all the while downplaying the potentials of class-based tensions and relations of production in the city's docks and factories. What was neither imagined nor desired by Nkrumah or Doxiadis was intraclass mobilization, whether born of infrastructure-based struggles or industrial ones. That is, implicit in the plans for the new city was the fantasy of economic mobility without the unpredictability of class-based activism in Tema's newly built harbor and industrial zone. With the conditions of employment and social reproduction all but guaranteed for its residents, at least in theory, Tema was conceived as a city without an urban body politic, whether based on the essentialisms of race and tribe, the essentialisms of labor, or the chambers of participatory rule. By no means is this to claim that access to modern sanitation was in any way inappropriate or misguided for Tema residents, or that Nkrumah's investment in urban infrastructure for the new nation was somehow misplaced or nefarious. The point, rather, is that large-scale infrastructural investments were inherently aligned with political interests and carried political implications, both intended and inadvertent.

More specifically, the city's "understory" serves as evidence of the Nkrumah government's fundamental ambivalence regarding class and labor-driven social transformation. On one level, the regime professed a commitment to social empowerment via grand planning and state-driven industrialization. On another, politicization was sidestepped through the securities and satisfactions offered by the promotion of "bourgeois survival" (a term borrowed from Ahlman 2017, 146) via the carefully orchestrated household and neighborhood designs for the city. While labor mobilization in Tema could never be completely avoided (Yedu Bannerman 1973, 15), with displacement of the locus of social transformation from worksite to the *oikos* via "self-rule" of and through home and body, the state could both exert control at a distance and narrow the scope of collective mobilization and mutual recognition.[25]

The inward-looking and individuating practices of urban housing and domestic infrastructure, in sum, mitigated the body politic. If Arendtian ideas of plurality attune us to an interplay of collectivity and differentiation, city planners tamped down both to offer a depoliticized vision of urban assembly designed to avoid conflict or cohesion. In short, in Tema, despite Doxiadis's, Nkrumah's, and Arendt's common philosophical footing, the indeterminacies of aggregation and collective freedom afforded by the polis idealized by Arendt were for Doxiadis and Nkrumah replaced by the affordances of security in the sheltered sphere of the household. Turning class to the ends of domesticity, this was an implicit project of what can be called "depluralization," where the conventions of daily life are made common to all but rarely shared or collectivized.[26] Reversing cause and effect, subject and agent, rather than a conformity sought by modern subjects, as in Arendt's critique of the rise of "the social," here conformity is produced by state suppression of difference. Governance, in turn, aspires to what Arendt (1958, 44–45) calls "pure administration ... withering away ... the state as a realm of participation."

Minipublics and the Infrastructural Inchoate

Public life in the new city could not be avoided. It could nevertheless be orchestrated, or at least circumscribed. Further inhibiting the possibilities of mass political mobilization in Tema, the inevitability of urban aggregation was matched by planning strategies geared to its containment. This is evident in the design of the city center, one of Doxiadis's earliest design proposals for the city (TDC Archives, DOX-GHA 3, 1960, 21). Relatively compact compared to the broad expanse of the Tema metropolitan area, the city center was tightly bounded from the start. All the core functions were predetermined, leaving little room for further growth or organic development. Besides a small central market and a few department stores, core functions were largely administrative, consisting of banks, a post office, a police station, and a magistrate's office and courts, along with a compact community center to stage performances. Like the elite polis of ancient Greece, this was not an arrangement geared to large-scale or spontaneous gathering. Arranged around three separate plazas, the community center was conceived as a transit zone designed to move people through and toward other parts of the city (TDC Archives, DOX-GHA 62, 1962, 15, 31). By no means reflecting a singular consensus among members of Tema's planning team, DA's Ghanaian counterparts repeatedly shot down DA proposals for a seaside recreational area that might have functioned as a central place in its own right, open to public mixing and interaction (TDC Archives, DOX-GHA 62, 1962, 46).

Alternative to a singular city center subsuming all urban functions, the city was instead organized on the premise of decentralization. Tema's twelve communities were each allocated their own commercial centers and central thoroughfares. These were then subdivided into smaller neighborhood quadrants with respective central places offering storefronts, schools, and recreation areas. In Doxiadis's (1968, 439) words, "Here in the basic community the machine scale ends and the human scale begins." With each neighborhood unit designed to contain three to five thousand people, proportionally speaking these were much more extensive in size and services than the city center. At the same time, promoting internalization both spatial and social, the designs turned public interactions toward private needs such as shopping and education.[27] For DA, such arrangements were driven by a distinctive brand of central place theory that saw each neighborhood as a microcosm of the whole, rather than a subsidiary piece of a larger hierarchy. Self-contained and built on the extension of domestic space, the

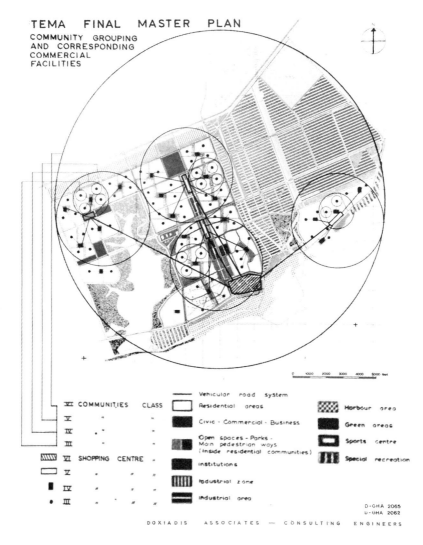

Figure 1.8. Circumscribed centers and minipublics, 1962 (Doxiadis Associates Report for Government of Ghana, DOX-GHA 62, Tema Development Corporation Archives)

neighborhood units engendered what might be called "minipublics" akin to the Greek village squares familiar to Doxiadis. Discounting DA's claims of culturally appropriate stylistics, Menoret (2014, 67) describes the approach as one of "containment urbanism."

With the earliest neighborhoods built to house workers from the new companies setting up shop in the city's industrial zone, a few of Tema's communities resembled miniature company towns. Current place-names in Tema continue to reflect these early corporate affiliations: Kaiser Flats, SSNIT Flats, Italian Flats (for employees of Ghana Italian Petroleum Company). Again, mitigating workplace mobilization even as they fostered community building, the neighborhoods were home to clubhouses, teams, and recreational space and were reserved for employees and their families. The Volta Aluminum Company (VALCO) club in Community 4 best illustrates these ideals, with courts, a bar, and playgrounds, with one side reserved for workers and the other for management. Just as city writ large resembled *oikos*, the company claimed the role of provider, further cultivating the domestication of public life and mitigation of class mobilization.

Very different from a full-blown public sphere enabling open-ended inclusion and interaction (Arendt 1958, 190), neither did these arenas qualify as what we might call "minor publics," drawing on Robert Dahl's terminology (1989).[28] Indeed, so much did the design of the new city delimit the possibilities of mass gathering, Tema's earliest planned neighborhoods lacked designated houses of worship. Among the very first social mobilizations in Tema involved pleas to city planning authorities for space to gather. In response, congregations were permitted to use school buildings for purposes of worship (Yedu Bannerman 1973). In short, even when it came to the unavoidable contingencies of public life in the new city, Tema's urban plan sought the containment of collectivity under a rubric where household, domicile, and small-scale community prevailed. Informing the fabric of urban life—at least in theory—this was a logic of affiliation mitigating the sort of alliances or alienations that might spur politicization outright.

An irony of grand-scale city planning in Tema and elsewhere, this decentralized order, designed to keep people apart, depended on an underlying network of infrastructural interconnection (D'Auria 2010, 47). Dispersed and out of sight, it was largely unknowable in its totality to the average urban resident. In planned New Towns like Tema, where the principles driving urban form are evident in modernist stylistics, the actual complexities of infrastructural arrangements are obscured by the apparent simplicity of surface-level design (Scott 1998). In this case, ideological prioritization of the human-scale and human needs relied on the operational prioritization of the machinic, foregrounding the one and backgrounding—or, in the case of sanitation, undergrounding—the other.

Sanitary Foundations and Machinic Fault Lines

Man adjusted himself to the environment of machines the moment he designed them. . . . Unlike the tools of workmanship, which at every moment of the work process remain the servants of the hand, the machines demand that the laborer serve them, that he adjusts the natural rhythm of his body to their mechanical movement.
—Hannah Arendt, *The Human Condition* (1958)

Sidestepping the perils of political mobilization, the careful orchestration of aggregation evident in Tema's master plan by no means precluded urban growth. Nkrumah's aspirations for the new city considered expansion the very engine of national development. Generating national prosperity and international status by means of industrial and infrastructure-driven productivity, from the Akosombo Dam and hydroelectric power plant to the city's aluminum smelter, factory sites, railroad, and world-class shipping harbor, this was a fundamentally machine-driven vision of human progress. As Nkrumah emphatically remarked in a speech commissioning Tema's new factory zone on September 28, 1963, "Since the attainment of our political independence, there has been no doubt in our minds as to the direction in which our duty lay, namely, to develop Ghana into a modern industrial state. It is only in this way that we can survive as an independent country" (1997a, 107).

Nkrumah's technology-centered ideals were fully in sync with DA's approach to urbanism. Transcending the specificities of the Ghanaian case, as Doxiadis saw it, cities must be planned with growth in mind, whether the expansion of individual settlements and structures or the unstoppable spread of urban systems overall (Doxiadis 1974). A decidedly mechanistic outlook, according to Doxiadis, along with size, urban plans need to anticipate growth of income, energy, and human mobility (30). This, he says, "turns the old static city into a dynamic city, the polis into dynapolis" (Doxiadis 1960; 1974, 23), the latter a term he coined in 1960, just as the Tema project was launched. Such spaces are dynamic "multi-speed" systems involving the "intensification of energy," the "control of nature," and the "maximization of contacts" through "networks created by man" (Doxiadis 1974, 12, 15, 29).

Integral to the orchestration of public life, from DA's perspective, just as the machinic must make space for the human at the microscale of community, in the ideal city human systems give way to the machinic (Doxiadis 1968). According to this outlook, large-scale infrastructure—whether roadways, power lines, or sewage systems—are central to urban modernity and must be planned alongside the core functions of human shelter. Knitting the urban polity together and guaranteeing its ordered operation, this was another way to avoid mass mobilization on the political front. From Riyadh to Dhaka, Islamabad to Baghdad and Aspra Spitia, DA's master plans were predicated on a total package of large-scale infrastructural outlays. Whether Riyadh's highways (Menoret 2014), the electrical lines and carefully paved footpaths that crisscross Aspra Spitia (Yiannados 2015), Islamabad's sewage outfalls and banks of office blocks (Daechsel 2013), or Dhaka's expansive educational grid (Karim 2016), these elements were shared across the many midcentury cities designed by DA. Part of the social contract of liberal modernity, in Tema as elsewhere, infrastructure provided the developmental benefits of industrialization without industry-inspired political activism posing a threat to new leaders or international policy makers.[29]

Sanitary Foundations

Tema was a city built on, around, and through large-scale infrastructure, not as a second thought but as the foundation of urban order. Due to the precedence of port and hydropower development in the path from colonial rule to self-government during the 1950s (Nwaubani 2001), investment in industrial and infrastructural outlays preceded DA's involvement in building and designing the city's residential zones initiated in 1960. Their considerable scope fit Doxiadis's vision well. Predating the microinstallations of individual household sanitation, by the time DA received the official commission for Tema's master plan, the fundaments of the city's sewage system were already in place, along with the waterworks, major roadways, and rail and power lines.

Bankrolled alongside the preliminary development of Tema's industrial zone, construction of the sewage system was initiated in 1959–60 to serve the soon-to-be-completed harbor and adjacent resettlement village of Tema Manhean. With shades of colonial-era infrastructural investment, it was designed and built by Balfour and Sons, a leading UK civil engineering firm (TDC Archives, DOX-GHA A 105, 1967, 2). The system consisted of three sewage mains, three pumping stations, and twenty miles of sewage pipes leading to a gravity trunk line culminating in a single seabound outfall at the far eastern edge of the city. These installations formed the infrastructural baseline of DA's plan to build private sanitary facilities for all residents of the new city.

The firm's early report documented its core features with thorough precision:

> The initial sewage system of the town designed by Messrs. Balfour & Sons and constructed by 1960. The system was designed for a 40.0 g/d per capita consumption of water and for a population of 80,000−120,000 persons. The whole system composed by gravity and pressure sewers comprised three pumping stations and one inverted siphon. One part of the pressure pipe passed through Chemu Lagoon. In general, the whole system has been designed as to be adjusted on the configuration of the ground, which was divided into three main basins, the western, the eastern and the southern one. The three main basins were furthermore subdivided into secondary mains, which presented considerable differences in elevation between ridges and watercourses. . . . The pumping stations form the main elements of the system. From these pumping stations, the sewerage is taken to the main sea outfall through a system of cast iron pumping mains. The 27″ steel sea outfall extends into the sea to a distance of about 2,000 yards from the shore. The end of the outfall sewer coincides with the edge of the continental shelf (at this point the bottom of the sea drops from 30–35 ft to a depth of 70–80 ft). The maximum capacity of the three pumping stations is 3,000,000 g/d. The 27″ steel sea outfall has a maximum capacity of 5,000,000 gallons per day. The maximum sewerage for the city up to now was 700,000 g/d with an average of 300,000 to 350,000 g/d. (TDC Archives, DOX-GHA 6, 1961, 2, 16, 18)

Independent of the new residential plan, Tema's sewage system was a national cause célèbre, commissioned by President Nkrumah himself, just as he commissioned the harbor to national fanfare (Jopp 1961, 33).[30] Fabricated and assembled in situ, Tema's sewage works were touted as a feat of sanitary engineering in the tropics on par with urban infrastructural achievements worldwide. In promotional publications celebrating national progress and commemorating Queen Elizabeth and Prince Philip's visit to the city, Tema was described thus: "For the first time in West Africa a community could be

TEMA - EXISTING OR UNDER CONSTRUCTION
MAIN SEWERS ON THE YEAR 1967

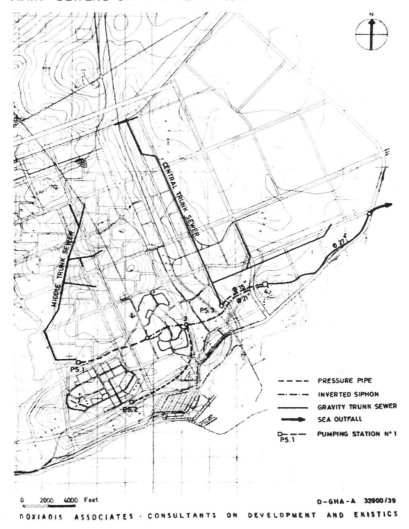

Figure 1.9. Sanitary baseline: Tema sewage system, 1967 (Doxiadis Associates Report for Government of Ghana, DOX-GHA A105, Tema Development Corporation Archives)

built up enjoying all the advantages of modern civilization—well designed houses, a well equipped hospital and comprehensive health, social and cultural services, piped water supplies and underground sewerage, planned and lighted streets, well laid out stores and markets, pleasant gardens and open spaces, well equipped schools and community centres. It would be a balanced community with a variety of industries" (Jopp 1961, 6).

The same brochure featured images of the outfall's fabrication by Tema's new population of skilled laborers. Extending more than a mile into the Atlantic, the sea outfall was noted as the second of its kind in the world, the first being Los Angeles' Hyperion treatment plant with its five-mile outfall (Jopp 1961, 33; Theroux 1957, 124). Putting the organic to technical ends, the success of Tema's sewage system was attributed to human effort and ingenuity as well as efficient use of the natural environment. Organized across the town's alluvial basins, the city's sewage works were designed to fit the slope and contour of the wider Tema Acquisition Area. Optimizing the force of gravity in the placement of pipes and siphons, the system likewise depended on the proximity of lagoon and sea to transport and dilute the accumulated waste. Like the famed Volta River Project that spurred the city's development, nature's potential could be harnessed via the efficiencies of infrastructure.

Sustaining Ghana's standing as sub-Saharan Africa's first industrial-hydraulic society (D'Auria 2010), a copious water supply was the guarantor of system success. Connecting individual persons to grand schemes, bodily needs were put into a common machinic calculus. Initially pegged at an average daily consumption of twenty-five gallons (Jopp 1961, 51), estimates of water usage quickly rose to forty gallons per day (TDC Archives, DOX-GHA 6, 1961, 16), a rate higher than the United Kingdom, "because of the need for bathing in the tropics" (Alcock 1963, 4). In this midcentury mindset, nature was a vital public good, necessary and available to those with the requisite know-how. From the perspective of midcentury theorists like Arendt, these interventions enabled progression beyond the gross dependencies of *animal laborans* driven by bodily needs that reduced humanity to "nature's servant" (1958, 139).

Rather, this next stage of industrialization at work in Tema involved the "use and imitation of natural process" (Arendt 1958, 148). Accessed and further improved by human input, nature—specifically, large-scale natural systems—was considered the basis of the new system's success. Reflecting this perspective, DA's first report on Tema's sanitary infrastructure emphatically states, "No sewerage treatment plant exists or is planned for Tema" (TDC Archives, DOX-GHA 6, 1961, 16). Tema's initial sewage system, in short, was doubly "naturalized," making use of and bolstered by the natural environment and uncritically embraced as a beacon of national progress and individual prosperity.

Machinic Fault Lines

Born of an infrastructural-cum-political inchoate, the public instantiated by these large-scale sanitary installations was meant to be invisible—remotely felt rather than immediately known. An uneasy alignment, this would ultimately seed the sorts of open-ended political action it was meant to contain. To be sure, the infrastructural arrangements put in place by Balfour and Sons provided a technical baseline for the actualization of Doxiadis's ideals regarding human bodily shelter and security by means of private, household-based sanitation. However, they existed in tension with Doxiadis's overarching intentions for Tema, not to mention the lived realities of urban occupation and the desires, needs, and lifestyles of urban residents. There was the simple problem of precedence, with Tema's residential tracts being designed by one entity and its sewage system designed at a different time by another. A fundamental dilemma of new nation-building was also the inevitable disconnect born of top-down institution of citywide systems when the details of daily life were barely worked out, whether from the perspective of planning officials or those living, working, and existing in the city. This disjuncture was further exacerbated by the considerable expansion of Tema's population and territorial footprint under the newly authorized urban scheme. Alongside all of these frictions and countervailing forces was the inexorable, insistent agency of bodily waste in its own right, never fully compliant with the infrastructures meant to contain it or the bodies producing it. In sum, although Tema's large-scale sewage system was central to the realization of the city's residential plan, the fit between the two was always imperfect and instable.

Yet we should not simply dismiss this as a case of failure like other "grand schemes to improve the human condition," to quote James Scott (1998). The process of sanitary repair, resistance, and recalibration that resulted, as subsequent chapters make clear, were formative to the waging and staging of urban politics and plurality over the next half century. Sparking compromises, adjustments, quick fixes, and alternatives that have marked Tema's infrastructural lifeworlds since, these unsettled middle grounds between public and private, municipal authority and city resident, individual bodily outputs and large-scale urban systems, are central to this book. Advancing Steven Jackson's (2014) argument that the work of repair can be a source of innovation and empowerment, I argue that it may spur deeper processes of transformation, especially when vital needs and vital materials are in play. In fading modernist cities such as Tema, where formal institutions of urban governance claim a partial yet waning presence, these hybrid forms of infrastructural assembly binding human and nonhuman, machinic and organic, resident, neighbor, community, and city are the substance of urban political life. Precipitating new material arrangements and modalities of urban functioning, they organize new formations of urban plurality, that is, recurring, interconnected ways of being together and apart. As Arendt (1958, 144) reminds us, with plurality comes the *vita activa* and the unsettledness of action: "Action, though it may have a definite beginning, never, as we shall see, has a predictable end."

In 1963, the ink barely dry on official reports of Tema's sanitary promise, optimism quickly gave way to concern regarding the sanitary system's adequacy. Upending the wishful vision of "the sewage system as automatic" (Alcock 1963, 3), the infrastructure on which the smooth functioning of residential life depended was rapidly becoming a problem to be solved, with flows threatening to exceed capacity, pumps and pipes near exhaustion, and sewer mains crossing the city's central thoroughfares.[31] Doxiadis Associates attributed the infrastructure's failure to live up to expectations to a number of factors. With rapid buildup of the city underway, rising population was a big part of the problem (TDC Archives, DOX-GHA 84, 1963, 5). When the sewage system was commissioned in 1961, only 35,000 residents were accounted for (Jopp 1961, 51). The quick construction of affordable houses under TDC-administered contracts alongside the expansion of industry and, with it, jobs, made for high rates of urban settlement. Once the Doxiadis plan took off, it was not unusual for two thousand, three thousand, or even four thousand structures to be completed in a single year. For every thousand homes built, the population increased by several thousand residents (TDC Archives, DOX-GHA A 105, 1967, 10). When it came to sanitation, trunk lines and pumping stations were quickly pushed to capacity.[32] The city planner's population projections soon went from 80,000 in 1964 to 120,000 by 1967, and soon enough doubled to 250,000 by 1980.

Doxiadis Associates' science-driven rendering of impending system failure drew on the close study of use patterns and projected system capacity.

With homes and residential patterns designed to protect and cultivate vital human needs—eating, sleeping, shelter, recreation, hygiene, recreation— soon enough, these same processes took on a life of their own. Turning from basic necessities to an emergent terrain of infrastructure's vital politics, the city plan could barely contain the bodily practices it sought to nurture. The city's waterworks, sewage mains, holding tanks, and even the long sea outfall were deemed insufficient (TDC Archives, DOX-GHA 84, 1963, 2, 16). Urban growth brought new standards of living. Connecting private habits and public infrastructure, water rates quickly rose to fifty-five gallons per day per person, leading to projections of sixty-five gallons per day by 1969, making breakdown inevitable (TDC Archives, DOX-GHA 84, 1963, 16). Converted into flows per minute and peak rates per pumping station, the numbers dramatized the unstoppable pressures on the fixed capacities of the city's newly installed siphons, pumps, and pipes (TDC Archives, DOX-GHA A 105, 1967, 10). Exemplifying a triple alienation mixing atomization and aggregation, and calculated through a law of sanitary averages, in these calculations people were reduced to the waste they produced and their unconscious impacts on the collective well-being.

In these scenarios, despite the fundamental intimacy of bodily waste, the agency of Tema residents was occluded in favor of technical solutions despite the fact that the problems at hand resulted from earlier schemes of technology-centered nation-building. The public in this sanitary equation was posed as a collective force by means of waste. Yet in the eyes of planning authorities the same public was considered not a collective intelligence but a collection of self-interested individuals to be managed via infrastructure. Sophia Stamatopoulou-Robbins's (2019) depiction of persistent sewage crises in Palestine, what she calls "waste siege," demonstrates a much more extreme version of this logic where inadequate infrastructural provision is used to blame residents and further limit their autonomy or input. In Tema we see the roots of a more subtle tug-of-war held in check, in part, by the state's limited capacity to expand or control the infrastructure under its grasp.

In a marked departure from earlier treatment of Tema's environment as a resource to be put to use in the service of modernization, in short order city planners came to see urban nature as an impediment rather than an asset. The carefully engineered outfall that made the most of the city's coastal location and nearby deep waters was soon construed as less than ideal. A limited infrastructural good—workable but not good enough—it was considered insufficient for the city's already changing conditions, given the "limits of diffusion method with increased sewage loads of untreated sewage, and necessity to link up with networks of pumping stations and pressure pipes ... and treatment where dilution alone formerly was sufficient" (TDC Archives, DOX-GHA 84, 1963, 6). Also part of this changing view of nature, the city's numerous lagoons were treated as barriers to the efficient installation of urban infrastructure, sanitation-based and otherwise (D'Auria 2010, 47). Not long after the sewage system was up and running, the firm would report, "It should be noted that the lagoons of the Metropolitan Areas present special difficulties.... The lagoons do not create sanitation problems only, but also interfere with both communication and land use. No final design of road works or community developments can be prepared without complete reclamation of the lagoon's areas" (TDC Archives, DOX-GHA 84, 1963, 8–9).

An approach to sanitation bringing together water supply, sewage, urban waterways, and solid waste (TDC Archives, DOX-GHA 84, 1963, 1), the system took on a life of its own increasingly separate from household conditions and individual residential needs and interests that initially preoccupied city planners. Nature was considered disruptive. Infrastructure was to keep nature as well as residents in check. A triumph of instrumentality, DA's response is illustrative of Arendt's (1958, 148) description of *homo faber*'s use of technology as a means to separate and defend humanity from nature, denaturalizing it "for worldly ends." But rather than the strictly private aims of *animal laborans* or the marketplace, the technology-driven domination of nature in Tema was geared to public outcomes, transcending both nature and base needs: "Unlike *animal laborans*, whose social life is worldless and herdlike and who therefore is incapable of building or inhabiting a public worldly realm, *homo faber* is fully capable of having a public realm of his own, even though it may not be a political realm properly speaking" (Arendt 1958, 160).

Assuming the private while constituting the public anew, DA's technical fix was premised on administration and agglomeration. In turn, the "public" of "public good" was increasingly generalized. Reverting to the firm's preoccupation with the formation of continuous urban zones, the planning team advocated again for the amalgamation of Accra and Tema sewage systems to generate a single urban sanitary scheme with linked lines, budgets, and operations. The plan was allied with another promoting the formation of a dedicated agency to direct and coordinate the unified system (TDC Archives, DOX-GHA 84, 1963, 13). While neither directive was executed in full, both reveal core political suppositions. The scaling-up and cordoning off of

Figure 1.10. Trunk sewer lines cutting across Tema's Chemu Lagoon, 1965 (© Constantinos and Emma Doxiadis Foundation)

administration can be construed as an attempt to further remove sanitary matters from the general realm of public policy and deliberation. Further distanced from the lived experience of urban residents, the proposed interventions also suggest a penchant for administrative "flattening" on the part of urban authorities, lumping urban locations and urban problems together as if they could all be viewed and managed through the same lens. There was also a slippery assumption that system scale signaled the staying power of infrastructural modernization over the *longue dureé*. The conflation of scale and temporal scope marks a recurring aspect of what Appel, Anand, and Gupta (2018) call "the promise of infrastructure" intended to stand for state destiny over the long term (Stamatopoulou-Robbins 2019, 45). In Tema, this supposition would not take long to prove false.

Within a short time, more pointed proposals to further restructure infrastructure and its associated publics were beginning to emerge. By the mid-1960s, in an eerie parallel of nation and sewage system echoed in the excreta-centered literary work of Ayi Kwei Armah (1969),[33] claims of infrastructural breakdown in Tema coincided with the 1966 coup d'état. Sparked by allegations of elite corruption and self-interest, the coup forcibly removed Nkrumah and the Convention People's Party from power. With the city's prime patron now waylaid, in Tema reports on sanitation cited "near exhaustion of system" and called for "urgent amelioration." Still holding on to their place at TDC, the Doxiadis group sounded the alarm that "this situation will become crucial in the near future" (TDC Archives, DOX-GHA A 105, 1967, 10, 15). Mobilizing Ghana's growing relationship with Israel as a partner and a role model of infrastructure-driven nation-building earlier initiated by Nkrumah (Levey 2003), the Tel Aviv–based Tahal firm, initially established as Israel's national water planning agency, was tasked with redesigning the sanitary sewer system for the combined Tema-Accra metro area alongside DA (TDC Archives, DOX-GHA A 105, 1967, 1).[34]

Fully recognizing the inadequacy of the late-colonial designs of Balfour and Sons in light of the massive urban growth that came with the Doxiadis plan, the proposal called for scaling up nearly all elements of the earlier scheme. Reinforcing the divide between private life and large-scale systems, household facilities and connections were the singular and notable omission of the upgrading plan. Tahal recommended two new sea outfalls, two new pumping stations and several additional pumps, five new trunk sewers, major rerouting of sewage flows, and two dedicated treatment plants to process waste before evacuating it seaward (TDC Archives, DOX-GHA A 105, 1967, 12). Signaling the city's limited capacity for large-scale change, although proposed in 1964, only two of the five new sewers were completed two years later, in 1966.

In its role as intermediary between the grand propositions of externally based expert consultancies and conditions on the ground, Doxiadis Associates firmly endorsed implementation of the new plan. Despite a prevailing logic of aggregation, whether the meshing of Tema and Accra's sanitary outlays or the massing of neighborhood and household sewage rates, the new proposals strongly advocated partition of a once integrated urban whole. The proposed divides were as much about separating urban functions as further partitioning Tema's already divided residential zones and their associated populations. Regarding the former, the plan advocated strong controls over dumping industrial waste and an ordinance requiring separation of residential and industrial waste streams (TDC Archives, DOX-GHA A 105, 1967, 8, 18). The new plan, most of all, promoted the separate development of east and west ends of the city, a divide that reflected the city's starkest class differences that the initial urban design had suppressed. On the western edge of the city, Tema's newest bedroom communities were under construction along with the early stages of upwardly mobile middle-class occupation. With new gravity lines being installed there in 1966, Tema's first stand-alone waste treatment site was on the drawing board, as was a new dedicated sea outfall (TDC Archives, DOX-GHA A 105, 1967, 6, 12).

To the east was Tema Manhean, where the city's designated "native" residents had reluctantly resettled. Here, the focus was less on waste treatment and more on ramping up waste collection. It included the installation of new trunk lines from the city core to Tema Manhean, as well as two smaller pumping stations to facilitate movement of waste to and through Manhean to the original outfall at Gao Lagoon, soon to be renamed "Paradise Beach" (TDC Archives, DOX-GHA A 105, 1967, 12, 13, 16). With Tema Manhean increasingly positioned as a waste way station, so too was Chemu Lagoon on its northern border (see plate 2). Additional gravity pipes were recommended for immediate installation from the city's largest pumping station through the lagoon and its adjoining wetland. Given the pressing needs for expanded capacity, they were posed as a temporary fix, "to cope with urgent present needs only," and the planners promised, "It shall be dismantled after the construction of the new sewage works" (TDC Archives, DOX-GHA A 105, 1967, 20). Despite the many carefully wrought recommendations of Tahal and partners, few were fully realized. With TDC's authority consolidated while other state bodies dissolved with the fall of Ghana's First Republic, the agency's scope exceeded its reach. There were eventually new pumps, but no new pumping stations, few additional trunk lines, and no treatment plant for years to come. Promoting division by the very means of connection, the pipes through Chemu Lagoon, however, were put in place. Sixty years later they remain, as do remnants of DA's master plan, left on the premises of TDC (see plate 3).

In the face of untenable grand schemes, claims of impending breakdown and limited resources would drive provisional short-term solutions across Tema's vast sewage system. In these infrastructural false starts and partial fixes, a logic of repair spread across the underbelly of the new city at the very moment of its construction. Unsettling the social compact, the city's sewage works, which were intended to provide a guarantee of public services and private well-being to all residents, were set on edge. Amid the uneasy project of new nation-building and the shock of regime change, external shifts added to the sociopolitical and technical instabilities of public infrastructure. Supplanting the bilateral partnerships of nonalignment pursued by Ghana's Greek and Israeli counterparts was the rising weight of rapidly consolidated multilateral development agencies backed by the United States (Cooper and Packard 1998). These agents included the International Bank for Reconstruction and Development (IBRD). A precursor to the World Bank, the IBRD was slated to fund Tema's sewage improvements starting in the late 1960s.

Undermining the tight script of grand-scale urban planning promoted by Doxiadis Associates and the Nkrumah government at the inception, IBRD interventions marked the "end of the beginning" for the city of Tema. Still dependent on the consolidated authority of TDC, these piecemeal solutions contributed to rather than solved systemic inadequacies. New burdens on an already overstretched national administrative apparatus set the stage for the ongoing stream of breakdowns and fixes that continue to mark Tema's sewage system decades later. A near inversion of colonial strategies, in which the rhetoric and legislative codification of sanitation and hygiene loomed large but was accompanied by paltry investment, the rise of international development banks brought funding but little sustained oversight across sanitation systems, instead pursuing a scaled-down project-based approach.

Initiated in the late 1960s and early 1970s, multilateral influence on state and municipal investments and opportunities in Ghana continued to play out, evident in sanitation and other myriad public services (Konadu-Agyemang 2000). The piecemeal approach to sewage system repair that marked the later part of Doxiadis Associates' tenure at TDC became the norm. With Ghana's fate shaped by the ups and downs of the global economy, the oil price shocks in 1970s and subsequent structural adjustment programs of the 1980s did not help the matter (Chalfin 2004). Setting back Ghana's development trajectory, this was the very moment international financial institutions mandated the rollback of state expenditures and drastic cuts to public services in return for loans (Rothchild 1991). By the late 1980s, the Tema waste management director recounted that after almost thirty years in operation and receiving little sustained investment for system-wide improvement, the system was heading to full-blown crisis.

The World Bank Urban Environmental Sanitation Program was put in place in response, but it did little to address the widespread deterioration of materials that was already underway. Not only was the main sea outfall at Paradise Beach in disrepair but pipes in the older communities had also collapsed, which caused blockages and overflowing manholes in the city's core neighborhoods (Watertech 1994, 4). With fixes calibrated to immediate needs rather than future demands, the city's massive population growth was likewise overlooked (4). Caught up in the World Bank's Urban II program devoted to basic infrastructure (Aquaah-Harrison 2004; Watertech 1994), a substantial portion of promised funding went to evaluation and feasibility studies (Watertech 1998). It was a long decade before there were tangible results. A consultant's report from the 1990s notes, "Two of the pumping stations work sporadically due to pump maintenance difficulties and the emergency overflows become the main outlet from the pump station. The third pumping station is not operational due to theft and vandalism. The sewage flow is discharged into a surface stream. Ninety-five percent of the sewers suffer from sand depositions. Approximately 40 percent of pipes suffer a loss of cross-sectional area greater than 50 percent" (Salifu 1997, 84–85).[35]

Despite the intended goal of thoroughgoing rehabilitation of sewers, mains, and pumps, the most significant outcome was the construction of a sewage treatment plant on the west side of Tema in lieu of construction of a new sea outfall. Finally following through on recommendations from the 1960s to treat the city's waste before releasing it, the treatment plant was considered the ideal solution to the city's growing sanitary needs. After smaller-scale grants in 2003 through the World Bank Urban Environmental Sanitation Program, another round of investment did not materialize until 2010. By that time the sewage system was deemed a secondary concern and funds were instead devoted to septage ponds.

In the face of such programmatic gaps and failures, Tema residents pursued a range of alternative infrastructural solutions resulting in not always predictable social, political, and technical outcomes. In short, the sanitary infrastructure intended to constrain urban politicization under the Doxiadis-Nkrumah plan instead inspired individual and collective mobilization. As subsequent chapters detail, these solutions expressed collective discontent with the heavy-handedness of TDC aided and abetted by international agents, as fonts of city-making. Posing a "vital politics" against the faults and strictures of half-realized techno-political orders, these infrastructural outcomes wrestled with ideals laid out yet only partially realized by city planners, working with, around, and as an alternative to expectations and interventions of urban authorities both domestic and foreign.

Cobbled from the meager remnants of public resources and individual and collective imaginaries, spurred by vital remains, and sustained by infrastructural intimacies, these solutions would supersede the systems promised by urban and international authorities. The work of *homo infrastructurus*, here was a space of vitality carved out of the urban landscape, marked by the twin forces of human necessity and conditions beyond human control rooted in nonhuman materials and processes. Unsettled and unanticipated despite the narrow templates driving them, in political and material terms they stand apart from the combined self-determinations and overdeterminations of *homo faber* that are much better recognized in political theory, whether articulated by Nkrumah, Doxiadis, or Arendt.

Conclusion: Postwar Ideals Meet Infrastructural Realities

The intentions and interventions shaping Tema's mid-twentieth-century construction described above provides a baseline for understanding the distinctive cast and uneasy intersection of public and private life in the city via infrastructure in the early decades of the twenty-first century. Most prominent in this story are the efforts of the new city's founders to use large-scale infrastructures of urban sanitation to contain urban political life through a distinctive biopolitics geared to the satisfaction of basic bodily needs. As subsequent chapters bring to light, these grand schemes instead spawned a host of political fissures and emergences fanning the flames of public mobilization, discontent, and reimagining.

Triggering cracks in a façade of urban governance that promised equitable treatment of residents via attention to individual bodily necessities, the lines of flight within Tema's founding sanitary order are numerous. Despite TDC and DA's subscription to the trans-scalar ideals of ekistics theory, the larger and more complex the system became, the more disconnected it was from the small scale of the household and human lived experience. Overwhelmed by the growing numbers of bodies, and volumes of waste and water, the needs of Tema residents exceeded the capacities of the infrastructures designed to contain them. In another rupture from within, although the city's sewage system was initially predicated on harnessing natural forces, those forces too were deemed disruptive by system planners and overseers.

There was also the basic problem of the system itself. Instead of a seamless network of integrated flows, there were bottlenecks, partitions, and calls for urgent repair leading to stopgap fixes and continued malfunction. Consolidation of infrastructural control within a singular state agency staffed by handpicked experts and consultants was disrupted by the shifting winds of domestic politics and, with it, new strategies of international intervention under the rubric of multilateral development aid. Further unsettling the breach between Tema's suppressed past and promised future, planners' and consultants' scientific pretensions rendered "technical" multilayered human processes and communities with diverse histories and entitlements.

The myriad gaps between rulers and ruled, system promise and system performance, and vital matters and machinic form wrought by the grand schemes of national independence and international development offered unexpected political openings. These realities likewise challenge the premises of political theory. Not only do Tema's infrastructural breakdowns and ensuing processes of infrastructural recomposition confound the intertwined efforts and ideals of Nkrumah and Doxiadis; they also provoke reassessment of Arendt's rendering of postwar political life. Namely, as Tema's excremental infrastructural realities increasingly make clear, Arendt's (1958) tripartite conception of the *vita activa* founded on the hierarchy of labor, work, and action too quickly parses the political potentials of domesticity, infrastructure, industry.

Most of all, muddying Arendt's neat model as well as Nkrumah's and Doxiadis's political intentions, the instability of Tema's urban reforms indicate the possibilities of plurality emergent in infrastructural orders like citywide household-based sanitation, assumed to hold political mobilization in check. Instead, these infrastructural arrangements are always on the verge of eruption due to the uneasy alignments of their human users and overseers, the vitality of extrahuman substances that flow through them, and the mechanical wear and tear and decay of their material underpinnings, along with their charged status within Tema's top-down urban scheme.[36] Far from being prepolitical as envisioned by Nkrumah and Doxiadis and theorized by Arendt, they readily, if not inevitably, induce individual and collective material interests. Doubly charged by their lively content and heightened status within Tema's city plan, rather than inert infrastructure, they are in active assemblage (Latour 2005b). With exception and rule, structure and substance, agent and object difficult to disentangle, their standing as politically undecidable (Agamben 1998, 27) is harnessed by city residents for the ends of self-determination even as they advocate for resources and recognition from governing authorities.

A fact of life for Tema's engineers, administrators, residents, workers, and transients, these processes urge a reconsideration of Arendt's conception of *homo faber*—human fabrication of the material world through work. According to Arendt (1958, 7), "Work provides an artificial world of things distinct from natural surroundings." Just as the capacities of *homo faber* transcend those of *animal laborens*, the machines of *homo faber* exceed the rhythms and capacities of the human body to constitute a durable part of the lived world (Arendt 1958, 143–44), "offering mortals a dwelling place more permanent and more stable than themselves" (152).

A tricky formulation like much of her theory, these contentions sit side by side with Arendt's vigorous attacks on work's lost capacity to fully express human potential in the context of industrial modernity.[37] In this impasse lurks a meaningful distinction between industry and infrastructure appropriate to the case of Tema. Compared with the fleeting privations and satisfactions of industrial work and consumer society posed by Arendt (1958, 126), the world formulated by infrastructure retains the cast of longevity and human interconnection. In Tema, this obtains even in the case of breakdown, as the signs and substances of common humanity gain prominence amid the fragmented integuments of the built world.

An insight appropriate to the infrastructural dynamics found in Tema, Arendt tellingly speaks of the ancient practice of wall building, separating the public and private (Arendt 1958, 63–64; Markell 2011, 23, 26)—as Yar (2000, 5) puts it, "dividing the human realm from that of nature [to] provide a stable context (a 'common world') of spaces and institutions within which human life can unfold." As the chapters to follow make evident, the lived realities of excremental provisioning in Tema push us to reenvision Arendtian walls not as static forms but as active, vital entities. Rather than taking the permanence or fixity of the city's built foundations for granted, their ongoing negotiation in the face of the untrammeled force of urban waste and the inevitability of their own breakdown and decay generates a political and infrastructural inchoate where collective alternatives are possible.

These constructs, I argue, offer a nascent if under-recognized terrain of the *vita activa*. Resulting in neither deracinated polis nor disembodied plurality to which Nkrumah, Doxiadis, and Arendt aspire, as will become clear, these solutions orchestrate a material politics—lively, substantive, and embodied—in which waste and waste infrastructure, made and manipulated by Tema residents, come to do important political work. Intertwined with state claims and accountabilities, urban social hierarchies, and the legacies of preexisting communities and material cultures, they engender a vital terrain of urban coexistence.

2. Tema Proper
Infrastructures and Intimacies of Disrepair

Now I always look at this pump very well, like my own car. It's like I have a vehicle. So always I put my mind and I always put my eyes and ears to this car and maintain it very well and it is lasting for me. I always maintain the machine.
—Pumping station engineer, Tema, 2014

To think with ruins of empire is to emphasize less the artifacts of empire as dead matter or remnants of a defunct regime than to attend to their reappropriations, neglect, and strategic and active positioning within the politics of the present.
—Ann Stoler, *Imperial Debris* (2013)

The things that owe their existence exclusively to men nevertheless constantly condition their human makers.... This is why men, no matter what they do, are always conditioned beings.... The objectivity of the world—its object or thing-character—and the human condition supplement each other.
—Hannah Arendt, *The Human Condition* (1958)

Vital Remains in the City

Half a century after its founding, Tema is still intact, remarkably true to its original plan. The city's sewage system, however, is in the throes of collapse. Sewer mains still in use from the city's initial construction flood markets and streets with human waste. Household lines fail to drain, backing up in bathrooms and courtyards and inciting tensions between residents, neighbors, and local government officials. Defunct treatment ponds overgrown with weeds have become a go-to area for open defecation. The engines and gates of the city's pumping stations operate at half-capacity, making it impossible

Figure 2.1. Construction of Community 5, 1967 (© Constantinos and Emma Doxiadis Foundation)

to efficiently evacuate the accumulated waste of urban residents, causing influx in the city's surrounding lagoons and overloading of the sea outfall.

This chapter examines the strategies employed by residents, public officials, and waste management experts to cope with the inevitabilities of excremental infrastructural dysfunction and decline. Ann Stoler's (2013) thoughts on "ruination," inspired by Walter Benjamin (1999), serve as the theoretical fulcrum.[1] Apt with regard to the ongoing cycle of use, breakdown, and repair evident in Tema, Stoler asks, "How do lives accumulate around ruins and ruins around lives?" At the crux of the infrastructural adjustments and instabilities at work in Tema are a range of bodily and affective interdependencies among city dwellers, sanitary engineers, municipal officials, and the base substances and technologies of toilets, sewer mains, pumping stations, sewage manholes, and human excreta. I call these emergent attachments and identifications "infrastructural intimacies."

Across the expanse of the planned city, as bodily waste seeps into the public sphere, infrastructural intimacies come to the fore as private citizens take over municipal responsibilities, and individual sanitary engineers devise their own routines to slow the pace of system decay. An example of bodily matter spurring political assembly, errant excrement enlivens the "connective tissue" of community, to use Stoler's (2013, 7) term, as neighbors pool resources to clear pipes and clean spills. City sanitary workers exchange knowledge and bodily well-being to enable the functioning of public goods and uphold the façade of municipal capacity. Amplified by excrement's bioactive properties, Tema's sanitary infrastructure reveals the looming gap between public and private responsibility. The city's middle-class urban dwellers, who pride themselves on the privileges of private property, continue to look to city authorities for input and oversight. Viewing themselves as private citizens and property holders, they are reluctant to pursue collective action within the public sphere. Waste management employees reinforce residents' sense of autonomy, insisting that faults to the system are self-induced rather than a municipal responsibility and outcome of systemic decay.

Urban Form and Sanitary Decline in Late Modern Tema

On first glance, the city of Tema a long half century after its founding appears remarkably in line with the urban plan sketched out in the heyday of Kwame Nkrumah's reign with the assistance of Doxiadis's Athens-based planning team. The initial footprint of twelve communities has expanded to twenty-five, with an official population count of more than four hundred thousand compared to the eighty thousand originally anticipated.[2] More recently developed neighborhoods are suburban in style, with self-built detached single-family dwellings of diverse designs on large lots hiding self-contained septic systems. Despite modifications—enclosed yards, upper stories, and small shops in what was initially open space (D'Auria 2019)—the distinctive motifs of the original communities are readily recognizable in the city's core. The original layouts, house types, and materials are still visible: clusters of nearly identical sandcrete-block dwellings interspersed with modernist-style attached maisonettes and private homes, low-slung rooflines, geometric brise-soleil, playgrounds, greenways, and pedestrian thoroughfares just as they looked in Doxiadis's sketches and reports (see plates 4, 5, and 6).

The city's midcentury sewage system likewise remains in place, still essential to serving Tema's core communities. No longer controlled by Tema Development Corporation, the sanitary sewer network is under the auspices

Figure 2.2. TMA waste management yard, 2014 (Photo by Eliot Chalfin-Smith)

of the municipality's dedicated Waste Management Office. A few blocks from the rest of the city administration, now run by Tema Metropolitan Assembly (TMA), the waste management yard is full of dump trucks, porta-potties, and piles of cement blocks and sewage pipes. A narrow veranda connects a bank of offices designated for bills, registry, complaints, and repairs. There are separate sections for solid waste—namely, consumer and industrial waste— as well as liquid waste: the stuff of Tema's sewerage system. The director occupies a private office, with a private loo. The rest of the employees share workspace and dedicated male and female restrooms behind locked doors. At one end of the office complex is a shaded carport where the technical staff congregate and sort their gear before dispatching to the far reaches of the city's sewage network to carry out their daily assignments.

The system over which waste management employees preside claims a vast presence, at once highly organized and uncontained. It includes three sewage pumping stations, three treatment sites with detention tanks and settling ponds, three catchment basins, three lagoons, and two seabound outfalls. Forming an expansive subterranean network marked by manholes every few hundred feet, household sewer lines meet submains that flow into miles of trunk sewers. Linking Tema's residents and residential neighborhoods, commercial and industrial areas, fishing harbor and shipping port, these terrestrial installations merge with the surrounding sea and coastline, where city residents' barely processed fecal waste is ultimately released, much of it through the sea outfall at Paradise Beach.

Despite Tema's reputation as a place of urban attainment, the celebrated sanitary system is subject to frequent breakdowns, emergency repairs, spills, and ruptures. Though it is kept under wraps by the city's middle- and upper-class residents, who pride themselves on upholding standards of propriety, most who reside in Tema's core regularly contend with infrastructural disruptions and eruptions. These include storing numerous barrels of water to bathe, cook, and flush toilets during frequent water shortages, becoming accustomed to overflowing manholes on neighborhood streets, and coping in their own homes with disintegrating fixtures and hardware from the time of the city's founding. Echoing concerns voiced by the Doxiadis team in the early 1960s, problems have persisted for decades.

With system decline taking a progressive toll, Tema's waste management director described the near crisis condition of the late 1980s, an era coinciding with drastic cuts in state services and investments mandated by international donors. Precipitating partial fixes and continued deferral to external influence, Tema sanitation found itself caught up in World Bank's Urban II program during the early and mid-1990s (Aquaah-Harrison 2004; Salifu 1997; Watertech 1994), followed by smaller-scale grants in 2003 through the World Bank Urban Environmental Sanitation Program. Another round of investment did not materialize until 2010. By that time the sewage system was deemed a secondary concern, and funds were devoted instead to septage ponds to receive and treat waste collected from septic tanks installed by private homeowners in Tema's expanding suburban neighborhoods untethered to the centralized sewerage system.

By the time I started my research in 2010, the bulk of the original trunk sewers had yet to be replaced despite being half a century old. Tree roots growing in and around household lines caused cracks, allowing rodent penetration. The submains that serviced Tema's factories as well as residences were clogged with oil, sand, and other industrial waste that enters the system alongside human excreta (Awuah, Donkor, and Sanjok 2008, 15). The trunk line to the city's main retention ponds and outfall had collapsed. The new septage facility built according to World Bank construction and project management guidelines was already overflowing just months after its commissioning. Meanwhile, the municipality lacked sufficient funds for system maintenance and routine repair. Nevertheless, it is expected to uphold the city's legal "obligation to receive" human waste as set out in Ghana's *National Environmental Sanitation Policy* (Government of Ghana 1999).

Most problematic, the sewage treatment plant built in the late 1990s as the linchpin of a long-awaited overhaul had not operated for several years (Rohilla et al. 2018, 4). Located in a once remote area behind one of Tema's more affluent neighborhoods and funded by the World Bank for $6 million, the treatment process involved a series of large aerating ponds designed to purify the sewage sludge before sending liquid effluent out to sea (Salifu 1997, 84; Awuah, Donkor, and Sanjok 2008).[3] I was told that when the plant functioned, the water quality was so good it could be used for fish farming. Therein lay the plant's success and its demise. According to local lore, soon the tilapia the plant's overseers put in the ponds to test water quality were stolen, along with the aerators and the electricals powering them. When the generators stopped functioning, the aerobic ponds turned anaerobic, producing an odor so noxious the whole system was shut down. The city was left without any sewage treatment options (Awuah, Donkor, and Sanjok 2008, 16).

Unable to serve its intended purpose, treatment site's open space was informally repurposed for open defecation. According to a local blog, "The old waste water treatment plant located in Community 3 looks more like a meadow than the aerated lagoon it was designed as. The lagoon is however still collecting feces. Along the banks the local citizenry have deposited the waste of their metabolic processes. The irony of open defecation into a waste treatment plant is palpable" (K. David 2010). The Tema District Court regularly issued summons on behalf of the city's Environmental Health Department to those accused of "indiscriminate defecation," to little avail.

Adding to the dysfunction, the pumping stations at the heart of Tema's sewage system are in a state of rapid decline. Of the three original stations built during the early days of the city's development, only the smallest one serving the older neighborhoods close to the harbor still operates on a regular basis. Between the failing centralized sewage system in the city's core and the outlying neighborhoods dependent on public toilets and pit latrines emptied at local septage facilities, environmental sanitation experts estimate that 75 percent of the city's excreta is not adequately treated (Armaly 2016, 12; Rohilla et al. 2018, 35). Thus, for residents of Tema's twelve original neighborhoods with private water closets inside each house, the trappings

Figure 2.3. TMA sewage pumping station, 2014 (Photo by Brenda Chalfin)

of what development experts call "improved sanitation" by no means guarantees adequate sewage treatment or disposal.

The largest pumping station, built to receive the bulk of waste from Tema's residential area and industrial zone, is defunct. Indicative of interdependencies across the city's wider infrastructural grid, as with the sewage aerating ponds, the motor powering the pump stopped working due to frequent electrical blackouts, as did its control panel. In the process, the pump seized. With the pump deemed beyond repair, the station is shuttered. Waste instead runs through a bypass directly into nearby Chemu Lagoon. The third pumping station, built primarily to serve Tema's residential areas, is similarly hampered by electrical problems. With power to the station cut and repair long pending, it too is not operating, although the pumps are in working order. All of this means that domestic waste flows unprocessed into Sakumono Lagoon, which, like Chemu, is already choked with stormwater and plastic waste from the city's open drains before flowing out to the sea (Rohilla et al. 2018, 7, 11). Meanwhile, Tema's population continues to grow across the core areas of the city served by the midcentury sewer network, further taxing the already overburdened system.

Theorizing Vital Infrastructure and Dis/Repair

Susan Star's (1999) contention that infrastructure is both analytically and experientially visible in the case of breakdown is amply true when it comes to Tema's sanitary arrangements. Stoler's (2013) theorization of "imperial debris" builds on and goes beyond Star's core insight (1999, 385, 387). In order to trace the political implications of the system's enduring decline and the companion process of (dis)repair, Stoler's optic is apt for understanding Tema's midcentury sewage system as an inherently political formation. Embracing infrastructures' intertwined historical and material condition, Stoler (2013, 10–11) asserts, "Imperial remains are not inert but vitally reconfigured . . . actively positioned, and re-appropriated within the politics of the present." Apposite to Tema's sanitary order, Stoler (2013, 23, 29) attends to the way "ruins harbor particular biopolitics." In the case of waste and waste infrastructure's "vital politics," Stoler takes an important step toward a more open-ended paradigm, abandoning the synchronic "systems thinking" implicit in Star's analysis and the associated ideals of infrastructural integration.[4] Favoring the temporally and materially variegated network-centered paradigm of Bruno Latour (1993), Stoler (2013, 29) asks, "How do lives accumulate around ruins and ruins around lives?" This is surely a query readily transposable to human waste management.

Stoler's meditation on the lingering presences of imperial formations can be stretched to contend with the insistent twinning of system breakdown and repair found in Tema. Tema proves the fundamental fact that breakdown is rarely unidirectional, and more often is accompanied by attempts at amelioration that interrupt the downward slope of ruination (pace Jackson 2014). The case of Tema likewise forces a broader and more precise definition of "debris" than Stoler affords. Namely, imperial and colonial projects are not the only modern political orders that leave ruins in their wake. In fact, all infrastructural systems carry the seeds of breakdown and lodge their governing capacity in their staying power and inevitable degradation. Thus, it may be more productive to refer to "infrastructural debris" and probe the afterlives and deteriorations specific to the postimperial formations of high modernity such as those found in Ghana's midcentury city.[5]

Bringing Stoler (2013) to bear on Tema, and Tema on Stoler (2013, 13), reveals waste to be a particular sort of ruin, defunct but never inert: "Some remains are ignored as innocuous leftovers, others petrify, some hold and spread toxicities and become poisonous debris." The sewage, septage, and fecal matter that circulate through Tema's homes, streets, pumping stations, treatment sites, and watercourses resemble these substances only in part. Given their energy and vibrant afterlives, I treat them instead as "vital remains." Waste materials in their multifarious afterlives are an impetus for what Latour (2005a) calls "dingpolitics." Not only does the collective buildup of things anchor sociomaterial orders; so does their breakdown. An observation that puts Latour, Stoler, and Star in conversation, breakdown marks "matters of concern" much more readily and dramatically than stable configurations—a point the malfunctioning of Tema's sanitary system brings to the fore.

At once "making things public" (Latour 2005a) and "making things private," Tema's sanitary decline simultaneously activates individual bodies and otherwise hidden infrastructural attachments and interconnections. In the mix, private matters become vividly entangled with public life, recalibrating the terrain of urban governance and participation. The "parliament of things" (Latour 1993, 142), adjudicated by waste, spurs and sustains public assembly via infrastructure.

Shaped by this analytic outlook, the chapter proceeds in two parts. The first part recounts the wholesale crisis of Tema's sewage system from the vantage point of the city's sole functioning sewage pumping station and the technicians who sustain its operation. Here public good is contingent on the inner workings of a few private bodies. The second part of the chapter moves from an examination of systemic dis/repair to a consideration of individual and communal experiences of infrastructural malfunctioning and allied strategies of amelioration. It unfolds through an account of the sewage spills, pipelines, and manholes of a cluster of residents and residences in one of the city's original communities occupied from the city's inception.

The first section traces the devolution of matters of public provisioning and political accountability into individualized bodily processes by means of intimate infrastructural engagement. By contrast, in the second section, bodily evacuation becomes grounds for political recognition, with infrastructural breakdown and bodily waste mobilized to make collective claims on public space. Both scenarios confound expected conceptions of political ordering through the mediation of what Hannah Arendt (1958, 139) calls the "fabricated world" of infrastructure and bring Arendtian frames of inquiry to bear on contexts beyond Arendt's political imagination. In the one, the res publica is supplanted by the labor of "life itself" (7) lodged in the discrete bodies of the infrastructure's caretakers. In the other, biological pro-

Figure 2.4. Pumping station wet well, 2014 (Photo by Eva Egensteiner)

cesses and outputs open a space for collective discourse around the terms, sites, and configurations of human plurality to offer a fleeting instantiation of the *vita activa* and a fragile polis.

Intimacies of Dis/Repair: Sustaining Citywide Sanitation

Tema's sewage pumping stations, flat-roofed white structures accented by long black metal louvers, share the quintessential modernist geometry of the city. Until one goes around back and notices the gated sewage channels and deep open wells, it is difficult to know the buildings' dedicated purpose. Like a visit to Oz, a glance through the garage-style door reveals a wall-length control panel with illuminated plastic buttons and gauges embedded in an aluminum cabinet extending the length of the wall.

Although there is electrical power running to the facility, there are no working bulbs or overhead lights. Even with the doors open, the interior is dark, shrouding well-worn surfaces and years of accumulated dirt and dust. At the fore lie two underground chambers surrounded by metal railings, with ladders descending under the concrete floor. Archaic metal beams entwined with ropes and winches hang above, the casting mark "UK Lough Borough England 2 Tons" still visible. An old motor sits on a wooden chair. Personal possessions are scattered about: shirts, rags, a radio, a flashlight, a couple of TVs, and a stack of videotapes. The mechanics assigned to the station, along with the son of the resident watchman, charge their phones in a crowded outlet.

The technicians walk us through the sewage disposal process. This is Pumping Station 2, the smallest of the city's three pumping facilities, they explain. It receives waste from the adjacent harbor and industrial area, along with Tema's Community 2 and Community 3, through the old gravity-driven underground trunk lines. Waste also enters the pumping station's channels via the city's many sewage tankers, although they are supposed to discharge their loads at a designated disposal site at the city's outskirts. On my first visit, the sewage trucks were parked by the gate, and a pleated plastic sleeve ran from a tanker just barely reaching the edge of the sewage conduit. As sewage poured from the truck into the well, no one noticed the shit that splashed on my shoe.

In the mid-1990s the pumping station was retrofitted to channel its load into the waste treatment ponds constructed as part of the World Bank–funded Urban Sanitation Program. However, due to the plant's closure, the waste is instead pumped straight into the sea via the city's western sewage outfall close to Sakumono Lagoon. With the other two pumping stations out of order, the mechanics at Pumping Station 2 are on high alert, ever attuned to the challenges of keeping their equipment in good working order. Despite the fact that they are essentially shunting raw sewage out to sea—little different from the 1960 plan encountered by Doxiadis—the pump operators see their work as an earnest pursuit rather than a hopeless task already defeated by the system's decrepit condition.

Reminiscent of Stoler's (2013, 29) observation regarding the coformation of lives and ruins, Tema's sanitary engineers' work lives are clearly intertwined with the life of the well-worn equipment. Star's (1999, 386) insight that "ordinary infrastructure workers are vital to the social life of infrastructure" surely holds true here (see also Jackson 2014, 223). The five pumping station operators began their professional careers with the 1994 rehabilitation of Tema's sewer works. Under the supervision of foreign contractors, they were hired to dismantle the original pumps installed during the city's founding and mount the new machines in their place. Replaying the terms of late-colonial infrastructure, the new pump and motor and the rest of the working parts are all imported, just like the originals.

Foreign consultants oversaw the teardown and installation, and trained their Ghanaian counterparts to service the new equipment. Brought into the system to undertake the physical labors of transition, the Ghanaian mechanics identified with one another and the equipment they were called on to master. Now pushing twenty years on the job, Tobias recalled the intensive training he received fresh out of technical school: "We came when the new pumps were installed. We were all employed the same year and the same day. I had my certificate. Others learned on the job. We all had the same training and could do the same work." Binding persons, pumping machinery, and technical know-how—Tobi and his close colleague Matthew considered the skills and work sites of their cohort interchangeable. Assigned to Pumping Station 2, Tobi reported, "I can do the same work at Station 1 or Station 3. It's the same idea." Combining "scientific management with nurture" (Schneider 2011), from Matthew's perspective the ability to make this connection inheres in the person, not the mechanical apparatus. Matt remarked, "If a new man comes to work, I always teach him. Because I've stayed here a long time and I know the work. I'll show him before he is qualified." Lives give the run-down pumping station facilities both functional and historical coherence.

Turning renovation into its own sort of ruination, removal of the old fixtures left gaps and rough patches: from missing tiles to left-out and leftover mechanicals, such as the cast-iron crane and winch still in place. Though initiating their own professional advancement and assimilation, Tobi's workmate Matthew noted that the old pump that was replaced "wasn't spoiled." He recalled, "There were originally two pumps, only one was installed in its place. I don't know why. The old one had more power and lasted longer despite the style being different." Here, the old pumps' residues were a reminder of the simultaneity of going forward and going backward: of what once was, surpassing what could be. Confirming Stoler's (2013, 3,4) observation that the "uneven temporal sedimentations of earlier imperial formations" leave "bold-faced or subtle traces in which contemporary inequities work their way through," these recollections suggest that the 1990s renovations were as much politically as technically motivated.

As recounted in the preceding chapter, at its midcentury inception Tema's sewage system was managed by the Tema Development Corporation (TDC). With the new pump came new overseers. Waste management moved out of the hands of TDC and became the exclusive purview of Tema Municipal Authority. Under the midcentury plan, sanitation was an entitlement that came with a property dwelling. It was conceived as the backbone of the wider package of amenities that distinguished Tema from other towns: regular delivery of water and electricity, green space, a clean environment, paved roads, and streetlights. Under the aegis of TMA, waste management became one of an array of public goods to be provided by the city government. In turn, TDC was free to focus its attention on the much narrower and financially lucrative charge of real estate development.

In the meantime, TMA's portfolio became increasingly diffuse and politicized as elected representatives and party members at the city's helm vied for personal agendas and pet projects amid the complexities and constraints of municipal financing. Tema's sewage system lost its place as a high-profile, high-priority project. While it certainly was not too big to fail, in its totality the sewage system was too big to fix. It was reduced to a technical concern under the purview of the TMA Waste Management Authority. Low on the list of administrative priorities, financing of sanitary matters was all but ignored by the municipal authority. There were no separate accounts for sewer revenue, no dedicated budget for operation, and maintenance and fees often went uncollected (Awuah, Donkor, and Sanjok 2008, 16).

From the point of view of those operating the pumping system, TMA was a bureaucratic labyrinth. Accessing spare parts required several layers of approval. Requests within the waste management office and the wider municipal administration often went unanswered, especially when parts needed to be imported. Crew members, conveying frustration as well as vulnerability, explained how even servicing the pumping facilities incurred risks. On a visit to one of the other pumping facilities, a worker told me there was no power to run the pumps. As he recalled, TMA had finally summoned the Electrical Corporation of Ghana (ECG) to repair a fault. But before he knew it, the ECG contractor had removed all the copper wire, claiming he was going to replace it. Neither the repairman nor the wire was ever seen again. For those at the pumping station, the mix of bureaucratic buildup and technical breakdown meant that maintenance and, with it, self-reliance were key. When it came to the pump, Matthew and Tobi explained, "We are servicing three days a week. Every three days you put grease. To care for it, we change the down packing every eight months to prevent leakage." Keeping it all in the family, they were hesitant to invite anyone unfamiliar with the old equipment to assist (see plate 7).

At the edge of the pumping station and conforming to the original design of the sewer system, lines from the town merge with lines from the harbor to form a single stream known as the "Great Channel." When the pump and motor are in working order, the slurry of sewage and wastewater moves from the Great Channel to a giant holding tank abutting the backside of the pumping station. Termed a "wet well," the cement-lined receptacle is roughly fifteen feet by fifteen feet square and extends about fifteen feet belowground. The engineers control the flow between channel and well by manually adjusting a tall steel penstock to open or close the chamber between them. There is a mesh screen that captures rubbish and any large items mixed with the watery waste. With spare parts unavailable and repair unlikely—a hallmark of breakdown—the gatekeepers were inclined to improvise. Improvisations were more manual than mechanical, involving the bodily efforts of the waste technicians. With the platform damaged, rubbish retrieval required screwing shut the gate and climbing down to the concrete edge of the tank to dislodge the debris with a rake. Matthew described the setup: "We have some plate. It's a platform I can stand on it. I can pull it out. The platform is spoiled. That's why the rubbish has gone into the wet well. If you have the screen, no rubbish can enter."

Once the wet well starts to fill, the pump is activated to move the sludge into the dry well underneath the pumping station. Another gate stands between the two, preventing backflow into the wet well. A flow meter records the volume of waste moving from one to the other, activating the needle gauge on the control panel. For Tobias, there was no problem with the sewage. It came and went. That could be relied on. It was the pump that required care, and the electrical panel too. Without them, the system would be inoperable. All of this put demands on the pumping station operators, drawing on their technical know-how and embodied sensibilities—along with their bodies themselves. Indeed, in contrast to Latour's revelation of the ways infrastructures "make things public," in the case of Tema's pumping stations, breakdown "made things private." Ruination inspired intimacy: from intimate knowledge of and bodily engagement with the apparatus to the operators' reflexive "attachment" to it, similarly noted by Steven Jackson (2014, 232) in other cases of repair.

More than an attachment of people and things (Simone 2004) or between people through things, "infrastructural intimacy" here holds much in common with the "cultural intimacy" of bureaucratic regimes discussed by Michael Herzfeld (2005). Herzfeld coined the term "cultural intimacy" to describe the reworking of official rules and representations of political authority by state agents. Simultaneously asserting mastery over the terms and terminology of rule, and reinforcing divisions between insiders and outsiders, according to Herzfeld these manipulations ultimately affirm political institutions by inscribing them in daily life. Building on Stoler's (2013, 7) suggestion to view imperial debris as "connective tissue that binds persons to environments and to one another," I define the cognate "infrastructural intimacies" as connections, identifications, and attachments between people and publicly authorized infrastructure and the institutions they represent, as well as among people through such infrastructure and institutional traces (Chalfin 2015). Different from what Waqas Butt (2020, 246) calls "waste intimacies" regarding the ambivalent connections between urban waste producers and low-caste waste collectors in Pakistan, infrastructural intimacies at work in Tema serve to anchor the undecidability of waste itself—whether human excreta or the worn-out infrastructures and municipal institutions meant to channel, process, and contain them.

Rosalind Fredericks (2018) discusses an analogous imbrication of waste infrastructure and laboring bodies, what she calls "vital infrastructures of labor," among waste workers in the garbage dumps of Dakar, Senegal. Referring to the low-tech "participatory infrastructures" (94) of the city's informal sector, the interface of people and infrastructure at Tema's pumping stations is both similar and different. Notably, compared to Dakar, where those at the lowest ranks of the waste management chain experience as degrading the intimate technologies of waste work (116; see also Chalfin 2019), the engineers at Tema's sewage pumping station gained from them a source of pride and a sign of exclusive knowledge and expertise in the face of disorder. Moreover, in Tema, despite the shared bodily risks of waste work, these processes played out not in the context of informality but in realm of large-scale technology-dependent urban systems. All of this is to suggest that the character of infrastructural intimacy is not delimited by immediate material and sensory conditions alone but is shaped by the wider political economy of infrastructural systems and the human labors they entail.

Such infrastructural intimacies were abundant at the pumping station. The engineers, marginalized in the city administration and experiencing the sewerage system's collapse around them, felt personally responsible for keeping the pumping station in working order. Binding their professional lives to the buildup and breakdown of Tema's sewage installations, they expressed a multilayered identification with the equipment under their care. Describing his approach to the pump's mechanicals, Matthew told me, "Now I always look at this pump like my own car. It's like I have a vehicle. So always I put my mind and I always put my eyes and ears to this car and maintain it very well and it is lasting for me. I always maintain the machine." The engineers are very much "agents of repair" as described by Jackson (2014,

223), for whom repair is experienced as a moral relation (231). In addition to a sense of ownership and its attendant obligations, the mechanics convey a sensorial sympathy with the apparatus. They experience their own bodies and bodily ways of knowing essential to its ongoing operation, an attitude industrial historians identify as common among waste workers (Schneider 2011). Joshua Reno (2016, 40), with regard to the experience of sanitary engineers in US municipal waste dumps, discusses this permeability in terms of "leaky bodies" (see also Millar 2018). For Tema's pumping station engineers, as a sign of their expertise, this is experienced less as a threat to well-being than as a bodily endowment.

Arendt (1958, 9), in her discussion of the work of fabrication, perceptively observes, "The things that owe their existence exclusively to men nevertheless constantly condition their human makers," and goes on to say, "The objectivity of the world—its object or thing-character—and the human condition supplement each other." Along surprisingly similar lines, Stoler (2013, 10) remarks that imperial remains are "not inert but vitally reconfigured . . . within the politics of the present." Bringing these assertions to bear on the case of the pumping station, it becomes apparent that such vitality is reciprocal, at once giving life to the apparatus and enlivening the operator.

Shaped by the limited capacities of Tema's municipal authorities, the mutual imbrication of bodies and infrastructure found at the pumping station, more than simply a creative response to operational failure, reveals the structural conditions and constraints of infrastructure's vital politics. We witness a dynamic nexus of people and infrastructure, with infrastructure doubly present as immediate object and wider system, as opposed to claims about people "as" infrastructure (Simone 2004). Indeed, the case of the pumping station suggests that the greater the threat of breakdown of both object and system, the more intense the infrastructural intimacies of repair. Tobi went on to describe his close encounters with the pump's working and nonworking parts: "It chokes. It can choke at any time. The pump can choke. You have a place to open the pump and use our bare hands to remove the rubbish. I know how the machine works. If there is fault, I know it. If there is a fault that comes in right now, I know it. I have to take care of it. I open side chamber and remove rubbish with my bare finger."

Tobi's remarks point to the bodily perils of crossing over into the apparatus. What's more, for Tobi, the intimacies of repair involve monitoring the pump's vital signs along with his own. Effectively rendering "infrastructure as [if] people," these engagements signal the obverse of Simone's (2004) much-discussed couplet. Tightening Jackson's (2014) broad claims about the prevalence of repair, they also speak to the specific labor forms, and implicit and explicit political economies, necessary for sustaining large-scale systems perennially threatened by breakdown. As historian of sanitation technology Daniel Schneider (2011, 121) notes, craft-based knowledge and practice typically fill in for the gaps in scientific process and technical capacity. Thus, they interlace machinic and tool-based logics and practices—to borrow the terms of Arendt's (1958, 147) characterizations of "work." With the alienations of machines softened by the embodied rhythms of tool-based labor, this observation suggests why certain modes of fabrication, including repair, may be more conducive to infrastructural intimacy than others.

Deepening Star's (1999) baseline contention that infrastructural dysfunction attracts notice, at Tema's pumping station the move of infrastructure from background object to unsettled actant sparks a transubstantiation of a sort. In another case of infrastructural work impinging on if not reassembling the markers of human vitality, Matthew recounted his changing biophysical state across the infrastructural ups and downs of his career:

> You know we Africans, you see, God knows us as a poor country. Always God protects us and looks at us very well. This station, I stay here for seventeen years. I do this work here for seventeen years. I'm never sick. I never have any problem. I don't know. Maybe in future, in future if I'm sick. I don't know. As of now, I know I don't have any problem for my body. I never go hospital. But always I come here. The scent, I smell it. I smell it. I smell it. Now, no, I'm used to it.

Beyond the persistent interconnection of people and infrastructure characteristic of infrastructural intimacies, a third element is evident in this equation. Matthew's remark doubly registers bodily waste's inherent status as ruin and residue: defunct but never inert, as Stoler (2013, 13) notes of other debris. Moored in decay, human excreta are inherently vital due to their bioactive de-/recomposition. Sanitary infrastructures aggregate and to some degree intensify, rather than disperse, their expression. A tripartite relation of people and infrastructure and waste, when channeled into the public domain of Tema's pumping station, waste's vital residues refract back on the private bodies and self-reflections of infrastructures' operators and caretakers. Waste infrastructures are an especially "intimate technology," as Fredericks's (2018, 116) research in Dakar likewise affirms, given waste's inherent vitality, both repelling and inviting human action. What's apparent here is that if infrastructure enables transactions between public and private, waste in its fulsome vitality both augments and confounds the process, moving it in a direction of its own. Waste, to borrow again from Stoler (2013, 13), like infrastructure, is a "connective tissue," but a highly changeable one—undecidable—due to its dynamic "micro-ecologies." Human waste, a vital remain both necessary and bioactive, exerts a force of its own. This is part of what Sophia Stamatopoulou-Robbins (2019, 212, 221) refers to as the "doubleness" of waste, and waste politics, simultaneously serving as a "solution to another problem" and a "problem" in its own right.

In these examples we observe how the lived logics of decay and dis/repair at Tema's pumping station rework the expected purviews of public and private property and accountability. As they cope with gaps in municipal investment and oversight, municipal technicians assimilate infrastructure in a joint project of self-making and public provisioning. Liable to injure fingers in the apparatus or internalize noxious outputs and harbor future illness, they risk laying waste to their own bodies as they give life to municipal infrastructure.[6] With infrastructure as the platform and waste as its currency, we witness the melding of the multiple valences of public works as a mode of public service provision and a labor relation—a union that simultaneously underwrites and compromises the very possibility of private bodily reproduction. The breakdown of Tema's sewage system thus triggers the inversion of classic formulations of political order described by Arendt (1958). For those involved in its day-to-day operation, the sewage network in the throes of disrepair moves from a collective good organizing what Arendt (95) calls "human plurality" to a realm of work impinging on the bodily vitality—the labor of "life itself" (7). Infrastructure, the "artificial world of things," is the middle ground, the link or linchpin, in this real-life object-centered (per Latour 2005a) rendering of Arendt's (1958) *vita activa*.

The Public Life of Private Waste

With the pump and motor in operating order at Pumping Station 2, the mix of sewage and industrial waste flowing from wet to dry well, and from dry well to the underground outflow channel, moves one step closer to disposal. Because the settling ponds and aerators of the treatment plant have long stopped functioning, screening the waste as it leaves the great channel and controlling the pace of inflow and release must suffice as the primary form of sewage management. Minimal as they are, compared with the virtual inoperability of the other two pumping stations, these are substantial interventions.

At Pumping Station 3, due to the broken pump and motor and a problem at the main sluice gate, the entire waste load is instead diverted from the intake gutter to Chemu Lagoon, and from there to the sea outfall. With the outflow to Paradise Beach also in disrepair, waste from Tema New Town is likewise diverted to Chemu. All reports from those who work the system indicate that these measures are "temporary," "regrettable," "unfortunate," and "last resorts." They are, nevertheless, the city's prerogative. Authorized by Ghana's *National Environmental Sanitation Policy* of 1999 and associated statutes (section 6.1, "Control and Ownership of Waste"): "District Assemblies shall assure availability of facilities for safe-handling and disposal of excreta.... Water stabilization ponds, preferred. Marine Disposal if no alternative." In this formulation, both legal and practical, the state confers and confirms the Tema municipality's joint "monopoly of waste" and "waste disposal" (Government of Ghana 1999).

The city's right to dispose of waste matter by pushing it into surrounding lagoons and waterways offers limited relief from the fallout of sanitary disrepair. Overwhelming public space, invading daily life, and interfering with basic urban functioning, Tema's waste disposal problems cannot disappear so easily. As broken pipes and choked manholes send excreta into markets and streets, backing up toilets and flooding homes and compounds, system breakdown presents a problem with which city residents and authorities must jointly contend.

The discussion of sanitary problems is a fixture of Tema's news cycle. Reports such as these are common: "The broken-down sewage system has also led to a situation where some households in the metropolis continue to live with the discomfort of burst waste manholes due to inadequate pumping pressure from pumping stations to convey the waste to the sewage treatment facility" (Daily Graphic 2012). Replaying a now common occurrence (Glover 2014), a news flash from September 2015 describes a fact of life in Tema: "Parts of the Tema Community One market were on Sunday and Monday drenched in stench as burst sewer lines in the market gushed out human excreta. The incident left the entire place with the waste, leading to the inability of traders to open their shops or sit in the area" (GNA 2015). A radio host announced, "A mixture of feces, urine and dirty water has been spilling and running into residents' homes instead of gushing out into the sea as portions of the pipes have cracked.... The sewage leaking through neighborhood pipes is eating away at foundations of homes and apartment blocks . . . causing cracks . . . and razing buildings down" (Myjoyonline.com 2014). Tema residents complain, "It is an eyesore the fecal matter showing, the sewage central pumping units are threatening to blast. You can hear roaring waters. . . . The sewage is razing buildings down, buildings are cracked right down from the foundation level all caused by the sewage. If urgent measures are not taken, houses would be razed down, people within Tema Central will fall sick and die" (Myjoyonline.com 2014). Residents' complaints continue, unabated, about untreated fecal waste flowing through the city's open drains and the accompanying stench in the streets as well as their homes, especially for those who live in apartment blocks (Anderson 2019; Lartey 2020).

Top staff members of Tema's municipal administration readily admit that the system is in grave disrepair. I was told by one, "All the communities have problems with their sewage lines. In Tema, the most serious community problem is sewage." A former head of Tema's Waste Management Office recalled that when he entered the system in the 1970s, his office staff used to patrol the roads and arrest those defecating in the open. Now they are busy cleaning up their own mess.

Municipal authorities—much like the technicians who oversee the city's pumping stations without the means for large-scale renovation and repair—suggest that the presence of waste workers is an infrastructural fix in its own right.[7] Tema's waste management director and lead sewer technician walk through affected neighborhoods with local assembly members by their side, their knowledge of the system proportionate to its breakdown. Those at the waste office frequently consult the fragile vellum map from Doxiadis's days inherited from the TDC. Like the system itself, the map is a ruin: treasured, deteriorated, but largely left untouched. No matter, these individuals by dint of professional practice have bodily assimilated the layout of the city's underground routes. Similar to those who work pumping stations, as they walk the surface of the city they can recite which sewage lines they are crossing, where the manholes lie, and where the lines connect.

Stoler (2013, 9) speaks of the "elusive vectors of accountability" that accompany the "lasting tangibilities of ruin." In Tema, despite the vagaries of accountability, perennial infrastructural disorders break down into predictable forms of political conduct. Namely, different types of ruination incite different sorts of reactions from differently positioned political actors. When problems strike public areas like the city's central market, TMA's lead public

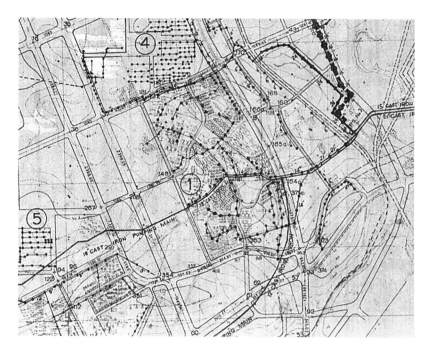

Figure 2.5. Original map of sewage manholes (Provided by Tema Waste Management Office)

affairs officer makes an appearance. Dispatching symbols of public order to counter the disorder of sewage "out of place," the mayor follows up with announcements that special work crews will be organized to respond to emergency spills, promising vehicles to dispatch them swiftly to areas in need.

In contrast with the largely symbolic "crisis-style" response of the figureheads of municipal administration, the actual management of sewage leaks is mired in bureaucratic procedure. This, too, is a highly discursive endeavor, but it departs from the mayoral pronouncements in its much greater deliberative potential. Though by no means resembling a Habermasian (1991) public sphere of open debate, of give-and-take, the management process nevertheless inserts a wedge to influence action, perception, and, ultimately, accountability.

Mornings at Tema's Waste Management Office begin with residents rolling in to lodge complaints. The office assistant explains, "It begins with booking a complaint. The homeowner or resident comes to the office to report a problem. We log the complaint in our ledger and collect a 20GH fee.

This is the fuel money—the cost of coming to inspect the problem. For domestic problems, there are typically two types of complaints. One is a sewage backup inside the house, when the water doesn't drain or the toilet won't flush." Flagging the prime point of connection between private sewer problems and public waste management authorities—the sewage manhole—the assistant continues, "The second type of problem is when the manhole is flooded and the wastewater flows from the manhole into the house."

After each complaint ("C"), waste management officials fill a final ledger column labeled "Remarks" ("R") indicating the corresponding course of action.

> C. Damaged 4" pipe. R. The 4" sewers must be changed to 6" pipe due to the increased populace and usage of the line.
> C. Damaged Main Line. R. It needs urgent replacement of 6" pipe to release community members from constant chokage and allow flow of effluent.
> C: Damaged 4" pipe (pitch fiber). R. It must be replaced with a 4" PVC pipe.

Concerns about the hundreds of manholes that link houses and neighborhoods to sewage mains abound. On a single week's list of problems, mention is made of flattened manholes, silted manholes, manholes missing covers, and those overcome by tree roots.

A site of infrastructural intimacy, the manhole is the point of diagnosis and point of entry for repair, and often a point of contention, an infrastructural middle ground both material and metaphoric providing a window onto the wider uncertainties of Tema's sewer system. It is worth noting, to return to Star's (1999) consideration of breakdown, that not all breakdowns are of the same import. When technical dysfunction meets social disruption meets cultural disorder, a "compound fracture" of the urban social contract is at hand, perhaps explaining why imperial debris is more potent as it deteriorates.

At the TMA Waste Management Office, a single day can easily bring ten to twenty complaints distributed to designated routing and construction teams on the TMA repair crew in addition to their system maintenance responsibilities attending to the city's sewage ponds, pumping stations, and public thoroughfares, as well as new building construction.[8] Crew members readily admitted to broken sewage lines across Tema's earliest-built planned communities. Breakdown has different valences depending on the part of the system one occupies (see plate 8).

Figure 2.6. Booking complaints, 2013 (Photo by Brenda Chalfin)

Manhole problems profoundly disruptive for affected households are normalized in the work routines of the waste management staff. When the Waste Management Office receives notice of overflowing manholes, its typical response is to send a "rodding" team to the affected areas. An age-old technique of sewage-system repair, rodding essentially involves the insertion of metal or plastic rods through the manhole into the sewage pipes to probe for blockages and clear whatever is choking a pipe (see plate 9). The rods may be attached in a series, allowing them to be introduced far along the line. The chief of the waste management repair team explained that rods come with different tips used for different purposes. He carried an array of them, along with extension pipes, to his jobs, noting, "Those with hacksaw blades attached are used to cut the roots that can invade a pipe. Even a small root can grow to fill a whole pipe. The rods tipped with spearheads can punch a hole in a blocked line. Those that look like corkscrews are used to fish out clothing. The fourth type is oval with a metal coil, [and] when spun can be used to bore through sand and soil that may be blocking a pipe."

A highly credentialed mechanic from one of the paralyzed sewage pumping stations, now reassigned to the manual labor of rodding, filled me in on the repair procedures. "The complaint office sends the rodding team out with a list of locations to attend to," he said. "Work is slow. On a good day, the team might cover five jobs. But if there are roots stuck in the pipes, it can take hours to dislodge." As is the case with the pumping stations, the amelioration of blocked pipes and manholes incited Latourian (2005a) "matters of concern." Just as repair compromised the bodies of pumping station technicians, rodding entangled private matters and public life. Simultaneously "making things public" and "making things private," to uncover—and in some cases unhinge—otherwise hidden attachments and interconnections, (dis)repair unsettled the accepted terms of the urban social contract in Tema.

The rodding process forced a confrontation between bureaucratic concepts of order and the intimate human economy of Tema's sewer system. Opening pipes, blockages, and fissures provided an opportunity to (mis)match technical and social concerns. Rather than attend to the actual infrastructural problem—the decrepit, narrow, pitch-fiber pipes meant only to last a decade or two but pressed into service for fifty years to accommodate an ever-growing population—workers on Tema's sewer repair team voiced a resounding concern with the stuff blocking the pipes. The repair team casts the private behaviors of private users as the problem to be solved and mistakes symptoms of breakdown for causes. They are quick to recount residents' rampant abuse of the sewage system, such as using toilets to dump trash and wastewater, or improperly modifying domestic lines. Without funds, equipment, materials, or a plan to rebuild the system, Tema's waste workers, in short, frame infrastructural breakdown as a human issue. Compared to Tobias and Matthew at the pumping station, who pose their bodily capacities as means of infrastructural amelioration, in the trenches with the rodding team, offering a different rendering of infrastructural intimacy, private bodies were treated as vectors of intrusion. Here we see what Kerry Ryan Chance (2018, 39), writing about South Africa's informal settlements, describes as the "double-edge" of infrastructure's promise, exposing urban residents to state surveillance as the price of infrastructural inclusion. Regardless, the vitality of waste materials and waste infrastructures in Tema eludes strict oversight.

Returning to Stoler's (2013, 22) consideration of the melding of lives and ruins, waste workers insist that private bodies bear a double blame as the source of infrastructural ruination. Not only do they peg private behavior as the cause of disrepair; they also malign the public actions of private persons. Staff, for instance, repeatedly complain that sewer problems are caused by

Tema residents' outright theft of manhole covers from the city's streets and byways. They claim residents sell the cast-iron covers as scrap metal, leaving sewer pipes exposed and vulnerable to damage. Taking this elision of errant persons and broken infrastructure a step further and generalizing it to the broader population, Tema's municipal chief executive went so far as to state that though the city has a "weak sewage infrastructure ... the attitude of residents has further worsened the problem" (Myjoyonline.com 2014). Again, humanizing a technical problem, these remarks are paired with the charge that residents illegally construct homes and other structures on top of manholes, interfering with the lines and preventing routine maintenance.

While these comments convey a view of infrastructure informed by the machinic logics of high-modernist thinking, the city's technical and administrative staff pose infrastructure not as anonymous or mechanistic but as empeopled. Authorities call on human intention to explain infrastructural malfunction, characterizing particular categories of persons as "disruptors." Although causality is always open to interpretation when it comes to sanitary faultfinding, these assertions turn the semantic ambiguity of waste and, by association, waste infrastructures into a discursive dumping ground for all sorts of social tensions.

As Tema's waste workers' increasingly urgent and extensive repair efforts pushed them further into people's homes and lives, the equation of errant infrastructure with errant domesticity was amplified and increasingly personalized. The complaint office clerk, inured to her clients' grievances, stated outright, "It's their problem, they are at fault, it's their part of the line." Curiously, I heard virtually no talk from Tema's waste workers about the unpleasantness of dealing daily with fecal matter. Every day they outfitted themselves in boots, gloves, and coveralls for the dirty job of rodding pipes and siphoning off the backed-up water and waste matter. Yet, taking the commingled wastes of private bodies in the collective waste stream to be the norm, waste workers singled out as problematic the signs of private lives.

Moreover, waste workers' disdain for the city's householders was distinctly gendered. Further deflecting blame by personalizing system faults as a function of mismanaged domesticity, a member of the repair team told me, "Every day people come to report on the sewage lines. Sometimes we meet bathing sponge, or jeans. We meet human being. They make abortion inside the sewage. Clogs the systems. Pads plenty. Food. Panties. Underwear." His superior continued, "When you open a choked sewer you find clothes, sanitary pads, condoms. Condoms aren't much of a problem. They burst and shred." He asked, "How does all of this get into the system? Some people throw wash water into the toilet since they don't have other drains available, and the clothes are occasionally dumped along with it. And sometimes people deliberately dump items."

Waste workers' commentary on "matter out of place" (Douglas 1966) in Tema's sewage pipes sheds light on the tensions between public authority and private life brought about by the city's sanitation crisis. With sewage breaks and spills ever more common and the system taxed by growing population and housing pressure, private matters—sometimes inadvertently and sometimes intentionally—physically materialized in the public domain of streets, gutters, and overflowing drains. Because all that Tema's waste staff could do was react to individual complaints rather than undertake systemic renovations, they were drawn deeper into domestic spaces and exposed to the intimate details of residents' private lives. In this confrontation between the forces of urban order and disorder, to cite Mary Douglas, the issue is not so much a structuralist one of new matters to classify. Adding to a sense of waste and waste infrastructures' undecidability, rather, it is a poststructuralist question of the unsettled terms and criterion of classification. In Tema, with the city unable to uphold its end of the infrastructural bargain, not only are the markers of public and private up for renegotiation; so too is accountability for them.

Private Lives and Waste-Based Publics

While Tema's waste staff attribute the breakdown of the city's sewer system to domestic ills and abuses, residents of Tema's planned communities engage in a countereffort to translate private concerns into bureaucratic language and logics. A close reading of the unfolding of a single complaint demonstrates how the commutation between public and private and back again plays out in rhetorical and material terms. The case involves four adjacent households continually plagued by the blockage of sewer pipes and flooding from a nearby manhole. Situated in one of Tema's older communities, this is an area where the municipal administration readily admits that sewage problems are acute. Such infrastructural "breaks," "blockages," and "overflows" are politically charged. Not only do they involve public officials and call into question the norms of civic life and governmental responsibility; they are also "undecidable" (Agamben 1998, 27). They bear new possibilities and recalibrations as well as uncertainties. In Arendtian (1958) terms,

COMMUNITY Nº 5
FINAL LAYOUT

DOXIADIS ASSOCIATES — CONSULTING ENGINEERS

Figure 2.7. Final layout for Tema, Community 5, 1961 (Doxiadis Associates Report for Government of Ghana, DOX-GHA 19, Tema Development Corporation Archives)

infrastructural breakdown mediates the translation of "practices necessary for maintenance of life itself" into objects of collective deliberation and engagement: that is, from "labor" to the *vita activa*. In this manner, playing on Raymond Williams's classic triad (1976), what is chronologically and experientially "residual" becomes historically "emergent," if not "dominant"—a conflation that helps to explain the enduring political valence of ruins, rendering them vital remains in the multiple significations of the term.

Tema's waste management officers treat written discourse and rational prose as the appropriate bridge between private concerns and bureaucratic authority, and require all sewage complaints to be accompanied by a letter explaining the problem. As a result of the bureaucratic state setting the terms of communication in public, without a document, the claim is moot. In the case at hand, the primary complainant is a professional who worked for several decades in Tema's industrial sector. I call him Nana.[9] On behalf of himself and his neighbors, Nana submitted a formal letter to TMA: "We wish to bring to your notice a broken underground sewer pipe for repair and replacement. Apparently, a sewer staff of your office on replacing a blocked sewer pipe identified a broken and damaged sewer to be the cause of the replaced sewer blockage. Almost every one and a half months we have had to invite workmen to repair the blockage, thereby spending lots of money. This has persisted for a year." On the surface, akin to the bourgeois public sphere described by Jürgen Habermas (1991), rational discourse gives political salience to private experience. But in this case, contra the Habermasian ideal, there is little room for debate, as both the message and the medium need to conform to an already formed public authority.

In her examination of the day-to-day political negotiations of South Africa's urban underclass to access urban water infrastructure, Chance (2018, 52) similarly discusses the necessity for urban residents to (over)perform compliance with bureaucratic norms, reinscribing their position of dependence as the price paid for social support. Nana confronts this obligation of administrative supplication in discursive terms. Exercising a capacity for self-determination not afforded to the urban activists described by Chance (2018), he is not entirely bound by it. Capturing the sensory excess of waste as well as waste infrastructure, the restrained tone of Nana's communication with TMA contrasts with the graphic description he volunteered to me during our interview:

> The old pipes are broken and collect mud and sand and soil for that matter. It chokes the entrance of where it enters the main. When that happens, the toilet rises. You see it rising. The manhole, you can see the manhole increasing. The water level comes up from the sewage in the shower area. It comes up. Because the sewer is choked it comes up. The water comes up in the bathroom and you are standing in the water. It happens in these four houses: nos. 5, 7, 9, and 11. There was one day it came from the street. My whole yard was flooded with sewage with the *poos* in it. It was like that for three or four days. It affected the whole street. It was very disgusting.

In contrast to this description, the letter written by Nana and his neighbors rhetorically sanitizes the intimate details of sewage spills and flooding feces, reflecting politically acceptable forms of "public reason" (cf. Calhoun 1992). Putting an envelope of propriety around unseemly events, the letter's reproduction of the nuances of bureaucratic language was also a plea to view a given complaint as a generic rather than purely personal issue. Semantically and socially neutralized, the intent was to induce the execution of an impartial public authority.[10] Instead, the unfolding of Nana's complaint incited a broader tug-of-war between Tema's waste managers and city residents over the boundaries of public and private life and the concomitant assignment of responsibility. Mentioned above, waste management officials actively renounced their public mandate by attributing private blame for systematic faults and asserting private responsibility for their repair. Refuting this point of view, residents argued for the responsibility of public institutions and representatives. However, rather than taking these as fixed and forever-opposed positions, their ongoing negotiation in the course of Nana's sewer case reveals the again unsettled, "undecided" (Agamben 1998, 27) political grounds between them. Simultaneously refuting and succumbing to TMA assertions of private ir/responsibility, city residents take on increasingly public roles. Filling in for the lapses of the municipal authority, they do so not as individual private citizens but instead act in a didactic role reversal "as if" public agents.

To interpret Tema's infrastructural struggles in terms of the proverbial if unspoken social contract (see Chance 2018, 58), TMA sought to assert a contractual logic in nonnegotiable terms. Residents of Tema's core planned communities such as Nana, who prided themselves on their status as model citizens, were not willing to reject it wholesale. They too held tightly to a normative framework of civic obligation and accountability but subtly shifted the assignment of responsibility from one part of the system to another, recoding the locus of private and public liability. These recalibrations, emerging in the context of chronic breakdown and (dis)repair, were premised on an array of infrastructural intimacies not entirely different from those pursued by pumping station engineers and their counterparts in waste management. In the same way the director of Tema's waste division knows the layout of the city's sewer system and the location of manholes by heart, Nana holds a detailed picture of the sewer lines and drainpipes beneath his neatly swept and cemented yard. He traced for me the invisible lines through which the toilet, tub, and kitchen wastewater flowed, where they drained, and where

Figure 2.8. Broken pipes and flooded manhole, 2014 (Photo by Brenda Chalfin)

they connected before being carried to the sewage mains beyond the house. Infrastructural intimacies encompass attachments between people and infrastructure as well as those among people through infrastructure. Nana also knew where the pipes traveled and met up with those of his neighbors' homes before reaching the nearest manhole. An artifact of the mass-produced building scheme of Doxiadis, the local contours of Tema's 1960s master plan are etched in Nana's mind. He knows well that, across his neighborhood, clusters of four houses share a common outflow.

Reflecting these subterranean and historical connections, Nana's neighborliness is as much technical as affective. He knows that when his bathroom drains started to overflow, it is because the sewer pipes in House 21 are clogged and that his neighbors in Houses 23 and 25 are likely to be experiencing the same problems. In the past, responding to shared infrastructural attachments and breakdowns, Nana and his neighbors sought private assistance when problems arose. With sewage backing up in yards and showers, and toilets inoperable, they took it on themselves to contract a private plumber rather than appeal to TMA and endure a long wait. First relying on moonlighting TMA repairmen, they more recently turned to journeyman laborers specializing in sewer problems and pooled funds to cover the cost of services.

Nana described the work: "It's not really for a plumber. It's not technical work. It's filthy. Not everyone wants to do it." Though they didn't have access to the special metal and plastic rods used by TMA, the laborers brought their own equipment, using long narrow PVC pipes to dislodge choked lines. Their interventions were effective but temporary. Lately the erstwhile sewage fixers had not returned the calls of Nana and his neighbors. With problems recurring on a regular basis and no easy way to solve them, Nana and his neighbors decided to pursue a more lasting solution. They chose to bring their case to TMA, enlisting the help of the local assembly member, as conveyed in the above letter. In an instructive parallel, Nikhil Anand (2018, 157) describes Mumbai residents' public pursuit of administrative accountability by city officials for household water services as a "domestic public" seeking official recognition of collective needs. Akin to the councilors who activate access to Mumbai's water system (Anand 2018) and municipal representatives in Palestine tasked with managing (unmanageable) waste crises (Stamatopoulou-Robbins 2019, 109), in Tema elected assembly members are crucial to sewage repair. Though their title refers to their position within Tema's Municipal Assembly devoted to formulating and negotiating district policy, true to a more literal designation, they are instrumental to assembling connections between persons and infrastructure in the city.[11]

Extensions, Exclusions, and Enclosures

Likely due to the local assembly member's influence, TMA responded in an unusually timely fashion. However, rather than resolving things, the arrival of the waste repair crew brought forth a new impasse that only added to the blockage of the neighborhood sewage pipes. A bottleneck as much conceptual as technical, the inter- and intrahousehold intimacies of shared waste were deemed antithetical to public responsibility. Compared to Manhean, described in the next chapter, where residents mount a clear defense against assembly members' claims and intrusions, here we see the complicated and complicating role of assembly officers as agents of mediation. In bringing in TMA, the already strained cooperative capacities of neighbors are disrupted and displaced, as municipal interference works to reinscribe the stark line between private and public responsibility. In these encounters the undecidability of both waste and waste infrastructure comes to the fore.

Once TMA came to investigate, they told Nana and his neighbors that although the problem was on the main pipe leading to the manhole and could be accessed via the manhole, waste management wasn't liable for the fault or the fix. Although the TMA team could repair it, the neighbors would have to cover the expense of replacing and repairing the pipes, at the substantial cost of a few hundred Ghana cedis (about eighty dollars). Waste management staff defended their stance on two grounds: one spatially proximate, the other, historically distant. The first line of defense was founded on domestic geography. Locating a break in the pipe near House 5 just inside the threshold of the compound gate, TMA technicians noted that the fault was in the confines of the household. A reverse tragedy of the commons (Hardin 1968), we might call this a "tragedy of private enclosure" cutting off Nana and neighboring residents from access to public goods.

The second line of defense—somewhat more complicated than the first—appealed to domestic history. It serves as an example of lives not only forming around ruins (Stoler 2013, 29) but also augmenting them. In this second case, waste management workers informed the homeowners that because extensions and apartments had been added to the original structures from Doxiadis's days and included modification to household drains and sewage lines, TMA could not be held accountable. Waste management team members made their charge knowing full well that the household additions were ubiquitous throughout the community, provisioned in Doxiadis's plan, and legally "permitted" decades ago by the city's original planning body (D'Auria 2014).[12] Challenging otherwise accepted norms, from TMA's perspective, the private modification of public works automatically turned them into private property and thus a source of private responsibility. While Nana and his neighbors countered the city's argument by drawing on their deep knowledge of the history of their household pipes and flows, TMA pressed its case despite residents' illustration that the faults were on the municipal mains leading to the house, not on add-ons made by homeowners (see plate 10).

In this example, the expanse of pipe between manhole and household lines exposed the looming rift between public and private responsibility in the city. Infrastructurally and politically indeterminate, or inchoate, the debate over techno-material breakdowns and stopgap repairs brought to the fore fissures of the urban social contract. Presenting this as an interpretive battle between "our extensions and their mains," Nana's neighbor Sister Henrietta explained, "The problem we are having we are thinking it's something they did in the 1960s. [They are] telling us it is what we (the landlords) have done [involving] the extensions we did to the houses behind. Therefore, it is our damage and our repair. There is a connection to this spot even without building the extension to the house. It is part of the original house before the extensions by the various landlords. If the house didn't have the extension, what would TMA do?"

Countering the questions and consensus-building potential of truly free public debate, TMA's pronouncements put the neighbors in a bind. When I suggested getting a private contractor to repair the fault for less than the amount demanded by TMA, Henrietta and Nana replied, "If the person doesn't do it well, you are in trouble. You will have to go back to TMA and they will ask, how could you do it without telling them? We are held liable if we interfere with their property." What's more, they explained, doing so would get TMA off the hook. Nana and Sister Henrietta were holding their ground to make it clear that the repair was TMA's responsibility. Creating an opportunity for TMA carry out what they considered the rightful public good, they asserted, "It is always proper to report [and] TMA can put it right permanently," voicing a still deeply felt sense of municipal accountability.

While Nana and his neighbors resisted pressure to pay for the repairs, they were not averse to investing in public resources. In the face of state contraction and the allied effort of waste management workers to broaden the parameters of private blame, Nana and company were involved in their own efforts to reestablish the parameters of public good. This was evident in their upkeep of the manholes beside their homes. Several months earlier, when the raw sewage overflowed the manhole and spilled into Nana's yard, waste management came to undertake emergency repairs. According to Nana, they siphoned away the sewage and cleared the pipe and blockage to the main near the manhole, but they failed to secure the manhole cover.

Taking on what they see as the rightful responsibility of waste management, Mr. Gideon, the owner of the house closest to the manhole, placed cinder blocks and other materials around it to protect it from damage. Gideon explained, "If it rains then water goes in. We covered it to protect the main. There should have been something from TMA to cover it after they opened it to make the repairs and TMA doesn't have a good way to secure it." Configuring a dually material and discursive public sphere (cf. Habermas 1991), however fleeting, Gideon and a neighbor from another house did the same to the manhole down the street. Before Nana pointed it out to me, I thought it was just a nondescript pile of rocks. In both cases, by privately yet collectively ensuring common benefits, the neighbors filled in the cracks of public service provision (see plate 11).

In this scenario, Tema's private citizens demonstrate intimate knowledge of the underpinnings of sewer lines and flows inside and across households. Their infrastructural attentiveness extends to what are rightfully public parts of the system. These informal "infrastructurations" (to wordplay with Giddens's [1984] alignment of structure and practice) hover between three registers of signification. Simultaneously "making things public" and "making things private," they can be understood all at once as private efforts to protect public infrastructure, examples of private persons acting "as if" they were public authorities and collectively protecting public goods, and as attempts to make public infrastructure private by assimilating it into the collective responsibility of linked domestic realms. Built on the reticence of middle-class residents to air individual bodily needs and outputs in public, and their strong commitment to ideals of state accountability, the self-determinations of what I call "deep domesticity" take a reluctant hold in the abodes of urban material attainment and respectability in the city.

The actions of Tema's middle-class householders certainly bear a resemblance to Mumbai residents' appeals to city officials to ensure household water supply, what Anand (2018, 157) calls "domestic publics." However, in Tema, residents move beyond discursive supplication to directly catalyze infrastructural transformation alongside wider process of sociopolitical recalibration. Residents call on, or "hail" (169), the state as well as performatively constitute state agency, at once covering up for its lacks and usurping it in the name of the domus. In Tema's core, rather than simply reinscribing more settled roles and relations of private consumer to public provider, state accountability is asserted and unseated at the same time. A sign of the infrastructural inchoate at work, figure and ground, provider and user, those who make and unmake infrastructure, shift positions. In this scenario, vital remains spur infrastructural intimacies to seed structural transformations of the domestic sphere unlocked and sustained by the infrastructural inchoate.

From this perspective, infrastructure, the locus of connection and contention, can be considered akin to Arendt's (1958, 52) proverbial table: "To live together in the world means essentially that a world of things is between those who have it in common, as a table is located between those who sit around it. The world like every in-between relates and separates men at the same time." In the throes of dis/repair, pushing bodily waste and domestic life into the public spotlight, in Tema's core, the table no longer holds a steady, readily knowable shape. Instead, it sets off a chain reaction of deliberation and negotiation at once material and discursive, social and political, rendering it, too, "under construction" even as it works to render durable the filaments of political accountability.

Conclusion: Privatization, Infrastructuration, and Public Intimacies of Disrepair

Recounting the ebbs and flows of Tema's sewage pumping station and improvisations of sewage engineers, the first half of this chapter traced the devolution of matters of public provisioning and political accountability into individualized bodily processes by means of intimate infrastructural engagement. The second half addressed the repair strategies of private citizens. In a situation both politically and infrastructurally inchoate, bodily evacuation becomes grounds for political recognition as infrastructural breakdown is mobilized to make collective claims on public space. Bringing Arendt's frames of inquiry to bear on contexts beyond Arendt's political imagination, both scenarios confound expected conceptions of political ordering by means of the mediations of what she calls the "fabricated world" of infrastructure. In the one, the res publica is supplanted by "the labor of life itself" (Arendt 1958, 7). In the other, individual biological processes and outputs incite critical discourse characteristic of a *vita activa*. Reworking the terms of human plurality, these embodied infrastructural engagements reorient public life. In the process, they open a space for deliberative discourse and a fleeting activation of the lineaments of the polis.

From Breakdown to Dis/repair

These snapshots of actual existing urban infrastructures home in on the sewage pumping stations and sea outfalls, treatment plants and settling ponds, toilets, trunk lines, and manholes that make up Tema's sanitary infrastructural underground and advance Stoler's (2013) injunction to focus not on "inert remains, but on their vital reconfiguration." By tracing the play of dis/repair across the city's part-working, part-defunct, but always lively sewage system, evidence from Tema indicates that the "freeze-framing" offered by theories of breakdown (Star 1999) does not adequately capture the political salience of urban infrastructural dys/functioning. More relevant to the grand-scale projects of midcentury modernity such as Tema is this statement by Stoler (2013, 11): "To think with ruins of empire is to emphasize less the artifacts of empire as dead matter or remnants of a defunct regime than to attend to their reappropriations, neglect, and strategic and active positioning within the politics of the present." In light of the realities of Tema's excremental infrastructures, this is the stuff of "vital remains."

Infrastructural Intimacies

Most of all, the close reading of Tema's sanitary system suggests that the "intimacies of infrastructural dis/repair" play a formative role in contemporary processes of political reconfiguration. Whether maintaining pumps and motors, mapping the city's sewage faults, rebuilding manholes, rodding blocked lines, or bailing out poo-laden courtyards, through the intimacies of dis/repair, the fabric of private and public life is both interwoven and remade. A form of active reassembly operating on technical as well as affective grounds, infrastructural intimacy turns inert structures to active social practice, transforming residual orders into emergent formations. In contrast to Latour's (2005a) revelation of the ways infrastructures "make things public," in the case of Tema's sanitary system, ruination and repair "makes things private"—from intimate knowledge of and bodily engagement with the apparatus to operators' reflexive attachment to it. Complicating AbdouMaliq Simone's (2004) much-discussed elision "people as infrastructure," managing waste on an urban scale in Tema depends on identifications between people and publicly authorized infrastructure, connections among people through such infrastructure, and renderings of infrastructure as if people. Similar to Herzfeld's (2005) notion of "cultural intimacy," these identifications also work to reference state bodies and accountabilities.

Waste Matter

Equally evident in Tema's urban core, while infrastructure serves as the armature for transactions between public and private, waste in its fulsome vitality augments and confounds this process. Waste, to borrow again from Stoler (2013, 13), like infrastructure, is a "connective tissue." However, it is a highly changeable one due to its dynamic "micro-ecologies." Not only does waste work on people when people work on waste (Chalfin 2019; Fredericks 2018; Reno 2016), waste works on infrastructure, just as infrastructure works on waste. Demonstrating the tripartite relation of people and infrastructure and waste, channeled through the partly functioning network of household toilets and shared sewage lines, the materialities and residues of human excrement refract back on the private bodies and self-reflections of infrastructures' operators, customers, and caretakers. In the mix of people, infrastructure, and waste, private matters become vividly entangled with public life, unsettling the accepted terms of the urban social contract in Tema. From sticking one's fingers into a pump motor to breathing in the noxious fumes of the city's collective ordure, repairing pipes connecting manhole and household lines, or shrouding the disgust of fecal backups in bureaucratic prose, the intimacies of sanitary infrastructure's dis/repair expose the looming divide between public and private responsibility in the city. In these sites and moments of infrastructural indeterminacy both political indeterminacy and political possibility come to the fore.

Vital Politics

Crossing between the domains of life-giving labor, the material world of work and human-made things, and the realm of contemplation and deliberation, the infrastructural intimacies that permeate waste management in Tema again complicate Arendt's (1958) classic rendering of political life and the human condition and offer unique analytic insight in their own right. Whether transfer of public provisioning and political accountability onto the bodies of pumping station mechanics, or city residents' mobilization of infrastructural breakdown and bodily waste to make claims on public space, infrastructural intimacy and dis/repair rework Arendt's frames of inquiry in distinctive and recurring ways. On the one hand, the common ground of the urban res publica is supplanted by the labor of "life itself" (Arendt 1958, 7) via the embodied sensibilities of infrastructure's caretakers. On the other, biological processes and outputs open a space for collective reasoning around the terms, locations, and configurations of human plurality and public accountability. Together these scenarios capture the lived instantiation of the *vita activa* by means of vital things as the urban social contract is severed, sutured, and reconfigured amid the messy realities of bodily needs, burst pipes, stagnant ponds, feces-laden lagoons, and the imperatives of collective existence in the shadow of Nkrumah's national urban ideal that is the city of Tema.

Plate 1. Tema Development Corporation, 2011 (Photo by Brenda Chalfin)

Plate 2. Trunk sewer lines across Chemu Lagoon from defunct sewage pumping station, 2014 (Photo by Eva Egensteiner)

Plate 3. Discarded Nkrumah-era maps and models on the premises of the TDC, 2010 (Photo by Brenda Chalfin)

Plate 4. Tema Central original house plans and modifications, 2011 (Photo by Brenda Chalfin)

Plate 5. Tema Central original house plans and modifications, 2011 (Photo by Brenda Chalfin)

Plate 6. Tema Central original house plans and modifications, 2011 (Photo by Brenda Chalfin)

Plate 7. Pumping station engineers, 2014 (Photo by Eva Egensteiner)

Plate 8. TMA engineer assessing pipe replacement and repair, 2013 (Photo by Brenda Chalfin)

Plate 9. Rodding team prepares for work, 2014 (Photo by Eva Egensteiner)

Plate 10. Objects of contention: Their mains and our extensions, 2014 (Photo by Brenda Chalfin)

Plate 11. Neighborhood and neighborly repairs, 2014 (Photo by Brenda Chalfin)

Plate 12. Fish processing in Tema Manhean, 2010 (Photo by Brenda Chalfin)

Plate 13. Awudung streetscape, 2010 (Photo by Marina Ofei-Nkansah)

Plate 14. Manhean public toilet exterior, 2014 (Photo by Eva Egensteiner)

Plate 15. Manhean public toilet and shower house, 2010 (Photo by Marina Ofei-Nkansah)

Plate 16. Manhean's multifunctional gathering space, 2010 (Photo by Marina Ofei-Nkansah)

Plate 17. Ziginshore panorama, 2014 (Photo by Eliot Chalfin-Smith)

Plate 18. Preparing fish for market, 2014 (Photo by Eva Egensteiner)

Plate 19. Floshin Taifi veranda, 2014 (Photo by Eva Egensteiner)

Plate 20. Emissah mopping entry, 2014 (Photo by Brenda Chalfin)

Plate 21. Floshin Taifi toilets: sitting style, 2014 (Photo by Eva Egensteiner)

Plate 22. Floshin Taifi toilets: squat style, 2014 (Photo by Eva Egensteiner)

Plate 23. Hostel exterior, 2014 (Photo by Eliot Chalfin-Smith)

Plate 24. Women create personal space in unfinished hostel, 2014 (Photo by Eva Egensteiner)

Plate 25. Building large-scale DIY excremental infrastructure: hand-dug wells, 2011 (Photo by Brenda Chalfin)

Plate 26. Biogas kitchen, indoor, 2014 (Photo by Eva Egensteiner)

Plate 27. Ashaiman street scene, 2014 (Photo by Eva Egensteiner)

Plate 28. Stomach Has No Holiday signboard, 2013 (Photo by Brenda Chalfin)

Plate 29. Stomach: male toilet entrance, 2014 (Photo by Eva Egensteiner)

Plate 30. Mr. and Mrs. Stomach, 2014 (Photo by Eva Egensteiner)

Plate 31. Adepa Modern Toilet signage, 2013 (Photo by Brenda Chalfin)

Plate 32. Adepa Modern's founder, Madame Halima (*right*), 2013 (Photo by Brenda Chalfin)

Plate 33. Adepa toilet stall, 2013 (Photo by Brenda Chalfin)

Plate 34. Adepa sanitary lane, 2013 (Photo by Brenda Chalfin)

Plate 35. Lady Di entrance and shower area, 2014 (Photo by Eva Egensteiner)

Plate 36. Kitchen turned filter room, 2014 (Photo by Eva Egensteiner)

Plate 37. Daughters turn waste into gold at Lady Di, 2014 (Photo by Brenda Chalfin)

3. The Right(s) to Remains
Excremental Infrastructure and Exception in Tema Manhean

No More Free Shitting.
—Toilet signage, Tema Manhean, 2012

One of the State's founding conditions is its application of the categories "public" and "private" to shit. In the discourse of the State, it is a contradiction in terms to speak of "public shit." Shit ceases to be shit once it has been collected and transmuted, and only exists in the form of symbolic equivalents. To "prefer public shit to private shit" is thus to knock down the partition that separates public from private, to deny the "totalitarianism of the State" its access to the private through the construction of this dialectical division.
—Dominique Laporte, *History of Shit* (2002)

The character of the public realm must change in accordance with the activities admitted into it, but to a large extent the activity itself changes its own nature too.
—Hannah Arendt, *The Human Condition* (1958)

Excremental Rights and Exceptions

Dominique Laporte's (2002) *History of Shit* begins with the heady proposition that public shit is an anathema to the modern state.[1] State power, from this "bottom-up" perspective, is founded not on public life but on the capacity to make things private. That is, before the public can be constituted it must be cleansed, and that which is foul and disorderly pushed behind closed doors. While Tema's urban core, in keeping with Laporte, was founded on the aspiration to sequester excrement as well as citizens in the private realm of the domestic unit, Laporte's principle is more outlier than rule across much of the rest of the city. This is the case in Tema's resettle-

Figure 3.1. Canoe harbor, Port of Tema, 2014 (Photo by Eliot Chalfin-Smith)

ment area, Tema Manhean. Here, an alternative excremental rubric prevails: public toilets designed, monitored, and administered by state authorities for residents of surrounding family homes. Put into place in the late 1950s, they continue to be used, maintained, and struggled over by Manhean's residents across backgrounds and generations in a long war of attrition challenging state entitlements to urban profit and property.

Manhean lies less than two miles from Tema's city center. Reflecting a meeting ground of late-colonial urban planning and modern nation-making, Manhean's design precedes the rest of the city. The two sections of the city are worlds apart when it comes to the technical and political contours of excremental infrastructure. Reflecting an earlier iteration of "containment urbanism" (Menoret 2014), in contrast to Tema proper, where individual household toilets are the norm and public facilities the rare exception, in Manhean private facilities are few and far between. Rather than hidden fixtures of urban life, public toilets in Manhean are used and managed in common. Transcending the claims and confines of individual persons and households, over time these installations have come to push against the gov-

Figure 3.2. Awudung streetscape, 2013 (Photo by Marina Ofei-Nkansah)

ernmental order from which they originated and extend the limits of what is possible and permissible within public space.

Perched on Ghana's western Atlantic littoral, Manhean is the earliest built of Tema's planned residential zones. In Manhean's Awudung quarter, the air is filled with the scent of vehicle exhaust, charcoal cooking fires, and fish-smoking ovens. Manhean residents remain tied to long-standing Ga livelihood strategies of canoe fishing (for men) and fish processing (for women) (see plate 12).[2] Within, alongside, and between the cement-block homes and compounds from Manhean's founding, evidence of fishing livelihoods prevail, from nets and buoys drying to furniture fashioned from worn canoes (see plate 13). Women, most of all, rely on the limited public space for their fish-processing operations. The corridors between residences and edges of roadsides are small-scale industrial zones, marked by fish-drying racks, clay and steel ovens for fish smoking, and round-the-clock operations. Other residents work within the factories, refineries, and power plants of Tema's officially recognized Industrial Area on Manhean's northern boundary.

The fenced premises of Ghana's Eastern Naval Command and the towering 150-foot Chemu Point lighthouse mark Manhean's southern boundary. The lighthouse offers a point of orientation for those on land as well as those at sea. Tema's fishing harbor occupies the cove directly west of Manhean, with separate berths for trawlers and wooden fishing canoes manned by local and migratory fishers. Next door is the container port, where massive tankers and container ships wait to discharge and receive cargo. To the east are remnants of ships run aground, and distant ciphers of canoes. The beach at Manhean's edge is strewn with boulders, seaweed, and heaps of debris washed ashore. Hard to discern from the roadside above, occasional figures crouch on wet rocks and face the cool sea spray, with their backs to the town, to attend to the elimination of bodily waste.

Along with the small portion of Manhean residents who enjoy toilet facilities in their own homes, only those who defecate at the water's edge for reasons of preference or extreme penury avoid the public toilets of this compact urban zone. The rest of Manhean's populace of forty thousand make use of public facilities. Public toilets here are central spaces, open to all for a small fee. They are managed by diverse collectives of residents in active contention with state agents and political elites.

Public toilets are fixtures of Manhean's urban landscape. They punctuate the thoroughfares of Manhean at regular intervals, accessible from the streets, lanes, and footpaths crossing the area, containing two rows of six to nine partitioned drop holes, one set for women, one set for men, with separate entries. The odors of urine, feces, and cleaning fluid come and go, depending on which way the wind is blowing and when the septic tank was last emptied. The toilets typically occupy fenced compounds with a kiosk near the entrance, where user fees are paid and customers can pick up squares of newsprint or, for an extra few cents, a small bundle of toilet roll. Male and female portraits point patrons in the right direction. Inside, stalls are divided by short partitions offering a modicum of privacy. Transoms cut into the surrounding walls and doorways allow for airflow and light during the day. A few bulbs light the way at night. Chalked announcements of football and boxing matches and posters advertising funeral observances, church crusades, and political candidates adorn their façades (see plate 14).

Benches or chairs for those waiting in line or visiting with the managers, cleaners, and attendants who staff each facility cut across the open space of each toilet compound, as do water tanks, buckets, and receptacles of various sizes. Also commonplace at Manhean's public toilets are brick inciner-

Figure 3.3. Manhean public toilet interior corridor, 2013 (Photo by Marina Ofei-Nkansah)

Figure 3.4. Manhean public toilet stalls, 2013 (Photo by Marina Ofei-Nkansah)

ators or metal drums to burn the soiled paper customers drop in the large baskets placed near each stall. A handwashing station may be positioned at the toilet's exterior, in the form of either a small porcelain basin or a plastic container with a faucet. Some public toilets have dedicated water taps. Many contain bathing areas where prepurchased buckets of water can be used for washing and laundry. More and more have pay-per-use public showers with cubicles built along the surrounding walls (see plate 15). In a settlement where most homes lack toilets, bathing rooms, and piped water, clusters of PVC pipes and rusty spigots towering above walls are common sights, signaling a standalone "shower house" or combined public toilet and shower facility.[3]

Most of Manhean's toilets were constructed in the late 1950s on the cusp of national independence. Although other sections of the new city were slated for self-contained private household facilities, planners insisted on equipping Manhean with public places of convenience. The rooflines of the blocky midcentury structures are easy to identify. Marking their presence along Manhean's streetscape, cement platforms encasing septic tanks create a tiered setback between the street's edge and the larger enclosure. Besides providing a comfortable place for sitting and relaxing, the manhole covers can be opened and accessed by sewage-emptying trucks that come to siphon out the accumulated waste. Bold letters and numbers in thick black paint—T1, T2, and so on—mark each lintel, reinscribing the toilets' original designations as government property.

At once in the middle of things and under the radar, in this unlikely crucible of public life Manhean residents pursue what Henri Lefebvre (1996) calls "the right to the city." Joining the political right to participate with the right to appropriate this manner of urban claims making has multiple faces (Purcell 2002, 102). According to Matthew Gandy (2006, 388), it can be productively understood "as a 'right to urban life' that combines the practical needs of everyday life with a substantive rather than abstract conception of modern citizenship." In Manhean, the "right to the city" (Lefebvre 1996) plays out via a multisided "right to shit." It involves, on the one hand, the right "to shit," that is, a practical entitlement to the act of shitting, and on the other, the right "to" shit as a material resource with both public and private value.

In this corner of Tema, the "right(s) to shit" are entwined with battles over the broader right to urban space and habitation. In a community built on forced relocation, the right to inhabit urban space was not guaranteed; neither were its terms consensual nor restricted to the base terms of survival. In Manhean the substantive rights to the city boldly refute Hannah

Arendt's (1958) narrow rendering of the "labors of living" as prepolitical. Instead, Manhean's toilets engage fundamental political concerns around inclusion, representation, and self-determination. Indicating the multiplier effects of infrastructural control (Jensen 2019), rooted in the inner workings of bodies and septic tanks, sewer lines, and drop pits, "right(s) to shit" in Manhean are predicated on and a platform for an expansive array of collective and individual entitlements that directly rebut state interventions.

Different from excremental politics in Tema's core, which ultimately seeks to reinstate established structures of authority, excremental politics in Manhean center on securing the fundaments of urban existence while rejecting the predations of the state and its proxies. This is a double move involving, first, repurposing government-built public infrastructure to keep the state at bay and, second, enlarging what is permissible therein and for whom in the absence and/or active refusal of state guarantees and protections. Far from government of, by, and for the private self, the public character of these processes remains at the fore. Offering an inversion of Laporte's (2002) thesis, the persistence of public excrement actively rebukes state authority and collectively sustains private bodies in public. The roots of this story lie in the prolonged course of forced removal and resettlement behind Manhean's founding.

Rights, Representation, and Resettlement

When the city of Tema was initially envisioned in the last years of colonial rule, a sixty-four-square-mile parcel was acquisitioned from the traditional "stool" lands of the surrounding communities, ethnically identified as Ga-Adangbe.[4] Government authorities subsequently decreed the removal of anyone residing in the fishing and farming villages occupying the area (Butcher 1966, 2). The village of Tema, perched on the ridge above the site of the new harbor, with a recorded population of four thousand permanent residents, was the largest among these long-established settlements (D'Auria 2019; Hilling 1966, 375). Considered prime real estate linking the port area to the rest of the city, it was slated for immediate demolition and resettlement deemed compulsory.[5] A special residential zone was proposed outside the confines of the tightly clustered communities of the new city. Called Tema Manhean in the Ga language (literally, Tema New Town) and also referred to as Tema Village, a six-square-mile plot hugging the Atlantic shoreline at the eastern edge of the new township was designated for relocation of those displaced.

Figure 3.5. Removal from Old Tema and resettlement in Tema Manhean, 1959 (Provided by Ghana Information Services Division)

Manhean, "from the outset, was treated as distinct" (Jackson and Oppong 2014, 479). Slotted into Giorgio Agamben's (1998) conceptual framework, it was a "space of exception." Different from the rest of the new city, which was posed as an exemplar of national progress to be copied, Manhean was deliberately held back to make way for this model of national promise. In Agamben's (1998) stark terms, when it came to Manhean, the codes of new nation-building were intentionally suspended by those at the helm of urban planning. A suspension of the law orchestrated by its makers, Manhean originated at this double-edged "limit," in the words of Agamben (15), at once "end and principle of the juridical order."[6]

Town planners were adamant about removing residents from Old Tema and instituting residential segregation, as they considered "tribal communities" to be poor candidates for assimilation into the multiclass and culturally mixed urban communities envisioned for the new city (D'Auria 2014, 340). Reports from the era indicate, "The Government is anxious that Tema village retain its individual character and not be absorbed into the new town" (Amarteifio 1966, 91). Claims of cultural preservation shrouded a sentiment that would long linger; namely, these persons were not qualified for full membership in the new city.

Manhean's status as urban exception was by no means met with acceptance. Similar to companion urban experiments of the day, such as Brazil's Brasília and India's Chandigarh, segregation of the city's underclass was both a prerequisite and a by-product of the construction and functioning of its core (Holston 1989; Prakash 2002). Relocation in Tema turned urban indigenes into urban outcasts—of the city but forcibly and permanently situated on its spatial social and political margins. Fanning the flames of contention, the relocation of Old Tema's residents was decreed by government authorities as not only necessary but to transpire without delay. Per the national development plan of 1951, construction of Tema Harbor was to commence immediately: "Harbour development took precedence over everything else . . . including the existing residents of the town" (Jackson and Oppong 2014, 492). Construction of Manhean in turn was initiated in 1952, before any other residential areas of the new city.

To incentivize Old Tema's inhabitants to move, authorities decided to offer all householders in the old settlement fully built homes in the new town (Amarteifio 1966; Jackson and Oppong 2014). At stake was what can be taken—and in some cases, mistaken—as the most basic right of all to the city, the right to habitation (see Doxiadis 1968 on "shelter"). In the case of forced removal, such rights were turned into obligations. Equally at issue was the right of representation, that is, the very right to decide or defer on another's behalf. With one confused for the other, housing was treated by urban authorities as a proxy for self-determination. That is, the right to habitation, one of the fundamental "labors of living" (Arendt 1958), was offered in lieu of participation in decision-making.

The rush to dismantle Old Tema on these terms incurred substantial resistance and would ultimately delay removal and resettlement for almost a decade, until 1960. The long gap between the initiation and completion of relocation from Old Tema says much about the political landscape of Manhean yet to come. Old Tema, though marked by designated hierarchies and specialized offices falling under the label of "traditional authority" (Field

Figure 3.6.
Wulomo and Tema Traditional Council members at Durbar, ca. 1962 (Tema Development Corporation Archives)

1940; Rathbone 2000), was crosscut by rapidly shifting coalitions and solidarities in pursuit of material outcomes as well as due process. Not to be breached, however, was the fundamental fissure between the populace and political elites who had earlier overstepped the boundaries of public good for personal advancement. Provoking dissent, resettlement authorities in the newly established Ministry of Housing gained the support of Old Tema's designated traditional leader, the Tema *mantse*. The *mantse* agreed to relocation and accepted token monetary compensation on behalf of Old Tema as a whole.

The plan ignited a chieftaincy dispute that remains unresolved to this day. While traditional authority among the Ga is highly regarded (Field 1937), the *mantse* is considered a ritual custodian of the land, not its owner, nor a chief.[7] Hence, when the *mantse* agreed to resettlement on residents' behalf, community members voiced accusations of wrongdoing on two counts: unauthorized transfer of common property, and unlawful acceptance and use of payment. As youth, elders, and well-off female fish traders allied against him, the *mantse* was further charged with failure to abide by expected conventions of public consultation and deliberation (Amarteifio 1966, 6, 8, 11). Finally, alongside loss of access to fields and fishing grounds, resistance to relocation was compounded by the prospect of leaving behind hundreds of ancestral and communal shrines.

These concerns incited protest and threats of violence, and resolving them took several years. One major problem was the terms of compensation. The Ministry of Housing promised to provide anyone living "rent-free" (and thus presumed to "own" a dwelling in Old Tema) with a new home of equivalent size in the resettlement zone (Amarteifio 1966, 7). In a move that aroused suspicion and limited cooperation, ministry representatives conducted initial surveys of residents and residential property in 1952. Surveyors ignored the possibility that one might not appear to have a permanent domicile but still have claims to place. As a result, many residents were denied the compensation they were due. Adding to the confusion, in the several years between the initial survey and the eventual relocation in 1959, newcomers and native sons and daughters established residence and acquired property in Old Tema, drawn to the opportunities afforded by the construction of a new city and harbor. At the end of the decade at least 40 percent of residents were calculated to have been born elsewhere (Butcher 1966, 24–25). From an original surveyed population of four thousand in 1952, by 1959 Old Tema's population was close to thirteen thousand (24–25). They too sought compensation for forced removal, raising the political and material stakes of relocation.

The ensuing dynamics of removal and resettlement are worth recounting in detail. A remarkable report (Amarteifio 1966) compiled in the immediate aftermath of relocation by a mixed team of Ghanaian and expatriate social scientists is a testament to the importance of bearing witness and the force of historical memory and forgetting. Little of this account appears in the city's official history, nor do current residents of Manhean overtly reference it. Nevertheless, the political currents it captures continue to surface in the present. The report indicates that

> the government's decision to remove the villagers . . . aroused great indignation. . . . They contended that the Government was taking away all their land from them, thus rendering them "landless people." . . . The people vehemently resisted resettlement for seven years. As a result of

this hostility, many violent acts were committed, including the destruction of the prototype houses by a section of the youth. . . . Some of them were arrested, tried in court and punished. This court action increased the tension between the Government and the people. Those punished became heroes and leaders, and any person who tried to persuade them to agree to the resettlement plan was regarded a traitor. This attitude led to the destoolment of the Mantse, who was accused of supporting the Government. A number of young men, supported by the Mankralo, who was appointed by the dissenters as the acting Tema Mantse, declared the chief destooled. The youths had the support of the Sakumo Wulomo and also of several other priests whose positions in the village were very strong. Many market women, mainly the fish sellers, rallied to the side of the Chief's opponents, and these powerful women provided substantial funds to finance the opposition. The Mantse himself was originally opposed to the Acquisition Act. But later, when he realized it would be foolhardiness to oppose the might of Government, changed sides and supported resettlement, and then agreed to accept compensation, failed to inform the whole community, as custom demanded, but instead used it to fight their opponents in the litigation which followed his destoolment. The Mantse appealed to the GA traditional council, which "sat on" the case for two years. The Government refused to recognize the act of destoolment and the litigation continued throughout the following five years. The main accusation against the Mantse was that he had sold stool lands (ancestral lands) to the Government, and with the financial support of the market women supplemented by their own contributions, the young men were able to fight until the end. Although the opponents of the Chief knew that they had no evidence to substantiate the charge, they realized that it was the only accusation which could win them the support of the mass of the people. . . . The conflict between the Chief and the people was a direct outcome of the scheme for resettlement. In order to enable the resettlement to proceed, the Government with great reluctance agreed to withdraw recognition from the Chief, perhaps acting on the assumption that it was better to sacrifice one person to achieve a desired and useful purpose. (Amarteifio 1966, 6–7)

Domesticating Urban Exception

In the maelstrom of transition from Gold Coast to Ghana the demands of Old Tema's residents were met by domestic schema devised by agents of the outgoing colonial regime. Again, sidestepping residents' pursuit of fair representation, not entirely different from Doxiadis's plans for Tema's core recounted in chapter 2, proposals for Manhean instead focused on the organization of domestic life. These concerns included dwelling design, proximity of extended family members, locations of household-based activities, and allocation of number of persons per room, along with where and how residents of the new settlement were to bathe and defecate.

The new settlement of Manhean was divided into four wards representing the major clans of the original village: Awudung, Ashamang, Aboitsewe, and Ablewonkor. Each ward contained clusters of nearly identical compound-style houses. Each house contained multiple rooms accessible via a shared veranda running the length of the structure and facing an inner courtyard. There were two house types. One, larger, identified as Type A, consisted of ten to twenty rooms per structure. Enclosed by high walls, every house bordered a common outdoor area. Known as a major compound, it was designed to be shared by multiple homes of a similar type. The other style, called Type B, had fewer rooms in each house. Linked by a veranda, these houses also faced a common area but largely lacked the high-walled enclosures of Type A. Bordered by a short fence or hedge, the buildings were arrayed in a circle around a common shared space (D'Auria 2014, 341; Whitham 1966, 59).

Prototypes were completed within the first year, and the designs were subject to a series of modifications. Consultation with a select group of Old Tema residents led to the alteration of the original barracks-style design (Jackson and Oppong 2014). Going unheeded, however, was the consensus that the area was too tightly packed. Those consulted complained that there was little room for inevitable extension of family homes to make room for the next generation, to accommodate tenants, and enable public activities, including outdoor industries such as fish processing.[8] According to Emmanuel Oko Adjetey (1964, 70), an architect who spent his childhood in Old Tema, in the original village "special attention was paid to open spaces, connected by narrow lanes which served as playgrounds and space for public meetings or social gatherings."

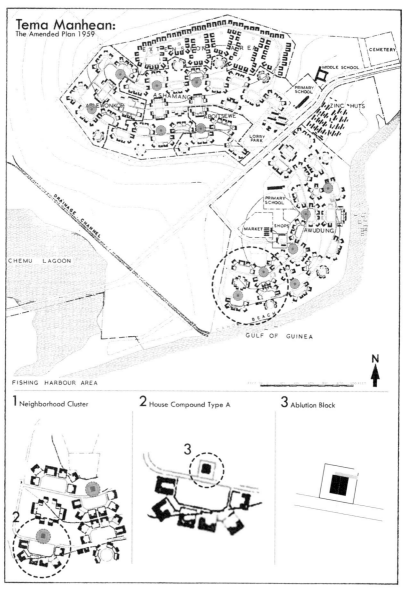

Figure 3.7. Final Drew and Fry plan for Tema Manhean, with residential compounds and public toilets, originally called "ablution blocks," ca. 1956 (Created by Kairon Aiken after Amarteifio et al. 1966)

Despite rejecting pleas for additional open space, in light of the imperative of removal from the area planned for the core of the new city, concessions were made for thousands of residents who had gone uncounted in the several years' interval between the Ministry of Housing's initial survey and the final attempt at relocation. Again, mistaking obligations for rights, housing authorities promised these residents homes in Manhean as a condition of vacating the village. For the four hundred compound houses already built, Manhean's settlement plan was revised to include an extension area beyond the demarcated wards. With a population above ten thousand and the likelihood of additional number of unrecorded inhabitants (Butcher 1966, 25), another one hundred compounds were constructed for those overlooked in the early housing surveys. Inhabitants of the originally planned structures garnered bona fide property rights via a seventy-five-year lease, and the rest were required to rent their accommodations. This section of Manhean is still known as the "U-compound," for "untitled householders."

Once the remaining structures were filled, to capture the influx of newcomers "temporary huts" made from zinc sheets were hastily assembled on the eve of relocation with the consent of resettlement authorities (Amarteifio 1966, 17), a further departure from the pledged room-for-room compensation that added to the uncertainties of resettlement. Far from the original intention of offering one house per family, these small structures often contained multiple households. In this way, Manhean, conceived as a space of exception (Agamben 1998) where old tribal order could be preserved relative to the new city, spawned exceptions of its own from the start. Mixing families of different origins and affiliations, Manhean's auxiliary structures muddied the clear division between wards at the core of the original resettlement scheme and contributed to the makeshift approach of the whole process (Amarteifio 1966, 27). Women's customary rights to property were also unsettled (D'Auria 2014, 342). Ga conventions of duolocal residence, with spouses living in separate households (Robertson 1984), were unevenly realized with resettlement. Some women remained household heads and others were allocated separate rooms in compound homes (Jackson and Oppong 2014), limiting their claims to both public and private space.

Rather than ameliorating the political divides already cutting across the community, resettlement intensified them. It was not clear which offices would carry out which public duties (Butcher 1966, 32). Given the lingering animosities between community factions for and against the Tema *mantse*, authorities were hesitant to hand over power. Instead, welfare officers were put in charge of community relations in a kind of temporary receivership—another exception reinforcing Manhean's residents' positioning at the spatial and political margins of the polity.

Architectures of Excremental Uplift

Side by side these upheavals and false starts were the last-gasp efforts of late-colonial architects and planners to harness tradition anew. When it came to final buildings and layouts, much of Manhean was designed under the direction of architects Jane Drew and Maxwell Fry, assisted by partners Kenneth Drake and Denyis Lasdun. T. S. Clerk, the first African director of the Tema Development Corporation, who worked with Doxiadis planning Tema's core, earlier served as a draftsman for Drew and Fry. With Africanization accompanying independence, Clerk eventually became their boss (Provoost 2020). A tight-knit circle, Drew and Fry were close colleagues of A. E. S. Alcock, who drafted the first plans for Tema in 1951. All three had earlier worked together as members of the colonial service. Drew and Fry had cut their professional teeth on large-scale urban planning projects in London (Bullock 2002, 29). In 1942 Fry arrived in the Gold Coast on assignment with the Royal Engineers. He was appointed town planning advisor for British West Africa in 1944 (Jackson and Holland 2014, 147). Fellow architect Drew, Fry's professional and marital partner, served as chief of staff, covering a territory from Gambia to Nigeria (148).[9]

Pacesetters in the tropical modernism movement, Drew and Fry designed schools, university campuses, and residences and urban master plans across the subregion (Chang 2011; Crinson 2003; Fry and Drew 1956, 1964; Liscombe 2006; Mumford and Frampton 2002). In the Gold Coast, they worked beside Alcock in the model village of Asawasi outside Kumasi. The village was a "laboratory in the field" (Kohler 2002). The trio experimented with building materials, structures, and layouts in situ, spawning design solutions that would later be adopted in Manhean. Drew and Fry soon published a popular how-to guide, *Village Housing in the Tropics* (1947), pitched to colonial officers and their assistants.[10]

When Alcock took up the master plan for the new city of Tema, Drew and Fry had already left West Africa for India to work on the city of Chandigarh with French modernist master Le Corbusier (Galantay 1975, 16; Jackson and Oppong 2014, 483).[11] They wrote to Alcock about participating in

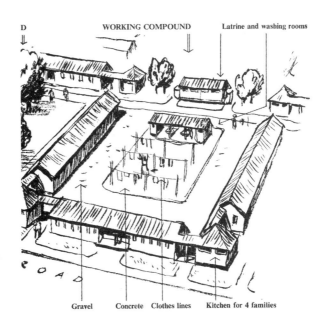

D WORKING COMPOUND Latrine and washing rooms

Figure 3.8. Compound design from *Village Housing in the Tropics* (Drew and Fry 1947)

Gravel   Concrete   Clothes lines   Kitchen for 4 families

Tema's design process. Save for a few clusters of showcase houses in Tema proper, the two were assigned to the much smaller settlement of Tema Manhean (Jackson and Oppong 2014, 484).[12] Drew and Fry's initial proposals for Manhean included "a village layout, with plans for schools, markets, churches, public byways, and the complete design for the new houses," including elaborate plans for the settlement's toilets (Butcher 1966, 55; see also Kulterman 1963, 16; Uduku 2006).

Though it was much less noted than their celebrated focus on climatic design (Fry and Drew 1956, 1964), the pair shared an overarching concern with health and sanitation. This agenda would substantially affect sanitary arrangements and the tenor of public, private, and political life in Manhean to this day.[13] Combining a baseline concern with sanitary infrastructure common to urban planning with a more targeted preoccupation with hygiene common among colonial authorities (Anderson 2006; Rabinow 1989; Wright 1991), Drew (1946, 57) conveyed her desire "to make the towns better and more healthy places for Africans." In an address to colleagues in London, toilets are central figures in this reformist frame (59): "The question of latrines is a very important one in Africa and it cannot be shirked.... The amount of illness occurring from lack of attention to this matter is terrible. . . . One of the great benefits we could give people was a decent septic tank latrine system in the compound, together with another great boon, a good water supply."

Drew and Fry's *Village Housing in the Tropics* puts water, waste, and sanitation at the fore, turning toilets into a near obsession. Drew and Fry treat "the question of latrines" as "the" problem to be solved and key to solving a host of other ills. A full chapter of the handbook is devoted to "Health and Hygiene," and nearly every layout and house plan includes a latrine and a wash area. The authors remark, "We know of no villages at all in West Africa with water closets and a proper water-borne sewage disposal system. . . . The commonest method is still to use the bush or forest as a latrine and fouling the earth brings its toll of disease. The situation becomes increasingly worse as the population becomes concentrated and there is the added danger of water pollution" (Drew and Fry 1947, 41).

An insight of lasting impact on the terms of public life and political contention in Manhean, Drew and Fry's signature sanitary solution is public toilets shared by multiple households. In *Village Housing in the Tropics* the pair suggests, "Latrines can be grouped with the houses so as to be easily accessible to them. Ten houses containing a hundred persons could use a six-seater septic tank latrine" (Drew and Fry 1947, 43). Drew and Fry go on to state, "Septic tank latrines if properly cared for do not smell and therefore can be placed nearer housing than pit latrines" (81). They add, "They require little upkeep and are cleanly" (49). This sanitary solution became the model for Tema Manhean. The settlement's first chroniclers note, "In addition to water supplied by communal standpipes and dust bins for every household, multi-seater public latrines fitted with pull-chain water-closets were installed across Manhean's new neighborhoods" (Butcher 1966, 28).

Taking the notion of sanitary collective to new heights in their plans for Manhean, Drew and Fry propose a distinctive arrangement of domestic infrastructure. Merging multiple domestic tasks and serving multiple domestic units, this is the "sanitary compound" on which the facilities of Tema Manhean would be based.[14] As envisioned years earlier in *Village Housing in the Tropics* (1947, 40), the sanitary compound is composed of a communal washhouse for laundry, communal kitchens for food preparation, shared refuse bins, and communal bathhouses and latrines. Though the structures in Manhean did not have adjoining kitchens, those initially built had both bathing areas and dedicated taps and washrooms for laundry.

In Manhean, rather than installing toilets in the individual compound houses as planned for the new city of Tema, facilities conformed to Drew and Fry's plan and were all, and only, public. This was so despite the considerable if not greater expense entailed in building public facilities rather than private toilets and bathrooms, as intended for the rest of Tema. Because building in Manhean cost considerably more than in Tema Township, the disparity cannot easily be attributed to financial constraints. It suggests instead a more deliberate decision not to provide comparable facilities. As the resettlement report notes, "The houses [in Manhean] were not cheap at £300 per room. At the same time Tema Manhean was being completed, Tema Development Corporation had started building . . . houses with full internal services. The total cost of development was about £550 per house, average size two to three rooms with water, electricity, bathroom, and WC in each house, street lighting and tarred roads" (Butcher and Whitham 1966, 68).

Filling in the little remaining public space in the new settlement, Manhean's public toilets were located between clusters of compound houses the architects designed to approximate the lost multifamily dwellings of Old Tema (Butcher 1966, 59). A sign of technological advancement despite their "transitional" character, rather than using septic tanks, the toilets were linked to Tema's newly built central sewerage system, an unusual and, as was soon evident, not entirely sustainable arrangement.[15] The result was a distinct sort of public space transcending both the familial and the household in the favor of collectivity, all the while promoting the progressive sequestration of bodily functions.

As in Tema proper, these arrangements channel long lingering Enlightenment ideals in which the cultivation of the private self is considered a mark of social order (Elias 1994; Mumford 1938). However, in Manhean's intermediary form, rather than the exclusion of others in the creation of private space, activities are performed in a specially designated common realm. As in Tema, this too is a space built by the state. Closer to the sanctions of colonial hygiene, in Manhean it is a realm whose inner workings and appearances were actively monitored by state agents despite being turned over to the public. Confounding Laporte's (2002) commentary on the problematic politics of public shit, as instituted in Manhean sanitation was not a modality for "governing at a distance" but a means of direct intervention in the management of bodily functions per individual and en masse. Confounding Arendt's (1958) ideals, the private body was made an active target of public management.

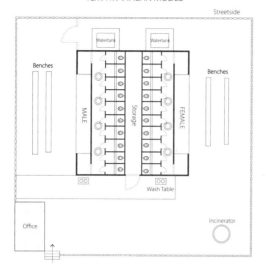

TEMA MANHEAN MODEL

Figure 3.9. Tema Manhean public toilet layout, ca. 2012 (Created by Kairon Aiken after V. Raets)

Drew and Fry considered sanitary design an active influence on personal and collective development. They recommend that washhouses include "a small seat, a soap ledge, [and] a peg to take clothing and towels" and also suggest that "interior walls will look more cheerful if slightly tinted" as an alternative to existing washing places, which "are ugly, and barren of even a seat or a dry shelf on which to place the precious soap . . . and there is no peg on which to hang the cover cloth or other clothing" (1947, 40). The architects stress, "Privacy is needed in the washing rooms as well as plenty of air and sunlight. This may be obtained by placing the windows high in the walls and only shutters in the lower section" (41). Further cultivating bodily and social propriety through the built environment, they suggest, "Little gardens and climbing plants near them will help sweeten their precincts. They need very clear labeling in good lettering, usually MEN and WOMEN in English and the local language is sufficient" (41).

In short, in Manhean, though ostensibly devoted by planning authorities to the preservation of tradition, sanitary infrastructure instead operated as "a mode of address whereby the . . . state offered development and technological progress in return for political subjection" (Larkin 2008, 245). In this case, the ratio of technological progress to political subjection was markedly uneven, with high rates of intrusion paired with limited infrastructural advancement.

Cultivating Excremental Accountability

The promotion of individual and collective hygiene was at the core of the relationship between state authorities and residents in the early years of resettlement. Very different from Tema's core, where the interiority of toilets and bathrooms within the space of the home presumed self-management, in Manhean state agents were involved in the regulation of private spaces and functions, giving government representatives a place in the daily life of the community via toilets. The latrines were cleaned and maintained by municipal employees, and residents were guaranteed access free of charge.

Once resettlement was underway, according to the site's lead welfare officer, G. W. Amarteifio (1966, 20), "welfare workers [were hired] to accustom residents to the new environment. They advised on house cleaning and tried to instill a spirit of cleanliness into housekeepers ... advising owners of fowls and other domestic animals, on how best to keep them, and whitewash fish smoking ovens to improve appearance." Of note, these interventions and associated infrastructures garnered considerable attention from Manhean's new residents. Indicating "buy-in" more often for the better, in surveys conducted by resettlement agents not long after the move, "good sanitation, rubbish removal, latrines and piped water" ranked high on the list of "good features of new houses" despite the purportedly frequent theft of flushing chains in public lavatories (Butcher 1966, 61). In comparison, "lack of latrines and poor water supply" ranked as "undesirable features" of their former living quarters (61).

Toileting habits formed a vivid interface between governing authorities and residents as well as among residents themselves. As noted by Amarteifio's coworker, social anthropologist David Butcher (1966, 32), "The gradual filling up of Tema Manhean with people from Old Tema brought new problems with it, such as the need for instructions on how to use flush latrines properly, and the use of dust bins." In response, forging a means to directly act on the bodies of Manhean's new residents, "the resettlement workers set about promoting a programme to ease the tension [of resettlement] and unite the community into a purposeful and harmonious whole. They concentrated first on sanitation; the sewage system was often blocked by stones and corncobs thrown by the people into the new lavatories. A campaign was started to sell toilet rolls to the villagers. The welfare workers purchased toilet rolls at wholesale prices, held demonstration talks with the people and sold toilet rolls to them" (Amarteifio 1966, 19).

Spurring the recognition of a new social order afoot, Butcher (1966, 27) tellingly recounts, "The forced mixing of families with different allegiances within one area has led to friction between them, which usually flares up in disputes about which families' children have made a mess in the public latrine." These seemingly petty quarrels and contestations about "the right (way) to shit" speak again to the substantive dimensions of urban citizenship captured in notion of the "right to the city" (Lefevbre 1996). They also bring to the surface deeper concerns about the fundamental contours of political organization. Namely, these confrontations reignited lingering generational divides and communal factions harking back to disputes over representation and redress that had charged the resettlement process, still fresh on residents' minds.

Here we see an early sign of shit's uneasy standing in the public realm noted by Laporte (2002). Human waste in Manhean was neither fully controlled by state, nor fully relegated to individual responsibility, readily turning it into a matter both politically and infrastructurally inchoate. While any public matter is open to debate, bodily waste occupies a perennially ambiguous in-between. Intimately individualized and widely shared despite its often-veiled production, excrement's "leavings" are available to external oversight. With the right "to shit," active and internal, and the right "to" shit, extrinsic and possessive, the clash of these logics in Manhean became evident early on. Again put to the test is Arendt's (1958) claim that the abject body is an inadequate basis for participation in political life, founded on norms regarding what can and cannot appear in public.

Agamben's (1998) insights amplify and provide an answer to Arendt's assumptions and blind spots. In Manhean, with political inclusion playing out in the terms of toileting, "bare life"—that is, natural or biological life (4)—is not outside the polis but institutionally scripted and enforced. For Manhean's early planners and overseers, as for Agamben, "bare life" is considered the minimal threshold, that is, the beginning and end point, of political membership and recognition. As Agamben (127) puts it regarding "inscription of natural life in the juridico-political order of the nation-state . . . the same bare life that in the ancien regime was politically neutral and belonged to God as creaturely life in the classical world . . . now fully enters into the structure of the state and even becomes the earthly foundation of the state's legitimacy and sovereignty."[16]

While again confirming to Laporte's (2002) claims regarding the complexities of "public shit," these arrangements confound Laporte's historical sequencing, which identifies the creation of a private realm and interiorization of the waste-producing body as a precondition of modern state power. Deliberately devised as a site of exception, in Manhean the production of the public-cum-"natural" or indigenous excremental subject is intentionally orchestrated to underwrite state authority. Here the body is renaturalized as the condition of state authority, and publicly so, as opposed to both an Arendtian (1958) and a Foucauldian (1979) rendering of biopolitics centered on the production of the self-disciplined body (Agamben 1998, 4). Agamben (6) famously asserts that the ascriptions of "bare life" are "the original—if concealed—nucleus of sovereign power." In the case of Manhean's founding, these arrangements occur in plain sight.

No More Free Shitting: From Abandonment to Reclamation

Despite receiving intense supervision early on, Manhean was increasingly peripheral to Tema's newly established municipal administration. This shift radically altered the political valence of bodily elimination. Urban authorities' dwindling involvement in Manhean became more graphic as time progressed and moved the settlement from urban showcase to space of exclusion and calculated underprovisioning. The neglect of public works in Manhean, starting with the unfinished sewer repairs and never-built extensions, coincided with the fall of the Nkrumah government in 1966. From roads and drains to housing stock, toilets, and sewage mains, a cycle of divestment and disinterest on the part of municipal bodies fed decline and discontent in Manhean. Exacerbated by national economic crisis and a long decade of political instability and underprovisioning, municipal neglect continued well into the 1970s, heightened by agricultural losses and world market oil and credit shocks (Rothchild 1991). Municipal withdrawal raised the stakes of self-reliance in Manhean while engendering residents' antipathy toward power brokers inside and outside the bounds of the settlement.

The abrupt shift from intensive government oversight to overwhelming neglect begat its own political dilemmas in the resettlement zone. Manhean's minimal qualification for political membership in the new city faded from the stage of governmental concern and turned Manhean from a space of exception to a "zone of abandonment," to borrow again from Agamben (1998). Shifting from a ground of marginal inclusion to a source of exclusion, the trappings of bare life represented by public toileting were no longer tethered to the polis. A remnant of political membership, however barren, caught in the contradiction of inclusive exclusion, Manhean's public toilets were among the little that remained of this earlier relation. Occupying a new threshold of "indistinction" (Agamben 1998, 27), now inchoate or undecidable, the political standing of public shitting in Manhean was up for grabs. In these "vital remains" of both infrastructure and policy, "new layers interact with preexisting ones, re-energizing some and closing off others," with none ever completely going away (Larkin 2008, 6).

Agamben (1998, 9) captures with remarkable precision the political stakes of the indeterminacy at play in cases such as Manhean, remarking, "The state of exception actually constituted in its very separateness the hidden foundation on which the entire political system rested. When its borders begin to be blurred, the bare life that dwelt there frees itself of the city and becomes both subject and object of the conflicts of political order, the one place for both the organization of State power and emancipations from it." Willem Schinkel and Marguerite van den Berg's approach (2011) is helpful in operationalizing Agamben's analytics and the intertwined processes of oversight and abandonment in Manhean. Overcoming Agamben's philosophical extremes, they suggest that the counterposing of bare life and political life, *bios* and *zoe*, "is active not only in an absolute sense, but also in various intermediary forms in which aspects of the exclusive inclusion of bare life into the community are actualized" (Schinkel and van den Berg 2011, 5).

The altered status of Manhean's residents from uniquely classified and protected urban subjects at the dawning of decolonization followed by descent into infrastructural incarceration born of municipal abandonment represents the lived complexities of states of exception created through intense oversight. With civic status for Manhean's residents substantively indexed by the terms of toileting, as municipal controls and capacities dwindled, Manhean's toilets turned into a charged terrain of negotiation and deliberation. Emptied of the investments of the past yet retaining the vestiges of earlier possibility along with the needs and resentments of the present, public toilets became a domain of vital politics. As the rest of this chapter explores, played out via the "right to participate" in the act of shitting (i.e., the right "to shit") and the "right to appropriate" its locus and substance (i.e., the right "to" shit) (Purcell 2002, 102), Manhean's toilets became a space where residents actualized Lefebvre's (1996) substantively construed "right to the city" in pursuit of more expansive claims to the right to survive on their own terms.

Poo-Populism Meets Privatization

With the rising tide of populism sweeping Ghana in the late 1970s in the aftermath of a coup d'état, state breakdown, and constraints of military rule (Chazan 1983), Manhean's toilets regained a place at the fore of community life. According to recollections of Manhean residents turned toilet operators, by the early 1980s toilets in Manhean had become a prime object of self-help and popular mobilization inspired by the populist-socialist platform of head of state J. J. Rawlings. Taking a cue from the People's Militias and Defense Committees of Rawlings's Armed Forces Revolutionary Council (Nugent 1991), residents of Manhean came together to clean, renovate, and run public toilets. Throughout Rawlings's reign during the 1980s and 1990s, public facilities were more or less managed by larger and smaller groups of neighbors, kin, and political affiliates. Putting to use patterns of proximity scripted in Fry and Drew's original town plan, managers collected funds from residents of surrounding homes and businesses to cover the cost of upkeep and introduced nominal user fees.

Fast-forward to 2001. With the replacement of Rawlings's National Democratic Congress (NDC) government by the market-centered New Patriotic Party (NPP), any remnants of populism at the state level were quickly supplanted by neoliberal ideals. Posed on the remnants of these earlier orders—spanning the gamut from late-colonial supervision to abandonment to populist reclamation—a very different system of privatized public toilet management followed. It relied on formally contracted franchises overseen by Tema Metropolitan Assembly (TMA), which had replaced the TDC as Manhean's official overseer. Each franchise was to include a slate of members and officers and register with municipal authorities. The franchise system required the imposition of mandatory fixed fees for toilet customers, from which franchise operators were to pay rents as well as dividends from monthly earnings directly to TMA.

Contracts for Manhean's several dozen toilets were distributed on a competitive basis in each ward. This was largely a community-based affair, with contracts in the hands of neighborhood associations and clusters of residents, sometimes registered under the name of a family head, fishermen's association, or general enterprise. Ranging in size from just a few members to a dozen and, on occasion, several dozen, most toilet contracts were held by groups of between five and ten members, more often male than female, and

Figure 3.10. Conversing with toilet managers in Tema Manhean, 2011 (Photo by Brenda Chalfin)

typically middle-aged with individual or collective assets to spare. Franchise registration was recorded in large ledgers held at the TMA Waste Management Office, including a running tab of fees paid and unpaid and the specific toilet under management.

With economic opportunities such as fishing, factory work, and government employment in decline, public toilets in Manhean were among the most lucrative economic options around. Toilets offered considerable profit on a consistent basis relative to other options available to Manhean residents. Open eighteen hours a day, 365 days a year, and attracting twenty-five customers an hour (and upward of one hundred patrons during the morning rush), at thirty pesewa per visit in 2018, a public toilet could easily generate upward of fifty thousand Ghana cedi in revenue over the course of a year.[17] With some franchise holders playing an active role in management and others serving largely behind the scenes as overseers, most toilets rely on a small group of employees for daily operations. Usually, facilities have one or two attendants on hire to collect user fees and hand out newsprint or toilet roll in return. Another employee is dedicated to cleaning and disinfecting the facilities, burning wastepaper, emptying baskets, sweeping and scrubbing stalls, and doing their best to keep the odors down with whatever blend of chemicals the management group can afford. Workers and owners, perhaps assuming I held expertise in public health, turned much of the conversation to access to cleaning supplies to dispel the stench of the accumulated waste.

Cleaners and attendants' monthly salaries, in the range of 120 to 150 cedi (forty to fifty dollars) a person, hardly made a dent in gross profits. Besides the fees for using the toilets, there were additional earnings from the sale of goods and services such as toilet paper, piped water for bathing and clothes washing, and access to shower stalls.[18] In Ghana's neoliberal milieu, even as other accumulative strategies dried up, the regularity of bodily functions in Manhean could be relied on and capitalized, bringing to life Laporte's (2002, 43, 78) recognition of the equivalence of shit and money within the early modern European sanitary economy.

A fertile source of value in neoliberal times, similar to the South African water privatization scheme described by Antina von Schnitzler (2018), excreta was put in the hands of the public yet legally retained in the grip of the state. Shifting the burden of management and upkeep to the franchisee while claiming municipal ownership and oversight, the TMA set the standards of operation. The municipal authority was legally entitled to collect revenue from each franchise despite their responsibility for almost all operating expenses. Toilet contracts with TMA, good for a three-year duration ("renewable"), detailed the division of labor, revenue, and responsibility between the "Franchisee" and the "Assembly" (TMA, n.d.):

> The Franchisee would undertake: twice daily cleansing of sanitary ware, floors and walls with approved cleanser . . . cleaning and polishing of pipe work to a bright finish . . . collect litter, replenish toilet paper, soaps . . . check operations of cisterns and taps, clean drains, gutters, clear debris from roofs and entrance way. . . . These duties would be performed with utmost accountability to the Assembly, as the Franchisee was expected to: Inform Assembly of any faults and repairs. . . . Supply all consumables, brand and type to be approved by Assembly officer. . . . Submit annual financial information. Most important, the Franchisee is obliged to pay: 20% of gross fee payments collected or a[n agreed on] fixed sum to the Assembly. The Assembly in turn would be responsible for: quality control and inspecting of cleaning and all other work including inspection of records. . . . The Assembly also had the authority to: sanction franchi-

see or terminate the contract, as did the Franchisee, if unable to recover costs or if the Assembly does not uphold its end.

The right "to" shit in this case was construed by law as partible, distributing public toilet proceeds between concessionaires and municipal authorities. With minimal investment in upkeep by government agents and the near-total devolution of responsibility to the franchisee, this was less a tariff for services rendered than a tax on bodily functions. As shitting turned into a public utility in private hands, human waste-making in Manhean was made a source of private profit and simultaneously reendowed with the specter of government control lingering from the settlement's founding nearly half a century earlier. As evident in the sign emblazoned on the lintel of one of Manhean's recently franchised facilities, "No More Free Shitting," under the neoliberal dispensation toilet users were expected to pay a political and economic price to shit.

Despite its contractual confines, tracing a course from exception to abandonment to neoliberal reclamation, TMA's toilet concession scheme did not work out as planned. For state actors and residents alike, public toilets were too hot a commodity, of too much importance, too much value, and too long a history to be easily slotted into a single contractual template. Combining a materialized right "to" shit and an ethico-practical right "to shit," the case of Manhean's Kutsho toilet reveals the multisided politics of privatizing public shitting. At Kutsho toilet, the promotion of private gain turned into a referendum on collective responsibility.[19] Run by a five-member committee harking back to the decline of TMA sanitary servicing and the early days of Rawlings's revolution, Kutsho toilet fell under community governance in the late 1970s. After twenty years, in 2000, discontent with the conditions of the toilet precipitated what Kwate Seth Boi, a middle-aged longtime toilet manager, described to me as a "toilet coup d'état." Mr. Boi recalled a group of local youth who took advantage of the yearly Ga *kleejo* festival (a traditional rite of reversal where youth express their opinion to local "powers that be," whether chiefs, elders, or elites) (Field 1937) to compose a song about the stench of the toilet, shaming its overseers.

The youth went further than most *kleejo* protests and locked Kutsho from the inside, militating for a change in management. As the story goes, they gained the backing of elders from the neighborhood, who accompanied them to the *mantse*'s palace in support of their request. With privatization newly in place, TMA insisted on turning the toilet over to a registered company. Fusing labor, location, and money through the common currency of shit (cf. Laporte 2002, 47, 78), individuals from the neighborhood volunteered their own funds and efforts to repair the facilities and eventually banded together to secure an official toilet franchise. Rather than consolidating management into a few hands, as TMA intended, the group was fifty persons strong, including a few better-off residents with toilets in their own homes and no need to use the public facility. The group made all decisions with the consent of an additional seventeen elders drawn from nearby residences, at once spreading accountability and safeguarding correct management. Privatization here was much more about collective ends and shared responsibilities than self-interest.

Propelling a different form of scatological collectivity with rights to place and property at the fore is a nearby toilet facility popularly known as Mang toilet.[20] In a reversal of the arrangements of Kutsho, where toilet oversight was a recent addition to the already established ambit of neighborhood leaders and elders, private management of Mang was an impetus to community mobilization and representation more broadly. Indeed, over time Mang's overseers became the public face of the neighborhood, providing material and social support to residents and fostering access to resources and recognition within a wider political-economic field. In the Mang case, the right(s) to shit, at once privatized and collectivized, underwrote the pursuit and realization of other rights.

The first toilet built during resettlement, Mang faced a long decade of decline between the fall of Kwame Nkrumah and rise of Rawlings. It was "brought back to life," the caretaker recalled, during the early years of the Rawlings regime by individuals active in the local Committee for Defense of the Revolution. By the late 1990s both the toilet and the management group broke down and were supplanted by an alliance of young men from the surrounding community. Already connected to the previous overseers by social, kin, and residential ties, national level political allegiances mattered little in the transfer of responsibility. With the franchise system established around the same time, they submitted bids to the municipal authorities and were swiftly designated the official overseers of the facility.

In the case of Mang toilet, much more of a challenge than TMA registration or community recognition was the actual operation of the toilet. The group's spokesman, Solomon Tetteh, recounted,

The septic tank was filled to capacity and the water and electric services were on the verge of suspension due to a string of unpaid charges and other debts inherited from the former managers. We sought out house-to-house contributions to pay the bills, to which we added to our own funds. I visited the Ghana Water Company to beg for a reprieve and negotiate an installment plan and sought out reimbursements from the former toilet managers. To little avail, the very day the water was reconnected, the electricity was disconnected, and we had to fight to get it back, too.

Due to these early frustrations and ensuing negotiations, Mang managers and facilities became well connected to utility company personnel, with infrastructural breakdown in the context of privatization serving as an impetus toward urban social networking. In addition, because TMA refused to pay for toilet repairs despite the stipulations of the franchise contract, Mang managers, carrying out the professed obligations of the state, covered costs with proceeds from the toilet supplemented by household contributions. They mobilized the same alliances with utility providers to get help with problems elsewhere in the neighborhood, extending the public influence of private toilet-based affiliation. This is an example of what Jean Comaroff (2007, 211), in her discussion of AIDS activism, identifies as a "counter politics of bare life," which works to garner resources and recognition and expand the range of social networks. Besides serving as the go-to person for negotiations with utility companies, Solomon Tetteh, the Mang franchise head, is the executive officer of the larger Manhean Toilet Operators Association. Over time he has come to function as the go-to person when there is a dispute to be adjudicated or when another association seeks advice about hiring.

In this example, Manhean's toilets shape-shift from a functionally specific public good to a foundation for cooperation and public life within the wider community. A comparison of Manhean with Arjun Appadurai's (2002) description of public toilet facilities in Mumbai helps to parse the political contours of these arrangements. Similar to Mumbai, public mobilization around toilets in Manhean is grounded in a subaltern sense of locality and the intimate proximity of daily life, driven by what Appadurai calls a "lateral" political ethos of "deep democracy" (45). As in Mumbai, public toilets in Manhean provide a basis for "the poor to work their way into the public sphere" and, in turn, "override the failed solutions and non-solutions of the state and elites" (39, 40). Though Manhean's toilet operators periodically pursue direct political recognition or redress from government authorities and participate in what Appadurai (39) calls the "transgressive display of fecal politics" (see the Kutsho toilet *kleejo* protests), the similarities between the two end there. While Manhean's toilet managers do forge local networks and alliances, a function perhaps of their combined experiences of exception and abandonment, they do not partake of wider forms of national and transnational affiliation, as in Mumbai.

Evincing what can be better described as a "deep" or "democratized domesticity" in contrast to Appadurai's (2002) "deep democracy," although collective opposition to municipal authorities endures across individual franchises in Manhean, there is little impetus to reach beyond neighborhood networks. In fact, when the Toilet Operators Association spokesman was tapped by municipal authorities to manage a toilet in another township, he immediately declined. Articulating a sense of urban territorial identification deriving as much from the specific matter at hand as from fear of co-optation by state agents, he shared his ardent belief that local residents should manage the toilets. In the wake of municipal abandonment, toilet privatization in Manhean spurs claims to place and collective property over and above individual entitlement. Excrement and the abject body had become a prominent part of a larger political puzzle. In a counterstrategy of political containment, while lateral linkages across the community's toilets were desirable, vertical linkages were rejected.

Toilet Concessions and Contentions

In the era of privatization, not only was public toilets' profitability a source of attraction, so was toilet operators' capacity to garner public influence. Whether reaching in to toilet customers, reaching across the collectivity of co-managers, reaching out to other concessions, or reaching up to public institutions and officeholders, toilets and their management groups accrued public standing. Along with the allure of income generation, all of this made Manhean's toilets an attractive sinecure along the pathways of political patronage. In turn, struggles to claim toilet franchises on political grounds spurred toilet managers to hold tight to their claims, inciting ties to place and joint property more often than not.

In Ghana, intense electoral competition creates a political field bifurcated along party lines. Seeding contention and coalition building, party

Figure 3.11. Public toilet plastered with political posters, 2010 (Photo by Marina Ofei-Nkansah)

loyalists in Manhean regularly compete for the spoils of public toilets. One toilet that was turned over to NDC supporters when the NPP lost power in 2008 was reopened a few weeks later after being converted from the older squatting style to what residents referred to as a "sit on" toilet. Taken as a sign of improvement or toilet "upgrade," along with the fresh coat of paint, the front of the toilet compound was emblazoned with an exhortation in English and Ga: "Sit on it!" (Ta Nɔ). Reminiscent of social welfare officers' efforts at community toilet education in the early days of resettlement, a mother and daughter toilet attendant team went around ensuring customers were sitting rather than squatting in the aftermath of reopening. Despite the investment in refurbishment by NDC loyalists hoping to garner influence in the name of public improvement, previous overseers allied with the NPP strongly opposed the transfer and challenged the interests of both local and national political authorities. It was resolved that the two groups, whose members were well-known to each other, would share the toilet's take, each claiming the proceeds on alternating weeks. Whatever one's party affiliation, attendants would enforce the new requirement to sit rather than squat.

A change in toilet oversight from an established set of managers to supporters of the incumbent party following the election was rebuffed with greater success at another Manhean facility. Here, refusal of the proposed change in management was less about interparty rivalry and more about protecting communal claims to public provisioning. Affiliates of the NDC unfamiliar to the members of the toilet management group were rumored to be in line to take over the franchise. Given its strong sense of ownership and the toilet's status as a primary income source, party affiliates could not upstage the management group's claim to the facility. In this case, political office and party affiliation did not guarantee access to toilet revenues, as in urban neighborhoods elsewhere in the city (Aryee and Crook 2010). Instead, in Manhean public toilets were at once a spoil of the state's meager midcentury investments and a rebuff of current state and party politics. That is, even as state bodies sought to reclaim their founding "right(s) to shit" in Manhean, residents asserted their own entitlements to the city's waste infrastructures. Falling into the category of "vital remains," they were one of the few public investments that still held value despite decades of institutional neglect. Manhean's public toilet franchises, in short, as "matters of [public] concern" (Latour 2005b, 41), due to their combined material and managerial contentions registered state claims without deferring to them.

Community-based toilet managers tend to "take excremental matters into their own hands" over and above political patronage. In the same way that it is misguided to treat defecation as a fundamentally private act, it is equally problematic to locate toilets in the realm of public life solely or primarily in relation to state authorities and elites. In this regard, Manhean presents a double challenge to the classic model of sanitary exclusion placing excrement in hands of the state on one end and relegating it to the hidden domains of private life on the other (Laporte 2002). Manhean's toilets occupy an intermediary realm (see Schinkel and van den Berg 2011). With various instantiations of publicness at the fore, they merge the recurring deprivations of bare life with the unstable residues of political life and engender a different sort of political terrain. To paraphrase Latour, "As infrastructures that matter," they are "the *res* that creates a public around it" (2005a, 14). Marking fissures recent and still resonating from resettlement, with toilets a material focus, this is a public forged in contention with formally recognized political authorities.

Adding a determinate layer to the political contests surrounding public toilets, Manhean's traditional authorities—the Tema *mantse* and Tema

Traditional Council—were designated by TMA as overseers of specific facilities bequeathed to the community by companies in the area such as VALCO Aluminum and the Volta River Authority. Beyond these few structures, the Tema Traditional Council was permitted access to a share of the profits of all, commanding a twenty-cedi toll from each toilet on a monthly basis. The contributions are nominal in the singular but significant in the plural considering the more than fifty public toilets across Manhean. These entitlements, drawing together representatives of individual toilet franchises, put the otherwise loosely organized Manhean Toilet Operators Association in pitched battle with the Tema *mantse* and Tema Traditional Council. Despite occasional appeals for funds, recognition, and audience with the current *mantse*, the Toilet Operators Association expressed a sworn animosity to the Tema Traditional Council, echoing the vehement opposition between community members, *mantse*, and *mankralo* during the drawn-out process of resettlement a half century earlier.

Local animosities became apparent during a long late-afternoon conversation with association executives from one of the settlement's four wards. They described the rift between a self-interested old guard who were guaranteed access to income and state-granted assets and Manhean's working-class residents forever struggling to get their daily bread. Expressing a moral as much as a political evaluation, operators shared their sentiment that the *mantse* and council already held claims to "stool lands" and benefited from the wealth and status therein. Why would and should they claim a share of the lowly gains of Manhean's public toilets? To these complaints were added the Tema Traditional Council's shameful housekeeping skills. The few public toilets under its purview were deemed to be a mess, run-down, and poorly managed and maintained. The executives noted that this was no different from the revenues the Traditional Council received—and mismanaged—from the aluminum and electricity companies who had built housing for employees on the edges of Manhean. Indeed, if Manhean's toilet operators saw themselves turning shit to gold, they saw the Traditional Council turning its God-given assets into shit. These were the places where the odor of fecal decay—*Emli samei ehii* (Ga for "It has a bad stink")—was unmistakable whichever way the wind was blowing.

Doing "Right" by Waste

Marked by sporadic alliances and interdependencies, a three-sided struggle emerged in debates over who did "right" by the settlement's waste. On display was toilet operators' capacity to make and defend claims in the face of material and structural disadvantage despite squabbling among those overseeing individual facilities. Franchise holders closed ranks when it came to interactions with Tema Metropolitan Assembly. In a bold move, after initially paying yearly fees to TMA and getting little in return, operators collectively refused to pay tax assessments to the city. Of the thirty-one franchises officially registered, half had refused to pay fees to TMA for upward of two years. Several were in arrears for four or five years and according to TMA owed several hundred to thousands of dollars. Complaining about the sheer cost of toilet upkeep, they criticized the municipal authority for not living up to its side of the bargain. Evident in the near total atrophy of the sewage lines that once connected Manhean to Tema's sewage main and outflows, this included failure to carry out repairs, offer discounted septic tank emptying services, or provide access to decent cleaning supplies.

Ordered to meet with Tema waste management officials to resolve the issue, the spokesman for the operators' association after a series of meetings crafted a succinct rationale to make his case. Appealing to historical precedent, he asserted that toilets could not be construed as state or municipal property. They should instead be considered "compound toilets," since they were built for the express use of the residents of the surrounding multifamily homes (per Drew and Fry 1947). A commons of a sort, this was as much a private space as a public one. Rooted in historical notions of domesticity, their private character was rather different from a neoliberal vision of marketable assets despite being enabled by the franchise system.

Battling over revenues, toilet operators took advantage of the bureaucratic labyrinth of Tema's city government to work with subsections of TMA to get what they needed. In a case of infighting among members of a single toilet cooperative, TMA officials recommended the group reconstitute with representation from each faction, avoiding the heavy hand of any single one. Sporadic and situational, the tactic presented less of a threat to toilet operators' autonomy than consultation with Manhean's traditional authorities, whose claims on toilet premises and revenues were too close for comfort given the close-knit clan and family ties between residents and the Traditional Council. Toilet association leader Tetteh opined that although disputes with TMA over unpaid taxes were still pending, working collectively with and against the city "actually reduced internal discord among toilet operators." Tema Metropolitan Assembly seemed to recognize toilet operators' authority, too, as it permitted the organization to serve as a go-between when issuing business licenses to toilet managers and even asking them to collect debts on its behalf. An indication of the distance between the bulk of Manhean residents and city authorities and the limited authority wielded over them by the municipality, the operator association was one of TMA's few legitimate lifelines to Manhean despite being in pitched battle with them.

It is not that Manhean's toilet operators were immune to government interference. Like other marginalized groups, deft at the ploys of rebuff (Chatterjee 2004), they used the state against itself. This is evident in their response to the entreaties of local assembly members. In contrast to the assembly members of Tema's core, who played a mediating role helping to smooth and suture differences and disagreements, assembly members in Manhean were ready and willing to assert claims of their own to public toilet franchises. In one case, an assemblyman convinced a member of a large toilet management team to let him on board. The assemblyman, I was told, then "brought his own boys" to occupy the toilet and demanded revenue from the group treasurer. Describing the situation as a "hijacking," and unsure about how to proceed, the rest of the management team waited a few days to resolve the matter. Working outside the ambit of TMA, the group leader then lodged a complaint with the local police. Though lacking absolute authority, the police had the discretion to independently follow up with TMA's waste division and seek information on the rightful franchise owner. Soon thereafter, they ordered the assembly member and his cronies to vacate the premises.

With public toilet facilities and operators in Manhean mapping out a political field that simultaneously subsumed, exceeded, and rejected the state nexus, municipal authorities in Tema could do little to reclaim or maintain the coercive charter of the founding era of public toileting in the settlement. Much less about looking to authorities, whether traditional or state-based, for aid or input, the "right(s) to shit" in Manhean was bound up with the pursuit and protection of collective possibility. Despite a clear interest in profit making, these stratagems were fundamentally oriented around the projection and protection of a multilayered and deeply localized public. Another emanation of "deep domesticity," this public—like the vital remains of the toilets they used and guarded—emerged as a function of and counter to the near internment of Manhean's inhabitants over the course of a long half century of late-colonial urban planning, uneven forms of state contraction, and neoliberal capitalist expansion.

Refuting Arendt's (1958, 65, 72) claims that "it has always been the bodily part of human existence that needed to be hidden in privacy" with "public life . . . possible only after the much more urgent needs of life itself had been taken care of," Manhean's toilets provided a stage for conjoining the intimacy of bodily functions with the loose affiliations of the open-ended social body that characterize Arendt's definition of publicness.[21] Here, Arendt's (1958, 72) "distinction between things that should be shown and things that should be hidden" implodes as the most base activities "connected to sheer survival are permitted to appear in public" (46) to be "seen and heard by everybody" (50).[22] Moreover, Manhean's excremental infrastructures framed open-ended forms of collective self-determination. Despite the structures' municipal origins and the ongoing claims of toilet managers and operators around the nominal exactions of fee collection and bodily propriety (i.e., "sit on it"), they refuted any singular or overarching source of authority.

Taking *Taifi* into Their Own Hands

In pursuit of enduring guarantees to the means of urban survival, Manhean's least-resourced residents leverage a narrow band of opportunity via the settlement's public toilets to launch a sustained refutation of the structural order of things. Sedimentations of urban habits and habitats, like the walls, tanks, sewage pits, and passageways left over from the settlement's founding, these amalgams of material things and human practice embody infrastructural intimacies and claim a persistent presence in the urban landscape. Despite the apparent disorder and decrepitude of Manhean's facilities, here we see a loose instantiation of Arendt's (1958, 55) observation that "the existence of a public realm and the world's subsequent transformation into a community of things which gathers men together and relates them to each other depends entirely on permanence." Different from the ruins (see Stoler 2013) of the old pumping stations of Tema's core forced into service by an insistent state and middle-class populace bound to the legitimations of the past, these vital remains are continually remade by dint of neglect, necessity, and residents' collective memory.

Largely abandoned by the powers that be, Manhean's toilets exhibit a tenacity continually enlivened by those on the margins of urban life who

Figure 3.12. Public toilet courtyard as worksite and living space, 2010 (Photo by Marina Ofei-Nkansah)

use and repurpose them on their own terms. Far from the top-down, internalized ordering of individual bodies and bodily functions "at a distance" at Tema's core, the well-used spaces of Manhean's toilets are plumbed by Manhean's populace to reveal possibilities unfathomed by the city's original planners or the social welfare officers assigned to manage them. Infrastructural intimacies here are likewise markedly different from the self-conscious pursuit of political entitlements by materially enabled middle-class householders in Tema proper who look toward the restoration of infrastructural ideal types by state authorities. Namely, Manhean's public toilets evince a distinct mode of publicizing private matters largely exclusive to the underclass, as the urban poor pursue a range of reproductive activities in and around the bounded public sphere of toilet premises.[23]

Arendt's associational notion of public space and political life is instructive here despite her professed discomfort with public revelations of bodily processes (Benhabib 1992, 78). In sync with Latour's (2005a) understanding of assembly, Arendt situates the self within a loose social body. As she eloquently puts it (Arndt 1958, 57–58, 52), "The public realm, as the common world ... gathers us together and yet prevents our falling over each other ... providing a sense of common object while permitting the expression of multiple perspectives." Advancing Arendt's intuitions regarding the material scaffolding of public life, Latour (41) points to the political side effects of such enduring if unexpected alignments of persons and things in the public sphere, "when matters of fact give way to complicated entanglements and become matters of concern." Part of the "sensual life of the city" (Larkin 2008, 250), though conversation and casual interactions were surely common, Manhean's toilets do not much resemble the rhetorically constituted public realm of self-conscious political deliberation as described by Jürgen Habermas (1991). Rather, in lieu of self-conscious claims directed to the powers that be (Benhabib 1992, 87; Frekko 2009, 228), as in the city's core, they are a nexus for quotidian copresence and practical interaction enabling individual and collective coexistence.

The infrastructurally embedded political propositions that emerge are evident at Mang toilet. At Mang, myriad facets of social reproduction are drawn into a single space alongside private bodily care and relief. Passages linking the toilets, bathroom, and entryway support the convergence of people and activities amid the sights and odors of waste, damp, and cleaning fluid. Describing one visit, my assistant, Marina Ofei-Nkansah, noted, "I met a lot of people, some standing and some sitting, chatting and listening to the music from the radio of a man on a bench. The facility is very dirty but lively." Fostering interaction, the anteroom leading to the men's facilities adjoins a washroom bearing remnants of taps from early phases of resettlement where children fill buckets and gather to do laundry. Left to their own devices, these again are remains, not ruins, despite their wear and disrepair.

Residents write proverbs and lessons in chalk on an interior wall painted black to serve as a notice board near the attendant's area. Apt in its double entendre, on one visit it reads, "Whatsoever goes into the mouth of a person does not defile the person but what cometh out." The author, Samuel Odoi, is the nephew of a longtime toilet attendant. A recent high school graduate, Samuel uses his perch to drill neighborhood children on the alphabet and sums between their work filling buckets and scrubbing laundry. When I expressed my fascination with his pedagogic aspirations, he explained that he had virtually grown up in the toilet compound, assisting his uncle and using the electric light of the anteroom to study. A rank illustration of Arendt's (1958) heady claim that "the character of the public realm must change in accordance with the activities admitted into it, but to a large extent the activity itself changes its own nature too," for Samuel, the sanctity of the word—written, spoken, and read—was made a part of this tainted space.

Further fostering unexpected political possibilities, the female wing of Mang toilet presents a crossroads of private and public life. Differently configured than the male wing, the female entrance is a combination of courtyard, throughway, storage area, dumping ground, and domestic space. Fostering social reproduction for its patrons and attendants alike, the expansive layout offers a common place for bathing and bodily functions, child and self-care, clothes washing and drying, food preparation, rest, and relaxation. The entryway is strewn with plastic and metal drums, old sail masts, toilet seats, spare parts, washbasins, pots, and dishware. At once evocative of and entirely different from the "mirrors, seats, pegs, soap ledges and tinted walls" mentioned by Drew and Fry (1947) decades earlier, these objects—part discards, part common property—are put to use by a cross-section of customers and related others.

A step up in comfort, income, and privacy from the open courtyard, the attendant's alcove contains a mattress and a bed. There is also a battered wood-and-wire kiosk where the attendant collects user fees for toilet management and hands out the compulsory sheaf of newsprint or few rolled sheets of toilet paper in return. Near a pile of coins she uses to make change and the small kerosene lantern, various items are arranged for sale. There are clusters of bath and laundry soap as well as locally prepared douches in recycled bottles, all of which the attendant sells for her own profit. Offering infrastructural intimacies of their own, like Mang, nearly every public toilet in Manhean serves as a makeshift living quarters, peppered with telltale signs of temporary and long-term habitation—laundry, cookware, sleeping mats—for those who service the toilet and for a shifting corps of customers.

Similar to Ga fish-smoking and -processing operations (Field 1940; Overá 1993) established in open spaces between compounds and gaps between residences and roadsides that are evident elsewhere in Manhean, it is largely women who engage in these forms of urban placemaking. Not self-consciously political, like the "quiet encroachments of the poor" described by Asef Bayat (2013), yet born of practical entitlement, they are strategies of active occupation combining pursuit of livelihood with place-bound routines of habitation. For public toilet attendants the option of temporary residence within a toilet compound has its attractions. Though unofficial and unstated, residential possibilities add value to the low wages of toilet workers. These spaces also guarantee access to washing and bathing facilities. In addition, the fenced and gated toilet compounds provide privacy and security not always found in a crowded family houses or the wooden shanties and unauthorized extensions that have continued to pop up since the first makeshift zinc compounds were constructed in the course of resettlement (Butcher 1966; D'Auria 2014).

At one toilet, the female attendant, along with her husband, who works as the toilet cleaner, reside in small structure next to the kiosk where fees are collected. The attendant at another toilet lives in the office with her three children. Modifying the premises to fit her own needs, she erected a bamboo fence between her living space and the larger toilet structure. Further cultivating the comforts of home within this much-used space, she used her own funds to purchase alum powder to spray inside the drop holes to keep the stench down. Another kiosk on the toilet premises is used as a bedroom for a member of the management committee's relative. Making the most of the availability of water and open space, many toilet attendants raise fowl or cultivate small stands of flowers or vegetables on the toilet compound's perimeter. Opportunities for enterprise can be cultivated from this meager base. Attendants can sell their own array of wares, soap, cigarettes, chewing sticks, bath sponges, mentholated rubs, and more. At "No More Free Shitting" toilet, the middle-aged female attendant said when she permits someone to sell food, she gets a free meal in return.

As at Mang, attendants are joined by other sectors of Manhean's populace who use public toilets as a domestic base. Along with the homegrown footloose lacking secure access to family housing or sufficient funds to obtain reliable accommodations on their own (Ofei-Nkansah 2003), Manhean continues to attract migrant laborers who find their way to the settlement in pursuit of work at the port and in the nearby industrial zone, as they did at its founding. There are also migrant fishermen and women living out long-standing patterns of coastwise movement across the fishing grounds of the Western Atlantic (Odotei 2002) who make Manhean their temporary abode and who pass through public toilet premises.

The female portion of this diverse demographic is particularly visible. Across a number of toilet compounds, a recurring network of young women and children can be found throughout the day napping, cooking, washing clothes, storing their wares, and caring for young ones in the open-air and shaded corners of toilet premises. Weaving together persons and things in the conduct of intimate bodily practices in the public space of the toilet, these arrangements confound Arendt's assertions that bodily labors properly precede the public life. Instead, in Manhean's toilets, a loose public is formulated around the very pursuit of private bodily matters, confirming Agamben's (1998, 127) observation that bare life can provide the threshold of belonging even in the face of extreme deprivation.

With regard to the other side of the Arendtian coin, however, here we find a ready illustration of her observation (Arendt 1958, 55): "It is what we have in common not only with those who live with us, but also with those who were here before and those who come after us. Such a common world can survive the coming and going of a generation only to the extent it appears in public." In this manner, the settlement's excremental infrastructure forms a bridge, connecting past and present, private and public, individual and collective, material and practical. A closed commons of a sort melding inclusion and a modicum of stability, Manhean's toilets are a centripetal force, anchoring and interconnecting multiple functions conditional to the social production of life itself. Enlarging the public realm through the inclusion of the so-called labors of the private, these practices fill an existential frame sustained by a wider arena of public life. Again, upending Habermas's (1991) classic rendering of the public sphere in which social actors arrive as preformed private persons (Calhoun 1992, 9), in Manhean's case the private is underwritten by the public. These arrangements effectively invert the operating order of Jeremy Bentham's panopticon as discussed by Michel Foucault (1979). While the public infrastructure of the panopticon aggregates and regulates private spaces and behaviors by dint of state authority, in the case of Manhean's toilets, self-directed private behaviors rework what is possible in a public space, actively rebuffing state interference.

Res Publicae as Vital Remains

Manhean's toilet facilities are in sync with the character of public space in Manhean in general, contributing to their standing as vital infrastructural adaptations and political devices. Recalling architect Oko Adjetey's (1964, 70) childhood reminiscence of Old Tema, where "special attention was paid to open spaces, connected by narrow lanes which served as playgrounds and space for public meetings or social gatherings," Manhean's neighborhoods are dotted with sites used and designed by residents for all manner of public congregation toward the broad ends of social reproduction. As terrains of daily life, these claim an enduring presence across Manhean's urban landscape. Cutting across the spectrum of Arendt's (1958) three-part model of human collectivity, these installations combine the routines of bodily labor, the permanence of infrastructural work, and the open-ended possibilities of social action. By functionally enabling urban living, they anchor collective and individual existence in the present and over the long term. Similar to Manhean's toilets and often in tandem with them, such material formations qualify as res publicae—"public things"—for Manhean's residents, evoking shared concerns and joint recognition alongside their substantive utilities (see plate 16).

Among the most noticeable of Manhean's "public things" that toilets echo and with which they are conceptually and functionally intertwined are the trees, or *tsoshishi* in the Ga-Dagme language, growing in the sandy soil in front of nearly every large compound house, including those built by Tema's municipal authorities at Manhean's founding.[24] A squat species with large leaves and dense clusters of short braided branches, the *tsoshishi* trees' deep shade is a welcome refuge from the intense heat and light of the Atlantic's tropical shoreline. Inciting congregation, *tsoshishi* are the literal and figurative basis of public gathering. The *tso* invoke the archaic meaning of "thing" as both material object and topic of public assembly (Latour 2005a, 12, 22). As people gather round the *tsoshishi*, so do other things. It is common to find stools and plastic chairs nearby, or tables and seats built onto roots and trunk. Residents bury medicine near the tree roots or tie it inside neat packages to upper limbs to ward off bad spirits and consecrate the trees. Under and around *tsoshishi*, residents, neighbors, visitors, and family members congregate. Coming together to talk, catch the breeze, repair fishing nets, make decisions, and hold celebrations, they acknowledge the lore of their elders that "whatever transpires under the tree will flourish," as Manhean's chief fisherman explained.

Manhean residents, united by kinship, friendship, and convenience, carve out a third type of public space enabling survival and a sense of collective history and (im)possibility. Forming a middle ground between the base functionality of public toilet and spiritual charge of *tsoshishi*, open-air porticos colloquially referred to as "ghettos" can be found across Manhean's wards.[25] Built from tarps and scrap lumber and furnished with broad benches that do double duty as seats, tables, and sleeping areas, the trunks and canopy of the *tso* sometimes anchor these structures. With or without a tree at its core, the ghettos turn urban detritus—zinc sheeting, rotting boards, fishing nets, and plastic sheeting—into functional forms. Objects of pride despite their humble origin, the ghettos, like household rooms and yards, are swept daily and often brightly painted. Manhean's ghettos are akin to other urban infrastructures configured from remains, such as the discarded bread that signals a publicly sustained collectivity in Palestine, despite their perishable form (Stamatopoulou-Robbins 2019, 28). Although Manhean's ghettos are constructed from similar materials, they contrast with the infrastructural assemblies of South Africa's urban shacklands described by Kerry Ryan Chance (2018), which are barely able to sustain individual habitation, much less operate as a sustainable platform for broader sociality, as in Manhean. Though public space is used by men and women alike by dint of need and cultural convention, it is important to note that women play a leading role in claiming and assimilating it in Manhean. Women's expansive fish-processing operations, patching together neighborhood open space, is a paradigmatic case.

Taken together, Tema's intimate infrastructures underwrite a "decentralized domesticity." Utilized by residents on a daily or near daily basis, they are in-between spaces, like the settlement's public toilets, bridging work and leisure, public and private, permanence and transience, survival and cultural production. Some ghettos appear temporary, while others suggest a fuller form of habitation. Each is the combined locus of a broad array of activities: cooking, eating and drinking, resting, napping and sleeping, clothes washing and drying, conversation, singing and Bible study, checkers and card playing. The space, in the words of project research assistant Marina Ofei-Nkansah, functions all at once as "bedroom, living room, and conference room." In the res publicae of a largely dispossessed urban strata, it is not unusual to find fishmongers talking about business, teenagers eating and relaxing, laborers washing and drying clothes, and fishers storing gear within the space all at the same time.[26]

These practices, combining "dwelling" and "survival" as Bhaskar Mukhopadhyay (2006, 230) describes in urban India, materially and experientially manifest "non-state formation" through the lived "negotiation of the city form." Built on unoccupied or unclaimed land at the interstices of community space, most ghettos are a stone's throw from public toilets. In a context marked by exclusion from the official deliberative domains of the polity writ large, the occasions for self- and collective reflection and interconnection spawned by these vital infrastructures map out an appreciable if obscured political space for Manhean's underclass. They are yet another way the pursuit of substantive "rights to the city" (Lefebvre 1996), including the aforementioned "right(s) to shit," by means of vital infrastructure actualize an expansive political topos shaping and shaped by essential practices of day-to-day survival.

Conclusion: Deep Domesticity and Excremental Rights

What happens to urban politics when excrement is a public matter? Evidence from Manhean, the first built section of the new city, indicates that public sanitation facilities, despite their magnification of the degradations of bare life, can wrest a space for urban existence outside the grasp of political institutions and elites. Along with accommodating the ends of individual bodily relief for Manhean's residents, the result is a public realm enabling collective claims and entitlements both tacit and express.

The realities of Manhean's excremental evidence prove and disprove Laporte's (2002) contention, likewise asserted by Arendt (1958), that public shit confounds the presumed premises of state authority reliant on a sharp divide between private subjects and the public realm. On the one hand, affirming state aspirations, pace Agamben's (1998) discussions of the political crucible afforded by states of exception, making shit and shitting public in the resettlement zone was an intentional aim of state authority at Manhean's midcentury founding. Municipal and national authorities' assertion of the "right 'to' shit" was a core modality of urban governance in the aftermath of the upheavals of forced removal and resettlement. Public toilets offered a prime realm for those who set the rules of urban life to work out their relationship with Manhean residents, as the remarkable archive of this period attests (Amarteifio 1966). On the flip side, residents' pursuit of the right "to shit" has proven a key means of establishing mastery of the legitimate terms of urban membership in relation to urban authorities.

In the course of relocation, per Mark Purcell (2002), in this rendering of the "right to the city" (Lefebvre 1996), via public shit "participation" was uneasily wedded to "appropriation." Within a decade of residents' removal from Old Tema, this strategy of excremental rule, which required extensive investment and prolonged presence by government representatives, not to mention functioning sanitary infrastructure, was retired. The shift in excremental policy turned Manhean from a space of exception combining exceptional infrastructures and exceptional oversight into a zone of abandonment (Agamben 1998). Vital remnants of the early excremental regime remained in play to lasting effect. That is, once entangled, shit could never fully free itself from the taint of the state, or the state from shit. To this day, the midcentury infrastructural installations designed by Drew and Fry endure: the squat concrete structures aboveground and their murky underground counterparts are inescapable features of Manhean's urban fabric, perennially calling out for notice due to their base utility.

Across an extended era of administrative neglect, the trappings of bare life in Manhean filled a latent force field of political possibility. Anchoring a lingering recognition of collective needs and entitlements, Manhean's sanitary installations index the inherent fragility of the social contract for rulers and ruled alike. Eventually subject to popular reclamation in the 1980s and 1990s as the country moved from military rule to democratic dispensations, Manhean's toilets brought forth the possibilities of collective management amid wider processes of state consolidation. Compared to the ruins of the sewage pipes, pumps, and mains of Tema's core awaiting repair by the city's official overseers in response to the pleas of service-seeking subjects, even in this era of populist political transition Manhean's excremental installations were and continue to be better understood as vital remains: that is, crucial built forms surrendered but still intact. A sign of state power as well as state fragility, they are an example of state afterlives fallen outside of state grasp (see also Stamatopoulou-Robbins 2019, 110).

At the millennium's turn, localized networks of accountability closed ranks as the rise of neoliberal logics pushed city authorities to monetize their latent "right 'to' shit" via private franchise of public facilities. Manhean's working-class residents, already factionalized and ever skeptical of infrastructural provisioning as a proxy for participation, pushed back against the entreaties of political elites, party faithful, and assembly members, just as they had rejected the claims of traditional authorities. Using the cover of privatization to promote collective entitlements, public toilets in Manhean gained new standing as a legitimate inheritance of the populace.

The legacy of public shit in Manhean again contrasts with Tema proper, where the ongoing breakdown and repair of sanitary infrastructure fuel appeals to municipal authorities, affirming expectations of state oversight and individualized ideals of accountability and responsibility. In Tema's core, where middle-class residents' pride in household and neighborhood infrastructure is paired with disdain for their own bodily outputs, articulations of political standing outweighed expression of bare life, placing *bios* above *zoe* (Agamben 1998). In Manhean, the limits and betrayals of the social contract are laid bare, prompting residents to take what was falsely promised into their own hands (see also Chance 2018). This differs from the mystique of individual accountability remaining in Tema's core, which renders collective action and collective refusal more difficult to muster for middle-class residents.

In Manhean, to the contrary, the "right 'to' public shit" is a means of making lateral connections, turning the substantive ends of toilet management as an urban right to more expansive and enduring solidarities. Here we see a convergence of the forthright claims against municipal authority articulated by toilet managers and concession holders, who are primarily male, and the practice-based strategies of customers and attendants, who are primarily female—each "holding their ground" in different ways. Evident in the multipurpose networks of toilet operators, these arrangements bear a resemblance to the public toilet activism of Mumbai, labeled "deep democracy" by Appadurai (2002). Better understood as a form of "deep domesticity" in Manhean, excrement-driven urban mobilization in this corner of Tema exhibits little of the associational scaling-up evident in Mumbai. It is contained and sustained by the settlement's infrastructural network and the interests, identities, and social and political histories of public toilet customers and operators. Underwriting more forthright political claims, in Manhean's public facilities, the recursive performance of a wide array of ostensibly private tasks and reproductive activities takes what is provisionally possible in public space to enlarge what is socially permissible and thus defensible. A far cry from the excremental pedagogy pursued by Drew and Fry (1947) and resettlement authorities in their original designs and managerial strategies for Manhean, these practices extend the functionality of the public realm while heightening the ungovernability of public life.

Staged on the remains of the infrastructural outlays of the city's early planners, these arrangements are buoyed by other amalgams of bare life and political life that populate Manhean's public sphere. Like the settlement's public toilets, they combine organic and inorganic matters, growth, decay, and the constant replenishments of the cycles of the body and daily life. From the *tsoshishi* whose shade and talismans call for gathering, or the ghettos that organize multifunctional congregation, the infrastructural intimacies of public, community-based toilets in Manhean turn Arendt's (1958) labors of living into durable material forms. In the process, they encode lived claims to rights, resources, and recognition with far more permanence than the fleeting discursive articulations of the classic Habermasian (1991) public sphere. These strategies exemplify what Alexei Yurchak (2008, 210), working from Agamben (1998), calls "the politics of indistinction." They build on and subvert the boundary between the public and the private established by the state while compensating for its gaps and limitations. Although it would be naive to label these capacities "empowerment," for a sector of society whom governing authorities care not to see or hear, these sites of public excremental evacuation function as a fully "lived space" (Lefebvre 1991, 39; Purcell 2002, 102) permitting the staging of intimate forms of self-determination.

The case of Manhean presents a multifaceted transgression of the ideal-typical terms of the political, attesting to what Larkin (2008, 249–50) characterizes as the "unruliness of infrastructure," where original meanings, uses, and political intentions are harnessed anew to unearth embedded and unexpected possibilities. Manhean residents' pursuit of the "right(s) to shit" from within the uneven remains of earlier installations actualize a double political move, at once severing the state from its assumed infrastructural claims and suturing the infrastructural connections and capacities of a community already excluded. These infrastructural arrangements, largely unhinged from the state though nested in its shadowy remains, provide a glimpse of what contemporary forms of public assembly look like if the "dome" of the state is no longer the prime container of the political (Latour 2005a, 31). An amalgam of Arendt's (1958) tripartite analytic divide, infrastructural-cum-sociopolitical restructuring in this corner of Tema not only occurs through the combined durability and flexibility of Manhean's infrastructural castoffs. It is also intensified by the ongoingness and vitality of excremental labors and intimacies and the ever-multiplying right(s) to the shit that flows through and alongside them.

4. Ziginshore
Infrastructure and the Commonwealth of Waste

I come from a pure science background. I have a physics degree. I incorporate scientific ideas into toilets. Sometimes science is being done in laboratories. We have it here. We have it in real life. We are trying to solve problems on the ground whilst doing experiments.
—Mr. Enyimayew, Ziginshore toilet proprietor, 2014

Each object gathers around itself a different assembly of relevant parties. Each object triggers new occasions to differ and dispute. Each object may also offer new ways of achieving closure without having to agree on much else. In other words, objects—taken as so many issues—bind all of us in ways that map out a public space profoundly different from what is usually recognized under the label of "the political."
—Bruno Latour, "From Realpolitik to Dingpolitik" (2005)

The World is Corporeall ... and consequently, every part of the Universe, is body.
—Thomas Hobbes, *Leviathan* ([1651] 1994)

Urban Wastelands, Bodily Infrastructure, and Political Projects

Just north of Tema Manhean along the Chemu Lagoon lies a wetland turned dumping ground turned shantytown. It was once a common, more specifically, a soccer pitch, referred to as Ziginshore, the rallying cry of Senegal's popular football champions, and the name stuck. Appropriately enough, its namesake is a contested border zone on Senegal's Casamance River. Tema's Ziginshore is also of uncertain jurisdiction. I was told it was earlier called "Abonko," a corruption of *Abrewankɔ*, an Akan (Twi) term meaning "old ladies don't go there." The settlement does not appear on any official map of the city although it lies at the crossroads of all Tema stands for: fishing fleets, factories, a container port, and modern middle-class aspiration. Nestled between Tema's port and industrial area, a stone's throw from the fishing harbor, ice houses, container yards, and canneries, it is built on the sediments of human, environmental, and industrial waste (see plate 17).

The marginality of the landscape is matched by the marginality of Ziginshore's residents. This is a community built from a shifting cast of largely transient young men, women, and children who lack permanent housing, reliable jobs, or the most basic guarantees of social and biological reproduction. They use the spit of reclaimed land for shelter and respite between stints of work at the harbor and movement to and from Tema and home-towns elsewhere. Without any "privately owned place," it is a fundamentally public realm where even the most intimate functions can be "seen and heard by everyone" (Arendt 1958, 50, 52).

Ziginshore's fluid ecology, human and otherwise, places it beneath the radar of official state recognition and oversight. Though sewage flows from Tema's city center are channeled across, and at times into, the Chemu Lagoon at the settlement's edge, Ziginshore is entirely off the grid when it comes to state investments. No municipal services are provided or planned. A more opportunistic sovereign has come to fill the void, one who has turned infrastructure into political experiment. A native son home from abroad has devised a massive toilet and bath complex and adjoining excrement-based biogas plant for public use. Containing upward of thirty water closets in one location, wholly different from the squalid drop-pit government toilets otherwise available, the place is popularly referred to as Floshin Taifi, a combination of "flushing" in English and *taifi*, meaning toilet, in Akan (Twi) and Ga. Over the span of a few years, Ziginshore's array of linked sanitary infrastructures has transformed this otherwise unstable locale from a putative "state of nature" into a "waste-based commonwealth."

If the sanitary installations of Tema proper are provided by public authorities for private use, and those of Manhean are provided by public authorities for public use, Ziginshore is a case of a singular private provider catering to public need. The centerpiece of public life and the proprietor's empowerment, Ziginshore's excremental infrastructures form the base of inclusion, accountability, and security in a space of extreme marginalization. Begat from the undersides of the planned city's lofty promise, the toilet, bath, and biogas complex has spawned an array of subsidiary functions and structures: schoolroom, hostel, meeting place, communal kitchen, and more. These waste-based infrastructural experiments organize and make

Figure 4.1. Chemu Lagoon management plan, ca. 1965 (Doxiadis Associates Report for Government of Ghana, DOX-GHA A90, Tema Development Corporation Archives)

Figure 4.2. Chemu Lagoon, 2014 (Photo by Eliot Chalfin-Smith)

Figure 4.3. Floshin Taifi interior: toilets, 2014 (Photo by Eva Egensteiner)

Figure 4.4. Floshin Taifi interior: showers, 2014 (Photo by Eva Egensteiner)

public Hannah Arendt's (1958) "labors of living." Entraining bodies and inculcating compliance by force, affect, and built form, they doubly instantiate and suppress the body politic in this overlooked piece of Tema's grand scheme. Public but by no means full-blown polis, Ziginshore's homespun biogas plant and associated waste-based built environment rule over sovereign and subjects alike as the ever-productive forces of human and nonhuman natures caught within are turned into crude Leviathan.

Ziginshore and *Leviathan*

With its renewed relevance to the contemporary political stage, Thomas Hobbes's *Leviathan, or The Matter, Forme and Power of a Commonwealth Ecclesiasticall and Civil* ([1651] 1994) offers a suggestive theoretical axis for comprehending the excremental politics of Ziginshore. An analysis of the workings and genesis of Ziginshore's infrastructural complex ultimately demonstrates that infrastructures of the body, including bodily waste, are a formative means of political substantiation in contexts where state authority is absent, uneven, or under threat. A rereading of *Leviathan* through the lens of Ziginshore reveals the mediating role of infrastructure in this equation, while weaving together notions of bodily immanence and political transcendence of concern to Hobbes.

Though Tema, with its exquisitely ordered master plan inspired by Ghana's president, Kwame Nkrumah, was considered a machine for making Ghana's future, Ziginshore appears a site of political evacuation, devoid of order or formal government. When the city was initially mapped out, what is now Ziginshore was lagoon, a marshy floodplain, and before that, a river flowing to the sea. A veritable state of nature, the area gradually drained—"died," as those who once knew it describe it—as Chemu Lagoon was choked by runoff from the Tema oil refinery nearby, opening the area to thoroughfare and eventual habitation. Along with the flow of excrement from severed sewage lines (Watertech 1995), the Chemu's eroding banks were turned into a dumping ground for domestic and industrial waste. Muddy lanes with makeshift gutters stand in for navigable throughways. Wood scraps abound, along with plastic sheeting and other discards layered not far beneath the sand and soil, deliberately added to speed the process of reclamation. Waste of every sort flows through the lagoon, too, pulled toward the sea by the tides and pushed by the torrents of urban runoff that flood the once sacred waterway after rainfall. The trees that manage to survive at the lagoon's edge are also laid to waste, poly bags and plastics suspended in their sharp branches like queer nests.

Ziginshore's precarious ecology is matched by its jurisdictional ambiguity. A no-man's-land just a few square kilometers in size, it is claimed by none yet abutted by many. It is outside the recognized jurisdiction of Tema Harbor and the nearby residential area of Tema Manhean, as well as the naval base on the bluff beside it. Neither is it within the official ambit of Tema's municipal or traditional authorities. I am told that no one would say they are "from" this place. Lacking permanent jobs or housing, residents and transients find temporary abode and a semblance of routine between stints of work, hustle, and unemployment and underemployment at the port, harbor, and nearby markets. Most who stay or pass through the area make a living as porters, drivers, pushcart operators, petty traders, fishers, seamen, fishmongers, and fish smokers, working short-term and seasonal jobs in which the human body is the most efficient instrument (see plate 18).

The structures that mark Ziginshore's human settlement are likewise temporary, cobbled together from cardboard, crates, and recycled metal sheeting, and scaled to the rhythms and needs of the individual body. None of them authorized, the shelters are hastily and inexpensively devised to service the bare necessities of social reproduction. Small kiosks, known in Twi as *adakem,* or "boxes," built from plywood and discarded crates and shipping containers, are the primary housing stock and among the few assets available to residents. Others perch for a few hours at time in makeshift dormitories and video parlors ringed by black plastic tarps to block out the daylight. Any infrastructure of scale is for the most part an afterthought: a function of adjacency or repurposing. Power lines pass over the area to service users elsewhere, and the few water pipes that flow are diverted from the port.

Amid this landscape of impermanence and degradation looms a strikingly different amalgam of infrastructure and waste. It houses not the discharge and debris of industry and rubbish dump but the waste of bodily evacuation. This is Ziginshore's pay-per-use public toilet and bath complex. A place of multipurpose self-care, it contains thirty-two flush toilets (eight sitting and eight squatting-style in the separate male and female sections) along with male and female bathing areas, standpipes, and water taps, all serviced by electricity, television broadcasts, and a team of clerks, cleaners, and plumbers-in-residence. The complex is distinguished by its size, popularity, range and quality of service, provisions, and origin. With a footprint

Figure 4.5. Floshin Taifi standpipe and entryway, 2014 (Photo by Eva Egensteiner)

Figure 4.6. Floshin Taifi veranda, 2014 (Photo by Eva Egensteiner)

of five thousand square feet and built from neatly laid and sealed concrete block, the toilet and bath facility stand apart from the surrounding structures. It is the only public place of convenience of decent size or standard in the whole settlement. The pitched roof, covered with yards of zinc sheets and, more recently, solar panels, and the surrounding giant water tanks make it easy to locate from afar. Differing in scale, condition, and materials, the infrastructural arrangements of the Floshin Taifi toilet complex reflects an order and intentionality little evident elsewhere in the area (see plate 19).

Accommodating upward of two thousand customers a day and open around the clock, the toilet complex is Ziginshore's central space of congregation and shared orientation. Residents and passersby use the facilities on a daily basis: at least once to draw water, another to bathe, and another to defecate. A regular patron explained in Twi, *"enbɔn koraa"* (there is no bad odor here). The facility is cleaned and disinfected several times a day. It is monitored inside and out as excreta move from individual water closets into a dedicated multichamber septic system installed belowground. In its entirety the complex offers a space of shelter, socializing, and security. Toilet staffers reside in a bank of rooms attached to the toilet and bath area. Benches on the toilet's veranda near the attendant's office and storeroom are popular spots to relax and chat. Children play and nap. The attendant on the day shift does her cooking on a coal pot here, as does the plumber's wife. Vendors hawk water sachets and snacks. During the early years of its existence, at night people would routinely sleep on the veranda and the open space surrounding the facility (see plate 20).

Ziginshore's toilet combines the intimately embodied and the collective. Despite its purpose of personal relief and self-care, the toilet complex is a defining feature of public life in Tema's wastelands. The facility provides a ready illustration of Filip De Boeck's (2012) observation that "infrastructure is a means to reflect upon the changing connotations of what constitutes the public sphere and the meanings of the categories of public and private." This insight resonates with Arendt's (1958, 52) characterization of the public realm as both a built and a shared space: "The term public signifies the world itself . . . not identical with the earth or with nature . . . rather, to the human artifact, the fabrication of human hands, as well as the affairs which go on among those who inhabit the man-made world together. To live together in the world means essentially that a world of things is between those who have it in common, as a table is located between those who sit around it, like every in-between, relates and separates men at the same time."

Drawing out this parallel, an Akan proverb states, "If we can eat together, we can shit together" (*Wo nkoa didi a, wo nkoa ne*, literally, "If you eat alone, you shit alone") (van der Geest 1998). Sharing these acts connotes sociality along with social parity. There is no shame in using the public toilet. With private compartments and clean upgraded facilities, it presents an opportunity for social betterment, setting one apart from those who defecate in the open. In this formulation, even if used for private purposes, Ziginshore's large-scale sanitary infrastructure is a technology of public life "assembling" human associations and instituting through its built form a "composite social body," to borrow from Bruno Latour's "thing-politics" (2005a, 15–16).

Rather than waste a vector of social retreat, waste and its infrastructures are an impetus for gathering, spawning other vectors of work and habitation. Once the toilet was established, a colony of fish smokers constructed brick ovens and work sheds in the lowlands between the toilet and lagoon using the dirt and rubble left over from excavation. A symbiotic relationship, they use the water, bath, and toilet facilities. Adjacent to the toilet, the shade provided by the thousand-liter water tank is its own site of congregation. One woman operates a hair salon in the cool space under the tank. At the toilet's perimeter, in the shadow of a shipping container that once held construction materials, another woman has a table with medicines for purchase and *bentuwa* (enemas) for rent.

In an area nearly entirely lacking municipal support and recognition due to a wider rollback of state services and a localized history of neglect, the toilet is one of the few things in this marginalized urban zone that approximates a public good (Samuelson 1954). Serving a vital human need while costing only the small fee of five to ten cents per use (depending on choice of newspaper or toilet roll), and free for children and the elderly, the public toilet is virtually nonexcluding—a classic feature of public goods. As it is large enough to accommodate many users at once with little or no waiting time, the toilet is also nonrivalrous—the other core characteristic of a public good (Ostrom and Ostrom 1978) (see plates 21 and 22).

Hierarchical in organization, Ziginshore's Floshin Taifi toilet facility is difficult to fully classify as a "commons" in the sense advocated by Michael Hardt and Antonio Negri (2009) in their postcapitalist reenvisioning of the multitude and the commonwealth. Though it is situated within a municipality earlier marked by the heavy hand of governmental planning, neither is it the purview of municipal or national authorities. To the contrary,

ZIGINSHORE MODEL

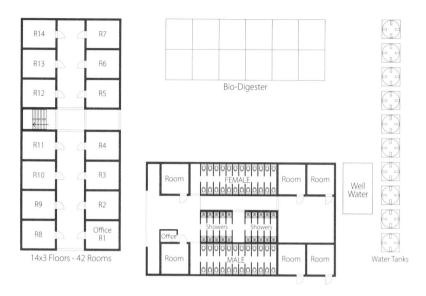

Figure 4.7. Diagram of Ziginshore's Floshin Taifi and surrounding infrastructure complex (Created by Kairon Aiken)

Ziginshore's sprawling public toilet facility is a wholly private enterprise. It was conceived and built and is managed by a single individual, Kwame Enyimayew, known by his employees as "Director" and referred to as "Uncle," a term expressing fondness and respect in Ghana, by those who use or reside near his facility. Most common, Enyimayew tells me, is the appellation "Uncle Director," which combines deference, familiarity, and recognition of his de facto leadership status. For ease of reference, I call him "Uncle" throughout.

Uncle is a master of "do-it-yourself" public works provisioning. By filling the gap opened by state contraction and growing public need (cf. Blundo and Le Meur 2009), he has become a highly successful entrepreneur of waste. The Ziginshore facility is the largest of three public toilets he operates in the Tema area. Uncle also owns a fleet of sewage disposal trucks used to service his own facilities and available for hire to empty municipal and household septic systems. He installed the underground drains, wells, and holding tanks that make up Ziginshore's septic system. Uncle is both held in disdain and relied on by city authorities for his penchant for clearing and reconnecting manholes and sewage lines abandoned by municipal waste management.

With a facility in the no-man's-land around the lagoon in mind, Uncle appealed to the Tema *mantse* and Traditional Council for permission to build. Their own claim on the wetlands being uncertain, the *mantse* could do little more than give tacit approval after successive visits and conversations.[1] Part pioneer, part colonist, Uncle was essentially deputized to go it alone, free to stake his claim on Tema's wastelands. Igor Kopytoff (1987) describes the internal political frontiers of rural Africa, where, spurred by domestic fission and weak political control, new settlements and political units appear. Uncle's exploits reveal what can be called an "internal urban frontier" enabled by novel forms of political evacuation and alliance staged across a veritable tabula rasa of formal governmental rule.[2] The fine-tuned infrastructural arrangements forged by Uncle and *citadins* of Tema's in-between "mark out a political space outside of the fragile margins of metropolitan civility" (Mukhopadhyay 2006, 230) yet carry their own codes of conduct, both intimate and public, novel and contained. In this uncharted middle ground attuned to profit and sustainability, Uncle's facility merges centralized planning strategies from the new city's founding with Ga practices of cultivating public space for collective ends, as evident in women's fish processing and the "ghettos" of nearby Manhean. Indeed, also exploiting this "internal frontier," as Uncle's complex has expanded so have women's fish-smoking activities surrounding it.

Conceptualizing the Commonwealth of Waste

A number of analytic riddles arise at this crossroads of waste, bodily infrastructure, and political ambition. One addresses the kinds of infrastructure that emerge in conditions of state absence. In what ways might the infrastructures—and attendant infrastructural intimacies—of Tema's wastelands, focused on the bodily processes of a diffuse body politic, bring to the surface modalities of political authority hidden in more established political systems? As discussed in earlier chapters, an array of social historians, for instance, remark on the privatization of bodily functions as a hallmark of modern state formation (Foucault 1979; Laporte 2002). By contrast, in Ziginshore, these common yet individuated processes are brought into the open and contained within a centralized apparatus with no effective state in site. Given Ziginshore's distance from the formal reciprocities and recognitions of state-based rule, could the infrastructural inchoate of the public toilet complex provide an alternative ground for political order—a space for "politics otherwise"—via its expansive domesticity?

These queries in turn beg the critical question of political projects where infrastructures and outputs of the body are at the fore. Namely, how do the nonhuman yet animate forces of bodily waste figure into the process? To unpack these concerns, I take a cue from science and technology studies (STS) (Callon and Latour 1981; Latour 1993, 2005a; Shapin and Schaffer 1985) and turn to the first principles of early modern political philosophy. Addressing the production of political community and civility via sovereign social contract, Hobbes's *Leviathan* ([1651] 1994) is central to this conversation. Along with my STS interlocutors, I read Hobbes to reevaluate the potentials of his political analysis. What resonances and impasses, I ask, are elicited if Hobbesian philosophy is ethnographically tested against the radically different social field of Ziginshore's toilet infrastructure?

A reconsideration of Hobbes's *Leviathan* is important to this endeavor for numerous reasons. First, the status of Tema's wastelands as a veritable "state of nature" suggests the fundamental relevance of a Hobbesian point of view. Beyond that, Hobbes ([1651] 1994, 134) harbors empiricist sympathies well in sync with anthropology. He states, "The varieties of Bodies Politique is almost infinite ... distinguished by their severall affaires, for which they are constituted, wherein there is an unspeakable diversity; but also the times, places, and numbers (134)."[3] Hobbes's theorizations of political order can likewise be turned to consideration of human assembly across multiple temporal and spatial scales. As Michel Callon and Latour (1981, 277, 295) assert, the emergence and reproduction of a body politic as conceived by Hobbes depends on "durable associations" of things across time and space. Urban infrastructure surely falls under this rubric. Moreover, aligned with the growing interest in the perceptual dimensions of infrastructure (Larkin 2013, 336), Hobbes's attention to sensory experience renders his work useful for investigating infrastructures in which bodies are prime. Arguing, "The World is Corporeall ... and consequently, every part of the Universe, is body" (Hobbes [1651] 1994, 412–13), Hobbes was a strong proponent of "plenism" (Malcolm 2002, 191), a philosophical stance asserting that the "universe is filled with different kinds of material bodies" (Leijenhorst 2002, 127). Hobbes's plenism was driven by a horror vacui both physical and political.[4] This body-centered sensibility is graphically captured in the famous frontispiece of *Leviathan*, in which the looming torso of the great sea monster is made up by a mass of densely packed human figures (Bredekamp 2007, 38; Martinich 2002, 201).

Similarly built around a multitude of bodies, Uncle's giant public privy enables the activation of what Hobbes considers the most basic laws of human nature ([1651] 1994, 28). Geared to securing the fundamental bodily requirements of survival and self-preservation, these include "the right(s) to shit" explored in the preceding chapter on Manhean. Hobbes (26) states, "Of appetites and aversions, some are born with men; as appetite of food, appetite of excretion, and exoneration (which may also and more properly be called Aversions, from some? what they feele in their Bodies), and some other Appetites, not many." Further consonant with Hobbes's characterizations, those who patronize Ziginshore's facilities "impose restraint upon themselves in the foresight of their own preservation" (97), a necessity, in Hobbes's view, since "to claim this right for oneself is to permit the same right to others" (74). A sentiment holding much in common with Arendt's (1958) view of plurality as a relationship of "equality and distinction," these formulations suggest it is possible to construe Ziginshore's toilet complex to tangibly express a Hobbesian contract built around human waste. One cannot discount its fundamentally nonegalitarian nature, however. Ziginshore's arrangements are both more hierarchical and more inclusive than any of the other excremental infrastructures devised by Tema residents.

Despite its popular appeal, Ziginshore is not exactly a site of politics from below. The nascent political community of the Hobbesian social compact is always more than the sum of its parts. As the celebrated frontispiece of *Leviathan* makes clear, with the looming body of the sovereign filled with the tiny bodies of his subjects, the contract must endow, or be endowed within, an overseer: "There be somewhat else required (besides covenant) to make their agreement constant and lasting, which is a common power, to keep them in awe, and to direct their actions to the common benefit. This done, the multitude so united in one person is called a Commonwealth. This is the generation of the great Leviathan . . . that mortal god under the immortal god to which we owe our peace and defense" (Hobbes [1651] 1994, 99–100).

Would Uncle not occupy this place? After all, his vision of Ziginshore's urban renewal was never about toilets, septic tanker trunks, or sewage systems alone. From the start, his infrastructural investments involved the cultivation of a loose-knit political community via calculated principles and controls. When we first met, he explained with a near missionary zeal that he saw public toilet facilities as a way to bring people together and improve

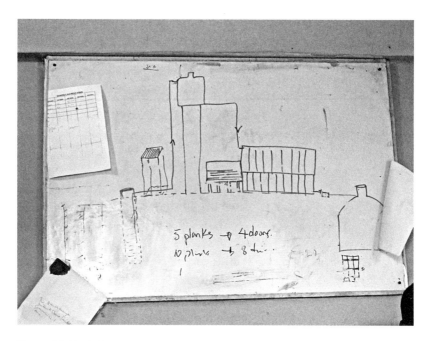

Figure 4.8. Uncle Director's proposal for self-contained waste and water infrastructure, 2014 (Photo by Brenda Chalfin)

their quality of life. In a later interview he asserted, "My role is to make people not feel deprived. The toilets make them feel they can achieve a certain level in life: a good level of hygiene and a good level of education for children. My toilets allow people to feel good about the communities they live in."

When his employees suggested building a fence around the structure, he emphatically refused. He shared with me instead his plan to build a library and community center on the lot, what he called "toilet schools." Worked out by infrastructural means, Uncle's strategies of oversight included the installation of closed-circuit television in public areas of the facility. Although the cameras were rarely activated or operable, Uncle made clear his intent to monitor his property and those who passed through it. He also installed several large televisions. Making broadcasts available to his customers, Uncle explicitly conveyed to me that this was not simply about providing entertainment but was a purposeful effort to instill civility by changing attitudes toward public toilets and associating them with prestige, pleasure, and proper behavior. Uncle recounted, "Everybody likes a good toilet, just like everyone likes good food. The only problem is not everyone can have access. We used to be embarrassed. We had no place to go decently. The provision of public toilets in this place gives us a new status. Customers come to me and say thank you and shake my hand."

To borrow Hobbes's ([1651] 1994, 120) language, Uncle sought to harness the social covenants surrounding Ziginshore's public infrastructures of waste to establish dominion (a term meaning "authority or possession over") in which he stood at the ultimate, sovereign helm. Although Uncle had not studied Hobbes, these are strategies he clearly grasps. Rather than an abstract illustration of political norms, he sought to actualize these strategies by demonstration.[5] As A. P. Martinich, a leading Hobbes scholar, writes, "Hobbes was an uncompromising materialist, mechanist and determinist. As a materialist he believed that the only thing that existed was matter. As a mechanist, he believed that all causes operated by one object coming into contact with another object. As a determinist, he believed that every event has a moving cause that determines the effect" (2005, 24).

Though the scale and scope of Ziginshore's Floshin Taifi was unprecedented, Uncle's use of sanitary installations as a key means of sociopolitical engagement was built on a hygienic history shared across the postcolonial tropics (Anderson 2006). The roots of Uncle's infrastructure-based political aspirations can be traced to his status as a first citizen of the new city of Tema, a place where infrastructure and urban planning reigned as the operative mode of societal transformation. Uncle's ancestors hailed from the original fishing village of Tema, forcibly razed in the late 1950s to make room for the new city and port. The residents (including Uncle's forebears) were resettled several miles away in Manhean.

In a prophetic tale, Uncle told me that he was the first child born in the new settlement when his pregnant mother left her husband's house to give birth among her natal family. While the compound-style houses of Old Tema were loosely replicated in Manhean, the standards of hygiene were wholly new. Uncle recalled the communal flush toilets and piped-water washhouses, replete with sparkling porcelain water closets and a central sewage system connected to the new city and harbor. Historical accounts note the active role of social service staff in managing the Manhean facilities, including instructing residents on their proper use (Amarteifio 1966). Uncle spent his early childhood moving between his grandmother's home and his father's house in an individually plumbed apartment block of the new city of Tema, in a neighborhood known as Kaiser Flats, named after the aluminum company involved in the Volta River Project. His interest in hygiene and sanitation was rekindled when he later moved with his elder brother, a doctor, to the staff quarters of a regional hospital.

By the early 1980s, in the heyday of the country's revolutionary populist struggle, Uncle left Tema to attend one of Ghana's prestigious public universities, where he earned degrees in physics and education. He was exposed to a different sort of idealism than that of the independence era. As mentioned in the preceding chapter on Tema Manhean, under J. J. Rawlings's Provisional National Defense Council (PNDC) regime, self-help and local defense committees became commonplace (Nugent 1995). Since few jobs were available at home during this period of economic decline, Uncle relocated to the United Kingdom on graduation. There, he established a family and pursued a career, first as a science teacher, and later as a London police officer, all under the expanding arc of conservative Thatcherist-state rollback. Radiating out from its North Atlantic epicenter, this policy marked a worldwide shift in the premises of modern government. Abandoning the postwar Keynesian welfare model in favor of a new neoliberal norm radically cutting state supports in favor of free enterprise (Harvey 2005), this policy's global spread would eventually bring Uncle back to Tema.

With Ghana's economy on the upswing in the face of a massive World Bank and International Monetary Fund finance scheme and privatization drive (Chalfin 2004, 2010), Uncle returned home in the late 1990s ready to invest. A few years later, he initiated plans for Floshin Taifi in Ziginshore. Illustrating the deep historical underpinnings of infrastructural systems (Larkin 2013, 331) and the ability to build connections across them in a manner at once new and anachronistic, Uncle's scheme for Ziginshore reveals the channeling of two political paradigms. On the one hand, radically rescaling the communal toilet blocks of Manhean, we see the remnants of the late-colonial state's infrastructurally hyperactive high modernity (332; Scott 1998). Reflecting the neoliberal moment, on the other, we see state supervision and service provision moving into private hands, motivated by economic and moral investment in the entrainment of individual bodies (Rabinow and Rose 2006). Ziginshore's public toilet facility lies at the juncture of these dual infrastructure-based political logics.

Infrastructure as Political Experiment

The resonance between Uncle Director's occupational background in physics and policing and his penchant for social and material engineering in Ziginshore should not be overlooked. Scholars note the mechanistic suppositions behind Hobbes's formulations, which assume human rationality to be much like "material objects in terms of pushes and pulls" (Minogue 1994, xviii–xix). Science historians Steven Shapin and Simon Schaffer (1985) describe the fierce controversy over the relation between science and politics that unfolded in the seventeenth century between Hobbes and the experimental chemist Robert Boyle. On this point, Uncle holds a firm grasp of the experimental nature of all political projects that is more in line with Boyle than with Hobbes. He explained, "I come from a pure science background. I have a physics degree. I incorporate scientific ideas into toilets. Sometimes science is being done in laboratories. We have it here. We have it in real life. We are trying to solve problems on the ground whilst doing experiments."

Indeed, Uncle's political experimentation, like Boyle's exploits in the lab, was contingent on the unpredictability of the infrastructural apparatus on which it relied (Latour 1993, 21). Aligning techno-material and social orders, Uncle's project, again similar to Boyle's, required public assent to succeed (Shapin and Schaffer 1985, 79). However, compared to Boyle's exclusive club of scientific witnesses (113), the popular character of Uncle Director's infrastructural realm complicated consent anew. Because Uncle's infrastructural assembly was publicly validated in a way Boyle's private experiments were not, their open-endedness generated a marked sense of social indeterminacy.

The experimental character of Uncle's infrastructural efforts was apparent as he pushed his project to new social and material ends. A year after I first visited Ziginshore, there was a multistory brick building under construction in the lot adjacent to Floshin Taifi. Uncle, alerted to the need for accommodations by the growing number of people who would congregate around the toilet compound at night to sleep, designed the ground floor with dormitory-style rooms. He planned to rent them to the area's transients at the nominal fee of one cedi (about forty cents) per bed per day. Once complete, the rooms held eight wooden bunks with vinyl-covered mattresses. There were tile floors, ceiling fans, and electric lights. The second story was to be a cafeteria serving inexpensive meals to his tenants. The third floor, yet unfinished, where Uncle often tethered his goats, was to be the classroom for the children who flocked around the toilet (see plate 23).

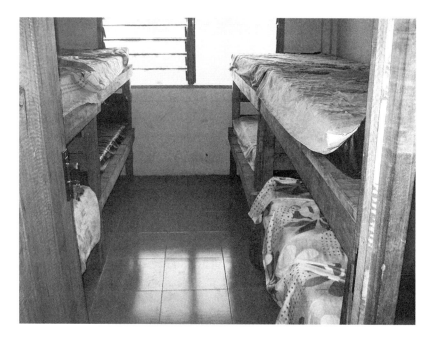

Figure 4.9. Hostel interior, 2012 (Photo by Brenda Chalfin)

Providing a slow-motion snapshot of the unfolding of Hobbesian dominion, this was a political structuration in formation, not yet, not quite, sovereign.[6] Although the building was still under construction, it could easily
accommodate one hundred people each night. While Uncle had expected
the hostel to host mostly male clientele, women, along with their children,
turned out to be the primary occupants. The numerous fish-smoking operations that had gradually filled the space between toilet and road leading to
the fishing harbor also had shelters of their own. These operated around the
clock, and women used them to rest and store belongings. Similar to fish
processing in nearby Manhean, operations in Ziginshore were scaled up in
size, labor supply, and output. Floshin Taifi's hostel offered more space and
privacy than the open-air processing sites and—for better or worse—did
not obligate residents to a single job or employer. Residents were required,
however, to acknowledge Uncle's expectations of domestic order.

Some paid the expected fee; others avoided payment, their presence noticed yet unchecked by Uncle and his staff. Most were in their twenties and
thirties and were brought to the area by friends or relatives in the fish trade
who needed assistance close at hand. One resident, Mary, explained, "My

sister who plaits hair at the water tanks brought me. I would come here to have my bath and leave my child with my sister and go sleep at the harbor. I heard you could pay 1GH and sleep, so I moved." Many, like Mary, shared ties to fishing communities along Ghana's eastern and western coastline. Some came from Ghana's economically depressed northern savannah. Others came from elsewhere in Tema seeking distance from their mates and extended family. One of these was Efi, who had been there for two years with her five children after a dispute with her husband. Men were certainly around too. Efua met her husband when he was staying in the ground-floor bunkrooms. They have a child together and private time when his roommates are out.

Initially most of the female residents planned to return home or find more appealing residential options. However, many end up staying for months if not years, leaving for a time to attend festivals, funerals, or markets, or to participate in planting and fishing seasons but then returning. On a most basic level people remained at the hostel because it provided a safe place to sleep, expressing a Hobbesian ([1651] 1994, 74) surrender of independence in return for the preservation of physical well-being. Although there was no permanent security force, two of the long-term male residents served as nighttime guards. Women spoke assuredly of not considering themselves or their children at risk of physical harm. Even Uncle Director himself, in pursuit of personal security after he had been robbed at gunpoint in his suburban home, decamped to a hostel room for a solid month before he returned to his house, and continued to spend a few nights a week there.

Sex is an obvious subtext. With no formal jurisdiction and a transient population, Ziginshore had a reputation for prostitution. The infamous Three Monkeys bar relocated from central Accra after being shut down by the authorities. The original block of bedrooms at the back of the toilet complex were sometimes rented "by the hour" until Uncle decided to use them to house the growing ranks of toilet employees. Uncle and his wife, who resides in the hostel, have three children together. She is left in charge when he is absent and managed the hostel restaurant until her third child was born.

These considerations come at the cost of tolerance for the discomforts of the hostel accommodations. Women complained about the rain and flies that swept through the unscreened second-floor windows, the goats that sometimes got into their food or knocked clothes off the line, and the ongoing construction. Even so, for many, life in and around Uncle's toilet complex guaranteed fundamental "liberties" ([1651] Hobbes 1994, 125). Worked out through a palimpsest of built and assembled forms, these possibilities were mediated by the infrastructural means put to use by Uncle. Twenty-year-old Gifty, who gave birth to her son in the second-story rooms furnished with simple wooden bed frames and a few crates, waxed poetic: "Nobody controls me here. I am not afraid of sleeping up there. At times you give a helping hand with some work. I love this facility more than where I sleep at my husband's place" (see plate 24).

With the bare-bones infrastructure of the hostel providing a foundation for self-determination as well as interdependence, Ata, a fishmonger, described a similar sentiment of individual and collective freedom that came with residence: "I like this place. This bed belongs to another woman. A friend sleeps here on the floor and I sleep next to her on a mat. I have my peace of mind here." Jojo, a pregnant hairdresser, seconded this: "You can use my bucket. You can use my pan. You can sleep on my bed. This is not my bed but I am sleeping on it. If the place is dirty, I sweep." Mary reiterated the necessity of infrastructural improvisation: "There is no bed where I sleep. The beds have been shared among residents already. If you have a mat, there is room for you." With attachments to people and place vital but unstable, evoking Arendt's proverbial table, rather than a gathering in, this was a gathering around, constantly reconfigured, as people came, went, and returned.

Resonating with Hobbes's ([1651] 1994, 73, 104) "rules of propriety," "whereby every man may know what goods he may enjoy," the women explained that along with personal safety, they sought a safe place to store their belongings. Most were careful not to leave money around, though personal effects were left in the unlocked rooms. They sometimes argued over small items but sought to avoid conflict, since Uncle made it clear he didn't like quarrels. They guarded some objects while sharing others, such as cooking implements. Suggesting that infrastructures can be scaled down as well as scaled up, the women crafted their own additions and partitions to Uncle's ready-made infrastructural environment. Elaborate arrangements of crates, beds and mosquito nets, buckets, bricks, and clotheslines took form in the second-story rooms to claim space, secure possessions, and nestle resting and restless children.

Signaling an internalization of the infrastructural properties of Uncle's grand experiment for autonomous ends, it was not unusual for residents to provide safekeeping for other people's possessions. Silver pans essential for work in the fish business could be found in tall stacks throughout the sleeping quarters as women stored those of friends who resided elsewhere. Extending women's own influence "by association" (Callon and Latour 1981, 292), such

Figure 4.10. Makeshift shelter established from excess construction materials on the roof of the Floshin Taifi hostel, 2014 (Photo by Eliot Chalfin-Smith)

infrastructural rearrangements both sidelined and affirmed the capacities of Uncle's realm. Akin to the new form of witness initiated by the chemist Boyle, this incited a sort of "regress of replication" (Shapin and Schaffer 1985, 226), repeating the master's work for private purposes (Latour 1993, 22).

With Uncle's unfinished housing scheme setting off what might be described as an "infrastructural chain reaction," the teenage boys and young men who squatted on the hostel's unroofed third story pursued infrastructural experiments of their own. Away from their mothers, sisters, and younger siblings on the second floor, and not obliged to pay like the men living in the fully serviced ground-floor bunkrooms, they constructed their own roofed shelters. At once reiterating the infrastructural logics of Uncle's rule while refuting any claims to his absolute authority, these were miniature versions of the larger edifice. They were crafted from bamboo posts earlier used in the hostel construction, plastic sheeting purloined from neighboring fish smokers, and foam packing, among other pickings from Ziginshore's detritus.[7]

In these exchanges we see how, in the words of AbdouMaliq Simone (2015, 375–76), "infrastructure exerts a force—not simply in the materials and energies it avails, but also the way it attracts people, draws them in, co-alesces and expends their capacities. . . . People work on things to work on each other, as these things work on them." Like the force of Boyle's scientific facts open to affirmation as well as adjustment via experiment (Shapin and Schaffer 1985), we are reminded how the insistence and intrigue of infrastructure lies in its fixity but also in its malleability.[8] The politics of this process, however, occurs not via the dramatic forms of visualization and testimony invented by Boyle but through much quieter materializations about self, sociality, and space that mark infrastructural intimacy. As Latour (2005a, 6) puts it, "Each object gathers around itself a different assembly of relevant parties. Each object triggers new occasions to differ and dispute. Each object may also offer new ways of achieving closure without having to agree on much else. In other words, objects—taken as so many issues—bind all of us in ways that map out a public space profoundly different from what is usually recognized under the label of 'the political.'" In the case of Ziginshore, residents' infrastructural adjustments were much more about creating a private place of security and self-determination within the common space of Uncle's sprawling infrastructural complex.

Living Bodies as the Matter and Form of *Leviathan*

In addition to Uncle's infrastructure doing its own "silent" work of assembly motivated by the needs and desires of residents, his political program operated through more direct means. Hobbes ([1651] 1994, 100) draws a distinction between two forms of social compact. "Commonwealth by institution," to which the infrastructural "adhesions" above conform, involves voluntary surrender to sovereign authority. "Commonwealth by acquisition" involves the imposition of sovereign authority: either "despotical" (by force) or "paternalistic" (via affective obligation). As Uncle's complex grew, the latter modality gained traction. Like the more voluntaristic covenants surrounding the Floshin Taifi, it too was bound up with infrastructure and the body. It entailed both entraining bodies via infrastructure, and conforming infrastructure to bodily logics and substances, mobilizing anew the classic patrimonial political strategy of accruing "wealth in people" (Pitcher, Moran, and Johnston 2009), a phenomenon pronounced in West Africa's rural frontier zones (Nyerges 1992).

It did not take Uncle long to realize that many of the women, who rose well before dawn to prepare for trade, travel, or work at the fishing har-

Figure 4.11. Children and infrastructure, 2014 (Photo by Eva Egensteiner)

bor, regularly left their children behind at the hostel. The enclosed quarters and the constant movement and congregation of people around the facilities made this a viable option. One woman went so far as to state that her coresidents would be insulted if she failed to leave her offspring with them when she was out. This put the children at the heart of Uncle's infrastructure-based political project. Although Uncle left it up to the children's guardians to enroll them in school, which many did, the children could also be schooled and properly socialized under his guidance. Because the classrooms on the hostel's top story were yet to be completed, the multipurpose space of the toilet veranda served as Ziginshore's learning center. Uncle covered the walls with posters of the alphabet and would take the time to drill the kids en masse. Sums and simple words and pictures were chalked on the still-unpainted walls of the hostel.

Uncle organized parties for the children. He purchased balls and balloons and distributed food and drinks for the kids while they watched television and danced to the sound system on the veranda. Taking advantage of the flexibility afforded by the unfinished hostel structure, and mirroring the residents' own infrastructural improvisations, Uncle had the wooden bed frames arranged in the open space between the toilet and the living quarters. Surrounded by benches and plastic chairs, they were used as party tables for the children. Retooling his own infrastructural agenda to accommodate his clientele and deepen his hold on an ever-dynamic space and population, Uncle fully invested himself in these efforts. While these children's hours, free meals, and learning sessions can easily be seen as a benefit of residence in Uncle's domain, they indicate a relinquishing of parental control in favor of the aspirations of this microsovereign. Transferring to Uncle in return for security what Carole Pateman (1989) in her feminist reading of Hobbes sees as the first-order social contract between mother and child, not entirely different from Doxiadis's (1968) equation of shelter with the mother-and-child bond, in these exchanges Ziginshore's child residents are made diminutive political subjects.

With many of the younger children defecating at the lagoon's edge despite the option to use the toilet for free, they were not necessarily fully compliant, but they were nonetheless actively enrolled in Uncle Director's project of infrastructure-based social reform. Adolescent Elijah recalled carrying mortar when the hostel was built a few years earlier. It was common to see much younger children carrying gravel in head pans near the construction site, either working or playing at imitating workers. Nearly every day when Uncle's water truck arrived, children flocked to assist, connecting hoses to spigots, filling jugs from wells, and hanging on the vehicle with delight. Infrastructure worked through the children's bodies, at once extracting labor and triggering affect, what Brian Larkin (2013, 336) calls "aesthesis." Indicating the varied ways infrastructure is distributed across bodies, in this scenario children become "durable forms"—to borrow from and upend the ideas of Callon and Latour (1981, 284)—through which infrastructure and the political projects that drive it are reproduced. Both durable and active, these infrastructural intimacies take on a momentum of their own, offering one way the "micropolitics of infrastructure ... multiply future possibilities" (Jensen 2019, 105).

Here we circle back to the heart of Ziginshore's infrastructural body politics. Callon and Latour (1981, 283), speaking to the subtitle of Hobbes's text *Leviathan, or The Matter, Form, and Power of a Commonwealth Ecclesiasticall and Civil*, argue, "When living bodies are the form and matter of Leviathan, there is no Leviathan." Associations of bodies are fleeting, they assert: "In order to stabilize society everyone need[s] to bring into play associations that last longer than the interactions that formed them ... replacing unsettled alliances with walls and social contracts" (283). Uncle's pursuit of infrastructural dominion by means of the body involved not just embracing the offspring of those who resided in and around the toilet complex but building his authority on their very bodily output, marking a further impasse—but also a potential meeting ground—between Uncle and Hobbes's modern critics.

Despite the still-unfinished state of the hostel, Uncle confided his intention to build a large-scale biodigester in the lot behind Floshin Taifi. Fully aware of the energetic potential of vital remains, his idea to convert the toilet's accumulated fecal matter into the readily usable form of methane gas channeled one infrastructural project into another. Playing on what Latour (1993, 31) calls the two guarantees of modern political order claimed by both Hobbes and Boyle, these were bodily substances at once "immanent and transcendent."

Deposited within a spherical brick-lined underground anaerobic chamber designed to speed up the natural process of biodegrading organic waste, excreta's transformation from base substance to multivalent power source depended on Uncle's orchestration of artisanal engineers, moonlighting masons, and off-duty biochemists. My notes from a visit to the construction site read,

> Uncle's biodigester is underway. It is a single tank, not the double version he showed me in the drawing. A few hiccups: the backhoe was only able to get down about ten feet because of the soft soil collapsing around the edges. Then the crater cut through several water pipes that are now leaking into the pit. The tank is about halfway finished. It is built from red-clay bricks mortared with cement then sealed in and out. The foundation has a steel armature. According to Uncle, the foreman knows how to build and what the specs should be, but not always the reasons why.

Less than six months later, Ziginshore's biodigester was up and running (see plate 25).

With the tacit consent of the toilet's many users, their bodily waste had become Uncle's property, accumulated and aggregated through the biodigester. Uncle could use its output in any way he chose, including enforcing assent anew. As a first step, a series of tubes, filters, pipes, valves, and gauges conveyed the compressed methane from the digester to a gas range on the toilet veranda. Aiming to entice his employees and hostel residents

Figure 4.12. Building large-scale DIY excremental infrastructure: biogas, 2011 (Photo by Brenda Chalfin)

Figure 4.13. Building large-scale DIY excremental infrastructure: septic system, 2013 (Photo by Marina Ofei-Nkansah)

Figure 4.14. Biogas kitchen, outdoor, 2011 (Photo by Brenda Chalfin)

to cook with the harvested biogas, Uncle set up an outdoor kitchen. Part magic show, part science experiment resembling Boyle's laboratory displays, he cooked meals for himself, for his underage fan club, and for whoever else cared to eat. I was invited to do my own sort of "Julia Child–esque" cooking demonstrations, with Uncle hoping my foreign status would dispel the taint of preparing food from the dregs of bodily waste. Adding a further layer to an already expansive vision of domesticity, Uncle invited me to return on the weekend with my family to cook for the children in the area on their day off from school.

The next year the biogas pipes were diverted from Floshin Taifi's entryway and rerouted to the hostel. By then the second story was roofed, screened, and partitioned, and Uncle's plans for a mess hall was finally underway. The methane was piped directly to the premises of a chop bar Uncle supplied with produce from his up-country farm. He hired a woman to help his wife Kekey run the kitchen and cook and serve for a daily wage. With so much output from the heavy toilet traffic, Uncle said he was barely tapping the full potential of the methane gas supply. When I saw him next he was looking for a generator to convert the gas to electric power. The plan was to use the power for the toilet and the hostel's electrical needs and to sell the surplus to others nearby. Through these arrangements a self-contained public settlement in the heart of a densely populated urban area, nearly entirely off the grid yet fully serviced and under his sole control, was on the way to becoming a reality (see plate 26).

Perhaps, after all, it was the biodigester, not Uncle, that functioned as the Leviathan of Tema's Wastelands. In the words of Hobbes ([1651] 1994, 47), "The greatest of humane powers is that which is compounded of the Powers of most men united by consent in one person, natural or civil, that has the use of all their powers depending on his will, such as is the Power of the Common Wealth . . . for they are strengths united." The digester's very possibility was built on the consensual surrender of bodily waste by toilet patrons. Combined, amassed, and anonymized, this collective was made a singular yet fully versatile substance under the authority of a single individual. In continual demand, the output served to fuel further dependence while it propelled Uncle's vision and ongoing plans for infrastructural expansion.

However, the biodigester, with its ever-renewable contents and expansive potential, seemed also to rule over Uncle, inspiring his awe and compelling action. Uncle continually monitored the inflow of water and waste, building new tanks for runoff, flaring excess gas, and supervising his employees to maintain the valves and filters. Connecting toilet and hostel, kitchen and play area, urban margin and up-country farm, the biodigester guided his investment strategies and his vision for the future. Indeed, Uncle's self-made sanitary infrastructure did not transform the waste products of living bodies into the durable forms discussed by Callon and Latour (Callon and Latour 1981; Latour 1993, 2005a). Instead, it enabled their animation, producing a life force that could be channeled but never stabilized. The biodigester, in short, unlocked what Jane Bennett (2010, 38, 36) describes as the "vital materiality" of nonhuman materials (in this case bodily waste), "giving them an active role in public life." The political force of this once human yet now nonhuman agency lay not in its endowment of a singular transcendent human sovereign but in its intrinsic vitality or immanence out of that sovereign's control. Though nonhuman, this Leviathan, privileging the age-old insights of Hobbes over the claims of Callon and Latour (1981, 293), remained more "body" than "machine."

The last time I saw Uncle Director, I was passing the municipal administration in Tema Township. The successful operation of the biodigester had resulted in release of clean, watery effluent near the Chemu Lagoon producing a bright green crop of lush grass at the water's edge. A sharp contrast with the usual array of sludge and waste, it piqued the interests of the Health Department. The vitality of his project captured the attention of a larger Leviathan: Uncle had been summoned for questioning by TMA.

Conclusion: Between Immanence and Transcendence — Infrastructure and Urban Body Politics

A number of lessons can be learned from the Ziginshore case, some practical and proximate, some more general and abstract. The most basic is the viability of public toilet facilities: public places of convenience can effectively serve large urban populations, even those that are highly transient, under-resourced, and largely disenfranchised. There are more politically tinged lessons here, too. Among them, Tema's wastelands expose the unexpected political potentials of urban frontier zones, what Igor Kopytoff (1987) calls "interstitial spaces": political vacuums or breaking points ripe for mobilization and rearrangement.

The core issue under investigation is not urban space or urban public life per se but rather what such arrangements reveal about the politics of infrastructure and the politics of waste. This is where the work of and on Hobbes is relevant anew. As public entities, the infrastructures described above serve as prime arenas for observing the unfolding of the urban social contract. Comparable to a public version of Boyle's private laboratory (Shapin and Schaffer 1985), they are a focal point from which to track day-to-day practices, experiments, improvisations, and replications, along with the tacit forms of consent and coercion that frame them. Such public forums provide empirical grounds from which to comprehend how people manage to live together: to gather round in Arendt's (1958) sense, and to configure the very objects and infrastructure around which they gather. In the microcosm of Uncle's infrastructural enterprise, it becomes possible to grasp both how infrastructure orders the social field and how members of that social field order infrastructure. In an era when state supremacy is on the wane, replaced by private partnerships, unofficial authorities, and zones of near abandonment, these spaces of infrastructural commonwealth, though not the singular "great" Leviathan of Hobbes's scheme, map the operative political landscape.

There are other ways in which Hobbes's perspective is generative, indeed prescient, for the study of infrastructure. This prescience derives from

Hobbes's fundamental concern with the body: its appetites and aversions, senses, motions, and bodily security and survival, that is, "what they feele in their bodies" ([1651] 1994, 26). Reading infrastructure through the body advances the current anthropological effort to invest infrastructure with analytical purchase. Susan Leigh Star's (1999) attention to infrastructural breakdown initiated this move. A host of works highlighting the unruly, malleable, and mobile character of contemporary infrastructure (Larkin 2008; Stamatopoulou-Robbins 2019; von Schnitzler 2016) bring new momentum to the discussion. Treating infrastructure "as if" a body, and body "as if" infrastructure, as in Tema's sewage pumping stations, might be considered simply metaphoric, enabling its conceptualization in more flexible, fluid, and lively terms. In the case of Ziginshore, at least, the very ground of infrastructure consists of bodily materials, precipitating the potentials as well as uncertainties of the infrastructural inchoate. This is the means through which restructuring is possible, sustaining new institutional formations through the channeling of plurality.

In this regard, a reconsideration of Hobbes reveals a productive tension between the interpretations of Callon and Latour (1981), which emphasize the durable and machinic qualities of the political, and Hobbes's original physical and sensorial sympathies. Close consideration of Uncle's apparatus, in which the needs and substances of the body are at the fore, pushes us to ask where the body lies in other infrastructural orders where its presence is not so obvious. Does the durability of infrastructure occlude or suppress the body, and, in turn, the body politic? Alternatively, why and how do the bodies of some political constituencies, such as the inhabitants of Ziginshore, fall outside of official infrastructures, uncontained by the infrastructural norms of states or other governing entities? If, as Larkin (2013) suggests, taking a long view we can read history for infrastructural high-water marks characterized by grand schemes and sweeping innovations, we might further ask at what historical junctures infrastructures of the body come to matter.

Using one historical optic to unseat another, analyzing infrastructure through the lens of Hobbes's bodily "plenism" upsets high-modernist conceptual divides such as those between persons and things, the material and the corporeal, and figure and ground. Moreover, this approach reveals a surprising alignment between the early modern ideas of Hobbes and late modern concerns with "vital materialism" (Bennett 2010). Evident across the vital remains that make up Ziginshore's landscape of garbage, surplus bodies, and spent things, the real force of materiality is its ongoingness and convertability: from hand-dug wells feeding flush toilets, and bed frames turned into school tables, to the animated bodily wastes of the biodigester fueling the hostel kitchen and sowing seeds of new life in the lagoon. For infrastructure to do political work, it cannot be stable. Recirculation of, around, and through waste fostered a chain of reciprocity drawing people together in networks of interdependence and interaction centered on Uncle's infrastructural complex. While not a common, the unclaimed, unstable terrain offered a shared space built from the circulation of things across bodies and landscapes. Though a different setting and substance, Uncle's reliance on tactics of recirculation to create connection resonates curiously with Sophia Stamatopoulou-Robbins's (2019, 149) portrait of bread disposal in Palestine, where the public circulation of discarded bread contributes to the expression of a latent, or lost, collectivity. However, in the case of Palestine, this community emerges intrinsically, without any need for permanent infrastructure to trigger these flows. In Ziginshore, Uncle intentionally orchestrates latent processes and sentiments of reciprocity by means of infrastructure.

In this figuration, drawn from an urban margin reeling with both political possibility and neglect, infrastructure turned inchoate is not a stable ground but an active political matter, more immanent than transcendent, but never fully one or the other. In the words of Latour (2005a, 31), "The assembling is done under the provisional and fragile Phantom Public, which no longer claims to be equivalent to a Body, a Leviathan or a State"—but, I would add, contains some elements of all. Rather than a mark of political authority already stabilized, Ziginshore's infrastructure, built of and on the body, is a means of popular political substantiation. Replete with political possibility despite its inchoate, unfinished form, Uncle's ontological experiment reassembles social relations by making tangible, scalable, and public the collective—and undecidable, ambiguous, and ever changeable—force of bodily waste. Unlike excremental infrastructural experiments in other parts of the city, where domesticity precedes publicity around waste matter, Uncle Director's apparatus reverses the usual order of operations. First amassing and inciting the hidden potentials of vital remains, these spark an array of infrastructural intimacies, and ultimately build and sustain the wider structures and interdependencies of deep domesticity, offering a model of polity both technical and organic.

5. Dwelling on Toilets
Tema's Breakaway Republic of Ashaiman

It used to be shameful to be a toilet attendant. Toilet work was the purview of reviled night soil collectors. Now we are going through a status upgrade and called "toilet managers." The Asantes have a proverb: "Before you realize the python is a good delicacy the northerners would have finished it." It's the same with the toilet business.
—Toilet operator, Ashaiman, 2014

The heterogeneous world includes everything resulting from unproductive expenditure. This consists of everything rejected by homogeneous society as waste.... Included are the waste products of the human body.
—Georges Bataille, *Visions of Excess* (1985)

The only indispensable material factor in the generation of power is the living together of people. Only where men live so close together that the potentialities of action are always present can power remain with them, and the foundation of cities, which as city-states have remained paradigmatic ..., is therefore indeed the most important material prerequisite for power.
—Hannah Arendt, *The Human Condition* (1958)

Making Waste Public, Making Waste Private in Ashaiman

Ashaiman began its urban existence in the late 1950s as the unplanned counterpart to the new city of Tema. Composed of surplus persons, unused materials, and leftover space at Tema's eastern edge, Ashaiman was conceived as Tema's inverse. Similar to Brazil's capital Brasília, split between a high-modernist core and an informal periphery (Holston 1989), Ashaiman started out as a peri-urban catchment area on whose labor, goods, and services the planned city relied, yet was denied the basic supports of urban develop-

Map 5.1. Map of Ashaiman within Tema Acquisition Area (Kairon Aiken)

ment. Ashaiman's prolonged history of neglect produced not abjection but aspiration marked by intense community activism and a drive toward upward mobility. Half a century after its founding as a lowly adjunct to Tema, Ashaiman, bent on "home rule," in 2008 fought for and won standing as an autonomous municipality with its own budget, representative assembly, municipal executives, and channels of national accountability (Debrah 2009; Owusu 2015). A handful of neighborhoods, zones of contention, continue to be overseen by the Tema Development Corporation despite being in the confines of Ashaiman municipality.

While Ashaiman's Municipal Assembly (ASHMA) is the seat of legal authority, self-determination brings its own challenges in the face of ever-intensifying growth, successive decades of inadequate servicing, and the economic burdens of political decentralization. As Ibrahim Baidoo, the leader of Ashaiman's succession movement and eventual mayor, noted, "Ashaiman was self-governed for so long, it is governing institutions that now need to be enabled." By 2014 Ashaiman's estimated population grew to over three hundred thousand as the city shifted from Tema's bedroom community to Greater Accra's main migrant catchment area. Further taxing municipal capacity, new arrivals come daily from elsewhere in Ghana and the wider West African subregion (Chalfin 2019; Cudjoe, Sepah, and Anarfi 2013, 109; Kissieh 2007). The ensuing social and infrastructural pressures test the limits and possibilities of urban self-governance anew (see plate 27).

Ashaiman's housing stock is largely composed of single-story multiunit cement-block dwellings and wood and zinc shanties (Asare, Osae, and Pellow 2015). As the city struggles to manage population growth alongside in-adequate municipal provisioning, when it comes to sanitation, Ashaiman has come to hold much in common with other parts of Tema metropolitan area where Doxiadis's midcentury ideals fall short. Like Manhean and Ziginshore, the case of Ashaiman turns "inside out" the modernist norm of public provisioning of private sanitation (Laporte 2002; Melosi 2000; Harvey 2008). Most homes do not have toilets, whether septic, plumbed, or pan latrines, and none are linked to Tema's centralized sewage system despite Ashaiman's founding as part of Tema Acquisition Area. Accommodating newcomers as well as long-term residents, because of high demands on housing stock, the large majority of homeowners tend to turn usable space into a source of rental income rather than provide in-home toilets to their tenants or family members.[1]

Markedly different from other parts of the city, in Ashaiman public sanitation is provided in select private homes by private persons to all comers. Indeed, in marked contrast to sanitary solutions found elsewhere in Tema, a dedicated tier of private dwellings operate as public places of convenience to serve the large majority of Ashaiman's residents. These facilities are operated by an enterprising corps of private homeowners who convert a portion of their dwelling into public toilets. Ashaiman thus represents a "fourth way" different from individual toilets for household use that continues to be promoted as the modern sanitary ideal, as in Tema's core. Ashaiman also stands apart from government provisioning of public toilets for the urban underclass, as in Manhean. It differs as well from Uncle's purpose-built mass-scale public facilities in Ziginshore. Ashaiman's unique infrastructural arrangements accommodate the urban population and provide the primary source of sanitary servicing in the municipality. Compared with public toilet usage in the entirety of the Greater Accra region, at 33 percent, in Ashaiman 63 percent of the documented population use public facilities, suggesting even higher actual rates (Cudjoe, Sepah, and Anarfi 2013, 114).

While some of Ashaiman's public toilets are stand-alone structures in places of dense thoroughfare—bus stations, markets, and shopping districts—similar to government-provided facilities, the large majority firmly depart from the typical public model. Rather, these multiunit structures, with few to dozens of toilets each, are located within privately owned homes in residential neighborhoods and are fully accessible to strangers, kin, neighbors, and passersby alike. Neither historic holdovers, as in Manhean, nor the one-off experiments found in Ziginshore, they are a conventional modality of

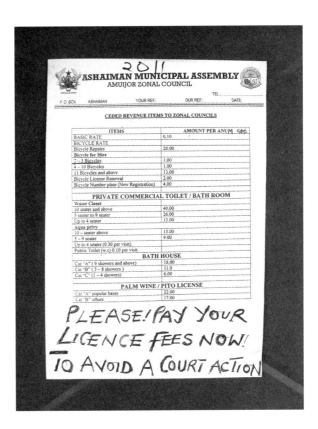

Figure 5.1.
Ashaiman's private commercial toilets tax rates, 2011 (Photo by Brenda Chalfin)

human waste management and continuously maintained, replicated, and updated. Transcending simple principles of neighborly reciprocity, these toilets are dedicated for-profit enterprises designed to serve a high number of users on a regular basis. Such infrastructural arrangements visibly affect urban political order and public life. Shaping localized configurations of authority and interdependence, they domesticate the public sphere in the face of a weak state apparatus.

Officially termed "private commercial toilets" (PCTs), the infrastructures abound in Ashaiman. Survey research from 2014 identified more than 150 separate installations diverse in quality, size, and associated services, from the commonplace pairing of toilets, showers, and water sales to the coincidence of toilets, sundries shops, snack bars, leisure spots, and religious observances. In the face of high demand, these home-based toilet businesses all but guarantee financial gain. So rampant are they that an urban opinion leader described Ashaiman to me as a "toilet town," with PCTs "mushrooming all over the city," regardless of class, ethnicity, or religion and without substantial statutory regulation.[2]

The facilities are remarkable in the aggregate coverage they provide. Simple arithmetic tells the story. If each of the 150-plus PCTs serves an average of five hundred customers a day, this means that nearly one hundred thousand people, about one-third of Ashaiman's population at a low estimate, rely on these facilities. Challenging the temptation to pose Manhean and Ziginshore as urban sanitary outliers, the stupendous scale of Ashaiman's public sanitary servicing makes it clear that Tema's sister city represents not the exception but the rule. As one PCT proprietor put it, "In a political environment of self-aggrandizement and party grandstanding, they are a collective solution—by and for the people—that caters to the quiet majority." Extending Hannah Arendt's (1958, 201) claims regarding the potentiality of action arising from living together in the city, in Ashaiman, these possibilities are muddied and multiplied by the dense social processes of living and shitting together.

Theorizing a General Economy of Private Commercial Toilets

The broad institution of private yet collective sanitary arrangements in Ashaiman calls for a theoretical frame all its own. Though sharing numerous overlaps and resonances with them, Ashaiman stands apart from the infrastructural intimacies of Tema's broken sewage network, the state-society struggles that play out in the res publicae of Manhean's community-based compound toilets, and the Hobbesian social contract of Uncle's toilet-cum-biodigester in the wastelands of Chemu. Notably, Ashaiman's PCTs depart from these other cases in the pronounced association of "public" private sanitary infrastructure with urban social mobility and political claims and the progressive delinking from state and municipal controls. Whereas the political field of Ziginshore is open-ended, characterized by shallow ties and transient personages, Ashaiman is densely populated by community organizations and alliances, and its residents maintain an active associational life that has long made up for weak state investment and oversight.

In conversation with Arendt's (1958) reading of political life explored in earlier chapters, two theoretical perspectives offer suggestive entry points where waste is the crux of social order: Georges Bataille's (1988) "accursed share" and Thorstein Veblen's ([1899] 1994) notion of "conspicuous waste."

These shed light on the entanglements of the public, private, and political in the management of basic bodily needs while blurring the boundaries of Arendt's tripartite framework. They do so without privileging or idealizing centralized governing institutions—a perspective especially appropriate to a politically diffuse setting such as Ashaiman.

For both Veblen and Bataille, relations of domination emerge from materially based social practice. Bataille's political economy is a framing of material life in its totality: what is made, what is shared, what is squandered, and what is pushed to the wayside and deemed unusable. Bataille (1988, 20) labels this the "general economy." Objects and energetic forms, including human bodies, are at the fore of Bataille's formulation. According to Bataille, all engender waste and excess in the form of outputs that resist productive use or assimilation. Bataille (37) labels this the "accursed share": that which is deemed extraneous and denied incorporation into the official order of things but which is crucial to its very functioning—a much broader category than Marxian (1968) notions of surplus.[3] As Bataille (1988, 27) sees it, waste is part of our species: "Neither growth nor reproduction—or the extravagant expenditures of warfare—would be possible . . . without waste." From the perspective of those who oversee and utilize Ashaiman's PCTs, neither would the promise of collective attainment and recognition be possible without waste.

For Veblen, waste is central to power, but differently so. Challenging the utilitarianism of the economic theories of his day long before his mid-twentieth-century French counterpart Bataille, Veblen attends to the human propensity toward wastefulness. He brings to light the panhuman tendency to squander useful resources in acts of conspicuous display, interpreting these practices as appeals for social recognition and influence. Advancing understandings of "conspicuous consumption" across archaic and modern eras, Veblen homes in on what he calls "the canon of conspicuous waste" (Veblen [1899] 1994, 56): the fact that the more flagrant the wastage, the more prestige—and social power—accrues to the one who wastes.[4] As he puts it, "In order [for expenditure] to be reputable, it must be wasteful" (60).

Following Bataille's and Veblen's injunction to put waste at the heart of political economy, in Ashaiman there is no shortage of waste despite the municipality's material deprivations.[5] Expanding on these theorists' core claims, the waste matter found in Ashaiman—including individual and collective dispositions of human fecal output—are critical to what Bataille (1985, 139) calls political "heterogeneity." Heterogeneity for Bataille contrasts with the "homogeneity" of state constraint and its neatly conceived political hierarchies.[6] Like the subterranean matrix of urban sewage systems Lewis Mumford (1961) refers to as the "invisible city," these relations constitute the political substrate of the city, at once serving basic needs and giving order to urban life while sowing the seeds of new arrangements and uncontainable substances. Heterogeneity, I argue, is the material basis of undecidability.

The public order that results is more variegated than singular and reflects the substance as much as the structure of Ashaiman's sanitation system. The excesses of bodily waste on which it is premised are full of possibility. As Bataille (1985, 140) boldly asserts, "What is heterogeneous is impossible to assimilate." Indeed, Bataille is one of the few social theorists who considers excreta and bodily waste in more than a metaphorical sense, stating (142), "The heterogeneous world includes everything resulting from unproductive expenditure. This consists of everything rejected by homogeneous society as waste. Included are the waste products of the human body and analogous matter: trash, vermin, impoverished classes." Generalized, Bataille's notion is unbound, encompassing what he terms "non-subjugated nature" (138), "violence, excess, delirium . . . everything resulting from unproductive expenditure" (142).

Bataille's conceptual play, taking excreta at face value while treating it as representative of an array of irrepressible social excesses through which power is forged, finds fertile ground in Ashaiman when jointly applied with Arendt's conception of political action, the *vita activa*. As part of a broader project to "ask Arendtian questions and be ready for non-Arendtian answers" (Benhabib 2000, 198) in order to comprehend the role of bodily processes in shaping urban political order, the interplay of these theoretical optics reveals surprising resonances despite their very different philosophical foundations.[7] Though Arendt focuses on bodily needs and Bataille on bodily excesses and outputs, both connect social power to bodily processes. Bataille, thinking with and against the received order of things, connects somatic and material excess to broader structural "formations of social heterogeneity," noting, "Social heterogeneity does not exist in a formless and disoriented state." It is in tension with the "social homogeneity" of "the State," "which delineates it by exclusion" (Bataille 1985, 139–40). Here we see a succinct articulation of what I call the "infrastructural inchoate."

Strange bedfellows as they may be, putting these perspectives together to analyze Ashaiman's PCTs surely upends the hard-and-fast distinctions of Arendt's (1958) classically inspired rendering of political action. At the same time, it gives Arendt's conceptual vocabulary new relevance. Notably, consideration of the crisscrossed social, organic, and technical "heterogeneities" of Ashaiman's privatized sanitary systems through the lens of Veblen and Bataille further demonstrates the potential of infrastructure—a suppressed component of Arendt's notion of work (Markell 2011) and little-explored aspect of her notion of labor—to mediate between basic bodily processes, urban status distinctions, and the collective and individual potentials of the *vita activa*.

Excess and Evacuation in Historical Perspective

Ashaiman's standing within the Ghanaian nation-state is rooted in waste. As recounted in earlier chapters, spurred by decolonization and post–World War II modernization, the Volta River Scheme in the late 1940s and plans for the new port shortly thereafter drew thousands to Tema. Three out of four newcomers were male, bringing their laboring bodies to bear on the prospects of the new nation. Identified as "Northerners" and "Nigerians" in government reports (Pellow 2008), they were further classified as traders, tradesman, and skilled and unskilled laborers; among them were drivers and watchmen, masons, quarrymen, rail and pipe layers, road builders, brickmakers, excavators, welders, and machinery operators (Jopp 1961, 22).

The catch-22 of urban development soon reared its head. The new port and city couldn't be built without workers, but workers required the basic trappings of urban life, from housing and markets to rudimentary infrastructure and social supports. Initially the transplants joined the existing migrant community living within the fishing village of Tema known as Tema Zongo, a Hausa term meaning "strangers' quarters" (Schildkrout 1978). As the story of Tema Manhean recounted in chapter 3 details, both recent arrivals and longtime residents occupied areas slated to be demolished for the new city (Butcher 1966, 31). By the time relocation finally rolled around in 1959, 40 percent of Old Tema's residents were identified as non-native-born. Regardless, the official resettlement area of Manhean was designated for Tema's "original" inhabitants, not the "strangers" from the Zongo.

While some contractors set up labor camps for their workers, these arrangements were temporary, inadequate, and unavailable to most members of the casual labor force. To fill the gap, the wilds of Ashaiman were posed as a convenient adjunct to the still largely imagined metropolis of Tema, all the more appropriate for "outsiders" whose assimilation into the heart of

Figure 5.2. "An immigrant removed from Tema Zongo outside of his house in Ashaimang," ca. 1959 (Amarteifio 1966)

the new nation remained in question. Government documents referred to the location just six miles from the core of Tema, but without services or a designated town center, simply as "Mile 17 on the Accra-Ada Road." Hosting a recorded population of just 185 in the 1948 census, by 1960 there were nearly three thousand people residing in the area that would soon become Ashaiman, "most of whom had been removed from the Old Tema Zongo or 'strangers' area'" (Butcher 1966, 25, 31).

The new settlement was the antithesis of the assiduously planned Tema. Little regulated by government authorities, it displayed only the barest outline of formal order, as evidenced in the recollections of a resettlement official:

> The 50 ft. × 50 ft. plots which were allocated at Mile 17 cost a mere 10s. per month each to rent, and some speculators from Accra came and managed to obtain leases on land which they hoped would become valuable as building sites. The effect that this had on the new settlement was to leave large patches of unkempt grass and rubbish interspersing the houses which the ex-Zongo people had built, and because the land was leased no one else could build on it. Due to the difficulty of finding out who the tenants really were no one could be compelled to keep the plot tidy and the grass cut. (Butcher 1966, 26)

A fact demonstrating the enduring interplay of political heterogeneity and homogeneity, the largely informal order of Ashaiman—geographically near yet conceptually far from the new city of Tema—was initially mandated by the authorities rather than organic to the settlement itself. Apropos the consideration of Ashaiman's waste in the present, the materials for the town's early structures were wrought from Tema's rubbish. The settlement's early chroniclers note, "The 1960 census recorded 299 houses and 2,624 persons, most of whom had been removed from the Old Tema Zongo.... The fortunate among the immigrants were permitted to salvage building materials after the bulldozers knocked down the old houses.... Of the householders allocated plots at mile 17, of these 95 percent wanted to houses built of iron sheets [salvaged] from Old Tema.... Those who could not obtain old sheets decided to build in swish after the rains" (Butcher 1966, 25, 26, 31, 32).

Twenty-first-century Ashaiman is a sprawling urban agglomeration with a range of neighborhoods and housing stock extending far from the original concentrated cluster of zinc shacks at mile 17. Underwriting its ongoing contrast with and connection to Tema, large-scale infrastructural investment in Ashaiman remains limited. While Tema in the early 1960s was celebrated for its centralized sewage system, Ashaiman continues to lack large-scale network sewage infrastructure. Long neglected by the TDC despite its proximity and deep dependence on its labor force, sanitation challenges have long been endemic in Ashaiman. As early as 1968, a petition issued to the TDC by community representatives listed among Ashaiman's major problems "insufficient latrines [which] force people to ease themselves throughout the town in open spaces" (Yedu Bannerman 1973, 9). Though Ashaiman's urban settlement is contemporaneous with Tema Manhean, it was not serviced by communal ablution blocks.[8] Instead, in Ashaiman human waste management was initially informal and self-supplied, with residents using the bush or proverbial pan and bucket latrines emptied by the type of low-status "night soil carriers" noted in Keith Hart's (1973, 69) pioneering essay defining the informal economy.[9]

The government of Ghana disrupted these practices when it issued a revamped *National Environmental Sanitation Policy* in 1999. Reprising the mandates of colonial-era hygiene, the policy sought to reassert state oversight of urban bodies and spaces. In the late twentieth century, as in the earlier era, sanitary order was imposed not through state provisioning but via prohibition in the name of public good. The 1999 policy, manifesting a neoliberal logic of state rollback (Chalfin 2010), traded government writ large

Figure 5.3. Government toilet exterior, 2013 (Photo by Mustapha Mohamed)

Figure 5.4. Government toilet interior, 2014 (Photo by Eva Egensteiner)

for government *minimus*. Two key directives were included in the new sanitation code. One was a ban on pan latrines, and the other was a refusal to build or upgrade municipal sewage systems.

To replace household-based pan latrines, Tema's municipal authority—still Ashaiman's overseer at the millennium's turn—built twenty-three public toilets in Ashaiman. Known colloquially as "gov'ment toilets," available for use for a nominal charge, each contained eight male and eight female toilet stalls and fed into a dedicated septic tank. With Ashaiman's official population pushing a quarter million by the early 2000s—not counting the growing number of undocumented residents and transients—"gov'ment toilets" could little accommodate the bodies and the bodily outputs of Ashaiman's populace. Indicating their sheer inadequacy, simple calculations show six thousand people per one toilet stall, with only fifteen seconds of access per person each day during peak use. Avoided by many in favor of the "free-range" (open defecation) option, the government toilets were a mess of disrepair, stench, and overflowing fecal matter. When the World Bank and the World Health Organization decided to tackle urban sanitation, they proposed a fifty-fifty split of the costs to build or convert one toilet per household to a Kumasi Ventilated Improved Pit Latrine (KVIP) or a water closet (World Bank 2015) predicated on the municipal-civic ideal (Mukhopadhyay 2006, 226) of individualized household toilets as the sole standard of improved hygiene. Despite the program's mobilization elsewhere in Ghana, not only was Ashaiman left out the plan; the myriad sanitary solutions in existence in the city were also completely off the World Bank / World Health Organization radar.

Toilet Typologies: Enterprise, Extension, Enclosure

Ashaiman's private commercial toilets flourished in the void between the banned household pan latrine and the soiled government structures. Some originated as household toilets with open access for friends and neighbors who lacked decent facilities at their disposal. In a spirit of "sanitation entrepreneurship" (Mazeau 2013, 173), others were built and founded with the express intention of accommodating all comers. Beyond catering to local need, these enterprises compete broadly for clientele. Requiring property, capital, and collateral, they are by no means a lowly public good but a source of upward mobility and wealth accumulation. As one toilet operator explained, "It used to be shameful to be a toilet attendant. Toilet work was the purview of reviled night soil collectors. Now we are going through a status upgrade and called 'toilet managers.' The Asante have a proverb: 'Before you realize the python is a good delicacy the northerners would have finished it.' It's the same with the toilet business."

In Ashaiman, in a twist on the bourgeois privacy principle, the most upscale private commercial toilets are the most domesticated and most buffered from state and municipal exactions. They are likewise well integrated into the domestic space and the domestic life of the proprietor, and conducive to social mobility and collective recognition for toilet customers and toilet owners alike. Both affecting urban public life and political order, here again we see the link between deep domesticity and the state, as well as deep domesticity and class.

An example of vernacular architecture meeting improvised infrastructure at scale, the form and layout of Ashaiman's PCTs appear wide-ranging at first glance. Each combines domestic space and public toilet facilities in different proportions and degrees of integration. On closer inspection, however, they exhibit a more restricted range of variation. As reflected in Ashaiman's varied housing stock, neighborhood histories, settlement patterns (Mazeau, Scott, and Tuffuor 2012), and diverse social makeup, the different ways public toilet infrastructures merge with domestic arrangements and living space are captured in the typology in table 5.1.

These arrangements build on the different residential templates prevailing in the upwardly mobile working-class neighborhoods of Ashaiman. Modeled on housing initially issued to government workers, one template can be called "quarters-style." Consisting of a cluster of structures that share a common lot, the main structure is typically a modest self-contained residential unit. Toilets and bathrooms are located in detached outbuildings. Other smaller structures may contain additional residential space. What I term "Domestic Sanitary Enterprises," they are found most often in association with "quarters-style" homes. Augmenting the original one- to two-unit detached toilets that are part of the home's original design, with a Domestic Sanitary Enterprise, sanitary facilities are expanded to include multiple toilets, or multiple blocks of toilets, and sometimes showers too, all within the bounds of a single lot.

The second residential template for Ashaiman's PCT is associated with the compound house. A defining feature of the residential compound is a central courtyard. The flexibility of the compound structure, which houses multiple generations of kin in rural settings, has fostered its adaption to urban settings to enable the accommodation of kin and nonkin alike in

Table 5.1. Ashaiman's domestic public toilet typology

Type	Characteristics
Domestic Sanitary Enterprises	Toilet facilities detached from residential space
Domestic Sanitary Extensions	Toilet facilities added on to residential space
Domestic Sanitary Enclosures	Toilet facilities built into the existing residential space

separate rooms. The rooms share a common central space built around the open courtyard. I call these PCT designs "Domestic Sanitary Extensions," as they augment the original footprint of a compound house. Residential compounds may also be associated with PCT designs that I call "Domestic Sanitary Enclosures." Toilets and other sanitary facilities are incorporated into a compound's internal layout, as opposed to Domestic Sanitary Extensions, where they are external to yet contiguous with domestic space. Domestic Sanitary Enclosures are also found in conjunction with a third residential template: the self-contained house, where living quarters are under one roof and share an entrance. While a self-contained house, like the compound, may have a courtyard, they often contain exterior verandahs and open space and may also lend themselves to Domestic Sanitary Extensions.

To put these examples in comparative perspective, it is helpful to refer again to Norbert Elias's *The Civilizing Process* (1994) and Lewis Mumford's *The Culture of Cities* (1938). Both remark on the emergence of a privatized interiority among Europe's ascendant middle and upper classes in which the bodily functions of sleep, sex, and excretion are progressively separated from other activities and collectivities and confined to discrete spaces within the home. Tracing this arc from the early modern era through the eighteenth century among elite and ascendant classes, the sequestration of bodily functions in the domestic realm was considered a sign of status. These new excretory habits all at once demonstrated a command of space, command over the intrusions of undesired others, and avoidance of the shame of public bodily exposure.

Of particular relevance to Ashaiman, Mumford not only attributes the expansion of private life and private space to rising prosperity but also sees it as evidence of the exclusion of the growing middle class from public affairs as political institutions become increasingly exclusive and consolidated. As Mumford puts it (1938, 114), "Among the middle classes there was a natural tendency to substitute private life for public affairs. Deprived of his liberties, unable often to vote for his municipal officers . . . it was natural that citizens' interest should shift. To use a Victorian catchword: the middle classes began to keep themselves to themselves."

While Ashaiman's PCTs likewise augment the domestic realm in terms both spatial and functional, effectively replacing government intrusions in the face of limited state capacity, they depart from the European model outlined by Mumford in one significant way. Namely, Ashaiman's PCTs mark not the withdrawal from public life but the incorporation of the public into the domestic arena. In a notable twist on Mumford's and Elias's "privacy equals status" thesis, Ashaiman's PCTs are built to attract and accommodate public consumption and entrain the private and public behavior of a wide swath of Ashaiman's residents. Neither rejecting "undesired others" nor attributing shame to bodily processes, here domestic propriety much more than privacy is a marker of status. Lending further comparative insight on Ashaiman, Habermas's *Structural Transformation of the Public Sphere* (1991, 142) captures an inverse course of sociopolitical reordering in the eighteenth century. In the European settings described by Habermas, the state's selective incorporation of distinct class fractions triggers the dissolution of the public sphere of open cross-class exchange. In Ashaiman the opposite process is at work. Rather, state exclusion prevails, and the city's vast network of private commercial toilets serves as a prime arena of cross-class mobility and interchange.

The following three portraits of PCTs illustrate the myriad ways private infrastructures turn waste into a medium of public order and social attainment in the face of limited state provisioning. They include a Domestic Sanitary Enterprise associated with a quarters-style dwelling, a Domestic Sanitary Extension of a residential compound house, and a Domestic Sanitary Enclosure within a self-contained dwelling. Close examination of each shows how Ashaiman's home-based PCTs eclipse state-based hierarchies and homogenies of command and control to structure urban plurality and self-determination, all the while fueling urban status contests. Arendt (1958, 7) famously asserts, "While all aspects of the human condition are somehow related to politics, this plurality is specifically *the* condition—not only the *conditio sine qua non*, but the *conditio per quam*—of all political life." Exactly how this occurs in Ashaiman—contra Arendtian categories yet toward Arendtian ends (viz. Benhabib 2000; Markell 2011)—comes into view below.

Case #1. Stomach Has No Holiday: From Labor to Leisure

Domestic Sanitary Enterprise Quarters-Style

No class of society, even the most abjectly poor, foregoes conspicuous consumption.
—Thorstein Veblen, *The Theory of the Leisure Class* ([1899] 1994)

Working-Class Waste

At first glance, the heavily trafficked corner across from Ashaiman's new administrative headquarters appears to be the usual cluster of low-budget commercial enterprises composed of shipping containers, wood, wire mesh, and assorted side tables. Eye-catching signage invites a second look: "Stomach Has No Holiday Refreshing Spot," "Stomach Has No Holiday: Dealers in Used Papers. Sachet Waters. Purified Water, Voltic Water, Etc." Nearby a signpost proclaims, "Public Toilet and Shower." Painted on one side is a woman's torso under a flowing spigot. On the other, a male figure sits on a box, pants to knees. The reverse contains a similar illustration, this time a man under the shower head, soap and sponge in hand. Pointing away from the road toward the dense neighborhood within, an arrow underscores front and back (see plate 28).

Following the narrow lane between the structures, the cues fall into place. In sight are an expanse of deep green walls, tanks, vent stacks, and roofline of one of Ashaiman's many PCTs. This one is known as "Stomach Has No Holiday." The proprietor goes by the name of Stomach. He is builder, owner, and manager all in one. Stomach falls under the category of Domestic Sanitary Enterprise, in which public toilets and baths are detached from nearby residential space. Painted the same shade of green as the rest of the complex, the quarters-style home of the owner and his family lies adjacent. The entry to the home is not more than twenty meters from the entrance to the toilet.

Like other public places, Stomach's enterprise is context-dependent: in this case, the context is the surrounding working-class neighborhood whose needs it serves and transcends. The area adjacent to Stomach's place contains residential structures of various sizes, quality, and permanence that reflect the working poor's struggle for urban prosperity. Shelters constructed from scrap are found side by side with partially completed concrete-block

STOMACH MODEL

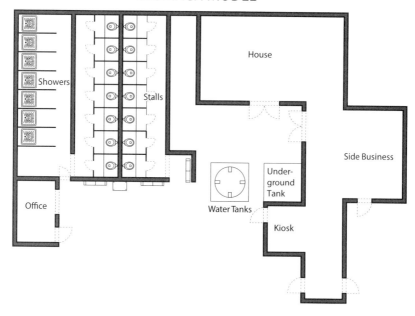

Figure 5.5. Stomach toilet layout (Created by Xhulio Binjaku)

houses and multiroom wood-framed dwellings. Nearly all lack their own toilets, and no other private commercial toilets are close by. The nearest government toilet a few blocks away is far from alluring, with filthy squat holes, no lights or privacy between stalls, and a cloud of stench emanating from its graffiti-covered walls. Stomach is a beacon of economic and bodily well-being in this hard-luck corner of the city. Costing only slightly more than the timeworn government structure (thirty pesewa compared to the "gov'ment" toilets' twenty pesewa), it is an affordable alternative to shitting "free-range" and the scourge of black poly-bag "flying-toilets," also known as "take-aways" (Mazeau 2013, 164).

Stomach's stand-alone outbuildings containing the toilet and baths are built atop an underground sewage pit. There are seven male and seven female drop holes, with separate tiled cubicles. A porcelain hand sink is situated between the male and female entryways, each marked with a carefully painted portrait labeled with elegant script (see plate 29). An attached enclosure holds seven tiled shower stalls that drain into a cement-lined channel at the rear of the structure, the runoff carving a path from the packed earth alleyway into the roadside gutter. An airy office anchors the other end of the complex. It faces the twisted trunk of an old mango tree and a few wooden benches in its shade, the ground between them bare and neatly swept. A large water tank sits on a raised cement platform a few feet away, with a massive in-ground water cistern a few feet farther behind. In front, there is a small kiosk stocked with sundries: soap, sponges, sanitary pads, and more (see plate 30).

Stomach, the proprietor, shares the profile of other longtime Ashaiman residents. He arrived in Ashaiman from Ghana's Volta Region in 1975 and for thirty years was a wage worker in government employ at the Port of Tema. Stomach embodies urban migrants' idealized path of stepwise economic and infrastructural attainment. He recounted his own sequence of acquisition as follows: "Requiring the consent of both TDC and Tema Traditional Authorities, I purchased a house plot a few years after I got here. The water pipe was added in 1985, and some years after, the tank and the cistern." Only when Stomach contemplated retiring did he create a plan to construct a PCT by extending the typical logic of domestic construction along with the footprint of his domestic unit. Stomach explained, "I started to prepare cement blocks and put money aside for building materials. I eventually hired a contractor and we worked out a plan for the facility, including the large underground septic tank. This required permits from ASHMA and the services of a local mason."

In 2010, on the heels of retirement, the toilet was finished. True to Stomach's motto, it has been open every day since. Combined, the bathing area and toilet stalls are much larger than his own residence, and more accessible. With Stomach's eponymous drinking spot and paper shop extending from the edge of his home to the well-trafficked road, it all appears a brilliant exercise in vertical enterprise integration and urban property development. Despite the end of his participation in the world of waged work, Stomach returns as *homo faber*: "the builder of walls (both physical and cultural) which divide the human realm from that of nature and provide a stable context (a 'common world') of spaces and institutions within which human life can unfold" (Arendt 1958, 198–99; Yar 2000).

From Waste as Labor to Waste as Leisure

Stomach's toilet is well patronized by those who reside nearby, proving Veblen's point that "no class of society, even the most abjectly poor, foregoes conspicuous consumption" ([1899] 1994, 53). A snapshot of Stomach's neighborhood includes young families for whom the kiosk is home and workspace, the middle-aged woman who occupies a modest house across the way built from scrap lumber where she prepares food for sale, and the owner and tenants of the half-finished block house where a common toilet may never be installed. In addition to this local customer base, Stomach is also patronized by a more transient section of Ashaiman's populace who lack any fixed address or domicile: pushcart operators, load carriers, day laborers, and the like. Spatially and vocationally unsettled despite their clear aspirations for material security, these individuals represent the lower rungs of Ashaiman's working class (Kissieh 2007; Chalfin 2019). For those without a permanent abode, the comforts of Stomach's toilet a few minutes' walk from the center of town is one of the few luxuries within their grasp. Conveniently appointed with soap, bathing sponges, and other essentials available for purchase, the toilet opens at 4 a.m., well before dawn, to accommodate their peripatetic schedules.

In contrast to the surrounding unfinished and timeworn structures of the working poor and their more upwardly mobile and downtrodden cousins, the dazzling green outbuildings, neat rest area, and decoratively tiled stalls of Stomach's PCT exert a power of attraction. Marked by aesthetic excess above and beyond utilitarian need in a manner straight out of Veblen's ([1899] 1994, 41–51) playbook, Stomach's infrastructural installation is deliberately made conspicuous. Putting superfluity on display, Stomach's facility highlights the specific excesses of human waste production. Illustrative of Bataille's claims (1988, 23) that "man is not just the separate being that contends with the living world and with other men for his share of resources. The general movement of exudation (of waste) of living matter impels him, and he cannot stop it," Stomach's graphic signboards boldly depicting persons in the act of elimination broadcasts the inevitability of human scatological processes.

Yet the aesthetic and semantic play that come with Stomach's attention-grabbing self-representations also call up human waste's ambiguities, both similar to and different from other sorts of surplus. With the facility situated in an area of the city where toil is extreme and wealth slow to materialize, the very phrase "Stomach has no holiday" calls into question any firm boundary between cycles of the body and cycles of work, expenditure, and accumulation—to borrow the language of Bataille. On the one hand, the phrase's subject, "stomach," equates the toilet enterprise with the relentless

Figure 5.6. Stomach: making wealth conspicuous, 2014 (Photo by Eva Egensteiner)

demands and outputs of "life-giving bodily labor," to go back to Arendt's (1958, 7) terminology. "No holiday," on the other, invokes the toilet's customers, who have no escape from the necessities of work and the daily requirements of what Arendt calls "fabrication" (136). Ironically, in contrast to those who patronize his establishment, for Stomach the man, "every day is a holiday," as his aggregate claim on community members' bodily waste via the toilet relieves him of the demands of production.

It is this arrangement that frees Stomach to cultivate the *vita activa*—the consummation of Arendt's triad—characterized by plurality, public life, and self-expression (1958, 12, 180). With property a core qualification for membership in the polis according to Arendt (1958, 61), Stomach's economic ascendance derives from claims to immovable assets that further distinguish him from his neighbors: lot and residence, sewage pit, zinc and block structures enclosing the toilets and showers, mango tree, and water cistern. In Stomach's case, confounding any simple actualization of Arendt's ideal type are the complex political economies of waste on which it is premised, as Veblen and Bataille both remind us. While infrastructures of bodily care and evacuation bring urban residents together in public as equals, such pluralities are marked by status differentials in which waste is also a prime means of rank, thus revealing the political complexities of living (and shitting) together (cf. Arendt 1958, 201).

Conspicuous Consumption and Infrastructural Assent

The operations of Stomach's PCT, while cloaking the "conspicuous waste" of feces, sewage pits, and toilets with the profligacy of "conspicuous consumption," establish Stomach's hard-won membership in the leisure class—a position he holds over, and holds up as a model for, his neighbors. As described by Veblen ([1899] 1994), this involves combining "non-productive time" (29) and "unproductive consumption" (44) along with "learning to live [a] life of ostensible leisure in a becoming way" (47). Free from labor and toil in general and the specific taints of bodily waste, Stomach mostly sits in his spacious office, counting receipts, reading the daily papers, listening to the radio, and conversing with friends and passersby. Stomach has five employees who take care of cleaning, a far cry from his jobs with Ghana's Ports and Harbors Authority, where he worked on the docks as a tally clerk, and at the State Fishing Corporation, where he was employed as a manual laborer.

Embodying the very traits highlighted by Veblen ([1899] 1994, 29, 31), Stomach's routines are marked by "decorum, refined tastes, manners, and knowledge of good form." His office is decoratively appointed. Alongside the calendars, wall clock, and framed photos loom religious posters and a stereo system. Making the space more living room than office, the large corner fridge contains cools drinks for himself and guests. On my many visits, Stomach was always sharply dressed: on occasion a lace agbada, more typically a shirt and vest, or batik up and down. Whatever the outfit, gold neck chains, a jewel-studded watch, and closed-toe leather shoes were de rigueur. By no means appropriate to latrine and shower maintenance, Stomach's sartorial overstatement conjures affluence, not the waste deposited by his customers and collected within his septic pit. Distinguishing himself from the manual exertions of the cleaning crew and his own earlier jobs at the harbor, Stomach doesn't hesitate to walk well-outfitted through the facility to supervise and inspect. A commentary on his hard-earned class standing, however, is that he will not stoop to mop or scrub.

Further associating Stomach's infrastructural investments with affluence despite the sewage pit on which it is predicated, "Pay Your Bills" is painted in bold letters across the exterior of his office block opposite the toilet entrance. In this setting not only is monetary wealth free from moral taint (pace Laporte 2002), but so too is waste if it can be properly channeled, cleansed, or disguised, illustrating the ongoing conversion of waste to value described by Bataille (1988). Shit might stink, but despite occasional complaints from

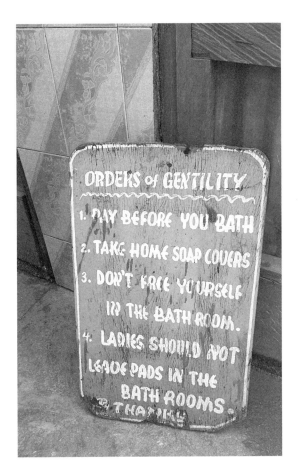

Figure 5.7. Orders of Gentility, 2014 (Photo by Eva Egensteiner)

neighbors, "*Ɛbɔn*" ("It stinks" in Akan [Twi]), about the lingering odor of the sewage pit and muddy shower runoff, in Stomach's hands money looks and smells sweet.

Just as Stomach's infrastructural array constitutes a public space on the basis of bodily parity at the same time that it demonstrates the spoils of class distinction, the facility offers the promise of social mobility in terms simultaneously inclusive and disciplinary. Surprisingly true to Veblen's ([1899] 1994, 52) observations that in the lower- and middle-class community "the leisure class sets the norm of reputability for the community," within Stomach's facility these norms are made explicit. Publicizing codes of domestic propriety, a large, carefully painted placard is prominently posted in the shower area listing "ORDERS OF GENTILITY," as follows:

Figure 5.8. Toilet stall augmented with rebar, 2013 (Photo by Brenda Chalfin)

1. PAY BEFORE YOU BATH

2. TAKE HOME SOAP COVERS

3. DON'T FREE YOURSELF IN THE BATH ROOM.

4. LADIES SHOULD NOT LEAVE PADS IN THE BATH ROOMS.

THANKS

The physical infrastructural compunctions of Stomach's toilets further direct the private behavior of his customers. Stomach worked with a local welder to install a kinked rebar support in each toilet stall to create a design that went beyond the typical verbal exhortation to "Sit on it"—of the type found in Manhean and also visible on the doors of Stomach's place. Poised above the middle of each drop hole, the bar makes it nearly impossible to squat on the raised box of the toilet. The bar instead requires customers to place their buttocks, not their feet, on the toilet seat. This infrastructure compels compliance with Stomach's standard of practice, making correct position incumbent on those using his toilet cabinets, warding off missed shots and preventing extra work for the cleaning crew.

Infrastructural Spot-Checks and Municipal Adjustments

Stomach's actions and material attributes speak louder than words. His infrastructural impositions of assent are not restricted to the members of the public who use and live near his PCT. His whole apparatus functions as a means of urban claims making to which the municipal authority in its own right is subject. Due to Stomach's proximity to ASHMA headquarters, the city's Environmental Health Department inspectors regularly visit his facilities, and I witnessed one such encounter when ASHMA's inspectors stopped by to "spot-check" the facilities. Stomach's tone conveyed the politesse of a host in his own space, not the tentative demeanor of a dependent. He eagerly pulled out a sheaf of records from his office, crisply laminated and neatly stored, confidently showing each one in turn. The ASHMA certificate of operation from opening day read "neat and clean" on all counts. Inspection records from subsequent visits showed the highest grade of "Very Good" for "General Housekeeping." Deferring requests for additional documents, he explained that the other certificates were in his house for safekeeping.

The Environmental Health inspectors announced that the visit's premise was "pest and vector control." Moving from room to room, the conversation went back and forth between the inspector's claims and Stomach's counterclaims. Acknowledging their complaints, Stomach defended his own managerial methods, expressing little concern about possible sanctions from ASHMA. He didn't mind the inspector's attention but was not going to defer unless it served his needs. From this perspective, the municipality was just another actor on the scene from whose input Stomach could pick and choose. The inspection transcript captures this dance of deference and indifference, in which infrastructure was the object of mediation.

"I" = ASHMA inspector; "s" = Stomach

I. The maggots are too much. Cleaning is not adequate. You need to intensify cleaning every day.

s. I don't know why. She has done it once today. Early morning people queue here. If you come here in the morning, you will see a queue.

I. But if she's cleaning, we won't see maggots.

s. We clean at a late hour in the night, at 10 o'clock, and then we close the gate. In the morning at 9 o'clock she will do it again. And in the afternoon, before she again cleans at night.

The inspector continued with her next complaint, and Stomach once again rebuffed the recommendations:

I. Fly breeding is too much. We advise a ceiling.

s. Because of the tree, the tree down there, always there are flies inside.

I. The gate won't allow them to get access.

s. When you close the gate, the odor is there. That's why the fan is there. I put on the fan and flies go away.

i. And the odor, we have chemicals to use. Our bosses have it.

s. I've been coming there. The odor doesn't go at once.

Only when they reached the showers did Stomach demonstrate any concern with the inspector's remarks.

i. (Pointing to mold) Common bleach will work on this. The workers can remove these things. The walls need to be cleaned.

s. Yes.

i. You can see where they are painted. If you are asthmatic or respiratory disease these things will trigger it. You begin to sneeze.

s. It will start the illness?

i. We don't allow it. It used to be new. Not properly maintained.

s. Thank you for giving me the advice. Next time you come here you will see a difference.

The last part of the inspection involved walking around the facility to check out the drains and vents. The senior inspector noted that the pit on which the whole facility was perched did not qualify as a septic tank, per minimum regulations for PCTs. Rather, they said it was a mere holding tank, where fecal waste builds up without processing before being siphoned out by the sewage truck. Again, this appeared to be a fact to which the city's Environmental Health team was resigned, and Stomach largely indifferent, despite the contravention of ASHMA's building codes. Just as the unofficial drainage channel guiding the shower runoff into the municipality's street-side gutter ensured the smooth running of Stomach's operation, the Environmental Health officers seemed to have little interest in upsetting an arrangement on which the municipal authority likewise depended. Whether the drain or the holding tank, or the toilet, water, and bath business as a whole, each enlarged Stomach's reach as property owner, permanently reshaping urban space while providing essential public services in lieu of the state.

The inspectors, like Stomach's customers, hemmed in by Stomach's infrastructural apparatus and waste products that sprawled and spilled above, below, and around them, were just one voice in a conversation in which collective needs, aggregate bodily outputs, and status aspirations prevailed. Mixing bodily life, work routines, built forms, and the exposures, interjections, power plays, and unpredictability of the public sphere, Stomach's place at once mapped and disordered the components of Arendt's (1958) *vita activa*, as bodily processes performed triple duty as the condition of labor, work, and action.

Discussion

Reminiscent of the reworking of the eighteenth-century public sphere in the face of state and class consolidation described by Habermas (1991), in twenty-first-century Ghana, Stomach extends the public via its merger with the domestic and its appeal to the lowest ranks of the working poor. Enlarging the spatial and operational boundaries of the domestic realm, Stomach aggregates his less prosperous neighbors' bodily outputs. As opposed to "the middle classes keeping themselves to themselves" as Mumford's up-and-coming nineteenth-century city residents (1938) would have it, at Stomach's the expression and satisfaction of basic bodily needs allies urban dwellers across class fractions in a publicly accessible space. In Stomach's PCT, one form of conspicuous waste intermeshes with another, melding the waste-based general economy of Bataille (1988) and the status plays and displays captured by Veblen ([1899] 1994). At this working-class PCT, the aggregation and transformation of waste promises social mobility for customer and proprietor alike. Arrangements at Stomach's place flaunt the markers of leisurely living and impose codes of conduct in the name of "gentility," all while capitalizing on the bodily excesses of the urban poor. Unlike Ziginshore's Uncle, however, Stomach has no interest in controlling his customers' lives in toto. He is too invested in building his private wealth and public status and serving as a more distant object of aspiration for others.

It is difficult to characterize Stomach's operations and ambitions as explicitly political working from an Arendtian (1958) rubric stressing publicness and plurality, deliberation, and self-expression as defining features of political action. Contra Arendtian standards, the practices and infrastructures on which Stomach and his customers depend downplay verbal debate as a central means of public claims making. Neither are they demonstrably deliberative despite their broadly inclusive character. Likewise, they are designed to deflect rather than promote confrontation, whether among neighbors, users, proprietor, or municipal officials.

Nevertheless, built on bodily routines and substances, Stomach's infrastructural complex projects and protects collective interests and interdependences via the manufacture of public goods from private means. Private infrastructural investments such as Stomach's put bodies and their outputs on the urban map by carving out a common space for the participation and provisioning of Ashaiman's working poor. Compensating for the lapses and lacks of city government, the excesses and innovations of Stomach's private sanitary works in turn bring municipal authorities to attention yet hold them at bay. Neither in the stead nor in the thrall of the state, coded as living space, worksite, and sewage hold, the open-ended domesticity, waste flow, and runoff of Stomach's place at once deflect government incursion and entice public participation.

Case #2. Adepa Modern Toilet: Making Waste Respectable

Domestic Sanitary Extension Compound Style

We do not have one type of electric light for the rich and another for the poor. All these instruments have an objective standard of performance, determinable by experiment: they are products of a collective economy and are meant to fit into a collective whole. One's economic position may entitle one to a greater or smaller quantity, but the quality is fixed.
—Lewis Mumford, *The Culture of Cities* (1938)

Building the Best Toilet

Adepa Modern Toilet embodies other trends shared across Ashaiman's commercial toilet enterprises. The form and operational norms of Adepa Modern Toilet, like "Stomach Has No Holiday," demonstrate how sanitary infrastructures refigure public and private life and sociopolitical order in the face of limited state capacity. But compared to Stomach's place, Adepa is more fully integrated into the life of the household and surrounding neighborhood. In turn, it offers greater possibility of status mobility and public recognition. In the Twi language, *adepa* means "it's nice." And it is (see plate 31).

This private commercial toilet, classified as a Domestic Sanitary Extension, offers thirteen stalls with cistern-style water closets, individualized hand sinks, and lighted mirrors. The facility is located in an older, predominantly Muslim neighborhood not far from the center of Ashaiman. A classic example of the "compound-house" style, the area consists of single-story cement-block houses each containing a central courtyard. Entered from within the courtyard, banks of rooms typically line two, three, or even all four walls of the home. The central space is used for household activities such as cooking and washing and socializing. In the case of Adepa, with rooms on two sides and the entryway on another, the far end of the courtyard contains a series of shower stalls. Some used for storage, some used for bathing, they are not available for public use but reserved for household residents.

Adepa's public toilets are contained within a narrow corridor at the home's rear, a literal embodiment of the Hausa term for toilet, *bayan gidaa*, meaning "behind the house." Built several years after the original residence, on a raised platform, the long row of toilet stalls has a separate entrance although it shares a wall with the rest of the house. Like other PCTs associated with compound living arrangements, Adepa fits the classification of "attached compound style." Rather than being located within the confines of the courtyard, which would put customers in the midst of domestic life, Adepa's location behind the house marks off a space that is of the house but not in it. This "separate but attached" style permits easy access and communication while allowing a degree of discretion for customers and residents alike. With an arm's-length intimacy created by its entrance adjacent to the back door of the adjoining residence, entry to the toilet affords a fleeting glimpse of the interior courtyard. The proximity provides an opportunity to exchange glances and greetings with residents and their visitors. The interactions are optional, not obligatory.

Given the size and high quality of the facilities, it should come as no surprise that the proprietors of Adepa may be counted among Ashaiman's better-off. Though Adepa's owners are similarly staking their status on the control of wealth and property, unlike Stomach they do not carry the yoke of a past life of industrial or wage labor, having earned their wealth as traders and merchants. As such they bear their status differently. The female head of household, Madame Halima, is a woman well into her seventies who lived the first half of her life in northern Ghana before moving to Ashaiman. She has a longtime stake in the local water business, selling water to neighbors by bucket and barrel. Demonstrating her relative prosperity, Madame Halima's waterworks required substantial capital as well as social connections, first to install a household water line, and later to invest in two huge water storage tanks, mounted just outside the house, and the cement-lined in-ground cistern inside the compound (see plate 32).

Because it is household-based, the water business made it possible for Madame Halima to generate income while abiding by the lingering proprieties of purdah befitting a respected, older Muslim woman (Schildkrout 1982). Taking advantage of the already good patronage and ample supply of water, Halima eventually augmented her business with pay-per-use shower stalls located within the confines of the family yard—the remains of which

ADEPA MODEL

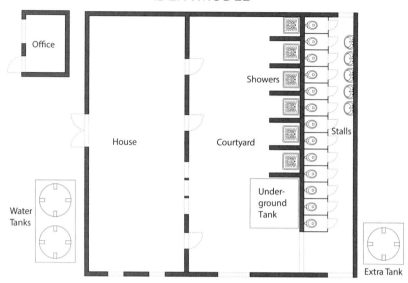

Figure 5.9. Adepa Modern layout (Created by Xhulio Binjaku)

are still visible. The traffic in and out of the house, a form of publicized domesticity afforded by the compound's enclosed yet accessible configuration, also provided an opportunity for sociability and increased the family's reach and influence in the community. Merging work and leisure while preserving status and respectability, Adepa is yet another reminder of how active investment in infrastructures integral to what Arendt (1958, 31) calls the menial "labors of living" can provide the very means to participate in public life.

Much like Madame Halima's water business, Adepa's toilets exhibit a similar combination of publicity and decorum, basic services and higher purpose. The move from water to showers to public toilets was spearheaded by Halima's adult son, Amir. A self-described "businessman and broker," Amir explained,

> I wanted to build the best toilet in the area: neat, attractive, and odor free—not like the government toilet down the street known for the overpowering stench and filthy drop holes. My neighbors were initially concerned. Fearing the smell emanating from the nearby public toilet would be even closer to home, they threatened to take me to court. I had to convince them that this is a beautiful toilet. It's one of the reasons I

try to make it so nice. I want it to be the best in Ashaiman, no two ways about it. Although it's not the largest toilet, I try to make it the cleanest.

The new toilet was an exercise in intentional design supplanting disgust surrounding human waste and filthy "gov'ment" toilets with desire for the clean comforts and civility of Adepa. Befitting its name, Adepa is exceptionally well-appointed. The stools and sinks are porcelain, and the basins plentiful compared to what is usually a single handwashing basin shared by all. The floors are tiled. The interior walls are neatly painted in contrasting tones. The exterior walls and dividers are plastered with the same stucco as the rest of the house and built from concrete block. Unlike the government toilets and some other PCTs, the individual stalls provide ample space and privacy. The doors to each stall are framed and painted in high-gloss finish. Above each stall, rows of perforated block in the classic Akan designs allow for air flow and light and add a decorative touch. It's all a neat, attractive setup.

Toilet Talk: Interpellating Interiority

With a raised roofline jutting several feet above the neighboring houses, Adepa is visible from hundreds of yards away. Bold lettering on all four sides spells out "ADEPA MODERN TOILET." As at Stomach's place, the eye-catching signage boldly communicates the toilet's purpose. On one side is a figure of a man, back straight, pants pulled down, sitting on a fully plumbed water closet. The other side bears a woman in the same pose distinguished from her partner by a string of waist beads. But here, different from Stomach in intention, neatly written in red next to each illustration is the word "Su-suka." An injunction to shun gossip and loud talk, *susuka* is an Akan (Twi) term that means "be discreet." Despite broadcasting the realities of human defecation, Adepa's very notice is bound up with calls for proper behavior. In other words, it's one thing to use a public toilet, and another thing to do so with the requisite decorum. Adepa PCT stresses the later. With its headlines "It's nice! Be discreet!" Adepa alerts customers and passersby not just about what to do but also about how to think and feel about it. Here we see how "specific canons of conduct" come to qualify generalized markers of conspicuous waste and expenditure (Veblen [1899] 1994, 56). Similar to the standards of "gentility" imposed by Stomach, Adepa associates public waste with what can be called an "aesthetics of propriety." In marked contrast to what Achille Mbembe (2001) describes as the "aesthetics of vulgarity" typifying the excesses of the state, Adepa's "aesthetics of propriety" signal a

Figure 5.10. "I care for you," 2013 (Photo by Brenda Chalfin)

counterpolitics acknowledging and overcoming the taint of waste through collective means.[10]

In the case of Adepa, these codes of conduct actively inculcate the dispositions of "honor, dignity, and worth" that are the signs and substance of the leisure class (Veblen [1899] 1994, 9). Meant to reflect the good graces of the toilet's source and target audience, Adepa's signage, to borrow from Louis Althusser (1971), interpellates toilet users and proprietors alike with polite injunction.[11] Going beyond the simple purpose of advertising to attract customers, Adepa's facilities are coated with verbiage pitched at those actively using the facilities. In contrast to the infrastructural obligations of Stomach's rebar, Adepa's signage assumes toilet users' literacy, voluntary compliance, and moral compunction. The interiors of the toilet stall doors are painted at eye level with flowery requests. One reads, "Please don't spit on the wall, we beg you." Another, "In the name of . . . I care for you." In these injunctions, use of the facilities is posed as a form of care akin to the moral compunctions of repair described by Steven Jackson (2014, 231) (see plate 33).

On the exterior wall, prefacing the common command "Don't urinate here," is the passively polite "Please stop." It is possible to read these verbal injunctions as explicit attempts to cultivate the very sort of "privatized interiority" regarding bodily functions described by Elias (1994) for Western Europe's ascendant urban classes in the context of modern state formation. In the case of Adepa, in a notable twist on Elias's historically derived model, the inculcation of norms of excretory comportment occurs in a manner that is externally mediated rather than self-imposed. Moreover, departing from Elias, it occurs in a space open to the intrusions of others despite the intensified sequestration of bodily functions.

In/Conspicuous Waste: Making Waste Respectable

Adepa is geared to the paired advance of toilet owners and toilet patrons alike, in contrast with Stomach's quest for social and economic distance from his customers by means of conspicuous waste. Combining displays of social decorum with displays of wealth, the very use of Adepa's facilities involves what Veblen ([1899] 1994, 17, 22) calls "invidious distinction," that is, "the valuation of persons in respect of worth—usually monetary." At fifty pesewa per visit, the cost of using the facility is among the highest in the area. Even more to the point, when it comes to luxe shitting, unlike other toilets in the greater Tema area, newspaper is not available as anal cleansing option in return for a lower toilet entry fee. At Adepa, which insists on grade "A" for all, only superior-quality toilet roll is offered to those who use the toilet.

Adepa exploits the qualitative diversity of sanitary services by providing top quality to all comers, contradicting Mumford's (1938, 419) observation that when it comes to the provisioning of urban public goods, there can be only one standard of quality. In line with Veblen's ([1899] 1994, 60) adage "In order to be reputable it must be wasteful," Adepa's proprietors and customers together make the most of "laying waste to waste." A kind of "superfluity" (Mbembe 2004) in reverse built on a double negative of wastefulness, in the name of respectability Adepa's owners and users invest substantial value and effort in making human waste conspicuously inconspicuous.

Mr. Amir stressed over and over his cleaners' use of special chemicals to minimize the odor of decomposing fecal matter in Adepa's septic tank. The toilet customers I surveyed remarked on the extraordinary condition of the facilities, which vastly outrank others in terms of neatness and cleanliness. Responses were consistent in sentiment:

"The facility has no scent like the others."

"There are many facilities around but I prefer using this toilet because it is very neat."

"It is far better and cleaner than the rest."

"Of a higher standard than the others."

"The others are not as clean as this particular one."

"I like the manner with which this facility is taken care of."

"This is better in terms of cleaning, painting, and water."

Customers went on to talk about Adepa's attendants, who not only clean and care for the place but also care for them. In terms of "likes and dislikes," one survey respondent noted the facilities' "neatness and the way the attendants swiftly respond to our needs." Another indicated that "the attendants are respectful and respond quickly to my complaints." Another mentioned "neatness and [that the] attendants are friendly." Here again, even more than Stomach's place, within the domesticated public realm of Adepa Modern Toilet bodily needs serve as a means of cultivating the sorts of plurality and participation mentioned by Arendt (1958).

Rather than a site of sensory offense and social disregard, customers experience Adepa as a site where their needs and preferences are duly recognized. Transcending Adepa's express function as a locus for the aggregation and deposition of human bodily waste, these remarks portray the toilet as a locus of respectability. From the inculcation of self-respect via toilet signage to the investment in labor and resources in making Adepa's toilets aesthetically and sensorially tolerable and the responsiveness of Adepa's attendants to customer requests, respectability was the defining feature of this PCT. Compared to Stomach's PCT, which emphasized social distance between customer and proprietor and explicit bodily discipline, Adepa's economy of waste maps a more intimate modality of infrastructure-based social and bodily transformation.

Respectability reflected well on Adepa's customers; even more, it reflected the wider project of Adepa's prime proprietor, Amir, for whom the toilet was both means and end. For Amir, by turning human excrement and toilets from an object of defilement to a source of income, and in turn a source of dignity and civility, Adepa's economy of waste marks his good repute, as

Figure 5.11. Adepa Modern entrance, 2013 (Photo by Brenda Chalfin)

it extends his public standing. Where Stomach's engagements with waste based on a fee-for-service model are more aloof, Adepa's sanitary service provision, to borrow from Bataille's concept of general economy, can be understood as a kind of "unreciprocated gifting" (1988, 38), or, more appropriately, an "unevenly reciprocated return on investment." With shit and money flowing back to Mr. Amir, the very sordidness of the transaction magnifies the status conferred to and by the toilet's proprietor, who is able to handle the base functions of waste management without being himself debased.

Unlike Stomach, who approached his duties in light of his past life as waged laborer and his current status as urban property owner, Adepa reflects Amir's reputation-bound sensibilities as a merchant. As indicated by the visible sharing of wealth, as Bataille (1988, 66) puts it, "the merchant defines himself by giving" in order to gain, parlaying personal reputation into public recognition. Amir told me that when he initially planned to build the toilet and his neighbors protested, they were backed by the member of Parliament (MP) from the area. Amir recounted, "Later, when the toilet was complete, the MP came back and apologized and told me he now understood the need for projects like mine." While it would be wrong to see in this shift from rebuke to respect a delegation of authority from public official to private citizen, it does indicate national and municipal deferral of responsibility to provide public goods.

In these exchanges it is also possible to observe how the character of public life comes to represent the investments and imperatives of urban elites rather than the self-conscious demands of urban residents or the priorities of state actors. The arrangement is curiously reminiscent of the classic, elite-dominated public realm of action described by Arendt (1958). Pointing to the diverse political correlates of a waste-inflected general economy, Bataille (1988, 71) refers to this sort of public influence as prestige, remarking, "Prestige, glory, rank should not be confused with power. Or if prestige is power this is insofar as power itself escapes the considerations of force or right to which it is ordinarily reduced." Here again, enabled by its infrastructural institutionalization outside the confines of state authority, waste underwrites political heterogeneity. Though mired in individual body processes and status contests, which Arendt (1958, 68) argues diminish the *vita activa*, when tied to collective recognition and participation, the open-ended possibilities of human plurality are nevertheless unleashed.

Rites of Passage: Domesticating Public Space

Adepa's impact on urban public life spills beyond the bounds of the toilet facilities, contributing to the "city-forming" character of household sanitary infrastructure. Pairing publicizing of domesticity with the domestication of public space, Madame Halima's water business extends to the home's exterior. Next to the massive water tanks beside the house, plastic buckets, yellow Kuffour-era water jugs, and an army of smaller receptacles line the home's exterior wall. Domesticating the public realm, the toilet business of Halima's son Amir similarly transforms the space surrounding the compound.

With Amir's permission and occasionally his presence, the rear passage separating the homes bordering the toilet is an informal meeting place for those using the facility and for others passing by. An infrastructural "in-between," this was not exactly a private space, nor was it a fully public domain where, in Arendt's (1958, 50) much-quoted phrasing, "everything can be seen and heard by everybody." And, though marking the boundaries between one household and another, as in the Greek city-states Arendt idealized, it did not conform to her (1958, 63) characterization as "a kind of no-man's land between the private and the public, sheltering and protecting both realms while, at the same time, separating them from each other." It was, instead, a space where public life was actively and deliberately domesticated. Previously operating as a "sanitary lane" in the days of the bucket latrines and night soil carriers, the off-street open-air corridor next to Adepa was now swept clean and lined with benches. This was where the toilet queue formed during the morning rush hour, via a mix of infrastructural insistence and bodily convenience. Near the table where the attendant collected fees and distributed toilet roll, it was a natural place to stop, converse, and relax once the rush subsided (see plate 34).

My field notes recount of the space:

> When I came to meet my research assistant [Mustapha Mohammed], I found him sitting with a few other men and drinking sweet green *ataya* tea. Prepared in classic Sahelian fashion, a Fulani man tends a well-worn kettle on a small coal pot on the ground. A tray filled with glasses is on the bench beside him. Customers come to the toilet while the attendant drinks tea. He tells them to leave the money and reach into the basket for their roll of toilet paper.

A public space anchored by the collective routines of bodily evacuation, the public toilet and the passage, as well as the rites attached to it, were both a function of and counterpoint to the shrouded yet insistent cohabitations of persons and excreta within its confines. The in-between space of the sanitary lane engendered its own forms of public order and sociality that transcended the shared humanity represented by the common production of waste matter. Decisively male, these arrangements ranged from loose to formally structured with an explicit hierarchy and purpose. An example of the latter is an occasion when I came to meet Mr. Amir in the lane too. My notes capture the encounter:

> A mat large enough to accommodate a half dozen or more is wedged in the narrow space between the houses. This not a private space but it allows for close interaction, a togetherness. Mr. Amir fills the center of the mat. He is at ease, chatting and relaxing, surrounded by an eager audience. A large man, his shoes are off and legs curled under him. As he spreads out on the plastic mat, young men and teenage boys sit around

him. Their numbers seem to grow over the course of our conversation. Amir tells a long story that starts out as a bluff and ends as a parable about political leadership in Ashaiman. The young men listen closely. When I introduce myself as a professor from the US, a few eagerly identify themselves as university and secondary school students. They ask me questions about my work and my research in Ghana. Taking a more formal tack befitting the gender codes of his station and generation, Mr. Amir wants to know about my children, if my daughter is old enough to marry, if I am a Muslim.

Built on the possibilities of the toilet, the drawn-out commensality of tea and talk depended on Amir's extension of domestic space and counsel. Another mode of "unreciprocated gifting" (Bataille 1988, 38), these exchanges can be considered akin to public festivities and sacrifices undertaken by archaic elites described by Bataille. Like sacrifice, this ad hoc part-public, part-domestic assembly "restores to the sacred world that which servile use has degraded and rendered profane" (55). As it overcomes the reduction of humanity to the commonality of excretion, "blending the individual indiscriminately with their fellows," it facilitates communion for a higher social cause (59). In contrast to Stomach's pursuit of distinction by flaunting his personal gain, the gathering around Adepa accentuated Amir's rank as it availed those present of his superior knowledge and standing. Amir's infrastructural in-between confounds Arendt's (1958, 85) divide "between activities which should be hidden in privacy and those that were worth being seen, heard, and remembered," as it dissolves the boundary between his status as household head and well-regarded public citizen and his customers' voluntary gatherings and involuntary bodily needs.

When I returned several months later, Mr. Amir was again holding court, but his presence shifted from social rite to religious ritual. On this visit the group congregated in the passage at the front of the house near the street, not the rear walkway.[12] It was Ramadan, and rather than the usual plastic mat and benches, they sat on a carpet underneath a white canopy. In honor of the holiday most wore long tailored outfits of fine cotton or wax print. Instead of watching films on someone's laptop, they quoted verses under Mr. Amir's tutelage. With Adepa's signboard looming overhead and the bank of water closets on the far side of the compound, the religious practices cannot be entirely separated from the operations of the public toilet or from the bodies who frequent them. Both activities are a means of correct training, individually interiorized yet publicly inscribed, and are at once equivalent and inverse: the toilet, conspicuously discreet, the prayer session, discreetly conspicuous. A source of taint, the toilet equally underscores the gathering's transcendence. Defilement begets purification, and so too religious rituals build on the body's daily passages. Made possible by Amir's moral leadership, instituted via infrastructure, and shored up by the relentless stain of human waste, the domesticated proprieties of Adepa toilet morph into pieties,[13] stamping their presence on a now domesticated public realm.[14]

Discussion

Ashaiman's Adepa Modern Toilet, joining Stomach, provides a compelling illustration of the way private infrastructures turn waste into a medium of public order and sociopolitical attainment in a context of limited state provisioning. Variations on a theme, Adepa's waste-based infrastructures configure and relate domesticity and publicity on their own terms. Compared to Stomach's toilet enterprise, which emphasizes social division while holding out the promise of incremental social mobility, Adepa's sanitary infrastructure operationalizes inclusion as a path to status, influence, and, ultimately, public recognition and legitimation. Closing the gap between commercial toilet operations and private household practices, at Adepa these potentials are inscribed in and activated via the spatial arrangement of sanitary installations. They are reiterated in the very meanings and values explicitly attached to infrastructural objects and functions. Drawing people into a social and locational middle ground poised between the domestic and the public realm, Adepa draws people into themselves by means of infrastructural interpellation. The excessive yet veiled visual and verbal allusions to waste—rendering waste conspicuously inconspicuous—are a medium of self-recognition and public association for Adepa's customers in this corner of Ashaiman.

With waste a source of respectability, tactics of collective self-regulation are in turn a source of prestige for Adepa's proprietor. The domestic is manifest in public space, underwriting Amir's presence in person and by infrastructural proxy in the public realm. Spilling into streets and alleys and merging with other collective rites of passage, such social and infrastructural sidelines overshadow the sordid outputs of the public toilet. In the process, they entice state actors to concede responsibility for both public waste and public good. Again, confounding Arendt's (1958) neat categorizations and demarcations, here control over the private disposition of waste serves not as means of "underground" infrastructural influence, as it is in the example of Stomach. Rather, Adepa's infrastructural apparatus, broadcasting private standards of propriety (e.g., Susuka!) serves as the basis of explicit recognition and legitimate presence in a public sphere that city authorities have increasingly domesticated and abdicated. Inclusive of the toilet and its immediate surrounds, the polis here is alive and well, but privatized in content and management despite its public locus. In the words of Arendt (1958, 198), "It is the space of appearance in the widest sense of the word, the space where I appear to others as others appear to me, where men exist not merely like other living or inanimate things but make their appearance explicitly."

Case #3. Lady Di and Daughters: Conviviality Begets Consubstantiation

Domestic Sanitary Enclosure, Suburban-Style

To live an entirely private life means above all to be deprived of the reality that comes from being seen and heard by others, to be deprived of an "objective" relationship with them that comes from being related and separated from them through the intermediary of a common world of things, to be deprived of the possibility of achieving something more permanent than life itself.

—Hannah Arendt, *The Human Condition* (1958)

Excremental Infrastructure as Domestic Centerpiece

The merger of domestic and public spaces and functions takes an even more dramatic form in the case of Ashaiman's Lady Di toilet. As in Ashaiman's other PCTs, in the void left first by state neglect and more recently by political deconcentration, waste-based infrastructure shapes the contours of a political heterogeneity that is a condition of life in the city. While Adepa pushes domesticity onto the street for purposes of mutual recognition and respectability, and Stomach's PCT promotes domestic propriety in the service of his own status attainment to entice the aspirations of others, Lady Di demonstrates its own alchemy of bodily waste, domestic infrastructure, and urban sociopolitical order. Here the form and function of Di's Domestic Sanitary Enclosure are productively aligned (see plate 35).

Showing the domestic realm to be a complex material order involving production and reproduction, labor and leisure, strangers and kin, consumption and evacuation alike, Lady Di's domestic enterprise gives further credence to Bataille's (1988) concept of "general economy." In Bataille's formulation, the generation and circulation of material excess prevails, unbound by substance or sector. This PCT is the combined workplace and abode of a prosperous businesswoman of middle age, "Lady Di," and her young-adult daughters, who range in age from late teens to midtwenties. Di's husband long ago relocated abroad. With an aggressive work ethic and sense of enterprise, Di is clearly head of the household. Di's toilet, bath, and water business is located in a large annex directly attached to the house. It is accessible from a well-marked side entrance and from within the residence. There are twelve showers and sixteen flush toilets spread across three rooms of the roofed annex. Contiguous with the family living area, Di's sanitary complex is equivalent in size to the already spacious home to which it is connected.

The infrastructural operations and configurations of Lady Di's place engenders a waste-based conviviality, drawing people into an ever-capacious domestic space to seed social interdependencies alongside waste's many excesses. In contrast to Stomach's place, which sows social divides as it models domestic ideals, Lady Di cultivates coeval participation to generate wealth and influence from the unmet needs and untapped resources of urban living. Compared to Adepa, where waste provides a pathway to status through its purification in the public sphere, Di's operates according to a more bounded centripetal logic in some ways similar to Manhean's toilets. But different from Manhean, where hierarchies are shunned and overcome, Lady Di's toilet concentrates infrastructure and social influence within the expansive space of her private household. Ever enlarging the household footprint while drawing new functions and persons within, Di's structure epitomizes the category of Domestic Sanitary Enclosure. Pulling customers and employees as well as technical operations inward, Lady Di's densely networked infrastructural array blurs the boundary between dwelling space and sanitary enterprise, customer and intimate, waste and wealth.

Among the most domesticated of Ashaiman's PCTs, Lady Di offers the greatest options for socioeconomic mobility likewise predicated on an "aesthetics of propriety." While this can be attributed to the intensification of infrastructural operations and options for customers and attendants to participate in the domestic realm, opportunities for betterment likewise hinge on Lady Di's relationship to Ashaiman's municipal authority. At Adepa, city representatives offer preemptive sanction and after-the-fact recognition of private sourcing of public provisioning. At Stomach's, sanitary infrastructure remains subject to sporadic municipal oversight and exaction. Infrastructure takes a different political form at Lady Di's, as ASHMA agents actively devolve resources and responsibility to the homeowner. In turn, at Di's, the operational scope and autonomy of the domestic is enhanced.

Bridging infrastructural and status divisions, Lady Di's centrality is also sociogeographic. Located more than a mile from Ashaiman's jam-packed commercial core, Di's is situated in an up-and-coming neighborhood characterized by a mix of income groups and asset classes. The area's name, Lebanon, comes from the Ghanaian military men who purchased land and settled there in the 1980s after participating in UN peacekeeping duties. Homes here are newer than those around Adepa, though not as uniformly built or as neatly planned. Many properties are under construction or undergoing renovation. On the whole they are much larger and more prosperous than the one-room shanties and kiosks around Stomach's. Representing a broad spectrum of incomes and housing stock, there are multifamily dwellings mixing residential and common space and exhibiting varying degrees of privacy, prosperity, and amenity depending on the owner's and residents' income levels.

Just across the lane from Lady Di's is a concrete-block home crowded with tenants. To accommodate additional residents in the already densely packed space, the courtyard contains a wood-clad extension. Laundry lines spill into the public thoroughfare. At the other end of the spectrum is a two-story stucco home adjacent to Di's. Self-contained, it is surrounded on all sides by a high concrete-block fence topped with coils of barbed wire. Lady Di's dwelling stands apart. Styled as a single-family suburban home, it occupies a large lot twenty-five meters long and bordered by vacant land. Impressive in size and condition, the home's public face is ostentatious yet tasteful, neatly painted in two-tone beige and brown. There are planters in front and a sculpted privacy wall. The front boundary is marked by a massive metal double-door driveway gate and a smaller front gate decorated with gold-toned fleur-de-lis and topped with razor wire. The infrastructures hidden behind the home's imposing walls activate a web of interconnected functions and configurations.

Making Infrastructure Work

In keeping with its classification as a Domestic Sanitary Enclosure, at Di's PCT, in contrast to both Stomach and Adepa, there is no concise divide between dwelling space and commercial sanitary operation. As its size and operational complexity have grown, Di's waste and water enterprise has spilled into areas once dedicated to family life. This crossover is reflected in

Figure 5.12. Infrastructural adjustments, 2013 (Photo by Brenda Chalfin)

and enabled by the dwelling's infrastructural underpinnings. Water storage tanks in front of the house fill overhead pipes climbing the walls and running across the roofing to serve taps and shower spigots in the rear. Drains carry gray water to gutters cutting through the courtyard before emptying at the home's edge. Sewage slurry from the flush toilets flows through sealed ground-level channels and from there to a subterranean septic tank on the other side of the house. A fragile repurposing of domestic infrastructure for commercial ends, the septic system is the original, built for household use, and must be emptied frequently to avoid overflow due to its modest size.

Just as commercial operations affect domestic infrastructure, commercial infrastructure reshapes domestic order. Exerting the most dramatic impact on household space and operations are Lady Di's waterworks. Consisting of an on-site borehole, multiple above- and belowground water storage tanks, and a dedicated room-sized water filtration and purification system, the waterworks have evolved rapidly since drilling contractors hired by Lady Di found water under the lot early in 2012. Because piped city water was unreliable and insufficient to serve a commercial facility of scale, Di appealed to the ASHMA Waste Management Office for counsel. She was advised to give up on city servicing and consider prospects belowground on her own property.

After being connected to a drilling firm by an ASHMA sanitation officer, Di's borehole struck "pay dirt." On more of a social call than official visit, the waste management official who provided the advice brought me to meet Di. After initially conferring with her in the district office, he was curious to find out how her water prospecting effort had fared. After we arrived, besides making small talk with an old schoolmate exiting from the toilet, the ASHMA officer congratulated her on her luck at so easily finding an auxiliary water source. Eager to show off the results, Di led us to the front of the house, just outside the driveway gate. She described the drilling process and pointed out the drill site, which was temporarily protected by an old oil drum. In this transaction ASHMA's representative acted less as frustrated overseer, as at Stomach's toilet, and more as a curious bystander available to facilitate a direct relation between a private property owner and a private service provider. Compared to the more passive interest of municipal authorities in Adepa's operations, at Di's, city representatives actively deferred to the private sector.

On my return to Ashaiman several months later, Di's hydrological standing took another turn, shifting her attention from what flowed into her sanitation system to what flowed through it. Though the water was plentiful, it was too salty to drink and required purification prior to use. An infrastructure all its own became necessary. The water is pumped from the borehole in front of the house to a one-thousand-gallon holding tank in the side yard. From the holding tank, it goes through a multistep purification process utilizing small, pressurized tanks connected to valved pipes and a series of filters, all reliant on electrical power. Further transforming domestic space, the water purification system—an infrastructure within an infrastructure—occupies the entirety of a room that formerly served as the household kitchen. White wall tile and the remnants of cabinets, a large picture window, and a cute alcove remained. All other fixtures were removed to make way for the purification tanks. From here, the filtered water is pumped into a 2,500-gallon polytank located near the garage fronted by the home's ornate gates. Looming large in the neighborhood skyline, the massive black storage tank made it easy to find Lady Di's place from afar. As an advertisement for itself, unlike the eye-catching graphics of Stomach and Adepa, no other signage is necessary (see plate 36).

Surrounding the house, jutting skyward and occupying the home's interior interstices, Di's infrastructural array at once encompasses the dwelling and is absorbed within it. In this boundary-blurring general economy of waste, to borrow again from Bataille (1988), Ashaiman's leisure class pursues its "on-going struggle for prominence" (Veblen [1899] 1994, 21) through the constant improvement and acquisition of waste-based assets. Here we see the marriage of utilitarianism and excess through the proliferation of domestic infrastructure. With the domestic realm providing form and cover for a complex worksite, Lady Di's is big business, though it is even more shrouded in domestic packaging than Stomach's satellite sanitary complex or Adepa Modern Toilet at the rear of Madame Halima and Mr. Amir's compound.

Lady Di and family live with and within this infrastructural assemblage as it encroaches on household space and functions. Adjacent to the pump room, the home's garage is a bedroom for the round-the-clock cleaning staff. Next to it is a small office. The office, the hub for the whole operation, is the conduit between living space and sanitary enterprise. This is where Lady Di or one of her daughters sits to collect fees and monitor operations. Just as the facility's workers and infrastructural add-ons push the boundaries of domestic space, for Di and her daughters, work and family life spill out across the premises of the public toilets and showers. The benches in the open courtyard, used by Di's daughters and customers alike, are a popular spot to sit and chat. Ringed by showers on two sides and a row of toilets on the other, the courtyard marks a continuum where household and enterprise, intimate and stranger, consumption and evacuation, overlap. Compared to what Veblen ([1899] 1994, 69) identifies as the shrouding of private life from observation keenly pursued among the "better classes," in Lady Di's case, domestic life is open for inspection.

If Stomach's enterprise reflects his past life as a waged worker, and Amir's Adepa reflects his status as a merchant, Di's economic location is of a different ilk. Di is demonstrably devoted to labor in accord with Arendt's (1958, 88) definition of the term: that is, labor power hidden in the private realm and geared to the reproduction of life. Yet departing from Arendt's strict divide between labor and work, Di substantially adds to the object world via her infrastructural investments and adjustments. Her efforts confound received distinctions between public and private, political and apolitical, the built and the bodily, male and female. Bending the classic category of *homo faber* in a matter unimaginable to Arendt (1958), Di can be construed as *femme faber*. Training her work on waste and water infrastructure to merge gender norms, bodily processes, and class aspirations to novel social and political effect, Di dramatically—if not radically—enlarges the social and operational boundaries of the household. Putatively private, the domestic under Di's charge, and further charged by the circulation of water, wealth, and waste, emerges as an ever-capacious domain.

Co-living and Co-laboring

Like Stomach, much of what Di does is supervisory: checking and overseeing the work of her cleaning crew. Her role, however, is more hands-on than Stomach's and involves much more of her own physical exertions to enable the bodily reproduction of others. Veblen ([1899] 1994, 50–51) observes of nineteenth-century modernity that women of ascendant strata toiled in a style demonstrably symbolic to avoid the impression of "idleness or indolence" yet ward against any suggestion of obligatory rigor. Veblen's assessment captures Di's work habits surprisingly well. Even as she labors alongside her staff, Di's canons of self-presentation are concise. She is always well-dressed and coiffed, makeup carefully applied. On the morning of one weekday visit, she was wearing a crisp multicolored lappa and blouse cut in a Nigerian style, complementing an ample figure suggestive of a plentiful lifestyle. As beads of sweat formed on her forehead in the aftermath of mopping and replenishing cleaning supplies, Di maintained a dignified bearing, her comportment well in line with Veblen's ([1899] 1994, 41) gender- and class-bound rendering of "vicarious leisure": "The largest manifestation of vicarious leisure in modern life is made up of what are called domestic duties."

At Di's, the "aesthetics of propriety" actively encompass both property ownership and proper terms of living. Di's labors involve the entrainment of not only employees but also toilet customers. Among other tasks, Di occupies herself filling the large blue barrels located near the first row of the toilets, a task that requires attaching a hose to the tap by the office and monitoring the flow of filtered water into the barrels several feet away. Plans were in the works to build a second septic tank. In the meantime, Di explained, due to the high cost associated with frequently emptying the existing household-sized septic tank, she decided to turn her water closets into "pour-flush" toilets. This requires that customers take a small bucket of water from the larger blue barrel and bring it with them to the toilet. When finished, they are expected to use it to flush their own waste. Di noted that the "reduced water usage allowed by pour-flush method means our septic

Figure 5.13. Conspicuous labor, 2014 (Photo by Eva Egensteiner)

Figure 5.14. Toilet stall with graffiti, 2014 (Photo by Eva Egensteiner)

tank would not fill so fast, delaying the need for expensive siphoning" (requiring the hire of a sewage "puller" truck). Di admits the briny borehole water would be sufficient to flush the toilets. Nevertheless, combining thrift with minor extravagance, she distributes the cleaner and more costly filtered water for the task, a vital remain in its own right. A common tactic of conspicuous consumption for an emerging leisure class striving to be noticed without being considered unduly profligate, Di here plays on the paradox that "an article may be useful and wasteful both" (Veblen [1899] 1994, 62).

An example of infrastructural intimacy at work, at Lady Di's, such colaboring generates a multiform conviviality—a term literally meaning "living together," "from *con-* 'with' + *vivere* 'live'" (*Oxford Dictionary of English* 2015). Proprietor and customer partake of a shared task, each working for the other when they would otherwise expect to do no work at all. Leveling the playing field and cementing their interdependence, proprietor defers to customer, and customer defers once more. At Lady Di's these interactions engender more affinal, consubstantial relationships, differing from the engrained hierarchies of Adepa and Stomach. In the transactional range of "communion" rather than "sacrifice," they blur the boundary between familial and commercial. Evocative of the training provided by Uncle to the youthful residents of Ziginshore, children are central to these exchanges. When surveyed, customer-respondents consistently remarked on the assistance provided to their family members, children most of all. One, a man who works as a clearing agent at the port of Tema, noted, "The cleaner helps my children fetch water to flush." Another, a man in his thirties, reiterated, "They consider my children when I go to work." A teenage girl recounted that when she goes to school early in the morning, the proprietors put aside three buckets of water for her to pick up at the end of the day: one for bathing, one for clothes washing, and the other to bring home. But in contrast to Uncle's, these are considered favors rather than investments.

Just as commercial and domestic space interpenetrate at Di's, so do social roles and relationships. Cultivating affinities and interdependencies in the course of attending to basic bodily functions, household membership is approximated. Not restricted to children, an expansive sense of household belonging demonstrates a form of co-living or conviviality stretching into cohabitation; customers of all ages comment on the intimate affordances that come with use of the facilities. Several commented on the "friendly seller" and "good customer relations." A regular customer confirmed, "If you forget soap and sponge, towel, the attendants will lend one to you." Frequent users bring clothing in garment bags to dress for work each morning after evacuating and bathing. One man bluntly remarked on the extended terms of his inclusion. Mixing money, bodily waste, and social contract, he said, "I shit on credit."

At Lady Di's conviviality extends from sanitary service delivery to living standards more generally as attention to bodily needs merges with leisure pursuits. Here Veblenesque "canons of taste" ([1899] 1994) are tried on and tried out as customers share in the pastimes and preferences of the toilet's proprietors. At Di's, the office TV is mounted on a high shelf for easy viewing from all angles and tuned to the latest films and serials. Like other patrons, a neighbor who works as a driver explained, "When I come here, I watch movies while I wait my turn." As one woman put it, "There are games like Ludo and cards that I play when I'm bored at home," regardless of her need to use the toilets and showers. Another, who described her occupation as "housewife," recounted that she regularly brings food to eat at the benches near the shower stalls and office. Showing none of the privations or isolations of the classic notion of privacy noted by Arendt (1958, 58), and making ostensibly private possessions available to others (71), Lady Di's domestic emerges as a site of everyday conviviality encompassing both common enjoyments and commensality.

Affective and infrastructural, such arrangements engender a space of plurality drawing people from without and incorporating them into domestic routines. Broadcasting the proper terms of self-care while expanding the social and spatial boundaries of the household, Di's daughters told me it was their intention to "teach people 'best practices' when it comes to sanitation" such as "using the hand basin with soap and towel." Though similar in spirit to Stomach's posted "Orders of Gentility" and Adepa's hand-painted "I care for you," no such signage is provided. Rather, in the shared domestic space of the toilet complex, Di and her family members are a near constant presence, involved in give-and-take with customers, monitoring the premises, and moving across the complex to ensure that the filters, drains, water pipes, and hoses are functioning as they go about their own lives. The infrastructural intimacies at Di's place precipitate the infrastructural inchoate as commercial toilet infrastructure and domestic space and operations vie for standing as figure and ground, intertwined and constantly trading places.

My discussions with Lady Di's middle daughter, Stephanie, required following her around the household interior and exterior, weaving a tight path between polytanks, filter room, borehole, and pump, as she adjusted valves, moved hoses, and checked water levels. Here, just as private needs turned into public matters, private space became publicly accessible via the day-to-day operations and adjustments of sanitary infrastructure. Harking back to the infrastructural intimacies in play at Tema's battered pumping stations and broken sewage lines, customers' and clients' relationship to sanitary infrastructure at Lady Di's was mediated by the lives and labors of the toilet's proprietors. These interventions, like Stephanie's adjustments, closed infrastructural loops. Others, from the TV and games, to assistance filling buckets, generated, if not imposed, social relations where none were technically necessary. Approximating the public, the private becomes "held in common." By means of waste and infrastructure, the radical intensification of privacy, so multilayered that it becomes a shared domain, is a far cry from the privations mentioned by Arendt (1958, 58) in the above epigraph.

Economies of Excess

Though routinized, the infrastructural mediations in place at Lady Di's were not immune to interference or outcomes beyond the proprietor's control. Driven by the inherent excesses of bodily processes, there was the inevitable public exposure to body odors, rhythms, and residues. For instance, in spite of toilet customers' and the proprietor's best efforts, the bucket-based pour-flush system made it difficult to fully clear the toilet bowls of feces. Toilets and showers were sites of other kinds of intimate expression. Notwithstanding the extensive monitoring by Di, family, and employees, the toilet stalls exhibited the same sort of graffiti, called "latrinalia" by Alan Dundes (1966), found in more transient public locations (Amevuvor and Hafer 2019). Channeling expressive excess, scratched into the wooden doors in Akan (Twi) were the phrase "*me wɔ ha*" (I was here); professions of love such as "*Adua ene me*" (Adua and Me); and raunchy epithets like "*Me pet we*" (I like cunt). Mixing the privacy of individual toilet stalls with expressive freedom, here are echoes of Arendt's (1958, 26) depiction of the polis as a space of discursive plurality.

Along with the expressive excesses of bodily outputs, there were other kinds of somatic surplus shaping social relations at Lady Di's. With impacts above and beyond the bare essentials of bodily need, waste infrastructure was an element in this process but not its end point. In the home's rear courtyard, on the high walls surrounding the shower and toilet stalls, remnants of Lady Di's earlier restaurant venture were visible. Signage with oversize lettering spelling out "Banku, Fufu, Konkonte," "Grilled Tilapia," and "Drinking Spot" was still discernable through the chipped paint. Indicating Di's abandonment of a food-and-drink business for a more lucrative foray into sanitary services, the faded decorations suggest the equivalence of private pay-per-use toilets and baths with dining out.[15] Harking back to Uncle's adage that "people liked a good place to shit, the same way they liked a good place to eat," no one expressed concern about the blunt juxtaposition of lavish meals and the necessities of bodily evacuation, least of all Di and family, for whom waste making and waste management was a mode of status attainment, regardless of its substantive form.[16]

At Di's there was little dividing line between luxury and waste, frivolous consumption and bodily needs, just as there was little differentiation between public and private in this self-made manifestation of the infrastructural inchoate. Inculcating canons of personal taste as those of rank are inclined to do (Veblen [1899] 1994, 71), this point was vividly illustrated one Saturday afternoon when I arrived at Di's. Her daughter Stephanie had just returned from downtown Accra loaded with baubles she intended to sell. The bundles of earrings, necklaces, and multipiece jewelry sets were discards of London brands still bearing price tags from Marks & Spencer and H&M. Stephanie arrayed them on the floor of the shower area atop a plastic mat to begin a venture in moneymaking and status-based social reproduction not entirely different from her mother's. We sorted through them with her older married sister, Lucy, a teacher and proprietor of a private school nearby. Lucy was fashionably if casually dressed as she sat on a stool by the toilets. Wearing a necklace culled from an earlier haul, she ably sorted through the best of the lot. Engrossed in conversation and dazzled by the mountain of costume jewels, we had forgotten that a man was in the shower stall behind us. Forcing the door open, he stepped over the wares as the sisters continued to sift through Stephanie's finds, barely missing a beat. A collective reverie born of vicarious co-consumption, contrasting with the rites of public sacrifice and purification at Adepa, here was yet another manifestation of communion at Lady Di's (see plate 37).

Visible proof that human excreta can beget metaphorical gold—both real money profit and fake metal—in this consubstantiation of wealth and waste, sanitary elites shined their prospects on a larger public while gleaning possibility from their neighbors' bodily excess. Whether in the case of jewels or shit, this was all about who had the means to turn waste into a source of public value, an intention linking the material foundations of Bataille's

(1988) general economy and the symbolism of Veblen's ([1899] 1994) vicarious expenditure. With infrastructure the linchpin in the equation due to its operation as a means of concentration, conversion, and accumulation, no wonder Lady Di and daughters attended to their sanitary assemblage with such fierce intent. About more than the production of material wealth, Lady Di's domestic infrastructural array was also a machine for manufacturing social order. Fostering both lateral parity and centripetal dependence, Di's network of borehole and storage tanks, water lines and purification tubes, sewage channels and septic system formed the armature and engine of a full-blown infrapolitics, fully acknowledged by city authorities and fully at home. Tentative in her analysis, Arendt (1958, 160) reluctantly admits, "*Homo faber* is fully capable of having a public realm ... even though it may not be a political realm properly speaking." Di's place presents an unanticipated manifestation of such a possibility.

Conclusion: Heterogeneous Power and Waste Work

In a city where most homes do not have toilets and government facilities are few in number and poor in quality, Ashaiman's private commercial toilets, such as Stomach, Adepa, and Lady Di, offer a viable sanitary option for urban residents. As bodily care is never simply a personal matter despite its intensive individuation (pace Elias 1994; Mumford 1938; Laporte 2002), Ashaiman's sanitary designs do more than provide a reliable space to shower and shit. Rather, as these cases make clear, they demonstrate the diverse ways domestic infrastructures turn the private disposition of bodily waste into an arbiter of social order and public life. Though not "governmental" in the classic Foucauldian (1979) sense of the term, these installations are inherently—though not always overtly or self-consciously—political in genesis and effect. Pursuing rank and resources via private means of public service provision, as in Manhean, Ashaiman's public toilets make the most of what the "state refuses and leaves behind" (Bataille 1985). But in contrast to the parities of Manhean's poor, Ashaiman's public toilet proprietors worked to encode infrastructure-based modalities of interdependence and status mobility through the accumulated agency of Bataille's (1985) "accursed share."

Fully of and in the household yet fundamentally public, the manifestation of deep domesticity at Di's place, as at Adepa and Stomach, is contra an orthodox reading of Arendt (1958). Notably, the "labors of living" put on display here cannot be separated from the material world of work and fabricated things. Given their popular and participatory character, and foundation in self-determination, choice, and consent, neither can they be separated from what Arendt calls "action": "the initiative to introduce the novum and the unexpected into the world" (Passerin d'Entreves 2019). A far cry from Arendt's endorsement of the classical ideal of the polis, Ashaiman's waste-driven versions of *vita activa* are admittedly highly conditional in their blending of expressive action, making, doing, and relationship building. They are rooted in private acts and domestic routines, which are public, plural, and participatory, if hierarchical. Organized around pragmatic ends and autonomous bodily processes, they claim an expressive domain where the somatic and performative vie with the declarative. Nevertheless, the recurring, popularly constituted contours of Ashaiman's private sanitary solutions render them a nodal and, indeed, vital feature of everyday politics and public life in an urban domain where the polis roves between nowhere and everywhere.

As opposed to the heavy hand of state oversight, as in the case of Tema's founding under the aegis of Kwame Nkrumah and Dinos Doxiadis at independence, or the incremental social engineering of Jane Drew, Maxwell Fry, and A. E. S. Alcock at the end of colonial reign, Ashaiman's excremental infrastructural organization and operations reflect and respond to the limits of state and municipal provisioning. In the process, Ashaiman's dwelling-based commercial toilets transform the nature and potential of the domestic realm, collectively organizing bodily rhythms and routines, shaping social status, and establishing the parameters of public interactions, outlooks, and locations.

While Ashaiman's infrastructural agglomerations are premised on an ethos of access, participation, and social betterment, the pursuit of parity vies with the preservation and projection of rank, providing further evidence of their political character, however veiled. Lady Di is founded on the wide-ranging possibilities of domestic interdependence and incorporation. Augmenting the scope of the domestic realm, these emplaced and embodied alliances boost the proprietor's material assets and oversight, along with the social potential of her customers. Stomach offers exposure to the trappings of working-class attainment, although their actualization, along with the proprietor, remains at arm's length. Adepa, in turn, promises inclusion in the social network and mores of an ascendant merchant class. All in the name of respectability, these social gains require the investment of time, money, private discipline, and public exposure for Adepa's customer base. Indeed, Adepa blurs the boundaries of the domestic realm as it diffuses into public space, augmenting public recognition and participation.

Sharing organizational propensities with Stomach Has No Holiday and Adepa Modern, Lady Di stands apart in notable ways. Situated at the heart of the proprietor's dwelling space and dominating the routines of resident family members, infrastructural intimacies at Di's are the most deeply internalized into household space, relationships, and operations of Ashaiman's commercial toilets. Di's also contains the most extensive infrastructural array, linking the home's original septic tank and newly discovered underground water source, low-tech pour-flush toilets, and high-tech water purification system with its tangles of hoses, pipelines, pumps, drains, and massive storage tanks. Thus configured, Lady Di's largely self-contained sanitary infrastructural installation pushes the internal and external boundaries of domestic space. Drawing persons and functions inward, the shared space of Di's toilet complex opens domestic life for inspection while turning domestic attention to the management and workings of public goods.

Though an exercise in infrastructural self-provisioning, a Latourian (2005b) network-centered analytic reveals these possibilities to be enabled by the nexus of forces—both natural and social—outside of Lady Di's immediate control. First are the circumstances not quite of state absence but, better put, of state abstention. Initially a by-product of Tema Municipal Authority's active disinterest, and more recently of ASHMA's passive refusal to provide adequate sanitary services, city authorities devolve resources and responsibility to residents and homeowners in Ashaiman. In Di's case, representatives from ASHMA's Waste Management Department tacitly encouraged her interest in drilling a well at her property's edge, indirectly enabling her to do so. In turn, adding the in/determinacies of nature to the mix, the plentiful, nearly potable water found under her home fueled the expansion of Di's sanitary infrastructural system. Demonstrating that connection does not necessarily imply extroversion, such entanglements enhance the autonomy of Di's domestic setup.

Stomach and Adepa's infrastructural operations, and thus their politics, are likewise entangled with the forces of nature and those of the state. At Stomach, the flies and fecal buildup in an unsanctioned cesspit are an affront to the municipality's regulatory claims. At the same time, the errant runoff from Stomach's showers comes to define the boundaries of his property—its scent both beckoning and deflecting users—and takes advantage of the city's overburdened roadside gutters and inspection team. Alternatively, at Adepa, the denaturing of bodily processes via social and religious ritual elevates toilets above the state in terms of social and moral good, with conversation and commensality covering up the debasements of co-shitting.

Harking back to Bataille's concepts of "general economy" and "accursed share," which recognize power as heterogenous and extraneous, Ashaiman's private sanitary enterprises are a testament to wringing value out of waste to generate an expansive circuitry of bodily expenditure and material accumulation. In Di's case, it is forged from excreta, groundwater, and the shreds and patches of underused domestic space. Across these locations, as Bataille recognizes and Veblen affirmed well before him, the political economy of waste is steeped in social and somatic signification. Illustrating this point, Stomach brings into relation the unfulfilled and overextended bodily cycles of Ashaiman's underemployed working poor and the surplus savings of a once-waged worker. Adepa aligns the small indulgences of sugared tea, leftover public space, and leisure time with Amir's freely offered counsel and spiritual wisdom to elevate neighborhood residents' quality of life and public reputation. These are not the superficialities of Arendt's (1958) category of "the social" but indicate deeper moral solidarities and conventions.

In his call for an integrated rather than segmented reading of Arendt's framing of *vita activa*, Patchen Markell (2011) locates "work" as a core operator in the rendering of political life. He writes, "Work is the specific activity that stands between and separates labor and action—two activities that are so perilously similar in their processual structure and lack of durable results that the former threatens to swallow up the latter unless they are held apart" (23). With Ashaiman's self-made sanitary installations in view, it is apparent that infrastructure—an often-overlooked component of Arendt's notion of work—is key to this dynamic. Rife with the heterogeneous materialities of the lived world potently theorized by Bataille (1985, 1988), the waste-based infrastructures of the body found in Ashaiman tread this fine line. Amid individuals' quest for bodily survival and social membership, these built and lived forms collectively translate "labor" to "action."

Like Bataille's "formations of social heterogeneity," in tension with the "social homogeneity" of "the State," "which delineates it by exclusion" (Bataille 1985, 139–40), these infrastructural solutions are outside of and in response to state practices. They emerge in the void of long-standing municipal underprovisioning under the TDC and more recent delegitimation of the long-used household pan latrine by Ghana's Environmental Sanitation Policy. Each of these waste management systems bears a distinct relationship to municipal bodies, actors, and regulations, which in turn shape and interface with their technical arrangements, domestic organization, and status plays. Stomach resists municipal overreach while taking advantage of municipal resources and installations to make viable and profitable its low-tech sanitary solutions. Adepa, alternatively, elicits governmental recognition and municipal renunciation of responsibility in return for cultivating public space, public services, and respectability in the public sphere. Di, in turn, incorporates municipal knowledge, networks, and protections to deepen the scope of domestic functions and social interdependencies despite the denial of government resources.

The household-based excremental experiments of Ashaiman's upwardly mobile capture a different nexus of infrastructural fabrication and urban political order than the urban planning schemes of Nkrumah and Doxiadis, which mobilized grand-scale urban infrastructure as means to thwart class politics. Ongoing, and continually recrafted and replenished, Ashaiman's infrastructural solutions may well be more enduring in their deep-seated patterning of urban plurality. Enlivened by the material and semiotic excesses of human excreta, Ashaiman's dwelling-based waste infrastructures in each of these instances stands as a nexus of domestic spatial organization, social aspiration, and regulatory reach. From a Domestic Sanitary Enterprise such as Stomach to the Domestic Sanitary Extension of Adepa to Di's Domestic Sanitary Enclosure, these hybrid configurations of public and private, biotic and inanimate, profit and expenditure, desire and disgust, claim a dynamic and insistent presence across Ashaiman's urban landscape. In turn, they push the limits of political possibility in this rapidly growing city. Vying with Tema for regional ascendance, Ashaiman's popularity and political dynamism render the planned city and its sewage system a remnant of an irreparable past. All the while, Ashaiman's residents respond to the realities of state neglect with solutions of their own.

In the background looms an emerging tug-of-war over urban sanitation between Ashaiman's fledging municipal authority, newly instated after years of neglect by the Tema Development Corporation and Tema Municipal Assembly, and community members such as Stomach, Mr. Amir, and Di. These residents turned public service providers fill the gap to sustain the public good. Now that a bona fide municipal government is in place, the sight of PCTs "mushrooming" is increasingly experienced by ASHMA leadership as an affront to their authority. Indicating ASHMA's weak hold on urban bodies and public life, privately based public provisioning is in growing tension with the aspirations of the municipality to assert a monopoly on urban waste (Chalfin 2019, 2020). Whether the dense ties of domesticity and infrastructural intimacy will serve as an adequate bulwark to dismantling is yet to be determined.

Conclusion. From Vital Politics to Deep Domesticity
Infrastructure as Political Experiment

Vital Politics and Urban Possibility

The stories of septic tanks, biogas flares, flush mechanisms, underground pipes, pumping wells, manholes, augur rods, ablution blocks, and repurposed pan latrines, and the persons whose lives and livelihoods propel their functioning, make evident that excremental infrastructures are vibrant arenas of urban plurality and political deliberation in the thriving West African urban zone that constitutes the city of Tema. Laying the foundation for what I call the "vital politics of infrastructure," on the one hand waste is a vital material, full of life and essential to it, exercising an agency of its own related to but separate from the bodies and agencies of its makers. On the other hand, the very infrastructures devised to channel and contain human waste reflect diverse social and political projects, turning waste into a subject of control as well as a basis for collaboration and challenge to systems of domination. Never fully settled, each excremental infrastructural solution harbors new tensions and vitalities as it answers to essential human needs and conditions urban coexistence. Centralized state authorities claiming a monopoly on waste, just as they seek to monopolize other forms of human excess (pace Bataille 1988; Tilly 1985), further color and complicate the contentions of urban excremental order.

The case of Tema is not exceptional in terms of system failures, fissures, or collateral effects. However, Tema's sanitary history brings to the fore forces otherwise suppressed, pushed to the backstage of urban administration and the backs of less fortunate communities in cities elsewhere. What makes Tema stand out is the remarkable variety and resourcefulness of the solutions posed to a common range of late modern sanitary challenges. Unraveling this reality—why, how, how generalizable, and to what effect—has been the object of this book.

Part of the explanation for Tema's exceptionalism lies in the heavy hand of high-modernist urban planning and nation-building that posed excremental infrastructure as a means of political containment at the city's founding and sowed the seeds of system inadequacy and faulty international fixes early on in the city's existence. The other part lies in the sheer resourcefulness of Tema residents striving for dignity and decency, income and investment opportunities, and the sorts of security and social support Tema's governing authorities were not fully equipped or inclined to provide, especially to those living at the city's geographic and socioeconomic margins, no matter their importance to urban functioning.

Besides these human intentions, this book has focused on a more complex in-between: the unexpected, not fully containable conjunctures and middle grounds where these diverse motives and their associated material manifestations meet. What happens in these spaces of intersection—what Actor Network Theory scholars call "gatherings" and "assemblies"; residents refer to as "ghettos," compound toilets, Susuka, Floshin Taifi, Stomach, and Adepa; and city administrators call private commercial toilets, contract toilets, unauthorized extensions, and illegally built structures—where new norms and routines take hold and new alliances as well as inequalities emerge? What staying power do they have? How do they inform the wider social and political fabric of the city?

Herein lies the book's driving concern with the distribution of power and the nature of public life and plurality made manifest in urban infrastructures. The book's chapters indicate that understanding what Arendt calls the *vita activa*—the actualities of living together in the world to enable individual and collective survival and fulfillment—cannot be separated from Latourian concerns with the full range of material forms and forces shaping and sustaining urban coexistence. This is where the vitality of excremental things, from the bioactive vitality of human bodies and bodily outputs to the vitality of landscapes, waterways, and human-made infrastructure—pipes, pumps, pits, courtyards, extensions, enclosures, showers, hand-wash stations, rebar, sit-and-squat toilets, methane-powered kitchens, water purifiers, holding tanks, siphons, mains, and more—come into play.

Several matters stand out in analyzing these arrangements. Most evident is the viability of excremental infrastructural solutions forged by Tema residents in the face of systemic faults. Different from a more familiar story of near overwhelming infrastructural collapse and dysfunction (Chance 2018; Hoffman 2017; Stamatopoulou-Robbins 2020), Tema residents turn the remaining elements of the city's midcentury infrastructural order to new ends. While it would be wrong to romanticize these excremental alternatives and downplay the very real health risks of poor sanitation, they are remarkably functional, if imperfect. Offering enduring solutions to urban needs, they are systemic interventions at scale that improve the quality of urban life. With designs and operations calibrated to reflect the distinct social and historical conditions of different sections of the city, Tema's novel infrastructural formations are fully incorporated into urban lifeways and landscapes. Despite their departure from proposed national and international models and standards, they need to be taken seriously as real solutions to real urban problems. This is not to endorse second-best outcomes for African cities. Rather, it is to recognize the value of what Matthew Gandy (2006) calls "urban life support systems" formulated from within. Would it not be appropriate for national and international experts to start here and work with Tema residents and waste proprietors to promote access, improve efficiency, and deter disease and health risk as opposed to importing another round of half-hearted, inadequate, and underfunded foreign fixes?

The case of Tema likewise confounds—if not disproves—the "sanitary-political paradox" that assumes private toilets, along with other forms of private, liberal personhood, to be the cornerstone of democracy and development. Tema's "unimproved sanitary facilities," downgraded by international agencies as developmentally substandard, in fact encode democratic principles of inclusion, participation, self-determination, and upward mobility. Built on resources, networks, and relationships internally generated and sustained, they offer essential public services to residents exceeding basic sanitation. Operating largely in the stead of city authorities, they simultaneously emulate and push back against the terms of municipal governance. Beyond the demarcation and recapitulation of state functions, Tema's excremental infrastructures, moreover, impinge on public space, whether domesticating public space in Ashaiman, claiming it in Manhean, creating it in Ziginshore, or protecting it in Tema's core. Though they shape the parameters of individual self-determination, Tema's excremental experiments call attention to the limits of state provisioning while building urban connectivity and collective life. Cultivating inclusion and interdependence among diverse urban dwellers and creating arenas for participation and mutual recognition, these are fundamental features of democratic coexistence.

In the very defiance of the high-modernist script of urban development wrought by means of division—of bodies, bodily functions, classes, spaces, production, and reproduction encoded in Arendt's discrete categories of work, labor, and action—Tema's examples of "deep" or "expansive domesticity" are part and parcel of democratization. Publicizing domesticity and defying the divisions between public and private life assumed to be essential to urban modernity, Tema's excremental arrangements expand what is acceptable and desired in public and alter public norms and expectations. More open-ended than bounded, these are largely nonexclusive infrastructural formations, not entirely privatized even if privately operated. Along with shaping the conventions of public life, Tema's excremental experiments extend the potentials of domestic life. These sanitary solutions augment the range of persons and interactions in domestic space; share norms of propriety, social interaction, and self-care; and seed new practices and desires. Such transformations directly shape the lived and fabricated world of the domus: from materials, aesthetics, and layouts to the types and interlinkages of technologies in and around domestic space and the range of persons who visit, reside, or otherwise dwell there.

Anchored in or building on the domestic realm alongside the day-to-day functions of the human body, Tema's excremental infrastructure-based transformations broadcast and legitimize domestic investment and innovation as a means of urban status and social influence and upward mobility for proprietors, operators, customers, and hangers-on alike. Certainly, these arrangements may limit the purported freedoms of self-determination protected by the mantle of privacy. However, for many if not most of Tema's urban residents in Manhean, Ziginshore, Ashaiman, and even in Tema's core, overcoming the very real privations of residential, income, and infrastructural insecurity trump the supposed premiums placed on privacy (contra Elias 1994; Laporte 2002; Mumford 1938). Surely you can "shit alone" just as you can "eat alone," to borrow from an Akan proverb (van der Geest 1998). However, joining the collective to satisfy private needs opens a much greater range of possibility for self-determination than going it alone, even when it comes to bodily evacuation.

Tema's novel excremental infrastructures, along with fostering collectivities in response to pressing individual needs, affect the urban built environment and broader political landscape of the city. In turn, they signal and act on a wider set of political economic transformations already afoot. By no means exclusive to West Africa, Ghana, Tema, or the global South, notably, the scope and capacity of the modern state form has substantially waned in comparison to its mid- to late twentieth-century high-water mark when Tema was built (Scott 1998). Nikolas Rose (1996, 327) characterizes this sea change in governmental ends, tucked under the vast umbrella of the neoliberal turn (Chalfin 2010; Harvey 2005; Sassen 1996), as "the death of the social," where society, public goods, and social justice are "no longer a key zone, target and objective of strategies of government."

Though not always portrayed as an integrated complex of global historical recalibrations, the shift in governmental ends and means is intertwined with several other factors. They include the breakdown of an infrastructural landscape inherited from post–World War II industrial modernity; the rise of project-based development fixes; worldwide urban agglomeration; and the untrammeled force of other-than-human and human-induced actants, otherwise known as the Anthropocene (Fortun 2014). All are in play in Tema, and all are registered in the quotidian operations of toilets, sewage trucks, severed trunk lines, disused settling ponds, frustrated residents, and overburdened city officials. Although Tema's infrastructural reordering might be considered a small facet of much larger adjustments, this book offers a reading of its significance as a telling sign of future possibilities to come. As eloquently put by Steven Jackson (2014, 221), "Many of the stories and orders of modernity (or whatever else we choose to call the past two-hundred-odd years of euro-centered human history) are in process of coming apart, perhaps to be replaced by new and better stories and orders, but perhaps not." Tema tells such stories.

Infrastructure and Excremental Politics in Tema

We cannot forget that Tema has long been an infrastructural forerunner. Evidence from this model West African city makes it clear that the quintessential modernist pact sanitizing and sewering the city to enforce state monopoly of urban waste and, through it, urban bodies (Elias 1994; Harvey 2003; Laporte 2002; Mumford 1938) cannot be taken for granted as natural, best, or inevitable. In Tema's case, this is not because it hasn't happened but because this rubric of urban rule has already proved inadequate. As the chapters make clear, the realities of twenty-first-century excremental provisioning in Tema chart a sweeping reimagination and retooling of mid-twentieth-century designs for the city devised under the leadership of

President Kwame Nkrumah with the aid of the planner Constantinos Doxiadis. For Nkrumah and Doxiadis, as for the theorist Arendt, the labors of bodily reproduction were best kept out of the public sphere. For all of Tema's successes in creating a haven for middle-class living, cosmopolitan outlooks, and industry-driven prosperity, this vision was inherently fragile when it came to the city's infrastructural underground.

Prone to breakdown, lacking routine maintenance, overwhelmed by the volume of waste, and subject to piecemeal expansion and repair, Tema's idealized infrastructural order failed to meet expectations even before its planned residential neighborhoods were complete. The inadequacy of sanitary arrangements was evident in the communities built under the mantle of Tema Development Corporation in partnership with Doxiadis Associates. It was even more apparent in the resettlement "village" of Tema Manhean, built and designed prior to the city center. The limits of the planned system were evident, too, on Tema's outskirts, in Ashaiman, where virtually no viable provisions were made for migrants forcibly relocated from Tema's core yet still under the ambit of TDC. The celebrated sanitary system was also of little merit in the settlements that emerged in the very crosshairs of the infrastructural grid, such as Ziginshore, located at the juncture of Tema's industrial area, fishing harbor, and sewage trunk lines leading to the original sea outfall at Paradise Beach. As a result, Tema's officially scripted excremental arrangements spawned alternative waste management solutions marked by intentional as well as unexpected revitalizations of forms and materials otherwise deemed defunct.

Sites of contention where residents challenge the limits of centralized authority, whether state, municipal, or customary, Tema's infrastructural alternatives stand apart from the recursive yet largely ephemeral impacts of everyday activism (pace Chance 2018; Robins 2014). This is due to their embedding in the urban built environment and incorporation into day-to-day routines and bodily practices. That is, they are not examples of what "might" be. Their very presence and operation do the work of transformation, aided and abetted by the unstoppable vitality of human bodies and bodily outputs. Tema's excremental solutions, to draw on the words of Bruno Latour (1993, 142), are examples of "democracy extended to—*and through*—things themselves," including human bodies.

Notably, Tema's novel excremental orders make public the very divisions city planners sought to shroud in the private domain of the household, complicating the received premises of urban life. Popular but not always egalitarian, they work from and around the class distinctions and expectations of economic mobility and security promised by the city's midcentury master plan. The private does not disappear, however. The domus remains central to the new system, but it is a much more open-ended configuration than assumed possible or appropriate. A modality of "domesticating" democracy and deepening and expanding the terms of domesticity, these homemade parliaments of bodily waste map abstract principles onto basic human needs. Evident across the city, Tema's infrastructural experiments actualize political possibilities that the city's original planners and their internationalist peers, including political theorist Arendt, could have little imagined, both defying the received order and mobilizing it to new ends.

To understand these dynamics, it is essential to recognize that human waste is a political matter, not just with respect to the impositions of colonial hygiene and modernist planning but also more generally. Excrement is caught in a categorical middle ground between public and private, individual and collective, state and society, resource and risk, and thereby unsettles the urban social contract. As evident in Tema, while it may be pushed out of site and rendered politically silent, bodily waste and its attendant tensions are always ready to resurface, at once subject to the claims and exclusions of centralized authorities. Scholars of political economy and political ecology, catching on to this truth and catching up with the insights of Tema residents, increasingly recognize waste—and waste infrastructures—not only as a source of degradation but also as an agent of transformation and collective and individual recognition and enablement (Chalfin 2019; Fredericks 2018; Millar 2018; Moore 2015; Reno 2016). In Tema, three aspects of this process rise to the fore. The first is the substantive force of "vital remains." Vital remains provide the substrate for the relational dynamics of "infrastructural intimacy." The second part of this work's proposed analytic triad, "infrastructural intimacy" is closely allied with the transformational potential of the "infrastructural inchoate." Third, these processes shape the expansion and institutionalization of "deep domesticity." These linked frameworks offer a conceptual tool kit applicable to other urban settings where vital materials are intimately entangled with infrastructure and where infrastructure is intimately entangled in reworking the contours and intersections of public and private life.

Theoretical Axes and Apertures: From Domus to Polis and Back Again

Along with providing comparative traction, the frameworks generated by the excremental solutions devised and utilized by Tema residents inspire new engagements with political theory. Via an inductive strategy of investigation borrowed from Latour (1993, 2005a, 2005b) and the theoretical insights as well as inconsistences of Arendt (1958), examination of Tema's excremental infrastructures inspire more abstract questions about the character and constitution of political life when the body politic is ostensibly privatized. Rather than the infrastructural elaboration of the domestic sphere serving as a means to truncate the polis, as imagined at the city's founding and by theorist Arendt (1958), the domus, encroaching, shaping, and morphing into res publica, reclaims these earlier suppressed political possibilities. In Ashaiman, for instance, the private bodily processes of a broad public are drawn into private households. Alternately, in Manhean and Ziginshore, public spaces are reclaimed to serve collective bodily needs and are increasingly privatized and politicized in the process. In Tema's core, the surfacing of private processes in the public sphere is an impetus to public action and recognition. All these arrangements confound the received divisions between public and private—polis and domus—on which modern political authority is ostensibly based.

On this deeper philosophical and historical journey, Arendt's *The Human Condition* (1958) has been a constant if inscrutable companion, offering both eye-opening insights and infuriating analytic blind spots. Most of all, Arendt offers a powerfully suggestive discussion of the public realm enlarging our understanding of the complexities of the human condition outside of the restricted realm of the classic polis. However, Arendt's acumen regarding publicness is paired with a maddeningly narrow rendering of the private. As already discussed, this is so despite Arendt's unusual treatment of and attentiveness to bodily processes for theorists of her day.[1] Yet she goes on to assert that the body is inappropriate and disruptive of the proper realm of politics in the modern polis.

In parsing the implications of Tema's urban exceptionalism through the lens of excremental politics, Arendt's ultimate refusal to recognize bodies in public as legitimately political might be reason enough to drop her along the way. However, Arendt is attentive to much that is at stake in Tema. Besides the public, she addresses the very elements of urban experience under scrutiny, speaking to matters of infrastructure as well as waste and decay, nature, the building of walls, and the subtle dynamics of work and fabrication (Arendt 1958). Hence, although the journey across Tema's excremental landscape could be taken without Arendt, she remains a worthy intellectual companion, offering insight as well as much to argue about. Notably, ethnographic investigation of excremental infrastructure in urban Ghana speaks back to Arendt and opens theoretical perspectives and conversations not anticipated.[2] Tema and Arendt (1958), we cannot forget, are contemporaneous formations, shaped by a shared crucible. It is fitting that the city's lived realities critique and expand on her intentions and ideals. It should be more than obvious that Africans are actors in, not passive recipients of, modernity's inheritance (Getachew 2019),[3] whether ideas of nation-building, seamless citywide sewage systems, or grand theories of human progress.

Offering a provocative point of comparison, the infrastructural configurations found in Tema instantiate in real life the abstract terms proposed in Arendt's *The Human Condition* (1958). This is true at the same time that Tema's excremental interventions situate intimate bodily processes and outputs in the public realm and draw public attention into the domestic domain. Arendt ardently dismisses such processes as examples of "the social" poisoning expressions of plurality with narrow self-interests and preoccupations (Canovan 1992; Pitkin 1998). Nevertheless, conditions in Tema reveal the unexpected configuration of the tenets of Arendt's all-important *vita activa* in the ostensibly private arrangements of excremental infrastructure. Tema's novel excremental arrangements bring together bodily processes (what Arendt terms labor), the fabrication of things (what she calls work), and the expression and negotiation of collective and individual interest separate from the administrative realm of the state (what she identifies as action). These concepts map onto the conceptual tool kit deduced from the case of Tema, with labor evident in the liveliness of vital remains, the fabrications of work apparent in relations and manifestations of infrastructural intimacy, and an action-based constitution of plurality in the institutional convergences of deep domesticity. I am not suggesting a one-to-one correspondence between Arendt's categories and the concepts proposed here. In play is a looser overlap that complicates the sharp divisions drawn by Arendt yet recognizes their substantive distinctions.

Three theoretical critiques emerge from this encounter. In the case of vital remains, Arendt's association of the *vita activa* with words, ideas, and deliberations is supplanted by a more embodied, dynamic, and materially based understanding of political action drawn from Georges Bataille (1985), for whom power derives from excess. Revealing and correcting Arendt's limited understanding of the political potentials of bodily labors, vital remains, like the energetic forms described by Bataille, are a source of power continually renewed despite their disorder and unpredictability. Built on vital remains, infrastructural intimacies also complicate Arendtian assumptions distinguishing between the fragility of bodily labors and the stolidity of built forms generated through the world of work. A distinction that maps onto Thomas Hobbes's ([1651] 1994) notions of immanence and transcendence, the social and affective investments and identifications around Tema's excremental infrastructure offer unexpected staying power. In turn, they effectively scaffold new configurations of public and private in the city, though they resemble neither the walls nor the machines envisioned by Arendt. Finally, the diverse formulations of deep domesticity cobbled from the remains of Tema's urban plan to serve a broad public in lieu of the state unseat the authoritative image of the classic polis offered by Arendt (Tsao 2002). Accompanying the expanded range of the domus is a transformed polis. The body offers the basis of collective rights and corecognition confounding the individuated and conformist character of the "social" feared and maligned by Arendt. Unimaginable to those whose ideas drove the city's design and founding, neither premodern nor countermodern, Tema's excremental infrastructural underground actualizes a social order born of modernity's limits and contradictions.

Vital Remains and the Ongoingness of Things

Among the clearest lessons learned from a close examination of urban life in Tema is the necessity of recognizing the liveliness or "vitality" of things — both human and other than human — and, more so, how that vitality endures, resurfaces, and erupts in expected and unexpected ways. As Gastón Gordillo (2014, 20), drawing on Benjamin, notes of the rubble of rural Argentina, these affectively charged matters propel their own afterlife. So too do Tema's waste matters. Indeed, Tema's excremental arrangements are multiply vital in their present and in their afterlives. Essential to life and composed of living matter, they are born out of living bodies' "life process, which have neither a beginning nor an end," to quote Arendt (1958, 144). Made up of bioactive things, they embody the "ongoingness of life" (Haraway 2016), fueling and enabling new relations and configurations of human and nonhuman.

While much political theory treats the body as an integrated entity that can be fully accounted for (Agamben 1998; Foucault 1979), experiences from Tema put bodily waste back on the table as a vital matter in its own right, not simply a source of subjugation or human control. Along with the bodies and bodily cycles of Tema's residents, the liveliness of the materials that make up and move through the city's infrastructural outlays are central to their political possibilities. As Rosalind Fredericks (2018) notes in relation to the burdens of waste's bioactive liveliness in Dakar, Tema's waste matter reveals a more multivalent materiality. Excrement crosses the line between human and not-human. A by-product of human life, bioactive fecal matter takes on a life of its own, enabling, competing with, and pushing back on human possibility. At the crux of human autonomy and coexistence in the city, people must live with one another and their own and others' shit. Apparent in Tema's core, when errant excrement erupts in courtyards and city streets, human gathering and contention commence. In contrast to the more reactive impulse evident in the city's planned neighborhoods, in Ziginshore the unruliness of shit incites innovation and inspires building rather than breakdown. In Ashaiman, too, it is ever present, available in abundance, up for grabs, and turned a source of status competition. In Manhean, shit is a long-term relic of communal copresence, as are the "U" compound houses still standing from the resettlement era.

As examples from across the city make clear, in the mix in Tema are another sort of vital remains. Namely, infrastructures, like excreta, are never inert. The infrastructures in which feces and other bodily wastes are entangled may break down. However, they never completely go away, degrading and resurfacing, like the old porcelain lavatories discovered in the rubble of Manhean. Ruination is a lively process, as Ann Laura Stoler (2013), Gastón Gordillo (2014), and Danny Hoffman (2017) all remind us. Infrastructure's material forms undergo decay and recomposition just as the bodies of city residents follow their own cycles of consumption and expulsion, production and evacuation. As Bataille's (1985) commutation of the law of thermodynamics to political theory asserts, matter can neither be created nor destroyed, nor completely captured. Neither can the excesses of human existence, whether bodily waste, built forms, or otherwise—including spiritual life, pace the prayer sessions and pieties of Ashaiman's Adepa Modern, or the glint of baubles and money wealth at Lady Di and Stomach's.

Across the city, given the "ongoingness of the life" and the "ongoingness of things," both bodily waste and infrastructures meant to contain them continue to produce new possibilities due to their inherent vitality. Elemental processes and essential needs drive collective life in the city, whether Stomach's errant effluent carving channels into city sewer lines, Uncle's biowaste fueling communal kitchens, Adepa's old sanitary lanes turned into sites of relaxation, or sewage leaks that reassemble households and neighborhoods in the city center. Gathering people and things together to anchor new social and material formations, these surpluses—never fully contained—enliven connections and tensions among urban residents and between urban residents and municipal bodies.

Beyond the human, yet intertwined with them, other living things extend the vital politics of Tema's excremental infrastructure at every turn: Groves of *tsoshishi* trees weave together neighborhood residents and throughways in Manhean. In Ziginshore, the polluted dregs of the once vibrant Chemu Lagoon gather the transient bodies of those who sustain Tema's port, fisheries, and factories. Pockets of life erupt within and alongside them: groundwater, patches of grass, children from the hostel drawn to the water's edge to defecate. Ziginshore's other-than-human elements—methane, sand, mud, oily effluent—are the force field on which Uncle's complex is delicately perched. These bioactive outputs likewise loom over him. Such elemental gatherings both distill and produce disruptions, inviting human attention and intervention, like the flies that inhabit Stomach's septic pits to the chagrin of Ashaiman's health inspectors. In Tema's core, when clothing, sanitary pads, condoms, and aborted fetuses are blamed for blocking sewage lines, vital remains of human lives similarly spark debate.

As with the old office blocks surrounding TDC's new headquarters, and heaps of records from the Doxiadis era filling its spare rooms, these contentions are structured by the vital remains of the city at large. Half-century-old sewage plans, beams, control panels, and the ancient engines of Tema's nearly shuttered pumping stations are monuments to lost possibility yet still somehow salvageable to those who live and work among them. Ruined, perhaps, but not ruins: by dint of routine and necessity they cannot be. They remain, ready to be revived by the labors of TMA's rodding team, the ingenuity of engineers, and the patient excavations of residents and roving private plumbers, all of whom make life in the city. Across Tema's varied neighborhoods and settlements, defunct infrastructure retains an insistent presence, deeply entwined with individual and collective lives and the antagonisms and alliances that fuel political projects.

Energetic and ever present, vital remains so conceived reopen discussions of body politics (including the Hobbesian [(1651) 1994] "body politique") that Arendt's restricted notion of bodily labors, relegated to meaningless routine, deem closed. Instead, the ongoingness of vital remains of and around the body, never fully captured or spent, upsets Arendt's reading of political plurality as forged foremost through verbal debate and deliberation. Proven by ongoing processes of bodily and infrastructural renewal in Tema that go beyond rote reproduction to produce urban order anew, the vitality of bodily and other remains in the city warrant recognition as a substantive means of political action. Fully evident in Ashaiman's private commercial toilets (PCTs), these forces are also on vivid display in Ziginshore as well as Manhean, and reluctantly yet insistently so in Tema's core. Revealing and correcting Arendt's limited understanding of the political potentials of bodily labors, vital remains, like the energetic forms described by Bataille (1985), are a source of power continually revived in the very process of breakdown and decay.

From Infrastructural Inchoate to Infrastructural Intimacy: Relations That Transform and Sustain

INFRASTRUCTURAL INCHOATE Cases from across Tema demonstrate that the vitality of persons and things, and that which sits in between, such as excreta—at once human and nonhuman—are infrastructure's reason for being and its perennial problem. This reality, ever present in Tema's excremental arrangements, challenges impressions of infrastructure as somehow already settled and inert rather than being lively as well. Grasping this truth helps to further dislodge the modernist smokescreen of infrastructural fixity. The notion of the "infrastructural inchoate," which normalizes situations of infrastructural incipience and indeterminacy, as Brian Larkin (2008) does for communications infrastructure, offers an alternative optic. Recognition of infrastructure as inchoate helps comprehend systemic transformations and recalibrations in cases where infrastructural figure and ground switch places and human-made systems and technologies are supplanted by or fused with functions and materials considered secondary or dependent.

Larkin (2013, 329) helpfully characterizes "infrastructure" as "matters that enable the movement of other matter. . . . They are objects that create the ground on which other objects operate." The infrastructural inchoate is about their admixture. Infrastructures are especially susceptible to these processes, given that their very purpose is to orchestrate the interplay of diverse entities. It is all the more apparent in the case of vital infrastructure, where day-to-day needs and routines render formal intentions susceptible to modification (K. Phillips 2020; Silver 2015) and the materials infrastructure is designed to channel are forceful in their own right (pace Anand 2018, on water; Degani 2018, on electricity). At these junctures, driven by the vitality of things—their necessity and ongoingness, even in the process of decay—the infrastructural inchoate is ascendant. In turn, unscripted amalgams of human and nonhuman, public and private, authority and society, are prone to emerge.

Indeterminate on multiple fronts, Tema's infrastructural inchoate is characterized by the never fully assimilated excess of bodily waste, a fractured built environment, and a perennially unsettled populace in pursuit of both material security and status mobility. Examples abound: half-functioning pumping stations activated by unprocessed waste; stagnant sewage treatment ponds used for open defecation; public manholes and overflow valves reconstructed by citizens; private toilets turned public leisure spaces; public toilets turned into private abodes; government-built facilities reclaimed as community property; and private homes providing basic public services. Making tangible the undecidable issues that characterize the collective life of interest to political theorists like Arendt (Honig 1991), such infrastructural apertures might be classed as "undecidable objects" (Hansen 1999, 21), or, in this case, "undecidable infrastructures." Inadvertent hybrids, these mixed infrastructural forms register and enable unexpected social-cum-political arrangements.

If the combination of citywide sewage tunnels, grand-scale pumping stations, and identical household toilets for all endorsed by Nkrumah and Doxiadis aspired to one sort of urban political order, Tema is the lived stage for multiple others, played out through the "infrastructural inchoate." In contrast to the singular, centralized, subterranean sanitary system made famous in Georges-Eugène Haussmann's Paris and presented as an invisible force that held the city together and the public in check (Harvey 2003; Laporte 2002), Tema's excremental armature and inputs rise to the surface and are actively debated and recomposed. Again, confounding Arendt's neat tripartite divide between reproductive bodily labors, concrete practices and objects of work, and the rarefied domain of political deliberation and expression, Tema's excremental innovations are a mixed meeting ground.

The infrastructural inchoate speaks (back) to Arendt's (1958, 52) discussion of the proverbial table, which she uses to offer a model of public life and plurality. What she presents as metaphor or "figurative space" of public good (Tsao 2002, 104) manifests, in Tema, in the material relations of excremental infrastructure. Sometimes the table is just a table; sometimes it starts to move and recompose as figure and ground switch, turning it from fixed form to inchoate. All infrastructural inchoates are not alike. They can be overloaded, as in Tema's core. They can be worn yet resilient, as in Manhean; can be strewn across a zone of abandonment, as in Ziginshore; or can exist only as a distant promise, as in Ashaiman.

Arendt scholar Roy Tsao is helpful in grappling with the implications of the figure/ground, action/making dynamics in theory as well as in practice. Tsao (2002, 108) notes that Arendt was inspired by Aristotle and Plato's treatment of "action as if it were making" yet ultimately rejected the implication of political forms as fixed and frozen. What if we turn the tide (or turn the table) and recognize making, whether tables, Arendtian conceptions of work, or infrastructure, as action? In this regard, the infrastructural inchoate unlocks and reflects the indeterminacy and negotiability of action, rendering action and making inseparable. Does the table support those who sit around it, or do those who sit around support the table, changing their relationship with one another, and the table too? Such uncertainty is at the heart of plurality. Pulled from underground to the fore, the resulting arrangements require considerable effort to hold in place and are further politicized in turn. This is evident in the never-ending exertions and negotiations of Tema's pumping station engineers, neighbors, and assemblymen; the unpredictable outputs of Ziginshore's subterranean tanks and biogas chamber; the precarious livelihoods of Manhean's toilet attendants; and the constant adjustments of Ashaiman's PCT operators to attract clients and harness public resources. Tema's excremental infrastructures are human fabrication and maker of relations. They are neither tools nor machines, neither gates nor walls, but something in between.

INFRASTRUCTURAL INTIMACY The infrastructural inchoate in Tema's excremental orders is routinized and stabilized—even if not technically or temporally "fixed"—through attachments between people and infrastructure and among people through infrastructure. This is the relational process I label "infrastructural intimacy." Sometimes the inchoate precedes infrastructural intimacy, as when the eruptions of manholes and neighborhood pipes in Tema's core cause neighbors to reassess relations and responsibilities. At other times, such as in Ziginshore, infrastructural intimacies may precipitate the intractable nexus of the infrastructural inchoate, as in Uncle's grand infrastructural scheme, built first and foremost on human relationships amid the wetland's unstable ground and unsettled jurisdiction.

Turning what is otherwise inchoate assemblage into a more recursive relational scaffold, infrastructural intimacies play out through an array of affective, sensory, intellectual, and technical correspondences and interdependencies across persons and infrastructural things. Similar to the moral compunctions of repair described by Jackson (2014, 231), they hinge on a sense of obligation, identification, and accountability. But beyond the more innocent relations of care mentioned by Jackson (2014, 232), they are tinged with interest, obligation, and a degree of inequality or insecurity. A reminder that infrastructural intimacies are political as well as material relations, infrastructural intimacies echo Michael Herzfeld's (2005) notion of "cultural intimacy" as they meld complicity and accountability. Infrastructural intimacies, in sum, convey interests and intentionality and work to harness the powers and unpredictability of vital remains, channeling and acknowledging them by means of human and nonhuman alliances and commitments.

Infrastructural intimacies in Tema enable a type of reciprocal assimilation simultaneously making "private things public" and "public things private." They encompass the critically important but more narrow rendering of "people as infrastructure" captured by AbdouMaliq Simone (2004) in which human bodies and labors substitute for infrastructural breakdowns and deficiencies. Tema, despite the clear lack of fully adequate public goods and services, is less a place of extreme infrastructural absence than a site of broad-ranging infrastructural presences and variations. Infrastructural intimacies here are much more about how infrastructures' technical and material forms are collectively empeopled in sync with human bodies and rhythms outside of either a totalizing modernist order imposed from on high or conditions of radical self-sufficiency without coordination originating from below.

Different from the externalized impositions and intentions of the state, even those transposed onto "techniques of the self" (Foucault 1979), infrastructural intimacies are more mutualistic in origin and operation. In line with what Willem Schinkel and Marguerite van den Berg (2011, 5) call "intermediation" in their critique of Giorgio Agamben's (1998) conceptual absolutism, these are middle-range, materially sedimented structurations. Neither spontaneous adaptations nor heavy-handed impositions, they are generated from within urban neighborhoods and communities in the shadow of earlier promises and failures. Infrastructural intimacies are not built on absence but are instead spawned from and in response to vital remains.

In Tema's core, for instance, infrastructural intimacies rise to the fore as bodily waste seeps into the public sphere. Private citizens take over municipal responsibilities to build and maintain urban infrastructure. In turn, they iteratively alter the terms of public and private life and municipal governance. In the planned settlements of the city center, pumping station engineers devise bodily routines to slow the pace of system decay and prop up the fading promise of municipal capacity. Infrastructural intimacies here hinge on a kind of "infrastructural identification" built on material copresence treating infrastructure as personified, reflecting a technician's lost labor and the misplaced properties and aspirations of residents. The vital remains of errant excrement spur technical connectivity as well as tensions among neighbors and municipal representatives. As the promise of the city's independence-era urban plan both looms large and proves false, these arrangements can be understood as private efforts to protect public infrastructure. They simultaneously exemplify private persons acting "as if" they were public authorities and attempts to make public infrastructure private by assimilating it into the collective responsibility of linked domestic realms.

In Manhean, infrastructural intimacies bear the imprint of earlier struggles surrounding the settlement's founding. Enmeshed in lateral associations of people and things, these arrangements emphatically reject the dictates of state authorities and political elites. Evident in the derisive *kleejo* protests and rebuff of tax assessments, these actions mix rejection with "radical conformity," turning the founding dictates of the resettlement zone initially imposed from above into a license for self-determination. Remains of structures earlier compelled by resettlement authorities are given over to individual and collective entitlement to do with as they please. Bound up with a host of "public intimacies," these collective refutations tie people together as they tie intimate bodily functions to public spaces. There are the public intimacies of toilet attendants who sleep, care for children, and locate their livelihood strategies within toilet premises, and those of Manhean's itinerants—largely females—who use the common space of the toilet complex to fulfill basic needs. Infrastructural intimacies in Manhean rest on other forms of infrastructure-bound copresence spurred by recursive bodily rhythms. Ghettos cobbled together from urban detritus offer a space for rest, shelter, and socializing. In contrast to toilets, where infrastructure precedes the inward pull of human practice, here "the public creates the *res* around it," to invert Latour (2005a, 12).

In Ziginshore, despite the vast scale and technical complexity of the settlement's multifunctional infrastructural order, infrastructural intimacies are mired in nature and affect. Pre- or proto-infrastructural, the surrounding wetland and chemistry of biodigestion and methane conversion provide an "elemental intimacy" for Uncle, his technicians, and those who use his services. Upending Arendt's (1958, 52) claim that "the human artifact, the fabrication of human hands," is "not identical with the earth or with nature," Ziginshore lies at their juncture. Uncle's elemental approach, seeking to harness nature's forces, finds a parallel in his cultivation of human dependence by means of base affect: from appetites and aversions to the need for shelter, security, and childcare. Catering to the vulnerabilities and aspirations of the area's overworked and underemployed, these are the core currencies of Ziginshore's infrastructural configuration. They spur customers' full-bodied coparticipation, from where and how to defecate, to where and how to sleep and raise one's children, involving them in processes of infrastructure building as they make the system their own. The ongoing expansion of infrastructure's functions and footprint in Ziginshore can be understood as a form of cohabituation despite the clear hierarchy between Uncle Director, his workers, residents, and customers. A mode of infrastructural intimacy transacted via bed frames turned tables, child's play turned work, excreta turned energy, and garbage turned solid ground, the result is a contingent collectivity, dependent on recursive rhythms of adjustment and renewal, growth, and decay.

Infrastructural intimacies in Ashaiman are far less encompassing than the expansive social and infrastructural interdependencies of Ziginshore. Rather than replicate the full bloom of state authority, as Uncle aspires to do, Ashaiman PCTs occlude the reach of the state by turning domestic dwellings into platforms for public provisioning. These arrangements sustain—and are sustained by—an infrastructure-inflected conviviality. Infrastructural intimacy here, true to the definition of "conviviality"—living together—builds on the collective execution of Arendt's "labors of living" in a private yet shared space. Bodily reproduction and self-care intermix with users' and proprietors' shared quest for social advancement, combining the pursuit of leisure with a demonstration of civility not unlike what Veblen ([1899] 1994) describes in other contexts of rapid social recomposition. Combining "coliving" with the promise of social mobility, Ashaiman's infrastructural solutions compensate for gaps in state provisioning and map out their own terrain of public order and influence. Each PCT cultivates distinctive codes of conduct by means of infrastructure-driven bodily assent. At Stomach's, users are infrastructurally compelled by the kinked rebar in each stall. At Adepa, they receive toilet paper, not newsprint. At Di's, they are instructed on the correct volume of water to flush. A more proximate and idiosyncratic biopolitics than the distant admonitions of Foucault's panopticon or the one-size-fits-all infrastructural orchestrations of Nkrumah and Doxiadis, these intimate injunctions are a form of "colaboring" on and through infrastructure and the self. Similar to "ideological state apparatuses" (Althusser 1979), they rely on processes of "infrastructural interpellation" to instill bodily and affective dispositions.

Taken together, infrastructural intimacies across the city build on the vital needs and vital remains of human bodies. They enable situations of political transubstantiation in which bodily immanence comes to structure and sustain more transcendent expressions of collective order. These processes complicate Arendtian assumptions distinguishing between the fragility of bodily labors and the stolidity of built forms and fabrications generated through the world of work. Taking a stance remarkably similar to Arendt, Michel Callon and Bruno Latour (1981) likewise dismiss associations of the human body for the expression and satisfaction of vital needs as sufficient armature for political life. Challenging the tenets of Hobbes, they assert ([1655] 1981, 283), "When living bodies are the form and matter of Leviathan, there is no Leviathan.... In order to stabilize society everyone need[s] to bring into play associations that last longer than the interactions that formed them ... replacing unsettled alliances with walls and social contracts."

Infrastructural intimacies, in contrast, by means of the recursive play of social, bodily, and affective investments and identifications, provide Tema's novel excremental infrastructure with unexpected staying power to scaffold new configurations of public and private in the city. Latourian (2005a) assemblage theory pivots on the concept of durable associations. In their capacity to transform and stabilize the uncertainties of the infrastructural inchoate amid the insistent force of vital remains, infrastructural intimacies generate durable ties to keep new infrastructural orders and attendant political relations intact in the midst of urban life.

The intersection of these forces to catalyze urban political shifts is far from inevitable and hinges on the critical alignment of infrastructural debris, human lives, and collective concern. Two counterexamples prove this point and bring the distinctive dynamics of Tema to the fore. In South Africa's shacklands, urban activism built on elemental needs is undermined by the infrastructural violence of the state, which systematically denies residents the right to fabricate, inhabit, or accumulate a semblance of material security to shore up their right to the city (Chance 2018). Posed in Arendt's terms, social movements here meld action and labor, but the potential of all that Arendt glosses as "work" is continually negated, inhibiting transformation. In Liberia (Hoffman 2017) ex-combatants occupy the extant infrastructure of Monrovia's postconflict landscape in the ruins of Brutalist-inspired concrete hulks. Yet no political community emerges in these shared sites of refuge. Though they are spaces of temporary safety, the atomization of labor and strategies of individual survival staged within the impenetrable bulwarks of leftover civic architecture impedes the vitality of fabrication or action. As in South Africa, infrastructural intimacy is unsustainable; neither can action be realized.

Deep Domesticity: Institutions That Matter

Integral to their political impacts and capacities, the diverse excremental arrangements forged and utilized by Tema residents are rooted in and transformative of domestic spaces and practices. This is because domestic arenas concentrate vital remains and cultivate infrastructural intimacies. Enabling the institutionalization of "deep domesticity," they provide a foundation for wider infrastructural and political realignments and are re-formed in turn. From the perspective of Tema's infrastructural innovations, domestic realms cannot be considered a subordinate or residual form simply sustaining or registering broader social and political processes. Rather, they are generative and determinative, demarcating and inflecting the terms of urban public and political life.

Each of the domestic configurations that characterize Tema's wideranging excremental orders has a distinctive political scope, articulating claims to resources, rights, and recognition and sustaining residents' coordinated response to state exclusions and intrusions. Each, in a different way, turns inside out Nkrumah and Doxiadis's founding plan for the city. As opposed to elaborating on and tightly enclosing the domestic sphere in order to delimit the possibilities of the polis as the founders intended, the domus melds with the res publica to unlock and reclaim urban political space. Collectively informing the political order in the city, these "parliaments of shit" institute access to the means of survival, security, and urban standing. While they may orchestrate inequalities along the way, they underwrite and sustain plurality.

As Ziginshore's Uncle Director is well aware, one can build a whole urban settlement in the shape of a household, weaving vital elements and intimacies into a political order. Or, in the case of Ashaiman, already-existing domestic space serves as a centripetal force, drawing in new vitalities and infrastructural attachments ultimately reshaping the scope of urban public life and status distribution. The dispersed domesticities of Manhean's toilets, ghettos, and *tsoshishi* offer islands of self-determination, making space for survival, self-expression, and solidarity. In Tema's core, more subtle forms of interhousehold cooperation surface to stave off failure of municipal functions. In each case, the domus is a locus and engine of political reorganization. The depth of "deep domesticity" lies in these multilayered linkages and entailments, at once state-facing, public-facing, and internally focused.

Expressions of "deep domesticity" in Tema share similarities with self-proclaimed "politics of shit" elsewhere (Appadurai 2002; Robins 2014; Robins and Redfield 2016; von Schnitzler 2018). Like the "deep democracy" in Mumbai's toilet protests described by Arjun Appadurai (2002, 29), excremental activism in Tema relies on horizontal ties arising from proximity and shared experience to inform political strategies and end points "built on what the poor know and understand." Challenging the impositions of experts and elites, those who use and manage Tema's novel excremental orders also engage in what Appadurai (35) describes as "counter" or "auto-governmentality" involving "self and collective surveillance and discipline" similar to the case of urban dwellers in Mumbai. Suggesting a realm of political life otherwise overlooked, however, Tema's excremental experiments depart in notable ways. Namely, the excremental politics in Tema are much more internally driven in both origins and end points than those in Mumbai or South Africa (Robins 2014; Robins and Redfield 2016). Difficult to characterize as forms of outright protest, excremental politics in Tema hinge on forms of demonstration that work through actualization. This is about "doing" rather than "appealing," "practicing within" rather than "performing without." In Mumbai, model toilets and demonstrations of building technologies amplify already-existing political alliances and end points (Appadurai 2002, 34). In Tema, the order of operations is reversed, with political possibilities emerging out of novel infrastructural arrangements.

Rooted in the domestic realm, Tema's excremental infrastructural innovations are public-facing, calling on the notice and participation of a wide range of persons, including public officials, and actively assimilate public spaces, responsibilities, and remains. Unlike the case of Mumbai, Tema's excremental innovations, despite reaching out to city representatives and reaching across neighborhoods and households, nevertheless rarely "reach up" to advocate for national recognition or involvement in transnational networks. Despite their eye-catching signage and distinctive architecture, as in Ashaiman and Manhean, and distinctive technical makeup, as in Ziginshore, public presence is never separated from use. This differs from toilet activists in South Africa and South Asia who stage toilet festivals (Appadurai 2002) and attention-grabbing toilet protests, dumping shit and portable toilets in public places (Robins 2014; von Schnitzler 2018). Though popular, participatory, and anti-elite, excremental activism in Tema does not reject class or status hierarchies. Instead, Tema's excremental infrastructural experiments build cross-strata solidarities and mobilities while upholding class distinctions and fostering class aspirations. Importantly, in Tema, such divisions, while grounded in domestic order and practices, shape the terms and limits of state authority.

Along with the widespread provisioning of public goods to a population with little access to state services and investments, class differentiation is a critical element of deep domesticity in Ashaiman. Here household-based excremental infrastructures expose customers and neighbors to norms of middle-class propriety and offer the opportunity for status advancement by publicizing standards of individual and collective conduct. Ashaiman's PCT operations spill out into public space via signage, ancillary activities, and convivialities, attracting customers and general notice as fixtures of the city's urban landscape. This includes the notice of municipal authorities, as the sheer expansion of the operations' domestic footprint and creep of operational infrastructure outside domestic bounds encroach on municipal property and functions. Overtaking state promises of urban provisioning by enlarging domestic space, functions, and participation, these conventions of urban living provoke both resentment and relief among city officials. Garnering recognition from municipal authorities, deep domesticity serves the commonweal in their stead.

In Ziginshore, deep domesticity is multidimensional, self-consciously harnessing bioactive processes for political ends. Uncle's multilayered infrastructural formation concentrates diverse persons and practices. Via the settlement's expansive excremental infrastructural array, public and private map onto one another. It is difficult to decouple system inside and outside: all is domestic, all is polity. Like the exemplary center of the theater state described by Clifford Geertz (1980), power is built on the capacity to gather people and things and convert control over one into influence over another. Here, it is infrastructure, not ritual, that does the double job of gathering in and extending out. A kind of personal rule based less on the body of the ruler than the bodies of the ruled, again similar to Bali's *negara* theater state (Geertz 1980), infrastructural capture and conversion must be constantly activated and renewed through the play of affective intimacies.

While Uncle's grand-scale domestic complex—toilet, hostel, kitchen, school, biodigester—are a tangible expression of authority, the elemental vitality of nature usurped is the ultimate source of power. Ziginshore's commonwealth of waste offers stability, security, and bodily sustenance for those marginalized by extreme poverty and mobility. Despite the steep hierarchy and deep dependencies that mark this infrastructure-driven and political order, incremental opportunities for self-determination and advancement are claimed by and ceded to the settlement residents' own infrastructural identifications and manipulations. That is, Uncle's singular apparatus spawns and contains many other domesticities within.

Deep domesticity in Manhean is more insular in organization than that in either Ziginshore or Ashaiman and evinces different political possibilities. More private than the unbounded excesses of Ziginshore's excremental economy or the ranked excremental options in Ashaiman, Manhean is a "closed commons," drawing some people and practices in while pushing others away. Vital remains in their own right, Manhean's toilets, like other structures in this densely packed resettlement zone, endure from the city's midcentury founding. Separate from designated residential space, they contribute to a decentralized domesticity erupted in spaces across the community. Manhean's compound toilets exert an insistent pull. They draw in customers by dint of bodily need and attract community groups in search of investments and municipal authorities seeking regulation and revenue. Compared to Ziginshore and Ashaiman, those who use Manhean's compound toilets frequently induce innovation. More self-directed than top-down, these accretions span cooking, childcare, sleeping, planting, and longer-term habitation. Staged on city property, private practices are a means to reclaim and assert rights to public space and individual well-being despite the limited resources at residents' disposal. Toilet operators' collective refusals to deliver taxes to Tema's municipal authority likewise turn their back to the state. Similar to the atomized yet aggregate acts of toilet customers and attendants, toilet management groups' reversions to the "cultural intimacies" of shared inheritance turn municipal abandonment into the basis for entitlement on collectively determined terms.

In the planned communities of Tema's core, deep domesticity comes full circle as middle-class professionals with the greatest sense of entitlement to state infrastructural provisioning confront chronic system failure. Offering a model of domestic self-management bearing the imprint of Doxiadis's designs and Nkrumah's political aspirations, the neatly arrayed private homes are equipped with their own yards, driveways, electrical hookups, water sources, and sewage lines. Given their sameness and sense of self-sufficiency, an arrangement much in line with Arendt's (1952) conformist and individualizing idea of "the social," these urban residents are least able to mobilize alternatives to inherited infrastructural orders. For Tema's middle-class householders, collective action is deliberately discouraged and designed away via the circumscriptions of public life and cultivation of individual accountability to city authorities. Only the eruption of vital remains of bodily excreta pushes the actuality and necessity of infrastructural interconnection to the fore. Igniting fleeting expressions of urban solidarity alongside collective pressure on TMA, the collaborations that result are more extrinsic than internalized. Rather than enlarging the boundaries of shared domestic space, expressions of deep domesticity here move across and outside of individual households and strive to reinstate, if not impersonate, the autonomous capacities of the state. Protecting points of connection, these investments are relatively tenuous compared with more routinized forms of infrastructural intimacy found in other parts of the city.

Taken together, Tema's infrastructural orders exhibit distinct formulations of deep domesticity. In Ashaiman, the private provision of private infrastructure for public use pushes domestic practices into public space in lieu of state. Deep domesticity here is functionally capacious, garnering status and the tacit recognition of city authorities. In Manhean, community members' takeover of independence-era public infrastructure alongside creation of other public spaces for productive and reproductive labor offers a pattern of decentralized domesticity that deliberately rejects state intervention. In Ziginshore, more apparatus than singular space, private provision of public infrastructure pulls people in and extends outward to integrate new functions and resources alternative to the state. Spurring replication at multiple scales, deep domesticity here takes a fractal form, iteratively enfolding and expanding through patterned replication. In Tema's core, residents call on the state as a transcendent order, which they replicate through collective investment in extrinsic fixes, both reinforcing and troubling the boundary between private property and public responsibility.

Looking Backward, Looking Forward

It is important to understand that the infrastructural innovations found in Tema are not idiosyncratic outcomes forged in the face of culturally inappropriate impositions. That conclusion would be mistaken. Rather, Tema's excremental interventions speak to the shared playing field of late twentieth- to early twenty-first-century urban modernity. The city is the product of the central forces of twentieth-century world-historical shifts of decolonization and post–World War II recovery and rebuilding. It continues to exist in the context of this conjuncture in the face of the failures and contradictions of these projects and the rise and fall of other world-historical agendas, from neoliberal capitalism to democratization to sustainable development. That is, Tema's novel excremental infrastructural solutions are forged from within modernity's sweep. Thus, as much as they tell us about the distinctiveness of time and place, they also reveal wider systemic tensions and potentials that may be otherwise and elsewhere submerged.

The public-facing expansion of the domestic realm found in Tema, encompassing more persons and functions; usurping public space, public resources, and responsibilities; and encroaching on the expected domain of the state to guarantee urban survival as well as status mobility, stands at this juncture. Although it may be tempting to characterize these shifts as a reversion to past forms, I suggest it is more accurate to view these dually political and infrastructural instantiations through a forward-facing lens and consider them diagnostic of a postmodern condition. Rather than the public domain of the rights-granting polis being overtaken by private social interests as in Arendt's (1958) discussion of "the social," Tema's excremental experiments map an alternative where the domestic realm and bodily labors offer space for collective participation and deliberation not possible in the formally constituted public arena. The domus exerts a centripetal pull, scaling up interactions and expectations, technologies included. Alongside body labors the domus is more and more about public matters, including public goods. Accompanying the expanded range of the domus is a truncated polis, reduced in reach, capacity, and aspiration. Neither premodern nor countermodern, this is a social order born out of modernity's limits and contradictions and radical decline of state interest and investment in social provisioning, a crisis that has little abated.

It is useful to situate discussions of deep domesticity and the unexpected, novel interface of vital remains, domus, and polis in Tema in relation to other conversations in anthropology challenging conventional understandings of domestication. Two works offer theoretic bookends to my analysis of Tema's excremental infrastructural innovations. One is Heather Anne Swanson's chapter "Domestication Gone Wild: Pacific Salmon and the Disruption of the Domus" in *Domestication Gone Wild: Politics and Practices of Multispecies Relations*; the other is James C. Scott's *Against the Grain: A Deep History of the Earliest States*. Both use the upheavals of the Anthropocene and a multispecies lens to rethink world-historical trajectories, in the present (Swanson 2018), and the past (Scott 2017). Their attention to other-than-human agency bears similarities to my concern with the vitality of non-human things, including bodily waste, polluted wetlands, urban plans, and infrastructural remains. As Swanson (2018) points out, domestication and domesticity are not identical, but they are linked. Considering what she calls the "home-domus-domestication trifecta," Swanson decenters the human in animal and plant domestication narratives without losing site of the domus. Taking a perspective relevant to deep domesticity and infrastructural restructuring in Ghana, Swanson views the domus as an expanse of interconnections rather than in the narrow sense of household. She uses this optic to attend to the margins of "domestication" and offers an instructive parallel for attending to the changing contours of domestic realm in Tema.

Undertaking a more expansive historical project, Scott (2017) examines the dynamics of ancient state formation through the lens of other-than-human environmental forces. Where Swanson addresses domestication and domus, Scott addresses domestication and state. Scott offers two arguments helpful to comprehending deep domesticity in Tema. First, Scott poses processes of domestication, in this case animal and plant domestication, as primary to state formation, not secondary or residual. Second, and related, he asserts that the state is a more dynamic and unstable political formation in human history than assumed, even in histories of urbanization, due in part to these environmental factors. Indeed, Scott argues that paired processes of state formation and state dissolution have been much more episodic than teleologies of modernity allow, and have been decisively shaped by other-than-human actants. Scott's recognition of the unstable boundaries between state and nonstate and human and nonhuman can be productively combined with Swanson in light of Tema's infrastructural dynamics. Made prominent is the role of the domus as a countervailing force anchoring the grand ordering schemes orchestrating relations among and between people and things in the swirl of uncertainty as states falter, dissolve, and regroup.

In Tema, as in many other parts of the world, global North and global South, the polis as conventionally conceived is no longer, even as it continues to assert its power to include and exclude, provide and deny, recognize or render invisible. At the same time, humanity's others—animals, climate, nature, waste, defunct infrastructure—are not inert background objects, but prime movers. Alongside these processes, the domestic is a decisive register of transformation and renewed space of politics in the present, as Tema's myriad excremental arrangements make clear.

Notes

Introduction

1 In a cultural system that prides itself on deference and propriety, to speak directly of feces and defecation in Ghana is inappropriate in public discourse. Like other linguistic conventions in this culture area, layered speech and the art of indirection is taken as evidence of maturity, knowledge, and respect. In Ghana, consistent with cultural convention, even the most base term for human feces, *ɛbini* in the Akan (Twi) language widely spoken in southern and central Ghana, is a euphemism, meaning "something that is part of something (eaten), literally *ɛbi* (some of it) *nɛɛ* (here is)" (Mohammed Mustapha, personal email communication, April 4, 2021). Despite the veiled reference, use of the term in common parlance is seen as vulgar. More acceptable is *taifi*, meaning "toilet" in Akan, and also used to denote bodily waste. Given my status as foreign professional, I revert to the linguistic conventions of those who occupy similar professional roles in Ghanaian society. However, as an anthropologist I also defer to the vocabulary used in the communities under discussion. In this text I primarily use the term "excrement" or speak more generally of "bodily waste." When it is used by my interlocutors, I also use the term "shit."

2 The term "undecidable," drawn here from Derrida (1981) after Hansen (1999), is also developed by Agamben (1998).

3 Long considered a fundament of modern sociality and civic order, this is labeled by Mukhopadhyay (2006, 226) "the municipal-civic master discourse."

4 This perspective is articulated by Jacky Bouju (2008, 159), who recognizes that recurring claims of "lack" regarding public sanitation usually hide political struggles and policy failures underwriting resource deprivation.

5 For a similar approach from a political science perspective, Paller (2019), also focusing on urban Ghana, offers a compelling example of studying informal politics in Africa to understand processes of democratization.

6 With reference to Palestine, Stamatopoulou-Robbins (2019, 212) speaks to the "doubleness" of waste as a matter both expended and portentous.

7 Kregg Hetherington (2019, 10–11) likewise recognizes the capacity of perspectives centered on "vitalism" to displace biopolitical paradigms in order to speak to the liveliness of infrastructures.

8 Though Kristin Phillips (2020) focuses on energy, her work on solar and wind power in rural Tanzania also insightfully unpacks the relationship between infrastructure and embodied capacity.

9 Drawing on the conceptual vocabulary of her interlocutors in South Africa's urban shacklands, Chance (2018) refers to the "living politics" of the urban underclass, which hinge on the mobilization of elemental matters, namely "fire, war, air, and land" in everyday tactics of protest, resistance, and community building. What I term "vital politics" are likewise a material politics. Rather than tactically politicized for self-conscious political ends as in South Africa, in Tema material forces are harnessed to fulfill essential needs. That is, while active and transformative and built from elemental forms of life, politics in Tema are more associative than agonistic, reflecting the different political histories and built environments of these contexts. In addition, vital politics in Ghana are more directly and consistently mediated by infrastructures with their own vitalities, which constitute what I call "vital remains."

10 The most graphic ethnographic example of the twin forces of scatological repression and resistance come from depictions of Northern Ireland's political prisoners' collective decision to cover the walls of their cells with their own feces and menstrual blood as a statement of self-determination under conditions of abuse and duress known as the "Dirty Protest" (Aretxaga 1995; A. Feldman 1991).

11 Reports indicate that more than half the country's population—56 percent—rely on shared facilities. The World Bank reports that 84 percent of the population was without access to "improved sanitation" (Armaly 2016, 1). Despite over a decade of government, multilateral, and NGO investment in meeting the UN Millennium Development Goal of private waterborne sanitation, rates shifted from 11 percent only to 15 percent between 2000 to 2015 (Appiah-Effah et al. 2019, 399, 402). Among rural households, open defecation was most common, followed by public toilets and pit latrines, and finally by water closets. In urban areas, with water closets used by 23 percent of the population, public toilet use prevailed, with a smaller percentage of open defecation (Armaly 2016, 3).

12 Colin McFarlane (2008a) makes a similar point about excremental politics in colonial India, including their continued imprint on contemporary practices.

13 "In the gold mining areas at the core of the colonial economy," Raymond Dumett (1993, 217) writes, "street sanitation, sewage disposal and anti-malarial preventive measures were entrusted almost entirely to the companies." These

were among the first urban areas to make widespread use of pan latrines (220).

14 Consisting of communal pan and pit latrines, these installations were considered sites of squalor and abjection despite the health benefits touted by medical officers. Marking their mutual taint, prisoners were put into service to clean and empty waste pits and buckets (Williamson and Kirk-Greene 2001).

15 Kru laborers emptied pan latrines each night. At first they waded into the surf to dump the contents, and later they made use of a "tipping depot" at the meeting point of the ocean and the Korle Bu Lagoon. An early example of makeshift urban sanitary infrastructure, "this facility allowed the contents of pans to be hosed out to sea in a long pipe supported by concrete pillars" (Patterson 1979, 254).

16 Accra's Jamestown area, for instance, in 1936 had a ratio of one toilet per ninety residents (Patterson 1979).

17 The city was named after the village of Tema that occupied the ridge above the port, itself named after the local calabash trees (*Lagenaria siceraria*) still common in the area and in some accounts referred to as *Torman*.

18 The Volta River Plan was a multifaceted megaproject, and its details were in flux for much of the 1950s. Coinciding with considerable political and economic upheaval regionally and worldwide, the location of the dam, smelter, and resettlement area changed considerably during the early years of project planning. As central elements of the larger project, plans locating the port and new city in Tema were fixed early on (D'Auria and Sanwu 2010). Following suit, when the US-based Kaiser Aluminum Company took over the smelter project from British industrial interests, the location was shifted from Kpong to Tema (Kirchherr 1968, 212) to make the import and export of aluminum inputs and outputs convenient to the port.

19 The new port of Tema would replace the antiquated surf port of Accra, which was little suited to large-scale bulk importation. The new port also supplemented the capacity of Takoradi Harbor, located hundreds of miles away and geared primarily to the export of raw materials (Kirchherr 1968).

20 The city of Accra, as a point of contrast, lacks a large-scale sanitary sewage system comparable to that of Tema. Accra contains an expansive, if imperfect, drainage system consisting of open storm sewers across residential and commercial areas and lagoons and wetlands that have been encroached on and re-routed to handle urban runoff and the pressures of urban settlement. Though the sewers may be used to dispose of and channel sanitary waste, they are foremost intended to capture stormwaters and household liquid waste from cooking, bathing, washing, and the like. Sanitary waste, i.e., fecal matter, is to be managed by residents through the use of dedicated household-based septic tanks, which have supplanted but by no means replaced pan latrines, or public toilets, also with self-contained septic systems. To reiterate, Accra, unlike

Tema, was never equipped with a citywide sanitary sewage system overseen by the municipality or national ministries. While sanitary codes remain widespread and exacting in scope, they focus largely on individual responsibility rather than state provisioning. The work of Accra's municipal authority with regard to waste was and remains largely devoted to larger-scale public works such as urban drainage channels and water courses, not those linking individual households to citywide networks, as in Tema's founding plan.

21 Given Tema's vast size, approaching half a million residents or more, and large expanse, spanning over fifty square miles, this book does not intend to be comprehensive in its discussion of sanitary practices across the city. It presents a representative sample drawn from Tema's core and its earliest-planned neighborhoods. Left out of the discussion are the more affluent and suburban communities at the fringes of the city's original expanse, such as Sakumono, along with those sections closer to the center with self-built and self-financed houses that rely on dedicated household septic systems. While they would surely offer a valuable source of comparison, the findings discussed here admittedly focus on excremental solutions that depart from the assumed modernist norm of municipal expectation and facilitation of private household facilities. Tema's oldest planned neighborhoods, Site 1 and Site 2 in Community 1, contain public toilets for its residents. These departures are more prevalent than meets the eye. Claims that the cases presented in this study are somehow exceptional or aberrant overlook the actualities of the midcentury system decline apparent to Tema residents, which they negotiate with grace, dignity, and tenacity and work hard to shroud from the view of visitors and casual acquaintances.

22 By no means is this a call to collapse the divisions between these domains: res publica, from Roman antiquity, and polis, from classical Greece. Arendt is sensitive to their different constitution. Although the polis is idealized by her, it is not always privileged. As a persistent subtext, Arendt notes the durability of material practice—of making—in the res publica versus the inherent insecurity of the polis grounded as it is in words, in the present, transformative yet fleeting (Ashcroft 2018). In this discussion I add the Latin *domus*, roughly equivalent to "household" (Swanson 2018). The Greek cognate, *oikos*, is widely used by Doxiadis. When quoting or referring to Doxiadis, I use the term *oikos* for accuracy.

23 In the case of waste, the chronic neglect and disempowerment of Black communities in the US South, as evident in Catherine Coleman Flowers's (2020) depiction of the fight for rural sanitation and sewage infrastructure in Perry, Alabama, makes these forces evident. In the case of water, the water crisis in Flint, Michigan, stands as an example of the convergence of all three and likely represents a phenomenon that is much more common than recognized.

24 Informed by Michael Herzfeld's (2005) discussion of bureaucratic intimacy, I initially formulated this term to explain the embodied and emotional disposi-

tions of Tema's waste engineers toward decrepit pumping station infrastructure (Chalfin 2015).

25 This term differs from what Butt (2020) calls "waste intimacies" with regard to garbage collection in Pakistan (see also Chalfin 2019). In the case of Tema, it is infrastructure rather than waste object that is the medium of intimacy. Butt furthermore stresses the ambivalences and inequalities of intimacy. My exploration of "infrastructural intimacy," by contrast, stresses intimacy as a means to build and stabilize material forms.

26 Elif Babül's (2017) discussion of "bureaucratic intimacies" in Turkey also draws on Michael Herzfeld (2005) to capture the collective moral frameworks and shared secrets of Turkish civil servants enrolled in international human rights training. Whereas Babül emphasizes the bureaucratic dimensions of Herzfeld's construct, I use the term "infrastructural intimacy" to draw attention to the insistent force of embodied processes and nonhuman agents in infrastructural transformation. Although experienced and enlivened by state actors and state-based and state-built material forms, ordinary citizens and state subjects are essential to infrastructural intimacies in Tema.

27 Driven by a shared interest in objects and contexts that orient urban political life outside the formally constituted realms of public administration and collective decision-making, Bonnie Honig's (2017) meditation on "public things" likewise joins the perspectives of vital materialism and Arendt's political thought. Offering little direct engagement with Latour, and making brief mention of infrastructure, it is primarily a conceptual work reflecting on political matters in the contemporary United States very different in object and orientation from this book.

28 From this perspective, Foucault's (1979) rendering of Jeremy Bentham's panopticon, in which both authority and fealty are absolute, is an infrastructural exception, not the rule. Among other things, in Foucault's reading, political relations are unmediated by the autonomous capacities of material objects.

29 In contrast to the late twentieth-century assessment of man-made waste as "unnatural," Mumford (1938, 46) mentions the prevalence in medieval cities of "organic waste materials, which decomposed and mingled with the earth."

30 Among the latter are new medical treatments utilizing fecal transplantation (Costello et al. 2017).

31 Vital infrastructures can be understood as a variant of critical infrastructure (Fredericks 2018). A concern with infrastructure's vital politics goes beyond this received understanding to consider how the fabrication, claiming, and taming of infrastructure's essence and essentialness are entangled with the expression and negotiation of political interest and contention.

32 The theoretical dispositions of Latour, a generation removed from Arendt and a student of Heidegger only in the indirect sense, are little discussed as bearing the burdens of Heidegger's political legacy, only his intellectual imprint.

33 Taking up Arendt's driving concerns around exile, human rights, forced mobility, and enforced stasis, the most prominent of these emergent intellectual trends combines the perspectives of migration and security studies, evidenced by the scholarship of Nicholas de Genova (2010) and Gregory Feldman (2013, 2015). De Genova (2010) addresses the most basic of human freedoms discussed by Arendt: the freedom to move outside of the sovereign logics of the nation-state. Feldman (2015) trains his lens on victims of what he calls the "migration apparatus" as well as its agents and perpetrators. Embracing Arendt's idea of the *vita activa*—a life for oneself that is at the same time a life for and with others—in the unfamiliar light of bureaucratic administration, Feldman investigates the possibility of political action through the act of speaking and thinking in common.

34 Mary Dietz (1995, 29) asserts, "*The Human Condition* carries a far more provocative gender subtext than most feminists have noticed." Building on this insight, I argue that *The Human Condition* carries a far more provocative "body" subtext than most analysts have noticed.

35 Tsao (2002, 105) discusses Arendt's "rather unconventional distinction between a public realm that is genuinely 'political'—allowing for human freedom—and one that is merely 'social.' Driven by the uniform, unceasing needs of their bodies and incessant cycles of labor and consumption, she argues that the demands of 'society' in this sense have increasingly overrun the public realm in modern times, bringing their inherent presumption of uniformity and unfreedom to human interaction."

36 Arendt (1958; Markell 2011) reads political life through the spatial and architectural arrangements of the classical city. She poses the enclosures of city walls as the protector of public life and the grounds for political participation, offering a durable context for human interaction and collective life of the *vita activa*.

37 Bonnie Honig (2017, 40) speaks of attachments to others via things as "adhesions," a term implying connection without the commitment of sameness implied by "cohesion."

38 Lucas Bessire and David Bond (2014, 449) voice a similar concern that ontological perspectives on their own run the risk of valorizing alterity and fail to speak to the wider political economic inequalities and injustices driving them. A notable exception, Gastón Gordillo (2014, 14), addressing large-scale rural ruins in Argentina, works to "politicize object-oriented approaches."

39 In *Overseas Building Notes*, A. E. S. Alcock (1963, 12) indicates that the town plan submitted by Russian experts included flats with communal kitchens. The plan was rejected on the basis of cost as well as style, as it "was not considered at all suitable to the Ghana way of life."

40 According to customary law, the core of the acquisition area was endowed in the chief of the village of Tema (D'Auria 2019). Chiefs of neighboring villages

Kpone and Nungua were also recognized as customary stakeholders because the tract extended into their traditional areas.

41 The ceding of land rights remains in contention to this day.

1. Assembling the New City

1 Danny Hoffman (2017, 16) notes that the large-scale transformation of West Africa's urban built environment in the aftermath of World War II was driven not just by shared postwar political-economic circumstances but by the same architects and pursuing similar planning paradigms (see also Uduku 2006).

2 An indication of a shift from piecemeal approaches to those driven by consistent policy, a master plan for Accra was established in 1944. Shortly thereafter, in 1945, alongside planning decrees for other areas of British West Africa, comprehensive town planning legislation for the entirety of the Gold Coast was put forth (Njoh 2007, 60, 63, 66).

3 These initial structures and layouts drew on the plans of A. E. S. Alcock and Drew and Fry (Provoost 2014).

4 Augmenting the scope and national significance of the city as a whole, in the same year a decision was made to locate the long-awaited aluminum smelter in Tema. President Nkrumah took the opportunity to embrace the prospects of the city anew and made the project a cornerstone of Ghana's "Second Development Plan," spanning 1959 to 1964. Infrastructure, including hydroelectric works of the Volta River Project, along with investments in housing, health, sanitation and water, were at the plan's core (Bissue 1967).

5 Pascal Menoret (2014, 68–69) offers an informative capsule biography of Doxiadis charting his rise to prominence.

6 Doxiadis's plan for the Greek city of Aspra Spitia, realized in 1961, closely paralleled his work in Tema. Not only was its execution coincident with Tema's, but Aspra Spitia's development also hinged on the takeoff of the country's aluminum industry (Theocharopoulou 2009, 128). Doxiadis Associates' involvement in Greek urban development followed earlier efforts by the firm in Baghdad spanning 1955–58. The master plan for Islamabad was launched with Doxiadis's first trip to Pakistan in 1954 supported by Harvard University and the Ford Foundation (Hull 2012; Harper 2012; Pyla 2008). Doxiadis's plans for Riyadh came later in 1968 (Menoret 2014).

7 Arendt's explicit engagement with Africa and the colonial predicament is uneven. In her discussion of German rule in Southwest Africa, she mentions colonial extermination of Herero people in present-day Namibia and argues that the roots of European totalitarianism lie in colonialism (Arendt 1973). Arendt goes on to assert that there are "unbridgeable gaps" between colonial genocide and the Holocaust (Stone 2011), an argument subject to extensive critique on the matter of race (Gines 2008; Lee 2011).

8   The rights, assets, and liabilities of the Tema Corporation were established under the Tema Corporation Ordinance of 1952.

9   Doxiadis's contract was finalized November 23, 1959. The first planning proposal, submitted December 12, 1959, was accepted on January 23, 1960, little more than a month later.

10 For Tema, as for DA's other planning projects, there were *Monthly Reports, Reports on the Town, Yearly Reports*, and *Five-Year Plans*, as well as reports on individual industries, building techniques, and special projects, from hotels and city centers to schools and recreation.

11 Among the mountains of discarded documents in the back rooms of TDC, DA reports from Dhaka and Islamabad regularly appeared, along with full runs of the DA-produced *Ekistics* journal.

12 These sentiments were echoed by J. H. Mensah, chairman of Ghana's National Economic Planning Commission, who asserted, "Socialists in developing areas should devote themselves not to the rearrangement of the ownership of the means of production. The central concern must be with the building up of the nation's stock of productive assets" (Fitch and Oppenheimer 1966, 110). Mensah and other members of Nkrumah's circle were described as "labor Aristocrats" who pinned economic progress to increased worker output, "not by changing economic structures or property relations" (104).

13 Tema Metropolitan Assembly was established to handle local government in 1974. Nevertheless, TDC long remained in charge of the city's physical planning, housing developments, land leasing, and public works, including sanitation.

14 By 1960, with the city building finally in full swing, TDC split into two wings (TDC Archives, DOX-GHA 64, 1962, 4). One, Tema Corporation (TC), was placed under the Ministry of Local Government and Justice. The other, Tema Development Organization (TDO), was devoted to the physical development of the town in conjunction with Ghana's Development Secretariat and the President's Office. Replacing this short-lived solution, soon thereafter, TDO was folded again into the Tema Corporation, which became the prime planning and governing body for the new city, recuperating the original TDC moniker.

15 The circulation of Doxiadis's Athens-based associates between Greece and Ghana for both short and extended visits began as soon as Doxiadis received his first contract. Records documenting projects from 1960 list a half-dozen DA employees undertaking work in Ghana: Messrs. Marinos, Deliyannakis, Ioakimides, Kavadias, Cleogenis, Andoniades, and Kryriakos (Doxiadis Archives, C-GHA 176, 11-10-60). Soon thereafter, Doxiadis placed high-ranking team members in their Tema office, with Yakas holding position of DA vice president and Chatiras serving as chief representative in Ghana (Doxiadis Archives, GHA-T 1602 [1964]). The flow of personnel between Athens and Ac-

cra was matched by the movement of Ghanaian politicians and technocrats to DA offices in Athens. As early as 1959, before the contract for Tema's master plan was finalized, the head of Nkrumah's Builder's Brigrade, John Tettigah, traveled to Greece (Doxiadis Archives, C-GHA 2, 10-12-59). Within the year, in April 1959, a delegation of Ghanaian officials, including Messrs. Ayensu, Thompson, and Afriyie, paid an official visit to the DA office, recorded in DA's picture album ("Pictures from the Visit of Ghanaian Officials at DA," Doxiadis Archives, C-GHA 55).

16 Discarded TDC personnel files found in the dust piles of the old library record hiring and terms of service for Ghanaians of many social and geographic backgrounds and professional skill sets: E. J. Quaye, assistant works superintendent, hired in 1958; D. B. Borketey, assistant plan printer, hired in 1962; and J. K. Dzeha, hired as management officer in 1965. Women were part of this professional workforce, including Cristina Irene Bossman, clerical assistant, hired in 1960; and Matilda Kumi, hired as a receptionist in 1962.

17 Further knowledge of Clerk's contribution to Tema's urban plan is of critical importance to understanding the interests and ideals driving the city's design. Additional information on Clerk's interactions with Nkrumah would also shed further light on Nkrumah's involvement in the city's realization. Evidence of their close relationship nevertheless attests to Nkrumah's recognition of and investment in urban planning as a formative mode of nation-building.

18 Doxiadis's belief in singular ideals of purportedly universal value is evident in ongoing reference to the Ancient Greek polis. He also believed it was possible to formulate a common set of principles of universal value to prepare humanity for the future. To this end, Doxiadis founded the Delos symposium, which included anthropologists, geneticists, psychiatrists, economists, and architects, as well as the leading public intellectuals of the day, from Marshall McLuhan to Margaret Mead to Buckminster Fuller, to debate and devise solutions to contemporary problems (Rezende 2016).

19 According to *Merriam-Webster's*, the root of "ekistics" in Modern Greek is *oikistikē*, from feminine of *oikistikos* (of settlement), from *oikizein* (to settle, colonize) from *oikos* (house).

20 This approach, decentering labor as the core realm of nation- and citizen-making, is in line with a wider argument that Nkrumah was ambivalent about the political potentials of the new nation's working class despite his government's professed socialist ideals (Ahlman 2017, 116; Biney 2011, 107).

21 As Dominique Laporte (2002) notes of seventeenth-century Paris, *non olet*, or odor-free sanitary facilities, are considered a civilizational achievement.

22 The earliest residential areas built in the new city were considered temporary housing for workers involved in the construction of the port and surrounding urban center. Known as Site 1 and Site 2, they are located on either side of

Tema's main market and still contain the original public toilets and ablution blocks.

23 A public secret of Tema's class-centered urban plan, this was so despite the city's founding on the displacement of individuals and groups identified and disenfranchised due to their "tribal" and regional origins as evidenced in the forced relocation of residents to Tema Manhean and Ashaiman.

24 Not restricted to Tema or the Nkrumah government, a similar mix of dependence on the working class and mitigation of their organization capacity was evident in the dissolution of Ghana's Trade Union Congress in the late 1960s after Nkrumah was deposed.

25 Further testament to the political unpredictability of using domestic conditions to suppress labor mobilization, one of the first successful social movements in Tema in the early 1970s revolved around domestic water rates and threats of mass disconnection (Yedu Bannerman 1973, 37).

26 While they may be recognized as a "common good" (see Arendt [1958, 35] on the medieval guild), they are certainly not public.

27 One of many examples of Doxiadis's application of a single urban planning template to multiple different locations, the urban plan for Riyadh, as Menoret (2014, 96,99) notes, was similarly designed to circumscribe public space and opportunities for large-scale public interaction. As in Tema, "residential neighborhoods were designed as self-sustaining . . . complete with shops, schools, parks, etc., limited to local access and pedestrian circulation while through traffic . . . pushed to the periphery." Riyadh's design also reflected the same logic of mixed-class and mixed-income neighborhoods (77).

28 Dahl (1989, 340) offers the idea of a "minipopulus," turned by others into the notion of a "minipublic," to denote a small-scale public sphere inviting inclusive debate and deliberation among its members.

29 Doxiadis, allied with up-and-coming national leaders and regimes, and garnering funding and recognition from the likes of the Ford Foundation, the United Nations, and other proxies of post–World War II US interests, was adept at playing both sides of the postcolonial power bloc (De Dominicis 2019; Provoost 2006).

30 Reuters' film clip "Ghana: President Nkrumah Opens Tema Harbour" captures the harbor's commissioning on February 10, 1962: https://reuters .screenocean.com/record/923005.

31 In the case of Palestine, Sophia Stamatopoulou-Robbins (2019, 53) speaks to a similar acceleration of "infrastructure's expiration dates" pushed forward by the actualities of use and population growth.

32 In 1967, Doxiadis noted "1,000 houses ready for occupation, 1100 under construction, 1800 programmed for upcoming year." Projections for the sewage system indicated that "by the end of 1968 about 4,000 houses or 25,000 peo-

ple will have to be taken care of by the system over and above the population served at present" (TDC Archives, DOX-GHA A 105, 1967, 10).

33   Ayi Kwei Armah's novel charting the dashed aspirations and material decline of Ghana's First Republic, *The Beautyful Ones Are Not Yet Born* (1969), inspired a literary genre described by Joshua Esty (1999) as "excremental post-colonialism."

34   Tahal's role in the project was not incidental and speaks to the close relationship between Israel and Ghana and the transfer of models and expertise between newly established postwar polities faced with similar challenges. Just as Tahal devised Tema's waste management plan, it also produced master plans for Palestinian waste management and was later involved in projects in the Israeli-occupied West Bank (Stamatopoulou-Robbins 2019, 31).

35   The report goes on to state, "Half of the original flow capacity has been lost in these pipes; and consequently the so called 'self-cleansing velocity' or 'minimum tractive force' is not achieved and further deposition occurs.... Blockages (caused by use of bulky anal cleansing material) can take between 8 and 20 weeks to clear from the moment they are identified [causing] backflows or emergence of sewage from inspection chambers into surface water drains that have become conveyance units of the sewerage system" (Salifu 1997, 85).

36   Anand (2011) makes a similar point in his discussion of "pressure" as the root metaphor linking Mumbai's overburdened waterworks and the constant demand for services by city residents.

37   As Markell (2011, 17) puts it, "We can learn something from the specific ways these seemingly contradictory formulations appear and interact in the text of *The Human Condition*."

2. Tema Proper

1   Stoler's consideration of ruins and ruination, centrally attuned to postcolonial conditions, is in dialogue with Walter Benjamin's (1999) treatment of urban space and the shadows of past lives that retain a hold on the urban landscape. The destruction and reordering of urban space is a concern both Benjamin and Arendt share with Heidegger as developed in "Building, Dwelling, Thinking" (1971); see Pensky 2011.

2   According to Ghana Statistical Service, the official population count for Tema in 2019 was 361,000. Ashaiman is 271,000 (Cudjoe, Sepah, and Anarfi 2013).

3   As E. Awuah, E. Donkor, and E. K. M. Sanjok (2008) confirm, well over a decade later, they were yet to be repaired. Over the course of my research, extending from 2010 to 2019, the problems remained, and repairs were still not complete. Rather than a new pumping station, World Bank funding was utilized to build a new facility for sewage-siphoning trucks to dump liquid waste.

The facility was over capacity soon after it opened, and the ponds built to handle the waste were inadequate to the daily sewage loads (Rohilla et al. 2018).

4   It is possible to attribute the limits of Star's (1999) insights when applied to settings such as Tema to the apparent gulf between the highly industrialized settings that are her point of reference and the developing world. However, more to the point may be the disconnect between her immediate point of reference—the virtual infrastructures of information networks—and the fully material worlds of sewage systems and human waste.

5   Gastón Gordillo's (2014) exploration of the layered resonance and affective "afterlife" of rubble in Argentina's Chaco, like Stoler (2013), bears the strong imprint of Benjamin's meditation on ruins and urban space. While also attuned to breakdown, the experience of Tema is more about repurposing than destruction.

6   Fredericks (2018) recounts similar bodily and health risks incurred by women in the course of garbage collection in Dakar. I address the interplay of physical risk and monetary reward for young men in Ashaiman's waste dump (Chalfin 2019).

7   Julia Elyachar (2010) refers to the network of social relations necessary to public problem solving in Cairo as "phatic labor." In the case of Tema's sanitation system, the elision of persons and infrastructure is inadequate, as the presence of waste workers without adequate tools and supplies can do little to repair infrastructural breakdown. In Tema, the waste worker operates instead as a sort of "phantom infrastructure" animating the promise of repair in the absence of material assurance.

8   Far from overriding past orders, new construction brings the vicissitudes of breakdown to the fore. On rounds with the repair crew one day, we checked on the new pipes being installed for an office building under construction. With the building sited on top of an existing sewage line, the pipes had to be moved. In the process a nearby water pipe was damaged and needed to be replaced.

9   A compelling point of comparison regarding the character of bureaucratic authority in weak states, Nana's letter—an example of epistolary tactics of bureaucratic access—strongly resembles the complaints received by the Palestinian Authority about waste dumping and overflows (see Stamatopoulou-Robbins 2019, 120).

10 Daniel Schneider (2011, 45) provides a parallel account of debates in the United States about whether sewage control was a private or public problem.

11 Jeffrey Paller's (2019) examination of political life in informal settlements in Ghana attests to the prime importance of assembly members in the production of political accountability.

12 Viviana D'Auria (2014, 2015) identifies "incremental housing" as fundamental to Tema's original design by Doxiadis, with the explicit intention of designing

dwellings and lots for residents to expand on as their families, assets, and living standards grew.

3. The Right(s) to Remains

Material from chapter 3 appeared in "Public Things, Excremental Politics, and the Infrastructure of Bare Life in Ghana's City of Tema," *American Ethnologist* 41, no. 1 (February 2014): 92–109.

1 Use of the term "shit" is increasingly charged in Ghanaian society. Depending on cultural background, generation, class, and religious persuasion, the term is considered vulgar and offensive by many, as it contravenes cultural conventions of deference and indirection, especially when speaking of sensitive matters such as bodily processes. For others, it is common parlance, widely used among youth and those in culturally mixed communities where multiple languages may be spoken and reversion to loan words allows for efficient communication. There is also a growing contingent of artists, musicians, and activists in Ghana who actively and intentionally address themes and vocabulary considered inappropriate in official discourse and public discussion in an effort to challenge conservative and hierarchical social norms and foster frank discussion of taboo topics. In this chapter I use the term in accord with community conventions and when quoting or paraphrasing the academic literature in which it is widely used.

2 Building on traditions as fishmongers and shareholders in canoe fishing fleets (Appiah et al. 2020), women's role in fish processing expanded with development of Tema's port and harbor, which offers access to the catches of fish trawlers and frozen fish in cold stores.

3 Even more than public toilets, public showers abound across Manhean. Easier to build than toilets, access to a water tank, overhead pipes, and a drain are all that's necessary for a shower business. Patronage is for the most part guaranteed if the price is fair and the premises are convenient and moderately clean. Crowded homes without toilets or bathing rooms, combined with the exertions of fishing, fish smoking, and other manual work in Ghana's hot climate, ensure a steady demand for shower facilities.

4 On Ga history and culture, see Field 1937; Kilson 1974; and Parker 2000.

5 Doxiadis's plan for the new city of Tema eventually designated the center of the original village for the ten-story, two-hundred-room Meridien Hotel. A massive construction project, the elegant yet short-lived state hotel has been reduced to a hulking shell, inoperable and uninhabitable for the past thirty years.

6 Agamben (1998, 15–16) draws on Schmitt's (1985) ideas in *Political Theology* regarding the "paradox of sovereignty." That is, "the sovereign stands outside the juridical order and, nevertheless, belongs to it, since it is up to him to de-

cide if the constitution is to be suspended in toto. . . . The exception does not only confirm, the rule as such lives off the exception alone." According to Agamben (17), "The state of exception is not the chaos that precedes order but rather the situation that results from its suspension. In this sense the exception is truly, according to its etymological root, taken outside (ex-capare) and not excluded."

7 Among the Ga, the role of *mantse* is similar to two other ritual offices, *mankralo* and *wulomo*. According to Butcher (1966), "Mantse—keeper of war medicine—was not initially a political office. Mankralo is considered the second Mantse. They hold ritual rights to land but are not landowners. Any rights to transfer land are family ('we' in Ga) or lineage based."

8 The Ga notion of household is complex and is not coterminus with any single residential unit given the convention of duo-local marriage (with husband and wife maintaining separate dwellings) and the common reference to a house in the dynastic rather than the dwelling-based sense. According to Claire Robertson (1984), the Ga household could be "a group of people who live together and eat from the same pot, although they may not all sleep under the same roof." It might also consist of numerous family groups living in separate rooms in the same dwelling unit (Jackson and Oppong 2014, 484).

9 Inspired by the International Congresses of Modern Architecture under the leadership of Le Corbusier, Drew and Fry were founding members of its British counterpart, the Modern Architectural Research Group.

10 Danny Hoffman (2017, 78), regarding urban design in Monrovia, Liberia, similarly mentions the impact of Drew and Fry's architectural experiments in West Africa in the interregnum between the end of World War II and the era of African independence, which connected emerging technologies in the tropics with the cultivation of new patterns of urban living.

11 Another modernist megaproject in the tropics, Chandigarh differs from Tema in its monumental aspirations and, unlike Tema, includes extensive civic space in addition to residential zones (Prakash 2002).

12 Jackson and Oppong (2014, 484) indicate, "As Fry and Drew were busy in Chandigarh, it is unlikely that in the first instance they were the lead designers for Tema Manhean, and is probable that the work was overseen by Drake and Lasdun until Fry and Drew returned to the UK in 1954."

13 With the recent reconsideration of tropical modernism, including the work of Drew and Fry, the duo's interest in sanitary matters is noted by Jackson and Holland (2014). They indicate, for instance, that Drew and Fry, on one of their earliest assignments in West Africa, took it upon themselves to redesign toilets for colonial officials in Bathurst, Gambia (153).

14 Drew's experience with industrial design via her work on kitchen appliances in the United Kingdom prior to her move to West Africa (Ayre 2014; Holder 2009) may have informed her proposals in the Gold Coast.

15 Although this was not the case in the Old Tema, per Oko Adjetey (1964), in Akan towns and settlements of central Ghana it was common to have public sanitary pits at the outer boundaries of the community (van der Geest 2002, 201). It is not clear whether Drew and Fry were aware of this practice.

16 Agamben discusses this premise in his critique of standard representations of human rights as a form of "natural rights" inherent to all persons. He directs this complaint at Arendt (Agamben 1998, 126, 131), who fails, in his opinion, to explore the contradiction between her treatment of bodily labor as prepolitical in *The Human Condition* (1958) and the stark politicization of the body in *The Origins of Totalitarianism* (1973). The difference may lie in their view of what counts as political life, with Agamben, like Foucault (1979), focusing more on repression, and Arendt (1958) invested in humanistic ideals of self-expression and collective recognition.

17 In 2018, this was about $12,000.

18 Children and the elderly may use the toilet for free.

19 These are pseudonyms. Kutsho translates to "subdivision" in Ga.

20 Also a pseudonym. Mang refers to "neighborhood" in Ga.

21 In Manhean, more important than exposure of the private body is proper comportment in public space. This point was made by a toilet manager who noticed a woman defecating by the beach while he conversed with friends a few hundred yards away. When he told her it was inappropriate to expose herself in clear view, she fully acknowledged her proximity but chastised him for failing to avert his gaze. Here, separate from the actuality of copresence, an act can be both public and intimate depending on the kind of bearing witness it allows, prevents, or incites.

22 Whereas for Arendt (1958) the modern era is marked by the troubling insertion of the social into the public, in *The Human Condition* the base act of shitting is among the very few social practices that remain properly situated in the private realm in the context of industrial modernity.

23 As Katz defines it (2001, 711), "Social reproduction encompasses daily and long-term reproduction. At its most basic it hinges on the biological production of the labor force both generationally and on a daily basis through the acquisition of the basic means of existence: food, shelter, clothing and health care."

24 Suggesting a more long-standing cultural convention, the house compounds in old Tema village sketched by Margaret Field (c. 1939) show trees in the interior courtyards (D'Auria 2014, 344). A more recent examination of changes to Tema Manhean's original structures indicates the enduring presence of large trees in shared spaces within and between compounds (D'Auria 2015, 113).

25 These gathering sites bear a formal resemblance to the *fada* men's tea and conversation circles of urban Niger (Masquelier 2019).

26 While some ghettos have a loose, peripatetic membership, others are more restricted in use and makeup. The most exclusive are those where young men get together to carouse, play cards, and practice the derisive chants of *kleejo*. Per the research of Marina Ofei-Nkansah, these sites thread through Manhean's dense urban landscape, tucked into alleyways, between houses, or over drains. They are adorned with striking graphics and monikers—Fabu, One Man, One Car, Peace and Love, God's Grace, Fun Club, and so on. Other ghettos are more flexible in size, membership, and purpose. Those better resourced through dues payments have TV hookups and blackboards listing gambling debts and telephone numbers. These spaces are often constructed from the worn hulls of old fishing canoes, enabling a competitive solidarity on land parallel to the sociality of the sea for the many fishermen who spend their time here.

4. Ziginshore

An earlier version of chapter 4 was published as "'Wastelandia': Infrastructure and the Commonwealth of Waste in Urban Ghana," *Ethnos: Journal of Anthropology* 82, no. 4 (January 2016): 648–71.

1 For a broader discussion of land and chieftaincy in the subregion, see Berry 2001.

2 Acting as an autonomous political agent, Uncle differs from other development entrepreneurs given his distance from established political authorities and lack of previously established ties to residents of the area (Kleist 2011).

3 Hobbes's employment of the term "Bodies Politique" is precise and deliberate. Distinguishing it from private orders, he uses it to characterize political systems made by the authority from the Sovereign power of the Commonwealth ([1651] 1994, 132).

4 First articulated in *De Corpore* ([1655] 1981), Hobbes's plenist convictions continue to be debated by scholars in terms of their inspiration by particular experimental observations and the diverse philosophical traditions of René Descartes and Aristotle, as well as their scientific derivation versus their political application (Leijenhorst 2002; Malcolm 2002; Schapin and Schaffer 1985).

5 Hovering between parody and serious inquiry, Slavoj Žižek (2004) famously discusses the symbolic resonance of toilet design for understanding national culture.

6 This arrangement does not conform to what Martinich (2005, 128) calls the "non-sovereign covenant." It signals a different sort of political partiality that could be labeled a quasi- or protosovereign covenant.

7 Occupations going hand in hand, several of the young men worked closely with the fish smokers behind the hostel, regularly transferring cartons of fro-

zen fish from cold stores near the port to the smoke ovens and bales of smoked fish to the roadside for transport to market.

8 Akhil Gupta (2018) makes a related point in his consideration of the lively temporality of infrastructure through the lens of ruins.

5. Dwelling on Toilets

Portions of chapter 5 can be found in "Excrementa III: The Leader in Upscale Sanitary Solutions?," in "Humanitarian Goods," special issue, *Limn*, no. 9 (October 2017).

1 In the case of landlords residing alongside tenants, toilet facilities are typically reserved for family members and off-limits to other occupants of a compound dwelling (Pellow 2008).

2 This comment alludes to an emerging tug-of-war over waste between Ashaiman's fledging municipal authority, newly instated after years of neglect by the Tema Development Corporation and Tema Municipal Assembly, and community members who filled the gap to sustain the public good. Now that a bona fide municipal government is in place, the inability to uphold a monopoly on urban waste is a sign of weakness (see also Chalfin 2019).

3 Marxian (1968) ideas of surplus focus on labor and exchangeable, profit-bearing outputs. Bataille, by contrast, concentrates on what can be appropriated but never fully assimilated. Rather than the Marxian triad of labor, surplus, and accumulation, Bataille's is a triad of energy, waste, and excess.

4 Despite claims that Veblen's and Bataille's outlooks are irreconcilable, Bataille can be understood as "Veblen's sinister double" (Preparata 2007, 62, 64).

5 Reliable income figures for Ashaiman are hard to come by. However, data from Ghana Statistical Service (2014) confirm the material challenges faced by residents, 73 percent of whom work in the private informal sector, and 5 percent in public-sector employment. A large majority, 78 percent, reside in compound houses, half of which are owned by nonresident landlords. Of those in compound dwellings, 69 percent are one-room households. Five percent indicate they live in improvised homes such as kiosks and containers. Regarding toilet facilities in Ashaiman, according to Ghana Statistical Service (2014), 64 percent utilize public toilets. Other studies place this at 83 percent (Mazeau 2013, 154).

6 Theories of political heterogeneity such as those proposed by Bataille both speak to and complicate theories of political plurality such as Arendt's. Plurality implies a multiplicity of similar forms and affiliations. Heterogeneity, however, is more diverse and unsettled. Refuting assumptions of political stability or boundedness, this framing serves as a reminder that Ashaiman, although a formally established and recognized political territory, like all urban spaces is made up of multiple overlapping and shifting publics. Private commercial toilets are just one space where demos is instantiated in the minor, fleeting

routines of everyday life amid the intense mobility and frenetic energy of this dynamic urban frontier zone.

7   Allied by their concern with violence and sharing intellectual roots in interwar Europe (Hegarty 2003), the political outlooks of Arendt and Bataille are largely distinguished by their different end points. Arendt distanced herself from Bataille and criticized his "aestheticization of violence" (Cavarero 2009, 48). Probing this apparent divergence, Charles Barbour (2012, 48) notes the similarities between Arendt's concept of action and Bataille's sovereignty, suggesting that Bataille reveals the "unspeakable repressed underside of Arendt's approach to action and politics." Although I agree with Barbour on the hidden resonance of their ideas derived from a shared concern with materiality and the body, in *The Human Condition* Arendt remains invested in classical norms of institutional closure, whereas Bataille sees power as part of the totality of human experience.

8   Ashaiman was barely provided with the most basic urban amenities despite its proximity to Tema. In 1970, there were only six government standpipes supplying water to a population of at least twelve thousand, and there was no electricity (Yedu Bannerman 1973, 9).

9   Other homes lack toilet facilities due to housing pressure, as nonresident landlords tend to convert all available rooms to revenue-generating living space. In the case of resident landlords, it is not uncommon to locate toilets in their private quarters, preventing access by those who rent space in the larger compound (Pellow 2008).

10 Not only do the "aesthetics of propriety" of Ashaiman's PCTs counter the filth and stench of the city's overused and poorly maintained "government toilets"; they also contrast with the deliberate if misplaced "aesthetics of vulgarity" evident in the city's new NGO-built public toilets. Here, graphic signage depicts defecating elders and infants, and piles of diarrhea. Images at once didactic and repulsive, they do little to attract patronage, in contrast to the aesthetic enticements of private facilities.

11 Hannah Appel, Nikhil Anand, and Akhil Gupta (2018, 21) also note how infrastructures "interpellate specific types of subjects."

12 Although mosques carved out in the process of prayer are common, the space may have been too close to toilets to be allowable for worship, especially during the holy month of Ramadan.

13 Rosalind Fredericks (2018) probes the interplay of Islamic piety and waste work among women in Dakar, showing personal sacrifice and humble abasement to be a path to spiritual purity.

14 The coalignment of mosques with toilets and urinals is a common feature of mosque architecture, as personal cleanliness and ablution is a prerequisite of prayer (Mokhtar 2003).

15 Slavoj Žižek (2004) speaks to the reversal staged in Luis Buñuel's film *Phantom of Liberty* (1974), in which guests sit around a table to defecate in public and retreat to private spaces to eat.

16 The association of defecation and eating well is graphically represented in the artwork of David Comrade Sedi Agbeko exhibited at BlaxTARLINES' "Orderly Disorderly" show, August 2017, KNUST End of Year Exhibition, Museum of Science and Technology, Accra, https://issuu.com/iubeezy/docs/od_print _brochure_final_final. Agbeko's installation includes facsimile faux coprolites formed from common foodstuffs and infused with the scents of air fresheners and confection flavorings that are displayed on dishware and arrayed as table settings to resemble plates of shit.

Conclusion

1 Arendt's treatment is fundamentally different from volume 1 of Marx's *Capital* (1968), for instance, in which bodily reproduction matters only for sustaining the conditions and capacities for production.

2 This dialogue with Arendt complicates the concept of "theory from the south" (Comaroff and Comaroff 2012) by challenging strict notions of theoretical emplacement tying theory to specific locations. Instead, both theory and places are tied to particular historical conjunctures.

3 Also reading Arendt against the grain, Adom Getachew (2019, 96) speaks to Arendt's investment in anticolonial struggles even if she didn't fully understand their roots or scope.

References

Archival Materials

Constantinos A. Doxiadis Archives, Athens, Greece (Doxiadis Archives)

"Letter from CA Doxiadis to John Tettagah, Ghana Builders Brigade." C-GHA 2 (10-12-59).

"Letter from CA Doxiadis to H.E. the Prime Minister Dr. Kwame Nkrumah." C-GHA 41 (26-4-60).

"To His Excellency Kwame Nkrumah." Cable. July 1, 1960. Athens. C-GHA 68 (1-7-60).

"Letter from CA Doxiadis to His Excellency the Minister of Works and Housing Mr. E.K. Bensah." C-GHA 131 (10-9-60).

"Data and Progress of Ghana Projects." C-GHA 176 (11-10-60).

"Tema." GHA-T 1602 (1964).

Photographs:

C. A. Doxiadis visit to Ghana, April 1960 (Archive Files 28558).

Community 7, Tema 1968, P-GHA-A 322 (7) (Photographs 34512).

C 7 Landscape, 1971, P-GHA-A 117 (7) (Photographs 34512).

Low-Income Housing, Community 5, Tema 1967, P-GHA-A 310 (38) (Photographs 34512).

Low-Income, Tema, 1971, P-GHA-A 148 (8) (Photographs 34512).

Low-Income, Tema, 1971, P-GHA-A 148 (13-11A) (Photographs 34512).

Low-Income, Tema, 1971, P-GHA-A 148 (14-12A) (Photographs 34512).

Pictures from the Visit of Ghanaian Officials at DA (1959), C-GHA 55.

Queen Elizabeth II, Exhibition of DA Projects, Tema, November 1961 (Photographs 30932).

Tema Sewerage Pipes, 1965, P-GHA-A 282 (47) (Photographs 34512).

Tema Spiral Road, 1965, P-GHA-A 280 (12) (Photographs 34512).

Tema Development Corporation Archives, Tema, Ghana (TDC Archives)

Doxiadis Associates for Government of Ghana. Tema Town Centre 1, DOX-GHA 3 (8-7-60).

Doxiadis Associates for Government of Ghana. Tema Main Roads 2, DOX-GHA 6 (10-2-61).

Doxiadis Associates for Government of Ghana. Tema 6—House Types—Preliminary Report, DOX-GHA 20 (22-8-61).

Doxiadis Associates for Government of Ghana. Tema 11—Thoughts on the Formation of the Town, DOX-GHA 27 (10-10-61).

Doxiadis Associates for Government of Ghana. Tema 14—The Five-Year Needs 1961–1966, DOX-GHA 31 (12-2-62).

Doxiadis Associates for Government of Ghana. Tema 19—Types of Dwellings in Tema, DOX-GHA 40 (10-3-62).

Doxiadis Associates for Government of Ghana. Tema 27—Hostels, Preliminary Report, DOX-GHA 52 (30-6-62).

Doxiadis Associates for Government of Ghana. Tema 30—Main Town Center, DOX-GHA 62 (28-7-62).

Doxiadis Associates for Government of Ghana. Tema 32—Administration of Town, DOX-GHA 64 (31-7-62).

Doxiadis Associates for Government of Ghana. Accra-Tema 4—First Approach to the Sanitation Problems of the Accra-Tema Metropolitan Area, DOX-GHA 84 (8-10-63).

Doxiadis Associates for Government of Ghana. Accra-Tema 45—Triennial Report, May 1961–May 1964, DOX-GHA A 91 (5-7-66).

Doxiadis Associates for Government of Ghana. Low-Income House Types 47, DOX-GHA A 94 (27-10-64).

Doxiadis Associates for Government of Ghana. Building Materials in Ghana 1, DOX-GHA A 96 (3-65).

Doxiadis Associates for Government of Ghana. Tema—Sanitary Sewer System, Urgent Amelioration Works, DOX-GHA A 105 (15-5-67).

Doxiadis Associates for Government of Ghana. Tema—Monthly Report No. 9, January 1962, MR-GHA 37 (1-62).

Doxiadis Associates for Government of Ghana. Tema—Monthly Report No. 11, March 1962, MR-GHA 43 (3-62).

Doxiadis Associates for Government of Ghana. Tema—Monthly Report No. 20, December 1962, MR-GHA 65 (12-62).

Other Sources

Adams, Samuel, and William Asante. 2020. "The Judiciary and Post-election Conflict Resolution and Democratic Consolidation in Ghana's Fourth Republic." *Journal of Contemporary African Studies* 38 (2): 243–56. DOI:10.1080/02589001.2020.1758639.

Agamben, Giorgio. 1998. *Homo Sacer: Sovereign Power and Bare Life.* Stanford, CA: Stanford University Press.

Agyeman-Duah, Baffour. 2005. *Elections and Electoral Politics in Ghana's Fourth Republic.* Accra: Ghana Center for Democratic Development.

Ahlman, Jeffrey S. 2017. *Living with Nkrumahism: Nation, State, and Pan-Africanism in Ghana*. Athens: Ohio University Press.

Alcock, A. E. S. 1955. "Tema, a New Town in Gold Coast." *Town and Country Planning* 23:51–55.

Alcock, A. E. S. 1963. "Community Development at Tema." *Overseas Building Notes: Housing and Planning in Tropical and Sub-tropical Countries* 87:1–12.

Alexander, Anthony. 2009. *Britain's New Towns: Garden Cities to Sustainable Communities*. New York: Routledge.

Allen, Danielle. 2004. *Talking to Strangers: Anxieties of Citizenship since* Brown v. Board of Education. Chicago: University of Chicago Press.

Althusser, Louis. 1971. *Lenin and Philosophy and Other Essays*. Translated by Ben Brewster. New York: Monthly Review Press.

Amarteifio, G. W. 1966. "Part I: The Story of Resettlement." In *Tema Manhean: A Story of Resettlement*, edited by G. W. Amarteifio, D. A. Butcher, and David Whitham, 5–20. Accra: Ghana Universities Press.

Amevuvor, Jocelyn, and Greg Hafer. 2019. "Communities in the Stalls: A Study of Latrinalia Linguistic Landscapes." *Critical Inquiry in Language Studies* 16 (2): 90–106.

Anand, Nikhil. 2011. "Pressure: The Politechnics of Water Supply in Mumbai." *Cultural Anthropology* 26 (4): 542–64.

Anand, Nikhil. 2017. *Hydraulic City: Water and the Infrastructures of Citizenship in Mumbai*. Durham, NC: Duke University Press.

Anand, Nikhil. 2018. "A Public Matter: Water, Hydraulics, Biopolitics." In *The Promise of Infrastructure*, edited by Nikhil Anand, Akhil Gupta, and Hannah Appel, 155–73. Durham, NC: Duke University Press.

Anderson, Gloria. 2019. "Poor Sewage System in Parts of Tema." GBC *Ghana Online*, April 8, 2019. https://www.gbcghanaonline.com/news/poor-sewage-system-in -parts-of-tema/2019/.

Anderson, Warwick. 1995. "Excremental Colonialism: Public Health and the Poetics of Pollution." *Critical Inquiry* 21 (3): 640–69.

Anderson, Warwick. 2006. *Colonial Pathologies: American Tropical Medicine, Race, and Hygiene in the Philippines*. Durham, NC: Duke University Press.

Appadurai, Arjun. 2002. "Deep Democracy: Urban Governmentality and the Horizon of Politics." *Public Culture* 14 (1): 21–47. DOI:10.1215/08992363-14-1-21.

Appel, Hannah, Nikhil Anand, and Akhil Gupta. 2018. "Introduction: Temporality, Politics, and the Promise of Infrastructure." In *The Promise of Infrastructure*, edited by Nikhil Anand, Akhil Gupta, and Hannah Appel, 1–39. Durham, NC: Duke University Press.

Appiah, S., T. O. Antwi-Asare, F. K. Agyire-Tettey, E. Abbey, J. K. Kuwornu, S. Cole, and S. K. Chimatiro. 2020. "Livelihood Vulnerabilities among Women in Small-Scale Fisheries in Ghana." *European Journal of Development Research* (October): 1–29.

Appiah-Effah, Eugene, Godwin Armstrong Duku, Naziru Yakubu Azangbego, Ransford Kojo Aduafo Aggrey, Barbara Gyapong-Korsah, and Kwabena Biritwum

Nyarko. 2019. "Ghana's Post-MDGs Sanitation Situation: An Overview." *Journal of Water, Sanitation and Hygiene for Development* 9 (3): 397–415.

Apter, David Ernest. 1963. *Ghana in Transition*. Rev. ed. New York: Atheneum.

Aquaah-Harrison, Richard. 2004. *Housing and Urban Development in Ghana: With Special Reference to Low-Income Housing*. UN Habitat. United Nations Human Settlements Programme, Kenya.

Arendt, Hannah. 1958. *The Human Condition*. Chicago: University of Chicago Press.

Arendt, Hannah. 1973. *The Origins of Totalitarianism*. New York: Houghton Mifflin Harcourt.

Aretxaga, Begoña. 1995. "Dirty Protest: Symbolic Overdetermination and Gender in Northern Ireland Ethnic Violence." *Ethos* 23 (2): 123–48. DOI:10.1525/eth.1995.23.2 .02a00010.

Arku, Godwin. 2006. "Housing and Development Strategies in Ghana." *International Development Planning Review* 28 (3): 333–58.

Armaly, Maha. 2016. *Ghana Project Performance Assessment Report: Second Urban Environmental Sanitation Project*. Washington, DC: World Bank Group.

Asare, Tony, Erika Mamley Osae, and Deborah Pellow. 2015. "Recreating Community: New Housing for *amui djor* Residents." In *Public Anthropology in a Borderless World*, edited by Sam Beck and Carl Maida, 350–75. New York: Berghahn Books.

Ashcroft, Caroline. 2018. "The Polis and the Res Publica: Two Arendtian Models of Violence." *History of European Ideas* 44 (1): 128–42.

Athens Technological Institute. 1963. "The Athens Center of Ekistics." *Ekistics*: 142–44.

Awuah, E., E. Donkor, and E. K. M. Sanjok. 2008. "Management of Sewerage System: Case Study in Tema." In *Proceedings of the 33rd WEDC International Conference: Access to Sanitation and Safe Water: Global Partnerships and Local Actions, Accra, Ghana, April 7–11*, edited by Hazel Jones, 13–19. Loughborough, UK: Water, Engineering, and Development Centre Loughborough University.

Ayee, Joseph, and Richard C. Crook. 2003. *"Toilet Wars": Urban Sanitation Services and the Politics of Public-Private Partnerships in Ghana*. IDS Working Paper. Vol. 213. Brighton, UK: Institute of Development Studies.

Ayre, Becky. 2014. "An Architect for Modern Times." *Raconteur*, February 6, 2014. https://www.raconteur.net/culture/an-architect-for-modern-times.

Babül, Elif. 2017. *Bureaucratic Intimacies: Translating Human Rights in Turkey*. Stanford, CA: Stanford University Press.

Baddoo, E. Offeibea. 2019. "When Opportunity Meets Determination: Working Together to End Open Defecation." UNICEF, January 17, 2019. https://www.unicef .org/ghana/stories/when-opportunity-meets-determination.

Barbour, Charles. 2012. "The Sovereign without Domain: Georges Bataille and the Ethics of Nothing." In *The Politics of Nothing: On Sovereignty*, edited by Clare Monagle and Dimitris Vardoulakis, 37–49. London: Routledge.

Barry, Andrew. 2006. "Technological Zones." *European Journal of Social Theory* 9 (2): 239–53.

Barry, Andrew. 2013. *Material Politics: Disputes along the Pipeline*. London: Wiley Blackwell.

Barton, Hugh, and Catherine Tsourou. 2000. *Healthy Urban Planning: A WHO Guide to Planning for People*. London: World Health Organization Regional Office for Europe / Spon.

Bashford, Alison. 2004. *Imperial Hygiene*. New York: Palgrave Macmillan.

Bataille, Georges. 1985. *Visions of Excess: Selected Writings, 1927–1939*. Edited by Allan Stoekl. Translated by Allan Stoekl, Carl R. Lovitt, and Donald M. Leslie Jr. Minneapolis: University of Minnesota Press.

Bataille, Georges. 1988. *The Accursed Share: An Essay on General Economy*. Translated by Robert Hurley. New York: Zone.

Bayart, Jean-François. 1993. *The State in Africa: The Politics of the Belly*. New York: Longman.

Bayat, Asef. 2013. *Life as Politics: How Ordinary People Change the Middle East*. 2nd ed. Stanford, CA: Stanford University Press.

Bear, Laura. 2015. *Navigating Austerity: Currents of Debt along a South Asian River*. Stanford, CA: Stanford University Press.

Benhabib, Seyla. 1992. "Models of Public Space: Hannah Arendt, the Liberal Tradition, and Jürgen Habermas." In *Habermas and the Public Sphere*, edited by Craig Calhoun, 73–98. Cambridge, MA: MIT Press.

Benhabib, Seyla. 1995. "The Pariah and Her Shadow: Hannah Arendt's Biography of Rahel Varnhagen." In *Feminist Interpretations of Hannah Arendt*, edited by Bonnie Honig, 83–104. University Park: Penn State University Press.

Benhabib, Seyla. 2000. *The Reluctant Modernism of Hannah Arendt*. Lanham, MD: Rowman and Littlefield.

Benjamin, Walter. 1968. *Illuminations*. New York: Harcourt, Brace, and World.

Benjamin, Walter. 1999. *The Arcades Project*. Translated by Howard Eiland and Kevin McLaughlin. Cambridge, MA: Harvard University Press.

Bennett, Jane. 2010. *Vibrant Matter: A Political Ecology of Things*. Durham, NC: Duke University Press.

Bernasconi, Robert. 1996. "The Double Face of the Political and the Social: Hannah Arendt and America's Racial Divisions." *Research in Phenomenology* 26 (1): 3–24.

Bernstein, Richard J. 2018. *Why Read Hannah Arendt Now?* Hoboken, NJ: John Wiley and Sons.

Berry, Sara. 2001. *Chiefs Know Their Boundaries: Essays on Property, Power, and Past in Asante, 1896–1996*. Westport, CT: Heinemann.

Bessire, Lucas, and David Bond. 2014. "Ontological Anthropology and the Deferral of Critique." *American Ethnologist* 41 (3): 440–56.

Biney, Ama. 2011. *The Political and Social Thought of Kwame Nkrumah*. New York: Palgrave Macmillan.

Bin-Kasim, Waseem-Ahmed. 2019. "Sanitary Segregation: Cleansing Accra and Nairobi, 1908–1963." PhD diss., Washington University.

Bissue, Isaac. 1967. "Ghana's Seven-Year Development Plan in Retrospect." *Economic Bulletin of Ghana* 11 (1): 21–44.

blaxTARLINES. 2017. *Orderly Disorderly: KNUST End-of-Year Exhibition*. Accra, Ghana: Museum of Science and Technology, June 30–September 1, 2017. Exhibition catalog. Accessed April 16, 2021. https://issuu.com/iubeezy/docs/od_print_brochure_final_final.

Blundo, Giorgio, and Pierre-Yves Le Meur. 2009. Introduction to *Governance of Daily Life in Africa: Ethnographic Explorations of Public and Collective Services*, edited by Giorgio Blundo and Pierre-Yves Le Meur, 11–37. Leiden: Brill.

Bohman, Anna. 2010. *Framing the Water and Sanitation Challenge: A History of Urban Water Supply and Sanitation in Ghana, 1909–2005*. Umea, Sweden: Umea University.

Bouju, Jacky. 2008. "Urban Dwellers, Politicians and Dirt: An Anthropology of Everyday Governance in Bobo-Dioulasso (Burkina Faso)." In *The Governance of Daily Life in Africa*, edited by Giorgio Blundo and Pierre-Yves Le Meur, 143–70. Leiden: Brill.

Bredekamp, Horst. 2007. "Thomas Hobbes' Visual Strategies." In *Cambridge Companion to Hobbes' Leviathan*, edited by Patricia Springborg, 29–60. New York: Cambridge University Press.

Bromley, Ray. 2003. "Towards Global Human Settlements: Constantinos Doxiadis as Entrepreneur, Coalition Builder and Visionary." In *Urbanism: Imported or Exported?*, edited by Joe Nasr and Mercedes Volait, 316–39. Chichester, UK: Wiley.

Bullock, Nicholas. 2002. *Building the Post-war World: Modern Architecture and Reconstruction in Britain*. London: Routledge.

Buñuel, Luis, dir. *The Phantom of Liberty*. Los Angeles: 20th Century Fox, 1974.

Butcher, D. A. 1966. "Part II: An Analysis of Resettlement." In *Tema Manhean: A Story of Resettlement*, edited by G. W. Amarteifio, D. A. Butcher, and D. Whitham, 21–26. Accra: Ghana Universities Press.

Butcher, D. A. P., and David Whitham. 1966. "Part IV Conclusion." In *Tema Manhean: A Study of Resettlement*, edited by G. W. Amarteifio, D. A. P. Butcher, and David Whitham, 67–69. Accra: Ghana Universities Press.

Butt, Waqas H. 2020. "Waste Intimacies: Caste and the Unevenness of Life in Urban Pakistan." *American Ethnologist* 47 (3): 234–48. DOI:10.1111/amet.12960.

Calhoun, C. 1992. Introduction to *Habermas and the Public Sphere*, edited by C. Calhoun, 1–50. Cambridge, MA: MIT Press.

Callon, Michel, and Bruno Latour. 1981. "Unscrewing the Big Leviathan: How Actors Macro Structure Reality and How Sociologists Help Them Do So." In *Advances in Social Theory and Methodology: Toward an Integration of Micro- and Macro-Sociologies*, edited by Karin Knorr-Cetina and A. V. Cicourel, 277–303. Boston, MA: Routledge Kegan Paul.

Canovan, Margaret. 1992. *Hannah Arendt: A Reinterpretation of Her Political Thought*. New York: Cambridge University Press.

Carse, Ashley. 2014. *Beyond the Big Ditch: Politics, Ecology, and Infrastructure at the Panama Canal*. Cambridge, MA: MIT Press.

Cavarero, Adriana. 2009. *Horrorism: Naming Contemporary Violence*. Translated by William McCuaig. New York: Columbia University Press.

Chalfin, Brenda. 2004. *Shea Butter Republic: State Power, Global Markets, and the Making of an Indigenous Commodity*. New York: Routledge.

Chalfin, Brenda. 2010. *Neoliberal Frontiers: An Ethnography of Sovereignty in West Africa*. Chicago: University of Chicago Press.

Chalfin, Brenda. 2014. "Public Things, Excremental Politics, and the Infrastructure of Bare Life in Ghana's City of Tema." *American Ethnologist* 41:92–109.

Chalfin, Brenda. 2015. "'Excremental Post-colonialism' Reconsidered: Waste as Political Diagnostic in the Post-millennial City of Tema, Ghana." Paper presented at the African Studies Association 58th Annual Meeting, San Diego, CA, November 19–22.

Chalfin, Brenda. 2017. "Wastelandia: Infrastructure and the Commonwealth of Waste in Urban Ghana." *Ethnos* 82 (4): 648–71.

Chalfin, Brenda. 2019. "Waste Work and the Dialectics of Precarity in Urban Ghana: Durable Bodies and Disposable Things." *Africa* 89 (3): 499–520.

Chalfin, Brenda. 2020. "Experiments in Excreta to Energy: Sustainability Science and Bio-necro Collaboration in Urban Ghana." *Cambridge Journal of Anthropology* 38 (2): 88–104.

Chance, Kerry Ryan. 2018. *Living Politics in South Africa's Urban Shacklands*. Chicago: University of Chicago Press.

Chang, Jiat-hwee. 2011. "Building a Colonial Technoscientific Network: Tropical Architecture, Building Science and the Politics of Decolonization." In *Third World Modernism: Architecture, Development and Identity*, edited by Duanfang Lu, 211–35. New York: Routledge.

Chatterjee, Partha. 2004. *The Politics of the Governed: Reflections on Popular Politics in Most of the World*. New York: Columbia University Press.

Chazan, Naomi. 1983. *An Anatomy of Ghanaian Politics: Managing Political Recession, 1969–1982*. Boulder, CO: Westview.

"Cleaner Toilets to Save Slums from Cholera." 2012. *New Humanitarian*, August 16, 2012. https://www.thenewhumanitarian.org/news/2012/08/16/cleaner-toilets-save-slums-cholera.

Comaroff, Jean. 2007. "Beyond Bare Life: AIDS, (Bio)Politics, and the Neoliberal Order." *Public Culture* 19 (1): 197–219. DOI:10.1215/08992363-2006-030.

Comaroff, Jean, and John L. Comaroff. 2012. *Theory from the South: or, How Euro-America Is Evolving toward Africa*. New York: Routledge.

Cooper, Frederick, and Randall M. Packard. 1998. *International Development and the Social Sciences: Essays on the History and Politics of Knowledge*. Berkeley: University of California Press.

Corburn, Jason. 2009. *Toward the Healthy City: People, Places, and the Politics of Urban Planning*. Urban and Industrial Environments. Cambridge, MA: MIT Press.

Costello, S. P., W. Soo, R. V. Bryant, V. Jairath, A. L. Hart, and J. M. Andrews. 2017. "Systematic Review with Meta-analysis: Faecal Microbiota Transplantation for the Induction of Remission for Active Ulcerative Colitis." *Alimentary Pharmacology and Therapeutics* 46 (3): 213–24.

Crinson, Mark. 2003. *Modern Architecture and the End of Empire*. Burlington, VT: Ashgate.

Crook, Richard, and Jonas Ayee. 2006. "Urban Service Partnerships, 'Street-Level Bureaucrats' and Environmental Sanitation in Kumasi and Accra, Ghana: Coping with Organisational Change in the Public Bureaucracy." *Development Policy Review* 24:51–73.

Cudjoe, Samuel Nii, Emma Sepah, and John K. Anarfi. 2013. *Population and Housing Census—Regional Analytical Report: Greater Accra Region*. Accra: Ghana Statistical Service.

Curtin, Philip D. 1985. "Medical Knowledge and Urban Planning in Tropical Africa." *American Historical Review* 90 (3): 594–613.

Daechsel, Markus. 2013. "Misplaced Ekistics: Islamabad and the Politics of Urban Development in Pakistan." *South Asian History and Culture* 4 (1): 87–106.

Daechsel, Markus. 2015. *Islamabad and the Politics of International Development in Pakistan*. Cambridge: Cambridge University Press.

Dahl, Robert Alan. 1989. *Democracy and Its Critics*. New Haven, CT: Yale University Press.

Daily Graphic. 2012. "Tema Sewage Treatment Plant Left to Rot: Broke Down 12 Years Ago." *GhanaWeb*, November 14, 2012. Accessed May 5, 2016. http://www .ghanaweb.com/GhanaHomePage/NewsArchive/artikel.php?ID=256310.

D'Auria, Viviana. 2010. "From Tropical Transitions to Ekistic Experimentation: Doxiadis Associates in Tema, Ghana." *Positions: On Modern Architecture and Urbanism/Histories and Theories* 1:40–63.

D'Auria, Viviana. 2014. "In the Laboratory and in the Field: Hybrid Housing Design for the African City in Late-Colonial and Decolonising Ghana (1945–57)." *Journal of Architecture* 19 (3): 329–56.

D'Auria, Viviana. 2015. "From 'Live Projects' to 'Lived-In' Environments: Learning from Six Decades of Re-design in Tema Manhean, Ghana." *Charrette* 2 (1): 106–18.

D'Auria, Viviana. 2019. "Re-centering Tema: From Isotropic Commercial Centres to an Intense Infrastructure of Street-Vending." In *Acculturating the Shopping Centre*, edited by Janina Gosseye and Tom Avermaete, 127–46. New York: Routledge.

D'Auria, Viviana, and Victor Kootin Sanwu. 2010. "Between Development and Experiment: The Volta River Project's (Un)Settling Communities." Paper presented at Urban Knowledge: Its Production, Use and Dissemination in Cities of the South, Brussels, October 28–30, 2010.

David, Kyle. 2010. "Tema Waste Water Treatment." *UEnergy*, November 30, 2010. https://uenergy.wordpress.com/2010/11/30/tema-waste-water.

Davidson, Basil. 1989. *Black Star: A View of the Life and Times of Kwame Nkrumah*. Boulder, CO: Westview.

Davidson, R. B. 1954. "The Volta River Aluminium Scheme." *Political Quarterly* 25 (1): 55–67.

Debarbieux, Bernard. 2016. "Hannah Arendt's Spatial Thinking: An Introduction." *Territory, Politics, Governance* 5 (4): 351–67. DOI:10.1080/21622671.2016.123 4407.

De Boeck, Filip. 2012. "Inhabiting Ocular Ground: Kinshasa's Future in the Light of Congo's Spectral Urban Politics." *Cultural Anthropology* 26 (2): 263–86.

Debrah, Emmanuel. 2009. "Assessing the Quality of Accountability in Ghana's District Assemblies, 1993–2008." *African Journal of Political Science and International Relations* 3 (6): 278–87.

De Dominicis, Filippo. 2019. "To Survey, Control, and Design: Doxiadis and Fathy on Africa's Future and Identity (1959–1963)." In *Routledge Handbook of Urban Planning in Africa*, edited by Carlos Nunes Silva, 139–208. New York: Routledge.

Degani, Michael. 2018. "Shock Humor: Zaniness and the Freedom of Permanent Improvisation in Urban Tanzania." *Cultural Anthropology* 33 (3): 473–98. DOI: 10.14506/ca33.3.08.

de Genova, Nicholas. 2010. *The Deportation Regime: Sovereignty, Space, and the Freedom of Movement*. Durham, NC: Duke University Press.

Deleuze, Gilles, and Félix Guattari. 1987. *A Thousand Plateaus: Capitalism and Schizophrenia*. Minneapolis: University of Minnesota Press.

Dietz, Mary D. 1995. "Feminist Receptions of Hannah Arendt." *Feminist Interpretations of Hannah Arendt*, edited by Bonnie Honig, 17–50. University Park: Penn State University Press.

Douglas, Mary. 1966. *Purity and Danger: An Analysis of Concepts of Pollution and Taboo*. London: Routledge and Kegan Paul.

Doxiadis, Constantinos A. 1960. *Dynapolis, the City of the Future: Lecture at the Oslo Arkitektforening, Oslo, March 3rd, 1960*. Athens, Greece: Doxiadis Associates.

Doxiadis, Constantinos A. 1968. *Ekistics: An Introduction to the Science of Human Settlements*. New York: Oxford University Press.

Doxiadis, Constantinos A. 1971. "Three New Cities in Africa." *DA Review* 7 (78): 3–13.

Doxiadis, Constantinos A. 1972. *Architectural Space in Ancient Greece*. Edited by Jacqueline Tyrwhitt. Translated by Jacqueline Tyrwhitt. Cambridge, MA: MIT Press.

Doxiadis, Constantinos A. 1974. *Anthropopolis: City for Human Development*. New York: Norton.

Doxiadis, Constantinos Apostolou, and J. G. Papaioannou. 1974. *Ecumenopolis: The Inevitable City of the Future*. New York: Norton.

Drew, Jane B. 1946. "Colonial Planning and Housing." *Arena: Architecture Association Journal* (November): 53–61.

Drew, Jane B. 1955. "West Africa." *Architectural Design* 25:137–39.

Drew, Jane B., and E. Maxwell Fry. 1947. *Village Housing in the Tropics: With Special Reference to West Africa*. London: Lund Humphries.

Dumett, Raymond E. 1968. "The Campaign against Malaria." *African Historical Studies* 1 (2): 153–97.

Dumett, Raymond E. 1993. "Disease and Mortality among Gold Miners of Ghana: Colonial Government and Mining Company Attitudes and Policies, 1900–1938." *Social Science and Medicine* 37 (2): 213–32.

Dundes, Alan. 1966. "Here I Sit: A Study of American Latrinalia." *Kroeber Anthropological Society Papers* 34:91–105.

Elias, Norbert. 1994. *The Civilizing Process: The History of Manners and State Formation and Civilization.* Translated by Edmund Jephcott. Cambridge, MA: Blackwell.

Elyachar, Julia. 2010. "Phatic Labor, Infrastructure, and the Question of Empowerment in Cairo." *American Ethnologist* 37 (3): 452–64.

Esty, Joshua D. 1999. "Excremental Postcolonialism." *Contemporary Literature* 40 (1): 22–59.

Ettinger, Elzbieta. 1995. *Hannah Arendt / Martin Heidegger.* New Haven, CT: Yale University Press.

Feldman, Allen. 1991. *Formations of Violence: The Narrative of the Body and Political Terror in Northern Ireland.* Chicago: University of Chicago Press.

Feldman, Gregory. 2013. "The Specific Intellectual's Pivotal Position: Action, Compassion, and Thinking in Administrative Society, an Arendtian View." *Social Anthropology* 21 (2): 135–64.

Feldman, Gregory. 2015. *We Are All Migrants: Political Action and the Ubiquitous Condition of Migrant-hood.* Stanford, CA: Stanford University Press.

Field, Margaret Joyce. 1937. *Religion and Medicine of the Gā People.* Oxford: Oxford University Press.

Field, Margaret Joyce. 1940. *The Social Organisation of the Ga People.* London: Crown Agents for the Colonies.

Fitch, Robert, and Mary Oppenheimer. 1966. *Ghana: End of an Illusion.* New York: Monthly Review Press.

Flowers, Catherine Coleman. 2020. *Waste: One Woman's Fight against America's Dirty Secret.* New York: New Press.

Fortun, Kim. 2014. "From Latour to Late Industrialism." *Journal of Ethnographic Theory* 4 (1): 309–29. DOI:10.14318/hau4.1.017.

Foucault, Michel. 1979. *Discipline and Punish: The Birth of the Prison.* New York: Vintage.

Fredericks, Rosalind. 2018. *Garbage Citizenship: Vibrant Infrastructures of Labor in Dakar, Senegal.* Durham, NC: Duke University Press.

Frekko, Susan. 2009. "Signs of Respect: Neighborhood, Public, and Language in Barcelona." *Journal of Linguistic Anthropology* 19 (2): 227–45.

Freud, Sigmund. (1905) 1947. "Three Essays on the Theory of Sexuality." In *The Standard Edition of the Complete Psychological Works of Sigmund Freud*, vol. 7, edited by James Strachey and Anna Freud, 123–246. London: Hogarth.

Freund, Bill. 2007. *The African City: A History.* Cambridge: Cambridge University Press.

Fry, E. Maxwell, and Jane B. Drew. 1956. *Tropical Architecture in the Humid Zone.* New York: Reinhold.

Fry, E. Maxwell, and Jane B. Drew. 1964. *Tropical Architecture in the Dry and Humid Zones.* New York: Reinhold.

Fynn, Shaun. 2017. *Chandigarh Revealed: Le Corbusier's City Today.* Princeton, NJ: Princeton Architectural Press.

Gadugah, Nathan. 2009. "Time Bomb in Ashaiman: NDC Taskforce Threaten Reprisal Attacks." MyJoyOnline.com, April 28, 2009. https://www.myjoyonline.com/time-bomb-in-ashaiman-ndc-task-force-threaten-reprisal-attacks/.

Galantay, Ervin Y. 1975. *New Towns: Antiquity to the Present*. New York: Braziller.

Gale, Thomas S. 1995. "The Struggle against Disease in the Gold Coast: Early Attempts at Urban Sanitary Reform." *Transactions of the Historical Society of Ghana* 16 (2): 185–203.

Gandy, Matthew. 2006. "Planning, Anti-planning and the Infrastructure Crisis Facing Metropolitan Lagos." *Urban Studies* 43 (2): 371–96.

Geertz, Clifford. 1972. "Deep Play: Notes on the Balinese Cockfight." *Daedalus* 101 (1): 1–37.

Geertz, Clifford. 1980. *The Theatre State in 19th-Century Bali*. Princeton, NJ: Princeton University Press.

Getachew, Adom. 2019. *Worldmaking after Empire: The Rise and Fall of Self-Determination*. Princeton, NJ: Princeton University Press.

Ghana News Agency. 2015. "Tema Community One Market Flooded with Human Excreta." September 15, 2015. Accessed June 22, 2020. https://www.ghananewsagency.org/social/tema-community-one-market-flooded-with-human-excreta-94443.

Ghana Statistical Service. 2014. *2010 Population and Housing Census. District Analytical Report. Ashaiman Municipality*. October. https://www2.statsghana.gov.gh/docfiles/2010_District_Report/Greater%20Accra/ASHAIMAN%20MUNICIPAL.pdf.

Giddens, Anthony. 1984. *The Constitution of Society: Outline of the Structuration Theory*. Cambridge, UK: Polity.

Gines, Kathryn T. 2014. *Hannah Arendt and the Negro Question*. Bloomington: Indiana University Press.

Glover, Benjamin Xornam. 2014. "Burst Sewage Pipe Spills Waste." *Graphic Online*, May 30, 2014. https://www.graphic.com.gh/news/general-news/burst-sewage-pipe-spills-waste.html.

Gold Coast Ordinance No. 38. 1952. "The Tema Town and Port (Acquisition of Land) Ordinance." Accra, Ghana: Gold Coast Government Printers.

Gordillo, Gastón R. 2014. *Rubble: The Afterlife of Destruction*. Durham, NC: Duke University Press.

Government of Ghana. 1999. *National Environmental Sanitation Policy*. Accra, Ghana: Ministry of Local Government and Rural Development.

Graham, Stephen, and Simon Marvin. 2001. *Splintering Urbanism: Networked Infrastructures, Technological Mobilities, and the Urban Condition*. London: Routledge.

Guardian: International Business Magazine. 2003. Tema: City @ the Centre of the World. Accra. January. Tema Development Corporation.

Gupta, Akhil. 2018. "The Future in Ruins: Thoughts on the Temporality of Infrastructure." In *The Promise of Infrastructure*, edited by Nikhil Anand, Akhil Gupta, and Hannah Appel, 63–79. Durham, NC: Duke University Press.

Gyimah-Boadi, Emmanuel. 2007. "Politics in Ghana since 1957: The Quest for Freedom, National Unity, and Prosperity." *Ghana Studies* 10:107–43. DOI:10.1353/ghs.2007.0004.

Habermas, Jürgen. 1974. "The Public Sphere: An Encyclopedia Article (1964)." *New German Critique* 3:49–55.

Habermas, Jürgen. 1991. *The Structural Transformation of the Public Sphere: An Inquiry into a Category of Bourgeois Society.* Cambridge, MA: MIT Press.

Halliday, Stephen. 1999. *The Great Stink of London: Sir Joseph Bazalgette and the Cleansing of the Victorian Metropolis.* Stroud, UK: Sutton.

Hansen, Thomas Blom. 1999. *The Saffron Wave: Democracy and Hindu Nationalism in Modern India.* Princeton, NJ: Princeton University Press.

Haraway, Donna J. 2004. *Crystals, Fabrics, and Fields: Metaphors That Shape Embryos.* Berkeley, CA: North Atlantic.

Haraway, Donna J. 2016. *Staying with the Trouble: Making Kin in the Cthulucene.* Durham, NC: Duke University Press.

Hardin, Garrett. 1968. "The Tragedy of the Commons." *Science* 162 (3859): 1243–48.

Hardt, Michael, and Antonio Negri. 2009. *Commonwealth.* Cambridge, MA: Harvard University Press.

Hargreaves, John D. 2014. *Decolonization in Africa.* 2nd ed. New York: Routledge.

Harman, Graham. 2014. *Bruno Latour: Reassembling the Political.* London: Pluto.

Harper, Annie. 2012. "Islamabad and the Promise of Pakistan." In *Pakistan: From the Rhetoric of Democracy to the Rise of Militancy*, edited by Ravi Kalia, 74–94. New Delhi: Routledge India.

Harris, Richard, and Susan Parnell. 2012. "The Turning Point in Urban Policy for British Colonial Africa, 1939–1945." In *Colonial Architecture and Urbanism in Africa: Intertwined and Contested Histories*, edited by Fassil Demissie, 127–51. Burlington, VT: Ashgate.

Hart, David. 1980. *The Volta River Project: A Case Study in Politics and Technology.* Edinburgh: Edinburgh University Press.

Hart, Keith. 1973. "Informal Income Opportunities and Urban Employment in Ghana." *Journal of Modern African Studies* 11 (1): 61–89.

Harvey, David. 2003. *Paris: Capital of Modernity.* New York: Routledge.

Harvey, David. 2005. *A Brief History of Neoliberalism.* Oxford: Oxford University Press.

Harvey, David. 2008. "The Right to the City." *New Left Review* 53:23–40.

Hegarty, Paul. 2003. "Undelivered: The Space/Time of the Sacred in Bataille and Benjamin." *Economy and Society* 32 (1): 101–18.

Heidegger, Martin. 1971. "Building, Dwelling, Thinking." In *Poetry, Language, Thought.* Translated by Albert Hofstadter. Vol. 154. New York: Harper and Row.

Heidegger, Martin. 2008. *Being and Time.* Translated by John Macquarrie and Edward Robinson. Cambridge, MA: Blackwell.

Herzfeld, Michael. 2005. *Cultural Intimacy: Social Poetics in the Nation-State.* New York: Routledge.

Hess, Janet Berry. 2000. "Imagining Architecture: The Structure of Nationalism in Accra, Ghana." *Africa Today* 47 (2): 36–58.

Hetherington, Kregg. 2019. "Introduction: Key Words in the Anthropocene." In *Infrastructure, Environment, and Life in the Anthropocene*, edited by Kregg Hetherington, 1–13. Durham, NC: Duke University Press.

Hilling, David. 1966. "Tema—the Geography of a New Port." *Geography* 51 (2): 111–25.

Hobbes, Thomas. (1651) 1994. *Leviathan, or The Matter, Forme and Power of a Commonwealth Ecclesiasticall and Civil.* London: Everyman.

Hobbes, Thomas. (1655) 1981. "De Corpore." In *Part I of De Corpore.* Translated by Aloyiusus Martinich. New York: Abaris.

Hoffman, Danny. 2017. *Monrovia Modern: Urban Form and Political Imagination.* Durham, NC: Duke University Press.

Holder, Julian. 2009. "The Nation-State or the United States? The Irresistible Kitchen of the British Ministry of Works." In *Cold War Kitchen: Americanization, Technology, and European Users*, edited by Ruth Oldenziel and Karin Zachmann, 235–58. Cambridge, MA: MIT Press.

Holston, James. 1989. *The Modernist City: An Anthropological Critique of Brasília.* Chicago: University of Chicago Press.

Honig, Bonnie. 1991. "Declarations of Independence: Arendt and Derrida on the Problem of Founding a Republic." *American Political Science Review* 85 (1): 97–113. DOI:10.2307/1962880.

Honig, Bonnie. 1995. Introduction to *Feminist Interpretations of Hannah Arendt.* University Park: Penn State University Press.

Honig, Bonnie. 2017. *Public Things: Democracy in Despair.* New York: Fordham University Press.

Hull, Matthew S. 2012. *Government of Paper: The Materiality of Bureaucracy in Urban Pakistan.* Berkeley: University of California Press.

Jackson, Iain, and Jessica Holland. 2014. *The Architecture of Edwin Maxwell Fry and Jane Drew: Twentieth-Century Architecture, Pioneer Modernism, and the Tropics.* Burlington, VT: Ashgate.

Jackson, Iain, and Rexford Assasie Oppong. 2014. "The Planning of Late Colonial Village Housing in the Tropics: Tema Manhean, Ghana." *Planning Perspectives* 29 (4): 475–99.

Jackson, Shannon, and Steven Robins. 2018. "Making Sense of the Politics of Sanitation in Cape Town." *Social Dynamics* 44 (1): 69–87. DOI:10.1080/02533952.2018.1437879.

Jackson, Steven J. 2014. "Rethinking Repair." In *Media Technologies: Essays on Communication, Materiality, and Society*, edited by Tarleton Gillespie, Pablo J. Bodzkowski, and Kirsten A. Foot, 221–39. Cambridge, MA: MIT Press.

Jensen, Casper Bruun. 2019. "Here Comes the Sun? Experimenting with Cambodian Energy Infrastructures." In *Infrastructure, Environment, and Life in the Anthropocene*, edited by Kregg Hetherington, 216–35. Durham, NC: Duke University Press.

Jensen, Casper Bruun, and Atsuro Morita. 2017. "Introduction: Infrastructures as Ontological Experiments." *Ethnos* 82 (4): 615–26.

Jobson, Ryan Cecil. 2020. "The Case for Letting Anthropology Burn: Sociocultural Anthropology in 2019." *American Anthropologist* 122 (2): 259–71.

Jopp, Keith. 1961. *Ghana's New Town and Harbour, Tema*. Accra, Ghana: Ministry of Information.

Joshi, D., B. Fawcett, and F. Mannan. 2011. "Health, Hygiene and Appropriate Sanitation: Experiences and Perceptions of the Urban Poor." *Environment and Urbanization* 23 (1): 91–111. DOI:10.1177/0956247811398602.

Karim, Farhan. 2016. "Between Self and Citizenship: Doxiadis Associates in Postcolonial Pakistan, 1958–1968." *International Journal of Islamic Architecture* 5 (1): 135–61.

Katz, Cindi. 2001. "Vagabond Capitalism and the Necessity of Social Reproduction." *Antipode* 33 (4): 709–28. DOI:10.1111/1467-8330.00207.

Kelly, John D., and Martha Kaplan. 2001. *Represented Communities: Fiji and World Decolonization*. Chicago: University of Chicago Press.

Killingray, David. 1986. "The Maintenance of Law and Order in British Colonial Africa." *African Affairs* 85 (340): 411–37.

Kilson, Marion. 1974. *African Urban Kinsmen*. London: Hurst.

King, Richard H., and Dan Stone. 2007. Introduction to *Hannah Arendt and the Uses of History: Imperialism, Nation, Race, and Genocide*, edited by Richard H. King and Dan Stone, 1–17. New York: Berghahn.

Kirchherr, E. C. 1968. "Tema 1951–1962: The Evolution of a Planned City in West Africa." *Urban Studies* 5 (2): 207–17.

Kirksey, S. Eben, and Stefan Helmreich. 2010. "The Emergence of Multispecies Ethnography." *Cultural Anthropology* 25 (4): 545–76. DOI:10.1111/j.1548-1360.2010.01069.x.

Kissieh, E. 2007. *Operationalizing the Subsidiary Principle in Ghana's Local Government for the Urban Poor: The Case of the Tema Municipality*. Accra, Ghana: Charles Kettering Foundation.

Kleist, Nauja. 2011. "Modern Chiefs: Tradition, Development and Return among Traditional Authorities in Ghana." *African Affairs* 110:629–47.

Kohler, Robert E. 2002. *Landscapes and Labscapes: Exploring the Lab-Field Border in Biology*. Chicago: University of Chicago Press.

Konadu-Agyemang, Kwadwo. 2000. "The Best of Times and the Worst of Times: Structural Adjustment Programs and Uneven Development in Africa: The Case of Ghana." *Professional Geographer* 52 (3): 469–83.

Kopytoff, Igor. 1987. *The African Frontier: The Reproduction of Traditional African Societies*. Bloomington: Indiana University Press.

Krimstein, Ken. 2018. *The Three Escapes of Hannah Arendt*. New York: Bloomsbury.

Kultermann, Udo. 1963. *New Architecture in Africa*. New York: Universe Books.

Kwei Armah, Ayi. 1969. *The Beautyful Ones Are Not Yet Born*. African Writers Series. Oxford: Heinemann.

Laporte, Dominique. 2002. *History of Shit*. Cambridge, MA: MIT Press.

Larkin, Brian. 2008. *Signal and Noise: Media, Infrastructure, and Urban Culture in Nigeria*. Durham, NC: Duke University Press.

Larkin, Brian. 2013. "The Politics and Poetics of Infrastructure." *Annual Review of Anthropology* 42:327–43.

Lartey, Nii Larte. 2020. "We Need $60 Million to Fix Poor Sewage System in Tema —TMA." CNR *Citi Newsroom*, August 12, 2020. https://citinewsroom.com/2020/08/we-need-60-million-to-fix-poor-sewage-system-in-tema-tma/.

Latour, Bruno. 1990. "Technology Is Society Made Durable." *Sociological Review* 38 (1 suppl.): 103–31.

Latour, Bruno. 1993. *We Have Never Been Modern*. Cambridge, MA: Harvard University Press.

Latour, Bruno. 2005a. "From Realpolitik to Dingpolitik or How to Make Things Public." In *Making Things Public: Atmospheres of Democracy*, edited by Bruno Latour and Peter Weibel, 14–41. Cambridge, MA: MIT Press.

Latour, Bruno. 2005b. *Reassembling the Social: An Introduction to Actor-Network-Theory*. New York: Oxford University Press.

Latour, Bruno. 2018. *Down to Earth: Politics in the New Climatic Regime*. Translated by Catherine Porter. Medford, MA: Polity.

Lee, Christopher J. 2008. "'Causes' versus 'Conditions': Imperial Sovereignty, Postcolonial Violence and the Recent Re-emergence of Arendtian Political Thought in African Studies." *South African Historical Journal* 60 (1): 124–46. DOI:10.1080/02582470802287752.

Lefebvre, Henri. 1991. *The Production of Space*. Translated by Donald Nicholson-Smith. Cambridge, MA: Blackwell.

Lefebvre, Henri. 1996. "The Right to the City." In *Writings on Cities*, edited by Eleonore Kofman and Elizabeth Lebas, 147–59. Cambridge, MA: Wiley-Blackwell.

Leijenhorst, Cornelis Hendrik. 2002. *The Mechanisation of Aristotelianism: The Late Aristotelian Setting of Thomas Hobbes's Natural Philosophy*. Leiden: Brill.

Levey, Zach. 2003. "The Rise and Decline of a Special Relationship: Israel and Ghana, 1957–1966." *African Studies Review* 4 (1): 155–77.

Liscombe, Rhodri. 2006. "Modernism in Late Imperial British West Africa: The Work of Maxwell Fry and Jane Drew, 1946–56." *Journal of the Society of Architectural Historians* 65 (2): 188–215. DOI:10.2307/25068264.

Loidolt, Sophie. 2018. *Phenomenology of Plurality: Hannah Arendt on Political Intersubjectivity*. New York: Routledge.

Lyon, Travis. 2016. "Ghana Says 'Let's Talk Shit' Because They're Fed Up with Open Defecation." *Global Citizen*, August 29, 2016. https://www.globalcitizen.org/es/content/ghana-says-lets-talk-shit-because-theyre-fed-up-wi/?template=next.

Mains, Daniel. 2019. *Under Construction: Technologies of Development in Urban Ethiopia*. Durham, NC: Duke University Press.

Malcolm, Noel. 2002. *Aspects of Hobbes*. New York: Oxford University Press.

Mamdani, Mahmood. 1996. *Citizen and Subject: Contemporary Africa and the Legacy of Late Colonialism*. London: James Currey.

Marcus, George E., and Michael F. Fischer. 1986. *Anthropology as Cultural Critique: An Experimental Moment in the Human Sciences.* Chicago: University of Chicago Press.

Markell, Patchen. 2011. "Arendt's Work: On the Architecture of 'The Human Condition.'" *College Literature* 38 (1): 15–44.

Martinich, A. P. 2002. *The Two Gods of Leviathan: Thomas Hobbes on Religion and Politics.* New York: Cambridge University Press.

Martinich, A. P. 2005. *Hobbes.* New York: Routledge.

Marx, Karl. 1968. *Capital.* 2 vols. Boston, MA: Dutton.

Masquelier, Adeline. 2019. *Fada: Boredom and Belonging in Niger.* Chicago: University of Chicago Press.

Mazeau, Adrien. 2013. "No Toilet at Home: Implementation, Usage and Acceptability of Shared Toilets in Urban Ghana." PhD diss., Loughborough University.

Mazeau, Adrien, Rebecca Scott, and Benedict Tuffuor. 2012. "Sanitation—a Neglected Essential Service in the Unregulated Urban Expansion of Ashaiman, Ghana." Paper presented at Sustainable Futures: Architecture and Urbanism in the Global South conference, Kampala, Uganda, June 27–30, 2012.

Mbembe, Achille. 2001. *On the Postcolony.* Studies on the History of Society and Culture. Vol. 41. Berkeley: University of California Press.

Mbembe, Achille. 2003. "Necropolitics." Translated by Libby Meintjes. *Public Culture* 15 (1): 11–40.

McFarlane, Colin. 2008a. "Governing the Contaminated City: Infrastructure and Sanitation in Colonial and Post-colonial Bombay." *International Journal of Urban and Regional Research* 32 (2): 415–35. DOI:10.1111/j.1468-2427.2008.00793.x.

McFarlane, Colin. 2008b. "Sanitation in Mumbai's Informal Settlements: State, 'Slum,' and Infrastructure." *Environment and Planning A* 40 (1): 88–107. DOI:10.1068/a39221.

McFarlane, Colin, and Jonathan Rutherford. 2008. "Political Infrastructures: Governing and Experiencing the Fabric of the City." *International Journal of Urban and Regional Research* 32 (2): 363–74. DOI:10.1111/j.1468-2427.2008.00792.x.

Melosi, Martin V. 2008. *The Sanitary City: Environmental Services in Urban America from Colonial Times to the Present.* Pittsburgh, PA: University of Pittsburgh Press.

Menoret, Pascal. 2014. *Joyriding in Riyadh: Oil, Urbanism, and Road Revolt.* New York: Cambridge University Press.

Miescher, Stephan F. 2012. "Building the City of the Future: Visions and Experiences of Modernity in Ghana's Akosombo Township." *Journal of African History* 53 (3): 367–90.

Miescher, Stephan F. 2014. "'Nkrumah's Baby': The Akosombo Dam and the Dream of Development in Ghana." *Water History* 6 (4): 341–66.

Millar, Kathleen M. 2018. *Reclaiming the Discarded: Life and Labor on Rio's Garbage Dump.* Durham, NC: Duke University Press.

Minogue, Kenneth. 1994. Introduction to *Leviathan*, by Thomas Hobbes, edited by Kenneth Minogue, xiii–xxxiv. London: Everyman.

Mitchell, Timothy. 2002. *Rule of Experts: Egypt, Techno-politics, Modernity*. Berkeley: University of California Press.

Mokhtar, Ahmed. 2003. "Challenges of Designing Ablution Spaces in Mosques." *Journal of Architectural Engineering* 9 (2): 55–61.

Molotch, Harvey, and Laura Norén. 2010. *Toilet: Public Restrooms and the Politics of Sharing*. NYU Series in Social and Cultural Analysis. New York: NYU Press.

Moore, Amelia. 2015. "The Anthropocene: A Critical Exploration." *Environment and Society* 6 (1): 1–3. DOI:10.3167/ares.2015.060101.

Morgan, Margaret. 2002. "The Plumbing of Modern Life." *Postcolonial Studies* 5 (2): 171–95. DOI:10.1080/1368879022000021083.

Moxon, James. 1969. *Volta: Man's Largest Lake*. London: Andre Deutsch.

Mukhopadhyay, Bhaskar. 2006. "Crossing the Howrah Bridge." *Theory, Culture, and Society* 23 (7–8): 221–41. DOI:10.1177/0263276406073224.

Mumford, Eric, and Kenneth Frampton. 2002. *The CIAM Discourse on Urbanism, 1928–1960*. Cambridge, MA: MIT Press.

Mumford, Lewis. 1938. *The Culture of Cities*. New York: Harcourt, Brace.

Mumford, Lewis. 1961. *The City in History: Its Origins, Its Transformations, and Its Prospects*. New York: Harcourt.

Murdoch, Jonathan. 1997. "Towards a Geography of Heterogeneous Associations." *Progress in Human Geography* 21 (3): 321–37.

Myjoyonline.com. 2014. "Tema Residents Fear Health Crisis as Sewage System Deteriorates." *Modern Ghana*, May 20, 2014. https://www.modernghana.com/news/542474/tema-residents-fear-health-crisis-as-sewage-system.html.

Nathan, Noah L. 2019. *Electoral Politics and Africa's Urban Transition: Class and Ethnicity in Ghana*. Cambridge: Cambridge University Press.

New Humanitarian. 2012. "Cleaner Toilets to Save Slums from Cholera." August 16, 2012. http://www.irinnews.org/report/96112/west-africa-cleaner-toilets-to-save-slums-from-cholera.

Njoh, Ambe. 2007. *Planning Power: Town Planning and Social Control in Colonial Africa*. London: University College London Press.

Nkrumah, Kwame. 1957. *Ghana: The Autobiography of Kwame Nkrumah*. New York: Nelson.

Nkrumah, Kwame. 1958. "African Prospect." *Foreign Affairs* 37 (1): 45–53.

Nkrumah, Kwame. 1962a. *Address to the Nationalists' Conference, Accra, Ghana, June 4, 1962*. Accra, Ghana: Bureau of African Affairs.

Nkrumah, Kwame. 1962b. *Gateway to Ghana; Speech by Osagyefo the President, on the Occasion of the Official Opening of the Tema Harbour on Saturday, 10th February, 1962*. Accra, Ghana: Ministry of Information and Broadcasting.

Nkrumah, Kwame. 1997a. "Formal Opening of the Oil Refinery, Tema, September 28, 1963." In *Selected Speeches of Kwame Nkrumah*, edited by Samuel Obeng, vol. 5, 107–10. Accra, Ghana: Afram.

Nkrumah, Kwame. 1997b. "Laying of the Foundation Stone at the Pre-fabricated Concrete Panel Factory, October 16, 1963." In *Selected Speeches of Kwame Nkrumah*, edited by Samuel Obeng, vol. 5, 175–77. Accra, Ghana: Afram.

Nkrumah, Kwame. 1997c. "Opening of the Unilever Soap Factory, Tema, August 24, 1963." In *Selected Speeches of Kwame Nkrumah*, edited by Samuel Obeng, vol. 5, 79–86. Accra, Ghana: Afram.

Norris, Trevor. 2002. "Hannah Arendt: Re-thinking the Social." Master's thesis, School of Graduate Studies, McMaster University.

Norton, Anne. 1995. "Heart of Darkness: Africa and African Americans in the Writings of Hannah Arendt." In *Feminist Interpretations of Hannah Arendt*, edited by Bonnie Honig, 247–62. University Park: Penn State University Press.

Nugent, Paul. 1991. "Educating Rawlings: The Evolution of Government Strategy." In *Ghana: The Political Economy of Recovery*, edited by Donald Rothschild, 49–68. Boulder, CO: Lynne Rienner.

Nugent, Paul. 1995. *Big Men, Small Boys, and Politics in Ghana: Power, Ideology, and the Burden of History, 1982–1994*. New York: Pinter.

Nwaubani, Ebere. 2001. *The United States and Decolonization in West Africa, 1950–1960*. Rochester, NY: University of Rochester Press.

Nyerges, A. Endre. 1992. "The Ecology of Wealth-in-People: Agriculture, Settlement, and Society on the Perpetual Frontier." *American Anthropologist* 94:860–81.

Odotei, Irene. 2002. *The Artisanal Marine Fishing Industry: A Historical Review*. Legon: Institute of African Studies, University of Ghana.

Ofei-Nkansah, Marina. 2003. "Factors Affecting the Knowledge and Use of Contraceptives among Adolescents: A Case Study of Tema." Bachelor's thesis, University of Ghana.

Oko Adjetey, Emmanuel. 1964. "Tema Manhean." Paper submitted to Faculty of Architecture, Kwame Nkrumah University for Science and Technology, Ghana.

O'Rourke, David K. 2013. *Oikos—Domos—Household: The Many Lives of a Common Word*. Vienna, Austria: Peter Lang.

Osinde, Rose N. 2008. "Framework for Promoting Pro-poor Water and Sanitation Governance in Urban Programmes and Projects." Nairobi: UN-Habitat, United Nations Centre for Human Settlements.

Ostrom, Vincent, and Elinor Ostrom. 1978. "Public Goods and Public Choices." In *Alternatives for Delivering Public Services: Toward Improved Performance*, edited by E. S. Savas, 7–49. Boulder, CO: Westview.

Oteng-Ababio, Martin. 2011. "Missing Links in Solid Waste Management in the Greater Accra Metropolitan Area in Ghana." *GeoJournal* 76 (5): 551–60.

Overa, Radnhild. 1993. "Wives and Traders: Women's Careers in Ghanaian Canoe Fisheries." *Maritime Anthropological Studies* 6:110–35.

Owusu, George. 2015. "Decentralized Development Planning and Fragmentation of Metropolitan Regions: The Case of the Greater Accra Metropolitan Area, Ghana." *Ghana Journal of Geography* 7:1–24.

Oxford Dictionary of English. 2015. "Conviviality." In *Oxford Dictionary of English*, 3rd ed., edited by Angus Stevenson. Oxford: Oxford University Press.

Paller, Jeffrey W. 2019. *Democracy in Ghana: Everyday Politics in Urban Africa*. New York: Cambridge University Press.

Parker, John. 2000. *Making the Town: Ga State and Society in Early Colonial Accra*. Portsmouth, NH: Heinemann.

Passerin d'Entreves, Maurizio. 2019. "Hannah Arendt." *Stanford Encylopedia of Philosophy*, January 11, 2019. https://plato.stanford.edu/entries/arendt/.

Pateman, Carole. 1989. "'God Hath Ordained to Man a Helper': Hobbes, Patriarchy and Conjugal Right." *British Journal of Political Science* 19 (4): 445–63.

Patterson, K. D. 1979. "Health in Urban Ghana: The Case of Accra 1900–1940." *Social Science and Medicine. Part B: Medical Anthropology* 13 (4): 251–68.

Pellow, Deborah. 2008. *Landlords and Lodgers: Socio-spatial Organization in an Accra Community*. Chicago: University of Chicago Press.

Pensky, Max. 2011. "Three Kinds of Ruin: Heidegger, Benjamin, Sebald." *Poligrafi* 16 (61/62): 65–89.

Peprah, D., K. K. Baker, C. Moe, K. Robb, H. Yakubu, N. Wellington, and C. Null. 2015. "Public Toilets and Their Customers in Low-Income Accra, Ghana." *Environment and Urbanization* 27 (2): 589–604.

Phillips, John. 2006. "*Agencement*/Assemblage." *Theory, Culture, and Society* 23 (2–3): 108–9.

Phillips, Kristin. 2020. "Prelude to a Grid: Nature, Labor and Cosmology on a Tanzanian Energy Frontier." *Cambridge Journal of Anthropology* 38 (2): 71–87.

Pieri, Caecilia. 2008. "Modernity and Its Posts in Constructing an Arab Capital: Baghdad's Urban Space and Architecture." *Middle East Studies Association Bulletin* 42 (1/2): 32–39.

Pitcher, Anne, Mary Moran, and Michael Johnston. 2009. "Rethinking Patrimonialism and Neopatrimonialism in Africa." *African Studies Review* 52 (1): 125–56.

Pitkin, Hanna Fenichel. 1995. "Conformism, Housekeeping, and the Attack of the Blob: The Origins of Hannah Arendt's Concept of the Social." In *Feminist Interpretations of Hannah Arendt*, edited by Bonnie Honig, 41–82. University Park: Penn State University Press.

Pitkin, Hanna Fenichel. 1998. *The Attack of the Blob: Hannah Arendt's Concept of the Social*. Chicago: University of Chicago Press.

Prakash, Vikramaditya. 2002. *Chandigargh's Le Corbusier: The Struggle for Modernity in Postcolonial India*. Seattle: University of Washington Press.

Preparata, Guido Giacomo. 2007. *The Ideology of Tyranny: Bataille, Foucault, and the Postmodern Corruption of Political Dissent*. New York: Palgrave Macmillan.

Provoost, Michelle. 2006. "New Towns on the Cold War Frontier: How Modern Urban Planning Was Exported as an Instrument in the Battle for the Developing World." *Eurozine*, June 28, 2006. https://www.eurozine.com/new-towns-on-the-cold-war-frontier-4/.

Provoost, Michelle. 2014. "Exporting New Towns: The Welfare City in Africa." In *Architecture and the Welfare State*, edited by Marc Swenarton, Tom Avermaete, and Dirk van den Heuvel, 277–95. London: Routledge.

Provoost, Michelle. 2020. "Tema: The Flagship of Nkrumah's Pan-African Vision." In *New Towns on the Cold War Frontier: Part 2*. In progress. Rotterdam: Crimson

Historians and Urbanists and International New Town Institute. Accessed July 17, 2021. http://www.newtowninstitute.org/spip.php?article1341.

Purcell, Mark. 2002. "Excavating Lefebvre: The Right to the City and Its Urban Politics of the Inhabitant." *GeoJournal* 58 (2/3): 99–108. DOI:10.1023/B:GEJO/.0000010829.62237.8f.

Pyla, Panayiota. 2008. "Back to the Future: Doxiadis's Plans for Baghdad." *Journal of Planning History* 7 (1): 3–19. DOI:10.1177/1538513207304697.

Rabinow, Paul. 1989. *French Modern: Norms and Forms of Social Environment*. Chicago: University of Chicago Press.

Rabinow, Paul, and Nikolas Rose. 2006. "Biopower Today." *BioSocieties* 1 (2): 195–217.

Rathbone, Richard. 2000. *Nkrumah and the Chiefs: The Politics of Chieftaincy in Ghana, 1951–1960*. Oxford: James Currey.

Reno, Joshua. 2016. *Waste Away: Working and Living with a North American Landfill*. Oakland: University of California Press.

Reuters. 1962. "Ghana: President Nkrumah Opens Tema Harbour." February 12, 1962. Accessed March 11, 2021. Reuters.screenocean.com/record/923005.

Rezende, Vera. 2016. "Urban Planning in Guanabara State, Brazil: Doxiadis, from Ekistics to the Delos Meetings." *History, Urbanism, Resilience* 6:251–63.

Robertson, Claire. 1984. *Sharing the Same Bowl: A Socioeconomic History of Women and Class in Accra, Ghana*. Ann Arbor: University of Michigan Press.

Robins, Steven. 2008. *From Revolution to Rights in South Africa: Social Movements, NGOs, and Popular Politics after Apartheid*. Rochester, NY: Boydell and Brewer.

Robins, Steven. 2014. "Poo Wars as Matter Out of Place: 'Toilets for Africa' in Cape Town." *Anthropology Today* 30 (1): 1–4.

Robins, Steven, and Peter Redfield. 2016. "An Index of Waste: Humanitarian Design, 'Dignified Living' and the Politics of Infrastructure in Cape Town." *Anthropology Southern Africa* 39 (2): 145–62.

Robinson, Denis Curtis, and Robert James Anderson. 1961. *Tema, 1951–1961: Report on Ghana's New Town*. Accra, Ghana. Copy held in Liverpool University Library.

Rohilla, Suresh Kumar, Henrietta Osei-Tutu, Bhitush Luthra, Shantanu Kumar Padhi, Amrita Bhatnagar, and Bertha Aboagye Essel. 2018. *SFD Report: Tema Metropolitan, Ghana*. New Delhi, India: Centre for Science and Environment.

Rose, Nikolas. 1996. "The Death of the Social? Re-figuring the Territory of Government." *Economy and Society* 25 (3): 327–56. DOI:10.1080/03085149600000018.

Rose, Nikolas. 1999. *Powers of Freedom: Reframing Political Thought*. New York: Cambridge University Press.

Rosen, George. 1993. *A History of Public Health*. Baltimore, MD: Johns Hopkins University Press.

Rothchild, Donald. 1991. *Ghana: The Political Economy of Recovery*. Boulder, CO: Lynne Rienner.

Salifu, L. Y. 1997. "Sewerage Maintenance Management in Ghana." In *Water and Sanitation for All: Partnerships and Innovations. Proceedings of the 23rd WEDC Conference, Durban, South Africa, 1997*, edited by John Pickford, 84–87. Loughborough, UK: WEDC.

Samnotra, Manu. 2016. "Provincializing Heidegger; Globalizing Arendt." *Contexto Internacional* 38 (3): 909–25. DOI:10.1590/S0102-8529.2016380300009.

Samuelson, Paul. 1954. "The Pure Theory of Public Expenditure." *Review of Economics and Statistics* 36:387–89.

Sassen, Saskia. 1996. *Losing Control? Sovereignty in the Age of Globalization.* New York: Columbia University Press.

Schildkrout, Enid. 1978. *People of the Zongo: The Transformation of Ethnic Identities in Ghana.* Cambridge: Cambridge University Press.

Schildkrout, Enid. 1982. "Dependence and Autonomy: The Economic Activities of Secluded Hausa Women in Kano, Nigeria." In *Women and Work in Africa*, edited by Edna G. Bay, 55–81. Boulder, CO: Westview.

Schinkel, Willem, and Marguerite van den Berg. 2011. "City of Exception: The Dutch Revanchist City and the Urban Homo Sacer." *Antipode* 43 (5): 1911–38. DOI:10.1111/j.1467-8330.2010.00831.x.

Schmitt, Carl. 1985. *Political Theology: Four Chapters on the Concept of Sovereignty.* Cambridge, MA: MIT Press.

Schneider, Daniel. 2011. *Hybrid Nature: Sewage Treatment and the Contradictions of the Industrial Ecosystem.* Cambridge, MA: MIT Press.

Scott, James C. 1998. *Seeing like a State: How Certain Schemes to Improve the Human Condition Have Failed.* New Haven, CT: Yale University Press.

Scott, James C. 2017. *Against the Grain: A Deep History of the Earliest States.* New Haven, CT: Yale University Press.

Shapin, Steven, and Simon Schaffer. 1985. *Leviathan and the Air-Pump: Hobbes, Boyle, and the Experimental Life.* Princeton, NJ: Princeton University Press.

Shaw, Annapurna. 2009. "Town Planning in Postcolonial India, 1947–1965: Chandigarh Re-examined." *Urban Geography* 30 (8): 857–78.

Silver, Jonathan. 2015. "Disrupted Infrastructures: An Urban Political Ecology of Interrupted Electricity in Accra." *International Journal of Urban and Regional Research* 39 (5): 984–1003.

Simone, AbdouMaliq. 2004. "People as Infrastructure: Intersecting Fragments in Johannesburg." *Public Culture* 16 (3): 407–29.

Simone, AbdouMaliq. 2015. "Afterword: Come on Out, You're Surrounded: The Betweens of Infrastructure." *City* 19 (2–3): 375–83.

Simpson, W. J. 1909. *Sanitary Matters in the Various West African Colonies and the Outbreak of Plagues in the Gold Coast.* London: Crown Agents.

Sowards, Adam M. 2018. "Sometimes, It Takes a Table." *Environmental History* 23:143–51.

Stallybrass, Peter, and Allon White. 1986. *The Politics and Poetics of Transgression.* Ithaca, NY: Cornell University Press.

Stamatopoulou-Robbins, Sophia. 2019. *Waste Siege: The Life of Infrastructure in Palestine.* Stanford, CA: Stanford University Press.

Stanek, Lukasz. 2015. "Architects from Socialist Countries in Ghana (1957–67): Modern Architecture and *Mondialisation*." *Journal of the Society for Architectural Historians* 74 (4): 416–42.

Star, Susan Leigh. 1999. "The Ethnography of Infrastructure." *American Behavioral Scientist* 43 (3): 377–91. DOI:10.1177/00027649921955326.

Stoler, Ann Laura. 2013. *Imperial Debris: On Ruins and Ruination*. Durham, NC: Duke University Press.

Stone, Dan. 2011. "Defending the Plural: Hannah Arendt and Genocide Studies." *New Formations* 71:46–57.

Swanson, Heather Anne. 2018. "Domestication Gone Wild: Pacific Salmon and the Disruption of the Domus." In *Domestication Gone Wild: Politics and Practices of Multispecies Relations*, edited by Heather Anne Swanson, Marianna Elisabeth Lien, and Gro B. Ween, 141–58. Durham, NC: Duke University Press.

Swanson, Judith A. 1992. *The Public and the Private in Aristotle's Political Philosophy*. Ithaca, NY: Cornell University Press.

Theocharopoulou, Ioanna. 2009. "Nature and the People: The Vernacular and the Search for a 'True' Greek Architecture." In *Modern Architecture and the Mediterranean: Vernacular Dialogues and Contested Identities*, 111–30. New York: Routledge.

Theroux, Robert J. 1957. "Enlarged Sewage Disposal for Los Angeles." *Sewage and Industrial Wastes Journal* 29 (2): 124–33.

Thrift, Charles. 2007. *Sanitation Policy in Ghana: Key Factors and the Potential for Ecological Sanitation Solutions*. Stockholm: Stockholm Environment Institute.

Tilly, Charles. 1985. "War Making and State Making as Organized Crime." In *Bringing the State Back In*, edited by Peter B. Evans, Dietrich Rueschemeyer, and Theda Skocpol, 169–91. New York: Cambridge University Press.

TMA (Tema Municipal Assembly). n.d. "Toilet Franchise Contract." Tema, Ghana.

Tsao, Roy. 2002. "Arendt against Athens: Rereading *The Human Condition*." *Political Theory* 30 (1): 97–123. DOI:10.1177%2F0090591702030001005.

Uduku, Ola. 2006. "Modernist Architecture and 'the Tropical' in West Africa: The Tropical Architecture Movement in West Africa, 1948–1970." *Habitat International* 30 (3): 396–411. DOI:10.1016/j.habitatint.2004.11.001.

UNDP (United Nations Development Programme). 2015. *The Millennium Development Goals Report 2015: Time for Global Action for the People and Planet*. New York: United Nations.

UNDP (United Nations Development Programme). 2019a. *Human Development Report 2019: Beyond Income, Beyond Averages, Beyond Today: Inequalities in Human Development in the 21st Century*. New York: United Nations. http://hdr.undp.org/en/content/human-development-report-2019.

UNDP (United Nations Development Programme). 2019b. *The Sustainable Development Goals Report 2019*. New York: United Nations.

UNICEF. 2018. "New Loan Scheme to Improve Household Sanitation." December 18, 2018. https://www.unicef.org/ghana/press-releases/new-loan-scheme-improve-household-sanitation.

van der Geest, Sjaak. 1998. "Akan Shit: Getting Rid of Dirt in Ghana." *Anthropology Today* 14 (3): 8–12.

van der Geest, Sjaak. 2002. "The Night-Soil Collector: Bucket Latrines in Ghana." *Postcolonial Studies* 5 (2): 197–206.

van der Geest, Sjaak, and Nelson Obirih-Oparah. 2008. "Liquid Waste Management in Urban and Rural Ghana: Privatisation as Governance?" In *The Governance of Daily Life in Africa*, edited by Giorgio Blundo and Pierre-Yves Le Meur, 205–22. Leiden: Brill Academic.

Veblen, Thorstein. (1899) 1994. *The Theory of the Leisure Class*. New York: Dover.

von Schnitzler, Antina. 2016. *Democracy's Infrastructure: Techno-politics and Protest after Apartheid*. Princeton, NJ: Princeton University Press.

von Schnitzler, Antina. 2018. "Infrastructure, Apartheid Technopolitics, and Temporalities of 'Transition.'" In *The Promise of Infrastructure*, edited by Nikhil Anand, Akhil Gupta, and Hannah Appel, 133–54. Durham, NC: Duke University Press.

Wald, Chelsea. 2021. *Pipe Dreams: The Urgent Global Quest to Transform the Toilet*. New York: Simon and Schuster.

Watertech. 1994. "Report on Tema Sewerage System." World Bank Urban Environmental Sanitation Project. Watertech Ghana Ltd.

Watertech. 1998. "Tema Infrastructure Rehabilitation Project." Watertech Ghana Ltd. Accessed June 16, 2021. https://www.watertechgh.com/projects/water-and -waste.html.

Whitham, David. 1966. "Part III: The New Village as Planned and Built." In *Tema Manhean: A Study of Resettlement*, edited by G. W. Amarteifio, D. A. P. Butcher, and David Whitham, 55–66. Accra: Ghana Universities Press.

Williams, Raymond. 1976. *Keywords: A Vocabulary of Society and Culture*. London: Fontana / Croom Helm.

Williams, Raymond. 1977. *Marxism and Literature*. New York: Oxford University Press.

Williamson, Thora, and Anthony Kirk-Greene. 2001. *Gold Coast Diaries: Chronicles of Political Officers in West Africa, 1900–1919*. London: I. B. Tauris.

Worboys, Michael. 2000. "Colonial Medicine." In *Companion to Medicine in the Twentieth Century*, edited by Roger Cooter and John V. Pickstone, 51–66. New York: Routledge.

World Bank. 2011. "Sanitation, Hygiene and Water Resource Guide." June 20, 2011. http://water.worldbank.org/water/shw-resource-guide.

World Bank. 2015. "World Bank/GPOBA Announce Ghana Output-Based Aid Project; DFID Funds to Support Construction of Sustainable Sanitation Facilities in Low-Income Areas." WorldBank.org, March 31, 2015. http://www.worldbank .org/en/news/press-release/2015/03/31/world-bankgpoba-announce-ghana -output-based-aid-project-dfid-funds-to-support-construction-of-sustainable -sanitation-facilities-in-low-income-areas.

World Bank. 2016. *Project Performance Assessment Report: Second Urban Environmental Sanitation Project and Small Towns Water Supply and Sanitation Project, Second Phase of APL*. Washington, DC: World Bank Publications.

Wright, Gwendolyn. 1991. *The Politics of Design in French Colonial Urbanism*. Chicago: University of Chicago Press.

Wright, Lawrence. 1980. *Clean and Decent: The History of the Bath and Loo and of Sundry Habits, Fashions and Accessories of the Toilet, Principally in Great Britain, France, and America*. London: Routledge and Kegan Paul.

Yar, Majid. 2000. "From Actor to Spectator: Hannah Arendt's 'Two Theories' of Political Judgment." *Philosophy and Social Criticism* 26 (2): 1–27.

Yedu Bannerman, Joseph. 1973. *The Cry for Justice in Tema (Ghana)*. Accra: Ghana Publishing Corporation.

Yurchak, Alexei. 2008. "Necro-Utopia." *Current Anthropology* 49 (2): 199–224. DOI:10.1086/526098.

Zarmakoupi, Mantha. 2015. "Balancing Acts between Ancient and Modern Cities: The Ancient Greek Cities Project of C. A. Doxiadis." *Architectural Histories* 3 (1): 1–22. DOI:10.5334/ah.cv.

Zerilli, Linda. 1995. "The Arendtian Body." In *Feminist Interpretations of Hannah Arendt*, edited by Bonnie Honig, 167–94. University Park: Penn State University Press.

Žižek, Slavoj. 2004. "Knee-Deep." *London Review of Books* 26 (17): 12–13.

Index

Note: Page numbers followed by *f* refer to figures.

Accra, 12–14, 17–18, 88, 199, 220, 261, 297n19; Ashaiman and, 213–14; Doxiadis and, 55; Jamestown, 297n16; master plan for, 301n2; sewage system, 86, 297–98n20

accursed share, 216–17, 262, 265

action, 27–28, 31, 42, 84, 93, 116–17, 208, 216, 263, 265, 271, 276, 282, 287, 312n7; collective, 8, 98, 179, 291; human, 112; political, 9, 29, 83, 218, 237, 277, 280, 300n33; public, 275; public realm of, 246; social, 175. *See also* labor; *vita activa*; work

activism, 7, 19, 54, 273; AIDS, 162; class-based, 73; community, 213; excremental, 8, 288–89; political, 79; public toilet, 179; urban, 287

Actor Network Theory (ANT), 25–27, 32, 269

Agamben, Giorgio, 26, 140, 154–56, 174, 177–78, 180, 284, 309n16; on sovereignty, 307–8n6; on the undecidable, 295n2. *See also* bare life

Alcock, A. E. S., 15*f*, 33–34, 63, 148, 263, 300n39, 301n3

Anand, Nikhil, 47, 87, 126, 129, 305n36, 312n11

animal laborans, 29, 54, 65, 82, 86, 94

Appadurai, Arjun, 162–63, 179, 288

Appel, Hannah, 47, 87, 312n11

architecture, 49, 60, 289; civic, 287; mosque, 312n14; vernacular, 224. *See also* Doxiadis Associates (DA)

Arendt, Hannah, 25–31, 38, 42, 47–48, 53–55, 64–65, 74, 92–94, 113, 170, 246–47, 250, 260, 262–63, 274–77, 281–82, 286, 299–300nn32–33, 301n7, 309n16; anticolonial struggles and, 313n3; on bodily needs, 218; on bodily reproduction, 273; discursive exchange and, 57; fabricated world and, 104; on fabrication, 111, 231; on labors of living, 240, 262; political outlook of, 312n7; public shit and, 177; self-determination and, 68; theory from the south and, 313n2; on urban space, 305n1. *See also* action; *animal laborans*; body, the; *homo faber*; *Human Condition, The*; labor; labors of living; life itself; plurality; polis; political life; privacy; public life; *vita activa*; work

Ashaiman, 5, 34–37, 41, 212–21, 223–27, 254, 266, 271, 273, 311nn5–6, 312n8; commercial core of, 252; deep domesticity in, 289–91; excremental infrastructural organization of, 263; infrastructural inchoates and, 282; infrastructural intimacies in, 285; leisure class of, 255; political leadership in, 248; population of, 305n2; public space in, 270; public toilets in, 262; relocation to, 304n23; shit in, 278; waste dump of, 306n6; working class of, 230; working poor of, 238, 265. *See also* private commercial toilets (PCTs)

Ashaiman Municipal Assembly (ASHMA), 213, 229, 235–36, 266–67, 311n12; Waste Management Office, 254, 264
Aspra Spitia, 50, 67, 79, 301n6
autonomy, 30, 85, 98, 167, 264; of the domestic, 252; human, 278; municipal, 41; worker, 60

Baghdad, 50, 79, 301n6
Balfour and Sons, 79–80, 83, 88
bare life, 40, 154–56, 162, 165, 174, 177–79
Bataille, Georges, 8, 23, 41, 216–19, 230–32, 237, 245–46, 248, 255, 311n3; Arendt and, 312n7; energetic forms described by, 280; political action and, 277; political economy of waste and, 265; Veblen and, 311n4. See also accursed share; general economy; heterogeneity
Bayat, Asef, 8, 43, 172
Benjamin, Walter, 38, 42, 97, 277, 305n1, 306n5. See also ruination; ruins
Bentham, Jeremy, 174, 299n28
biogas, 206f, 207, 268, 282; plants, 40–41, 182, 185
biopolitics, 73, 92, 103, 155, 286
bios, 156, 178
bodily care, 171, 262; infrastructures of, 231
bodily processes, 23, 33, 48, 54, 56, 104, 130, 237, 256, 263, 275–76, 307n1; Arendt and, 28–30, 170; denaturing of, 265; excesses of, 260; infrastructure and, 219; political assembly and, 37; shame and, 226; urban political order and, 218
bodily waste, 4–6, 8–9, 13, 17–18, 23, 112, 192, 231–32, 250, 259, 278–79, 293, 295n1; agency of, 83; biogas and, 205, 207–8, 211; collective management of, 29; disposition of, 38, 262; elimination of, 136; excesses of, 218, 281; human, 27, 42, 55, 244; as in-between, 154; infrastructural intimacies and, 284; as infrastructure of the body, 185; intimacy of, 85; parliaments of, 274; public space and, 104, 132; public sphere and, 97, 130. See also Kwei Armah, Ayi
body, the, 54, 65, 68; ANT's political ontology and, 30; Arendt on, 28–29, 312n7; Bataille on, 312n7; cycles of, 179, 230;

daily passages of, 249; excreta and, 27; Hobbes and, 210; infrastructural dominion and, 205; infrastructure and, 202; infrastructures of, 185, 192, 210–11, 265; political theory and, 278; politicization of, 309n16; politics and, 275; of the ruler, 290; state authority and, 155; Tema's urban plan and, 73; vital remains and, 280
body politic, 41, 73–74, 185, 210, 275
Boyle, Robert, 197, 201–2, 205, 207, 209
Brasília, 33, 64, 141, 212
Butcher, David, 153–54, 308n7
Butt, Waqas, 110, 299n25

Callon, Michel, 192, 204, 208, 210, 286
Chance, Kerry, 9, 119, 123, 176, 296n9
Chandigarh, 33, 64, 141, 148, 308nn11–12
Chemu Lagoon, 34, 80, 87f, 89, 102, 114, 181–85, 208, 279
Clerk, T. S., 15f, 63, 148, 303n17
colonialism, 301n7; excremental, 12
commonwealth, 189; infrastructural, 209; of waste, 290; waste-based, 40, 182
conspicuous waste, 41, 216–17, 232, 237, 241, 243
conviviality, 258–59, 285; waste-based, 251

Dahl, Robert, 77, 304n28
D'Auria, Viviana, 48, 306n12
decolonization, 14, 46, 48, 156, 219, 292
deep domesticity, 22, 24, 41, 211, 262, 288, 290–93; class and, 224, 289; excremental infrastructures and, 32; institutionalization of, 274, 276, 287; public toilets and, 168, 179; self-determination and, 40, 129
defecation, 165, 295n1, 313n16; human, 241; open, 18, 96, 101, 223, 281, 296n11
Deleuze, Gilles, 26, 64
design, 49, 72; dwelling, 145; industrial, 308n14; intentional, 241; of Manhean, 134, 146; of Riyadh, 304n27; sanitary, 14, 152, 262; sewer system, 108; of Tema, 33, 38, 45, 61, 65–66, 70, 75, 77–78, 86, 149, 277, 303n17, 306n12; toilet, 310n5; urban, 19, 49, 58, 65, 89, 308n10. See also Doxiadis, Constantinos "Dinos"; Doxiadis

Associates (DA); Tema Development Corporation (TDC)

Dhaka, 50, 57, 79, 302n11

dingpolitics (thing-politics), 26, 36, 104, 189

domesticity, 74, 93, 120, 167, 207, 211, 249–50, 274, 293; decentralized, 176, 290, 292; infrastructural intimacy and, 267; open-ended, 238; publicized, 240, 246, 271; public toilets and, 192

domestic realm, 73, 237, 250–51, 255, 287, 292–93; bodily functions and, 225; excremental infrastructure and, 43, 271, 289; PCTs and, 226, 263–64; privatization and, 129, 284; self and, 38

Domestic Sanitary Enclosures, 225–26, 250–52, 266

Domestic Sanitary Enterprises, 224–27, 266

Domestic Sanitary Extensions, 225–26, 238, 266

domestic space, 24, 39, 42, 65, 72, 121, 254, 265, 271, 288–89, 291; excremental arrangements and, 287; extension of, 77, 248; infrastructural add-ons and, 255; private commercial toilets and, 224–25, 258–59, 264; public toilets and, 4, 38, 41, 172; waste-based conviviality and, 251

domination, 9, 54, 86; relations of, 217; systems of, 268

domus, 18, 25, 274–75, 277, 288, 293–94, 298n22; fabricated world of, 271; infrastructure's vital politics and, 24; state and, 129

Doxiadis, Constantinos "Dinos," 38, 47–68, 73–74, 92–93, 98, 106, 115, 204, 214, 273, 281, 286, 302n15, 303n18, 304n29; biography of, 301n5; designs of, 291; *oikos* and, 298n22; plans for Tema, 46, 51, 55, 64, 69, 75–79, 83–84, 88, 91, 127, 145, 148, 263, 288, 304n32, 306n12, 307n5; urban planning and, 266, 301n16, 304n27. *See also* ekistics; Greece

Doxiadis Associates (DA), 34, 49–50, 55–61, 63–69, 72–73, 79–80, 86, 89, 273, 301n6, 302n10, 302–3n15; central place theory and, 75; containment urbanism and, 77–78; *Ekistics* journal, 302n11; ekistics the-

ory and, 92; midcentury cities designed by, 79; sewage system failure and, 84; Tahal and, 88; Tema's master plan and, 34, 38, 46, 49, 56f, 63, 66, 70, 71f, 79, 89, 125, 303n15; urban planning and, 90

Drake, Kenneth, 148, 308n12

Drew, Jane, 39, 148–52, 157, 172, 178, 301n3, 308n10, 308n12, 309n15; excremental pedagogy and, 179; incremental social engineering, 263; industrial design and, 308n14; Modern Architectural Research Group and, 308n9; tropical modernism and, 308n13. *See also* Manhean

ekistics, 51, 53, 57, 59–60, 303n19; theory, 64–65, 92

Elias, Norbert, 225–26, 243

Esty, Joshua, 21, 305n33

evacuation, 22, 250, 255, 278; bodily, 104, 130, 186, 231, 247, 261, 271; political, 185, 191; public excremental, 180

excrement, 4–5, 8, 39, 133, 179, 185, 274, 295n1; abject body and, 163; biogas plants and, 40, 182; errant, 98, 278, 284; human, 132, 244; infrastructures of, 18 (*see also* excremental infrastructures); public, 139, 177; state and, 165

excremental arrangements, 9, 20, 30, 33, 271, 273, 276–77, 280, 287, 294

excremental infrastructures, 8–9, 11, 18, 21, 23, 25, 33, 37, 42, 134, 169, 174, 182, 193, 206f, 271, 277; class and, 289; deep domesticity and, 32; infrastructural intimacies and, 286; material relations of, 282; plurality and, 30, 268; as political containment, 269; political life and, 275; public space and, 270; *vita activa* and, 276; vital politics of, 279

excremental orders, 20, 29, 268, 273, 282, 287–88

excremental postcolonialism, 21, 305n33

excremental solutions, 5, 21, 54, 29, 273, 275, 298n21

excreta, 27, 37, 101, 265; Bataille on, 218; bodily, 22, 291; conversion to methane, 205; errant, 39; human, 5–6, 97, 100, 110, 112, 114, 261, 266; infrastructure and, 278, 280, 285; neoliberalism and, 159;

excreta (*continued*)
public toilets and, 247. *See also* Kwei Armah, Ayi
excretion, 48, 225, 248; appetite of, 193; human, 24

fabrication, 49, 112, 188, 285, 287; infrastructural, 111, 266, 299n31; work and, 31, 42, 94, 231, 276, 282
fecal matter, 6, 18, 104, 115, 120, 278; conversion into methane, 205; government toilets and, 223; literature on, 4; septic tanks and, 243, 297n20
Foucault, Michel, 9, 26, 174, 286, 299n28, 309n16
Fredericks, Rosalind, 110, 112, 278, 306n6, 312n13
Fry, Maxwell, 39, 148–52, 157, 172, 178, 301n3, 308n10, 308n12, 309n15; excremental pedagogy and, 179; incremental social engineering, 263; Modern Architectural Research Group and, 308n9; tropical modernism and, 308n13. *See also* Manhean

Gandy, Matthew, 138, 270
Geertz, Clifford, 24, 290
general economy, 217, 237, 245–46, 250, 262, 265; of waste, 255
gentility, 233, 237, 241, 259
ghettos, 175–76, 179, 191, 269, 285, 288, 310n26
global North, 21, 42, 46, 294
global South, 21, 28, 42, 46, 50, 271, 294; sanitation in, 6
Gold Coast, 12–13, 48, 148, 301n2, 308n14; legislature, 14; transition to Ghana, 145
governance, 21, 74; community, 160; municipal, 270, 284; planning as proxy for, 46; self-, 25, 38, 47, 213; urban, 5, 12, 35, 84, 92, 104, 177, 213
Greece, 49–50, 58, 303n15; Ancient, 29, 53, 59, 75, 298n22 (*see also* polis); Ministry of Housing and Reconstruction, 49
Gupta, Akhil, 47, 87, 311n8, 312n11

Habermas, Jürgen, 123, 171, 174, 237; *Structural Transformation of the Public Sphere*, 226
health, 149–50, 301n4; benefits, 297n14; care, 309n23; environmental, 4; public, 6, 18, 21, 64, 159; risks, 270, 306n6; services, 82
Heidegger, Martin, 25, 28, 299n32, 305n1
Herzfeld, Michael, 109, 131, 283, 298n24, 299n26
heterogeneity, 8, 217–18; political, 221, 246, 250, 311n6; social, 218, 265
Hobbes, Thomas, 195, 197, 200, 202, 204–5, 208–10, 277, 286; Bodies Politiques and, 192, 280, 310n3; *De Corpore*, 310n4; *Leviathan*, 185, 192–93
Hoffman, Danny, 12, 278, 301n1, 308n10
homo faber, 31, 41, 86, 92, 94, 229, 255, 262
Honig, Bonnie, 26, 299n27, 300n37
housing, 12, 17, 46, 51, 63, 66, 68–70, 166, 219; developments, 302n13; family, 173; incremental, 306n12; investments in, 301n4; latrines and, 150; permanent, 40, 182, 186; pressure, 121, 312n9; programs, 59; repair, 61; self-determination and, 141; stock, 68, 155, 186, 213–14, 221, 224, 252; temporary, 303n22; urban, 74
Human Condition, The (Arendt), 25, 27, 30–31, 53, 275–76, 300n34, 305n37, 309n16, 309n22, 312n7
humanism, 64; techno-, 68
human waste, 4, 6, 11, 19, 42, 48, 96, 154, 160, 193, 241, 243, 249, 306n4; infrastructures of, 268; management, 103, 215, 221; obligation to receive, 101; politics of, 1, 274; production, 230; vitality of, 9; as vital remain, 113
hygiene, 6–7, 69, 85, 90, 153, 194, 196; colonial, 12, 67, 149, 151, 221, 274; standards of, 195, 223

infrastructural adjustments, 42, 97, 202, 253f
infrastructural arrangements, 9, 24–25, 78, 93, 180, 191, 289; Ashaiman's, 214–15; by Balfour and Sons, 83; of the Floshin Taifi toilet complex, 188

infrastructural breakdown, 37, 93, 104, 119, 122, 210; people as infrastructure and, 283; privatization and, 162; public space and, 130

infrastructural debris, 103, 287

infrastructural inchoate, 24, 83, 94, 129, 218, 261, 280–83; infrastructural intimacy and, 274; public toilets and, 192, 259; uncertainties of, 210, 286

infrastructural intimacies, 23–24, 39, 41, 97, 110, 112, 124–25, 132, 169–70, 204, 211, 259, 264, 283–87, 299n26; infrastructural inchoate and, 274; public toilets and, 172, 179; of repair, 111; of Tema's broken sewage network, 216, 260; of Tema's wastelands, 191; vital remains and, 129, 277, 286–87; waste and, 42; waste management and, 132

infrastructural intimacy, 22–24, 32, 39, 109–10, 112, 131–32, 202, 258, 276, 283, 285, 287, 291, 299nn25–26; domesticity and, 267; manholes and, 117; rodding and, 119; vital remains and, 274

infrastructural investments, 13, 79, 193, 221, 232, 237, 255; sanitary, 12

infrastructural provisioning, 24, 33; inadequate, 85; state, 291

infrastructure, 6, 33, 40, 46, 49, 64, 84, 86, 92–94, 103, 106, 113, 120, 186, 188, 190f, 195, 201–2, 209–11, 235, 249, 262, 265, 274, 279–80, 285–87, 289–90, 299n27; bodily, 191; children and, 203f, 204; defunct, 279, 294; domestic, 74, 150, 250, 253, 255; embodied capacity and, 296n8; fabricated world of, 104, 130; household, 73, 178; human-made, 269; improvised, 224; large-scale, 50, 79; mediating role of, 185; nation-building and, 88; people and, 23, 110–12, 125–26, 131–32, 282, 306n7; people as, 111, 131, 283; as political experiment, 182; political logics based on, 196; politics of, 209; potential of, 219; private, 226, 249, 291; productivity and, 78; promise of, 47, 87; public, 39, 85, 90, 129, 139, 174, 284, 291–92; public-facing, 42; pumping station, 299n24; ruins and, 311n8;

Second Development Plan (Ghana) and, 301n4; sewage, 120, 221, 298n23; toilet, 192, 224, 259; unruliness of, 180; vital, 17, 48, 110, 176, 281, 299n31; vital politics of, 9, 22–25, 27–28, 30, 85, 103, 111, 268, 279, 299n31; vital remains of, 156; waste-based, 9, 41, 249–50, 265; water, 19, 123, 194f, 255; Ziginshore's, 41, 192, 211. *See also* excremental infrastructures; infrastructural inchoate; infrastructural intimacies; infrastructural intimacy; Latour, Bruno: on infrastructure; sanitary infrastructure; urban infrastructure; waste infrastructures

internationalism: modernist, 17; postwar, 49

intimacy, 239, 299n25; of bodily waste, 85; bureaucratic, 298n24; cultural, 109, 131, 283; elemental, 285. *See also* infrastructural intimacy; waste intimacies

Islamabad, 50, 57, 60, 67, 79, 301n6, 302n11

Jackson, Steven, 22, 84, 109–10, 112, 242, 272, 283

kleejo protests, 160, 163, 284

Kopytoff, Igor, 191, 209

Kwei Armah, Ayi, 21, 88, 305n33

labor, 27–29, 31, 42, 112, 204, 232, 255, 265, 271, 276, 292, 300n35, 303n20; Ashaiman and, 41, 212; bodily, 174, 231, 309n16; conspicuous, 257f; division of, 159; domestic realm and, 250; essentialisms of, 73; expertise and, 60–61; infrastructure and, 219; investment in, 244; of life itself, 39, 104, 113, 130, 132; manual, 118; mobilization, 74, 304n25; needs of Tema's industries, 69; phatic, 306n7; shit and, 161; social movements and, 287; surplus, 311n3; *vita activa* and, 93, 122, 237; vital infrastructures of, 110; wage, 239

labors of living, 41, 139, 185, 262; infrastructural intimacy and, 179, 285; infrastructure and, 46; public life and, 240; right to habitation and, 141

Laporte, Dominique, 18, 139, 151, 154, 159, 177, 303n21; *History of Shit*, 5, 133

Larkin, Brian, 9, 22, 180, 204, 210, 280

Lasdun, Denyis, 148, 308n12

Latour, Bruno, 5, 25–28, 30–32, 103–4, 171, 202, 205, 208, 210, 273, 275, 285–86, 299n27; on assembly, 170; on body politic, 192; on infrastructure, 26–27, 63, 109, 131, 165, 204; theoretical dispositions of, 299n32. *See also* Actor Network Theory (ANT); dingpolitics (thing-politics)

Le Corbusier, 33, 148, 308n9

Lefebvre, Henri, 39, 138, 156. *See also* right to the city

life itself, 54, 169; labor of, 39, 104, 113, 130, 132; maintenance of, 28–29, 122; social production of, 174

lifeworlds, 4, 25; infrastructural, 83

machinic, the, 78–79; machinic logics of high-modernist thinking, 120

Manhean, 34–35, 41, 57, 79, 89, 126, 134–36, 139–41, 145–55, 159, 177, 180–81, 186, 219, 271, 273, 280, 291, 310n26; compound toilets in, 216, 290; deep domesticity in, 290; Fry and Drew and, 308n12; infrastructural inchoates and, 282; infrastructural intimacies in, 284; original structures of, 309n24; public showers in, 138, 159, 307n3; public space in, 176, 270, 275, 309n21; public toilets in, 36–37, 39–40, 134, 136–38, 150–51, 152*f*, 156–58, 160, 162–66, 169–75, 178–79, 182, 195–96, 214, 234, 251, 262, 288–89; shit in, 278; toilet attendants in, 172–73, 282, 284; Toilet Operators Association, 162–63, 166; toilet operators in, 157, 163, 166–68, 179. *See also* ghettos; resettlement; shit: right to; *tsoshishi*

manholes, 1, 67, 104, 114–21, 123–25, 127–32, 191, 268; covers of, 120, 138; infrastructural intimacy and, 283; network of, 99; overflowing, 39, 91, 100, 118; public, 281; sewage, 97, 116*f*, 117

Markell, Patchen, 265, 305n37

Martinich, A. P., 195, 310n6

materialism: Marxian, 31; new, 22; vital, 27, 210, 299n27

Mbembe, Achille, 8, 241

Menoret, Pascal, 51, 61, 77, 301n5, 304n27

minipublics, 76*f*, 77, 304n28

Ministry of Housing (Ghana), 35, 49, 142–43, 147

modernism, 12; tropical, 148, 308n13

modernity, 12, 18, 276–77, 292–94; high, 8, 10*f*, 11, 21, 42, 103, 196; industrial, 19–20, 30, 33, 46, 94, 272, 309n22; infrastructural, 14; midcentury, 131; nineteenth-century, 256; urban, 66, 79, 271, 292

modernization, 58, 68, 85; infrastructural, 87; post–World War II, 219

Mukhopadhyay, Bhaskar, 6–7, 176, 295n3

Mumford, Lewis, 72, 218, 225–26, 237, 243, 299n29

National Democratic Congress (NDC), 157, 164–65

national transformation, 4, 60

New Patriotic Party (NPP), 157, 164

New Towns, 45, 64, 77

Nkrumah, Kwame, 1, 14, 38, 46–51, 53–54, 57–62, 68–69, 73, 78, 80, 88, 91–94, 98, 132, 185, 263, 288, 303n17, 303n20; fall of, 161; government of, 49, 55, 64–65, 74, 90, 155, 304n24; infrastructure and, 281, 286; labor aristocrats and, 302n12; political aspirations of, 291; Second Development Plan and, 301n4; urban planning and, 266. *See also* Clerk, T. S.; Doxiadis, Constantinos "Dinos"

Ofei-Nkansah, Marina, 171, 176, 310n26

oikos, 65, 74, 77, 298n22, 303n19; modern, 32. *See also* ekistics

Oko Adjetey, Emmanuel, 145, 174, 309n15

Old Tema, 35, 140–43, 145, 151, 153, 174, 177, 309n15; compound-style houses of, 195; non-native residents of, 219; Zongo, 220–21

Paradise Beach, 89, 91, 100, 114, 273

parity, 38, 57, 67, 263; bodily, 73, 233; global, 54; of human needs, 66; intellectual, 59; internationalist, 58; lateral, 262; postwar, 50; sanitary, 70; social, 189

planning, 35, 38, 46, 49, 61–63, 301nn1–2; Ancient Greek city, 57; city, 77, 302n13; modernist, 274; national, 69; town, 48. *See also* urban planning

plenism, 192, 210

plurality, 25, 27–28, 30–32, 48, 74, 94, 210, 237, 259; bodily needs and, 244; human, 26, 105, 113, 130, 132, 246; infrastructural orders and, 93; parliaments of shit and, 288; polis as space of discursive, 260; public life and, 69, 269, 282; political, 280, 311n6; as relationship of equality and distinction, 193; the social and, 276; urban, 8, 22, 29, 33, 42, 64, 83–84, 226, 266, 268; *vita activa* and, 231

polis, 18, 30, 36, 41, 94, 105, 130, 154–55, 185, 250, 288, 292, 294; of Ancient Greece, 29, 75, 303n18; Arendt on, 53–54, 64–65, 74, 231, 260, 263, 275, 277; contemporary, 5; domus and, 24–25, 293; Doxiadis and, 53, 74, 78; Nkrumah and, 46, 74; res publica and, 25, 33, 298n22

political life, 23, 275, 286, 288; Arendt on, 25, 27, 29, 132, 154, 170, 216, 300n36, 309n16; bare life and, 156, 165, 179 (see also *bios*; *zoe*); bodily needs and, 29; body and, 54; domestic realms and, 287; excrement and, 5; in Ghana, 28, 306n11; in Manhean, 149; plurality and, 27, 226; postwar, 93; public space and, 170; urban, 19, 42, 84, 92, 299n27; work and, 265

political recognition, 163; bodily waste and, 104, 130

postwar reconstruction, 46, 49, 53

privacy, 6, 67, 136, 152, 169, 172–73, 198, 228, 241, 248, 252, 259–60, 271; bourgeois, 224; status and, 226

private commercial toilets (PCTs), 215–18, 223–24, 228–30, 232, 234, 236–39, 241, 244, 252, 261–64, 269, 280; aesthetics of propriety and, 212n10; Ashaiman's, 218, 224, 226–27, 250–51, 275, 282, 285–86, 288–89, 311n6; ASHMA and, 266; designs, 225. *See also* Domestic Sanitary

Enclosures; Domestic Sanitary Enterprises; Domestic Sanitary Extensions

private life, 3, 36, 46, 226, 255, 284; boundaries of, 124; excrement and, 165; expansion of, 225; of the household, 69; large-scale systems and, 88; public authority and, 121; public life and, 92, 271, 274; sanitary infrastructures and, 238

private property, 98, 113, 254; public responsibility and, 37, 292; public works and, 127

private space, 147, 151, 167, 246–47, 260, 313n15; expansion of, 225; of the household, 30; panopticon and, 174; regulation of, 153

privatization, 160–62, 196; of bodily functions, 191; of public works, 41; toilet, 163, 178; of waste management, 13; of waste production, 19; of water, 159

propriety, 124, 295n1; aesthetics of, 241, 251, 256, 312n10; bodily, 169; domestic, 226, 233, 250; norms of, 271, 289; rules of, 200; social, 152; standards of, 100, 250

public life, 4, 75, 26, 28, 30–32, 40, 42, 54, 169, 171, 174, 291; ASHMA and, 267; bodily needs and, 73; bodily waste and, 262; city walls and, 300n36; conventions of, 271; domestication of, 247; excremental infrastructures and, 182; infrastructural engagements and, 130; infrastructural inchoate and, 282; intimacies of dis/repair and, 131; labors of living and, 240; the machinic and, 79; nonhuman materials and, 208; plurality and, 69, 269, 282; private commercial toilets (PCTs) and, 215, 226, 263; private life and, 92, 271, 274; private matters and, 104, 119, 132; privatization of basic needs and, 47–48; public toilets and, 138, 150, 162, 165, 172, 188; sanitary infrastructure and, 189; state power and, 133; Tema's urban plan and, 77; ungovernability of, 179; urban, 18, 21, 33, 38, 209, 288; urban elites and, 246; urban infrastructures and, 269; urban politics and, 7–8, 25, 38; *vita activa* and, 231 public space, 18, 31–32, 135, 147, 151, 167, 175–76, 191, 202, 247, 265–66, 275, 292; Arendt on, 170; collective claims on, 104, 130, 132; the domestic and, 249–50, 264, 291; domestication of, 246, 270; excremental infrastructures and, 270, 289; objects and, 26; proper comportment in, 309n21; public intimacies and, 284; Riyadh and, 304n27; Tema's waste disposal problems and, 114; toilets and, 173–74, 179, 233

public toilets, 4, 17, 32, 38, 101, 134, 136, 138, 146*f*, 150–51, 157–58, 160, 164–66, 169–70, 177, 179, 190, 214, 223, 239–40, 255, 262, 281, 296n11, 297n20, 298n21, 304n22, 307n3, 311n5; aesthetics of vulgarity and, 312n10; changing attitudes toward, 194; deep democracy and, 162; as domestic base, 173; dwelling-based, 41; as in-between spaces, 176; privatization and, 163, 178; reproductive activities and, 40; status, 37; vital politics and, 156. *See also* Domestic Sanitary Enclosures; Domestic Sanitary Enterprises; Domestic Sanitary Extensions; private commercial toilets (PCTs)

Rawlings, J. J., 157, 160–61, 196. *See also* National Democratic Congress (NDC)
resettlement, 139–44, 147, 153–54, 161, 164–66, 171, 173, 177, 195, 278
res publica, 18, 24–25, 39, 104, 130, 132, 275, 288, 298n22
right to the city, 21, 39, 138, 154, 156, 177, 287
Riyadh, 50–51, 61, 79, 301n6, 304n27
Robinson, Denis Curtis, 15*f*, 63
rodding, 118–20, 131, 279
ruination, 38, 97, 103, 115, 131, 278, 305n1; infrastructural, 119; intimacy and, 109; renovation and, 107
ruins, 39–40, 97, 103, 106, 119, 122, 127, 169, 178, 287, 305n1, 306n5; of empire, 131; of high modernity, 21; rural, 300n38; temporality of infrastructure and, 311n8

Sakumono, 35, 298n21
Sakumono Lagoon, 34, 102, 106
sanitary engineers, 4, 97, 106, 111

sanitary infrastructure, 9, 13, 15, 36, 48, 64, 82, 98, 112, 149, 182, 189, 208, 238, 249, 251, 260; breakdown of, 3, 178; dis/repair, 132, 178; as equalizer, 73; household, 246; as mode of address, 152; public private, 216; urban, 297n15; urban politicization and, 91

sanitation, 6, 13–14, 17, 39, 48, 55, 66, 84, 88, 90, 100, 151, 153, 196, 259, 270; challenges, 221; crisis, 121; Drew and Fry and, 149–50; as entitlement, 107; household/household-based, 79, 83, 93; improved, 11, 102, 296n11; investment in, 12; the machinic and, 78; modern, 73; private, 36, 214; public, 36, 177, 214, 295n4; rural, 298n23; Second Development Plan (Ghana) and, 301n4; street, 296n13; systems, 19, 46, 90, 218, 254, 306n7; TDC and, 302n13; technology, 112; urban, 8, 18–19, 92, 223, 266; urban infrastructure and, 86

Schinkel, Willem, 156, 283
Schneider, Daniel, 112, 306n10
Scott, James, 83, 293–94
security, 37, 74, 83, 173, 188, 202, 204, 269, 274, 285; bodily, 210; commonwealth of waste and, 290; excremental infrastructures and, 182; material, 47, 230, 281, 287; parliaments of shit and, 288; personal, 199; studies, 300n33
self-care, 4, 30, 37, 40, 186, 188, 259, 271, 285
self-determination, 31, 37–38, 68, 92, 94, 123, 180, 200, 213, 270–71, 288, 290; collective, 47, 169; deep domesticity and, 40, 129; Dirty Protest (Northern Ireland) and, 296n10; excremental arrangements and, 9; housing and, 141; infrastructural adjustments and, 202; Manhean's toilets and, 139; PCTs and, 226, 263; public toilets and, 4; resettlement and, 284; working-class, 60
self-governance, 25, 47, 213
self-making, 46, 113
septage, 103; facilities, 100–101; ponds, 91, 100
septic systems, 12, 98, 188, 206*f*, 253, 262, 297n20; household, 190, 298n21

sewage pits, 169, 228, 231–33

sewage system (Tema), 11, 16*f*, 17, 38–39,
79–84, 86, 89–92, 96, 98, 100, 103, 107–
8, 153, 195, 214, 221, 297–98n20, 304n32;
abuse of, 119; breakdown of, 113–14; crisis of, 104; pumping stations, 101; repair,
118, 130

sewage treatment, 101–2; plants, 91, 101,
114; ponds, 281

sewerage, 17, 80; treatment plant, 83; underground, 82; waterborne, 11

sewerage system (Tema), 15, 17, 38, 99–100,
110, 151, 305n35

shit, 5, 7–8, 18, 166, 232, 261, 278, 289,
295n1, 307n1; art and, 313n16; money
and, 159, 161, 245; parliaments of, 288;
public, 133, 151, 154, 177–79; right to,
40, 138–39, 154, 156, 160–61, 165, 168,
176–80, 193

Simone, AbdouMaliq, 111, 131, 201, 283

social, the, 1, 30–32, 54–55, 74, 265, 272,
276, 291–92; public and, 309n22

socialism, 69, 73

solidarity, 9, 288; competitive, 310n26;
Pan-African, 53; social, 46; urban, 291

Stamatopoulou-Robbins, Sophia, 5, 21, 85,
113, 211, 296n6, 304n31, 306n9

Star, Susan, 103–4, 106, 112, 117, 210, 306n4

Stoler, Ann Laura, 39, 97–98, 103–4, 106–7,
109, 111–13, 115, 119, 130–31, 169, 278,
305n1, 306n5. *See also* ruination; ruins

stool lands, 139, 144, 166

Swanson, Heather Anne, 293–94

system decay, 98, 284

taifi, 1, 182, 295n1

Tema Acquisition Area, 34, 61, 82, 213*f*, 214

Tema Central, 34, 37, 115

Tema Development Corporation (TDC),
38, 61–63, 69, 73, 98, 107–8, 148, 151,
302nn13–14; affordable housing contracts administered by, 84; Ashaiman
and, 213, 221, 229, 265–66, 273, 311n2;
consolidation of authority of, 89–90;
Doxiadis Associates (DA) and, 65, 88,
90–92, 115, 279, 302n11; library, 67;
Manhean and, 157; personnel files,
303n16; promotional materials, 3*f*.

See also Clerk, T. S.; Doxiadis, Constantinos "Dinos"

Tema Harbor, 40, 46, 47*f*, 57, 73, 78–80,
100–101, 139, 186, 232, 307n2; construction of, 62, 141, 143; fishing, 100, 136, 182,
198, 273; sewage system and, 195; waste
from, 106

Tema Manhean. *See* Manhean

Tema Metropolitan Assembly (TMA), 123–
24, 126–28, 157, 159–62, 166–68, 209,
291; waste management, 108; Waste
Management Office, 99, 117, 158

Tema Traditional Council, 142*f*, 166–67, 191

Tema Zongo, 219–21

toileting, 154, 156; habits, 153; public, 155,
168

toilets, 48, 66–67, 70, 97, 114, 119, 126, 130,
149–51, 153, 155, 184*f*, 193–94, 197, 262,
265, 272, 285, 289, 308n13; communal,
37, 195; community-based, 179; compound, 167, 216, 269, 290; contract, 269;
drop-pit, 182; flush, 100, 186, 195, 211,
251, 253; flying, 18, 228; government,
223, 228, 241, 312n10; government-
built, 18; household, 132, 134, 223, 281;
in-home, 6, 11, 161, 214, 312n9; mosques
and, 312n14; pour-flush, 31, 256, 258,
260, 264; private, 6, 11, 151, 162, 270, 281;
private household, 38; privatization of,
41; public space and, 173–74, 179, 233; repairs, 162; shared, 11, 39; sit-and-squat,
269; vital remains of, 168; water-based,
13. *See also* private commercial toilets
(PCTs); public toilets

Tsao, Roy, 282, 300n35

tsoshishi, 175, 179, 279, 288

upward mobility, 3, 11, 34, 213, 223, 270–71

urban collectivity, 37, 46

urban development, 61, 219, 271; Greek,
301n6

urban infrastructure, 3–4, 130, 176, 192,
266, 269, 284; Nkrumah's investment
in, 74; political contentions of, 38; Tema's lagoons and, 86

urbanism: containment, 77, 134; deep, 9;
Doxiadis Associates (DA) and, 78; modern, 65; splintering/splintered, 35, 42

urban life, 35, 218–19, 270, 277, 287; logic of affiliation and, 77; public toilets and, 134, 169, 177; received premises of, 274; right to, 138

urban planning, 12, 140, 195; Doxiadis and, 51, 58, 90, 266, 304n27; high-modernist, 269; large-scale, 148; late-colonial, 134, 169; municipal-civic master discourse and, 6; Nkrumah and, 90, 266, 303n17; sanitary infrastructure and, 149

urban waste, 94; disposition of, 17; management, 18, 20; monopoly of, 267, 272, 311n2; politics of, 8, 33; producers, 110

van den Berg, Marguerite, 156, 283

Veblen, Thorstein, 217, 219, 230–33, 237, 243, 255–56, 262, 265, 286, 311n4. *See also* conspicuous waste

vita activa, 27–28, 31, 36, 93–94, 113, 122, 130, 132, 219, 237, 265, 269, 276, 300n33, 300n36; Ashaiman's waste-driven versions of, 263; plurality and, 84, 105, 231, 246; as political action, 218. *See also* action; labor; work

vitality, 9, 23–24, 92, 180, 208–9, 269, 273, 277, 279–81, 287; of excrement, 8; of extra-human substances, 93; human, 27, 112; of imperial remains, 111; of nature, 290; of nonhuman things, 293; of waste, 112–13, 119, 131

vital politics, 19, 21–22, 91, 296n9; from below, 38; public toilets as domain of, 156; of urban waste, 33. *See also* infrastructure: vital politics of

vital remains, 22–24, 29, 36, 38, 92, 129, 156, 210, 274, 278–80, 283, 296n9; bodily excreta as, 291; deep domesticity and, 293; energetic potential of, 205; excremental infrastructures and, 42–43, 131; filtered water as, 258; hidden potentials of, 211; human waste as, 113; infrastructural intimacies and, 284, 286–87; labor and, 276–77; public toilets as, 40, 168–69, 178, 290; ruins as, 122; waste infrastructures as, 165; waste materials as, 104

Volta River Project/Scheme, 14, 55, 82, 196, 219, 297n18, 301n4

waste. *See* bodily waste; conspicuous waste; human waste; urban waste

waste infrastructures, 4–5, 37, 95, 110, 112, 120, 260, 274; in Ashaiman, 266; investment in, 17; Manhean's, 165; Palestine's, 21; sensory excess of, 123; undecidability of, 12, 121, 127; vitality of, 119; vital politics of, 103

waste intimacies, 110, 299n25

waste management, 3–5, 19, 25, 98–99, 107–8, 110, 124, 127–28, 245, 261, 305n34; human, 103, 215, 221; infrastructural intimacies and, 132; municipal, 191; privatization of, 13; solutions, 33, 273; systems, 266; urban, 18, 20

Williams, Raymond, 21, 122

work, 27–28, 31, 42, 46–47, 51, 68, 84, 93–94, 112, 126, 176, 182, 186, 219, 230–31, 237, 240, 255, 265, 271, 276–77, 282–83, 285–87; human plurality and, 113; infrastructural, 175; infrastructural intimacy and, 258; manual, 307n3; material world of, 132, 263; routines, 236; toilet, 223; waged, 229; waste, 110; waste and, 189

World Bank, 101, 196, 223, 296n11, 305n3; "No Open Defecation" scheme, 6; Urban II program, 91, 100; Urban Environmental Sanitation Program, 91, 100, 106

World Health Organization, 11, 223

World War II, 48, 53–54; African independence and, 308n10

Ziginshore, 34, 36–37, 40–41, 181–82, 185–86, 191, 197–99, 202–4, 209–11, 214, 216, 258, 279–80, 289; biogas plant/biodigester in, 41, 185, 205, 282; deep domesticity in, 290, 292; detritus of, 201; infrastructural inchoates and, 282; infrastructural insecurity and, 273; infrastructural intimacies and, 283, 285; infrastructures of waste, 195; public space and, 270, 275; shit in, 278; toilet complex (Floshin Taifi), 186, 188–90, 192–93, 195–96

zoe, 156, 178